Praise for *The Eagles of Heart Mountain*

"[A]n absolutely stirring story . . . rigorous and important."

—*The Washington Post*

"Colorful, richly detailed, and deeply human, *The Eagles of Heart Mountain* mixes a fascinating history of the Japanese in the United States with a uniquely American story about one of the darkest chapters of our modern history. Brad's storytelling weaves together politics, race, and a wide cast of characters to show how sports carried a community of mistreated prisoners through World War II, a tale that ultimately stands as a testament to the resilience of the human spirit."

—Garrett M. Graff, author of the *New York Times* bestseller
The Only Plane in the Sky: An Oral History of 9/11

"This is an underdog story for the ages. Ripped from their homes by racist officials, Japanese American kids learn to play football in a remote Wyoming concentration camp—and soon become an unstoppable force. Pearson is a brilliant storyteller, and *The Eagles of Heart Mountain* will have you rooting for its young heroes as they defy bigotry and barbed wire."

—Jason Fagone, bestselling author of *The Woman Who Smashed Codes:*
A True Story of Love, Spies, and the Unlikely Heroine
Who Outwitted America's Enemies

"A remarkable piece of storytelling, *The Eagles of Heart Mountain* manages to be simultaneously devastating and uplifting. Pearson delves deep into one of the great blights on American history, and emerges with a story of humanity and resilience, played out on the rocky football field of a concentration camp.

This is a timely and utterly absorbing account of a country losing its moral way, and a group of its young citizens who never did."

—Evan Ratliff, author of *The Mastermind: A True Story of Murder, Empire, and a New Kind of Crime Lord*

"In *The Eagles of Heart Mountain*, Bradford Pearson weaves the greatness of the unlikeliest football team you'll ever meet into the history of Japanese American incarceration during World War II. Between fascinating details about how the camps came to exist and the on-field play-by-play narrated by Pearson, readers won't soon forget Babe Nomura and Horse Yoshinaga."

—Andrea Pitzer, author of *One Long Night: A Global History of Concentration Camps*

"Pearson succeeds in unearthing a feel-good story from a dark chapter in U.S. history. The result is a worthy portrait of triumph in the face of tragedy."

—*Publishers Weekly*

"A fresh look at the mass removal and incarceration of Japanese Americans during World War II . . . A deep-reaching chronicle of a shameful episode in American history."

—*Kirkus Reviews*

". . . an inspiring exploration of resistance and a timely examination of how the policy of Japanese incarceration impacted the lives of young people and their families."

—*BookPage*

"This well-written and researched book will strongly appeal to those interested in U.S. history and civil rights."

—*Library Journal* (starred review)

"[Pearson] renders people who are too often flattened by history into full human beings, and the reversal can feel exhilarating."

—*High Country News*

THE EAGLES OF
HEART MOUNTAIN

A True Story of Football,
Incarceration, and
Resistance in
World War II America

BRADFORD PEARSON

ATRIA PAPERBACK

NEW YORK · LONDON · TORONTO · SYDNEY · NEW DELHI

ATRIA
PAPERBACK

An Imprint of Simon & Schuster, Inc.
1230 Avenue of the Americas
New York, NY 10020

First Atria Paperback edition November 2021

ATRIA PAPERBACK and colophon are trademarks of
Simon & Schuster, Inc.

For information about special discounts for bulk purchases, please
contact Simon & Schuster Special Sales at 1-866-506-1949 or
business@simonandschuster.com.

The Simon & Schuster Speakers Bureau can bring authors to your live
event. For more information or to book an event, contact the Simon
& Schuster Speakers Bureau at 1-866-248-3049 or visit our website at
www.simonspeakers.com.

Interior design by Dana Sloan

3 5 7 9 10 8 6 4 2

Library of Congress Cataloging-in-Publication Data is available.

ISBN 978-1-9821-0703-1
ISBN 978-1-9821-0704-8 (pbk)
ISBN 978-1-9821-0705-5 (ebook)

For Freddy

CONTENTS

AUTHOR'S NOTE

Terminology

WORDS MATTER, AND often the words used to describe the wartime experiences of 120,000 people of Japanese descent in the 1940s are inadequate. "Japanese internment" is the most common inadequacy; both words are incorrect.

As this book attempts, in part, to explain, the mass removal known colloquially as "Japanese internment" was forced mostly upon Americans of Japanese descent. And the Japanese who were removed had been in the United States for decades but barred from naturalization.

"Internment," according to the Japanese American Citizens League, refers to the detention of enemy aliens during wartime. This applies to a smaller group imprisoned in U.S. Army and Justice Department camps—approximately eight thousand Japanese and smaller numbers of Germans and Italians—but not to the majority imprisoned in War Relocation Authority camps. The word "internment" was not widely used by scholars as a synonym for the incarceration of all Japanese Americans until the 1950s, according to UCLA Asian American Studies professor emeritus Lane Ryo Hirabayashi. In replacing "internment" I've followed the lead of Densho—a Seattle-based nonprofit dedicated to preserving and sharing the story of Japanese American incarceration—and called it just that: "incarceration." It's an imperfect solution, implying that those imprisoned had committed crimes, but it is the best option.

Following Densho's lead, I called the sites of imprisonment "concentration camps" or simply "camps." This usage is not meant to conflate the histories of Japanese American incarceration and the Holocaust in any way. Those imprisoned are "incarcerees." Other government terminology, such as "relocation center," "evacuation," and "colonists," is used only when referring to the formal name of a camp or in direct quotes; that reasoning is explained later.

One final primer on a few Japanese expressions used. *Nikkei* refers to the Japanese diaspora (to those emigrants from Japan and their descendants), and I use it in this book to encompass Japanese Americans and their Japanese families in America. *Issei* refers to the first generation of Japanese immigrants; *nisei* refers to their children, the first Japanese Americans. Though used much less, *sansei* (third generation) is also employed.

PART
1

PART

CHAPTER ONE

City of Good Neighbors

DO YOU KNOW what your people did?"

George Yoshinaga spent the Sunday morning of December 7, 1941, the same way he spent most Sunday mornings: with 10 cents in his pocket and his feet trained to Knight's Pharmacy. Since George was a little boy, his father or one of his older brothers would press a dime into his palm and send him on the five-minute journey to pick up the *San Francisco Chronicle*. The Yoshinagas subscribed to the Japanese-language *Nichi Bei Times*, but they made it a point to buy the *Chronicle* on Sundays.

Sixteen-year-old George had padded his way out of their Mountain View home and down the three blocks of Dana Street until he hit Castro, the main street of the farming community. He picked up the newspaper and paid, and then, as he was making his way to the door, his classmate Chuck entered and posed that question. *Do you know what* your people *did?*

"What do you mean *my* people?" George replied.

A popular if unmotivated student, George was one of only a handful of Japanese Americans in his class at Mountain View High School. His peers, recognizing his charm, had elected him class president that year, which had helped boost his otherwise dubious standing as a boy with only a C average.

"They bombed Hawai'i," Chuck said.

Hawai'i, George thought as his mind whirled. *Where is Hawai'i?*

Chuck scoffed and suggested that George listen to the radio when he got home. Sure enough, when George stepped back through the doorway of 267 Bush Street, his brother Kay informed him of the news: the fire, the deaths. The fighter planes lined up neatly along Oahu's Hickam Field, half-burned and bombed and destroyed. The eight battleships, three cruisers, and three destroyers damaged. Within a few days, the death toll would be 2,403.

The next morning, George walked into Mountain View High School as he typically did. But nothing was typical anymore.

————————

Usaburo Yoshinaga was born in 1867 on Kyushu, the southernmost of Japan's main islands. A rugged and rain-soaked wonderland covered in mountains and sulfuric hot springs, its most ominous feature was Mount Aso. One of the world's largest active volcanoes, it had the unsettling distinction of producing more explosive eruptions than any other.

Usaburo had grown up in a rice-farming family, well-off enough to own land, but not so well-off to prevent him from seeking opportunity elsewhere. By his early twenties he was on a boat headed for Seattle, for a job with the railroad. Usaburo owned a dead smile and an anvil of a haircut; the outsides of his eyebrows sat a half-inch higher on his face than the insides, creating the appearance of a permanent glower. He posed for photos with clenched fists, their veins bulging.

In 1910, and decades behind most men of his generation, Usaburo began his search for a wife. For an overwhelming number of Japanese men in America at that time, this meant a search for a picture bride. It was a crude form of matchmaking: men in America would flip through pictures of selected women and pick one, and the bride would arrive by boat months later. The men often put a thumb on the scale of the process, sending photos of their younger selves—or of entirely different men—to the women's parents. They'd lean on cars they didn't own or borrow suits just for the photo. Once the inevitably disappointed woman arrived from Japan, she and the man would be married in a mass ceremony along with the dozens of other couples meeting for the first time. The ceremonies took place right on the dock, some just minutes after the bride fainted upon seeing her husband.

Tsuru Fukuda was twenty-one years old and had smooth skin and dark black hair, parted at an angle that triangulated her hairline back and to the right. She had wide-set eyes and a third-grade education. Tsuru and Usaburo were married upon her arrival in San Francisco, and the two quickly began the work of starting a family. Seeing little opportunity to advance in the railroad, mining, or lumber fields in which Japanese immigrants often initially worked, many struck out on their own as merchants or farmers. Usaburo had already abandoned railroad work, so the couple moved south to California's Santa Clara Valley and began farming once again. Usaburo recognized that his ancestral skills in the rice fields would translate well to California's strawberry market, so he set his sights there.

By 1910 Japanese farmers were producing nearly 70 percent of the state's strawberries while cultivating less than one percent of the total farm acreage, an astounding efficiency that drew the jealous ire of white farmers. There was one problem with the model, though: after three or four years of harvests, the fruit would sap the land of its nutrients. So the Yoshinagas bounced around the lower San Francisco Bay area: San Jose to Redwood City, Redwood City to Gilroy, Gilroy to Sunnyvale, Sunnyvale to Mountain View.

This last city sat three miles inland from the southern wash of San Francisco Bay, squatting at the foot of the Santa Cruz range. Its name was self-explanatory. It had been founded as a forgettable stop on the stagecoach line between San Francisco and San Jose. By the time George entered high school, the Southern Pacific train stopped fifty-six times each day in downtown Mountain View, delivering travelers and commuters to San Francisco.

In 1931, the citizens of Santa Clara County raised $480,000 and purchased one thousand acres of farmland that lined San Francisco Bay. The land was then sold, for $1, to the United States government. The hope was that the government would improve the land and convert it into a military base, driving up property values and bringing even more jobs to the growing area. The parcel was ideal for an airport, as the Santa Cruz Mountains to the west blocked the fog that blanketed northern parts of the bay. Soon the government announced that the land would be turned into a naval air station to house the USS *Macon*. The *Macon* was the world's largest helium-filled rigid airship, and served the Navy as a flying aircraft carrier. The building constructed to house the airship, Hangar One, is still one of the largest freestanding buildings in the world. Large enough to fit six football fields, the aerodynamic, galvanized-steel wonder makes planes and cars appear like toys from above. Later renamed Moffett Field in honor of Rear Admiral William A. Moffett—the "architect of naval aviation," who died when the *Macon*'s sister dirigible, the USS *Akron*, crashed off the coast of New Jersey in 1933—the station was a boon for the economy, drawing more and more residents to the former hinterland.

The fields outside the small city were among the most fertile on earth. Nearly three hundred days of annual sunshine ensured robust numbers of apricots, pears, cherries, peaches, and plums. A 1936 municipal project brought six reservoirs to the Santa Clara Valley, enough to hold 16 billion gallons of water. Tomatoes and cucumbers were processed by the California Supply Company of San Francisco, which built one of the world's largest canneries two miles outside town. Two hundred 5,000-gallon salt brine vats cured hundreds of pounds of pickles a day, and the smell of tomatoes cooking into ketchup washed through the town.

Crime was nonexistent: the city spent only 25 cents a year per resident on police protection, the equivalent of less than $4 today. It dubbed itself "the City of Good Neighbors." "All creeds and races of people with almost every type of diverse interests [*sic*] are molded into a homogenous population," reads a 1944 pamphlet produced by the city's chamber of commerce. "A feeling of warmth and friendship is felt by the newcomers and long remembered by the visitor."

The jewel of the city was Mountain View Union High School. Built in 1926, the Mission-style structure could hold 650 students and was designed by famed California architect William Henry Weeks, whose aesthetic legacy persists in hundreds of schools and libraries across Northern California. In less than twenty years after its construction, Mountain View was rated as the third-best high school in California. Throughout the gymnasium the words of the alma mater rang during pep rallies and sporting events: "In a valley rimmed with mountains, covered by a sky of blue, stands our Alma Mater high school, with her colors brave and true. May her standards never waver, as we onward go each day, we'll fight for dear old Mountain View, and her colors blue and gray." The school's mascot was an eagle.

In class pictures, Yoshinagas and Yamijis and Okamotos stood next to Gruenebaums and Popoviches and Mendozas. The one place in the school where racial fault lines were most clear was the football team: of the twenty-eight players on the 1940–41 Mountain View Eagles squad, twenty-six were white. One was another Japanese American player, and the last was George. In a team photo, he can be seen in the lower left corner, almost slipping out of view.

George was the youngest of Usaburo and Tsuru's five children, and the only one with an English name. He was never told why his parents picked that name for him, but from birth it was immediately clear: George was different. As with his four siblings, George's mother sent him to Japanese-language school, but unlike them he was promptly thrown out for inattentiveness. When his family spoke at home, George would sit in confused silence, waiting to speak in English. His parents would return the silence. He was envious of the relationship others had with their parents and the easy way they communicated. His Japanese ability, he'd later say, was "zero." In elementary school, he was sent to the principal's office after hitting a bully with a two-by-four. There he was greeted by his sister, who was two grades ahead of him. She would serve as interpreter for her parents and the principal; all George remembers from the meeting is his father cursing in Japanese.

His relationship with his mother was warm, if quiet. In high school, he once baked a lemon meringue pie in home economics. Proud of his work, he brought the dessert home, excited to share it with his mother and sister. He tripped. The three scooped the pie off the floor and ate it anyway. His father was more volatile. When George was a boy the man stayed up one night with a baseball bat, waiting for George's older brother. When Kay pulled up to the house, Usaburo took the bat and circled the car, beating it. Kay had missed curfew. As George aged, he drew his father's attention both verbally and physically. He took judo and boxing lessons to defend himself from the abuse, and as he grew older, he found the football field. By the time he entered high school, George had grown bigger than the rest of his family. Standing at 5 feet, 10 inches, and weighing 170 pounds, he played tackle for the Mountain View Eagles. He wasn't first-string, but earned his letter when the team took back-to-back Santa Clara Valley Athletic League titles in 1940 and 1941. In an award from the Mountain View Kiwanis Club, the group honored "Yosh" for "fine spirit, good sportsmanship, team work, and athletic supremacy."

In between classes and practice he'd help manage the family farm, coordinating transportation and housing for its Mexican laborers. Usaburo died when George was thirteen, and Kay, then twenty-five, became the head of the household. As the grades ticked by, George saw his life spread before him. His father was a farmer, his brother was a farmer, and he too, would become a farmer.

Below the idyllic mist of Mountain View, the temper of the times quietly boiled. On the second floor of the Mockbee Building, right above Parkinson's Hardware, was the local chapter of the Native Sons of the

Golden West. Founded in 1875 by General A. M. Winn, the organization had been created to honor the legacy of the Gold Rush. Hundreds of parlors popped up throughout the state. Membership was limited to "only the sons of those sturdy pioneers who arrived on this coast prior to the admission of California as a state." By the 1920s the purpose of the organization had shifted from nostalgia to that of virulent anti-immigration efforts. (It wasn't difficult to foresee the shift. The man of the "sturdy pioneers" language was Willard B. Farwell, who, in 1885, wrote *The Chinese at Home and Abroad*. Chapter three of the book is simply titled "The Inhumanity of the Race.") Mexican, Chinese, and Japanese immigration was to be banned, the group argued.

"California was given by God to a white people," said Native Sons grand president William P. Canbu in 1920, "and with God's strength we want to keep it as He gave it to us."

CHAPTER TWO

Twinkletoes

THE BOARDINGHOUSE SAT one block north of the intersection of Santa Monica and Cahuenga Boulevards, across from Cole Field. The front steps of the low redbrick building were guarded by two cypress trees imported from Japan, their branches twisted and slanted. Hydrangeas perfumed the north and south sides of the building, popping into purples and whites and pinks at the first sign of summer. If you walked seventeen paces out the front door, into the middle of Cahuenga Boulevard, and craned your neck to the right, the Hollywood sign loomed over your shoulder.

Six bathrooms served the thirty-two units, each of which held a bed, a washbasin, and a single male Japanese immigrant. Behind the building was an eight-hundred-square-foot, two-bedroom space that the seven members of the Nomura family called home.

On June 12, 1907, the *Tosa Maru* docked in Victoria, British Columbia. Among the passengers disembarking was a stocky twenty-three-year-old with $75 to his name. Like every other passenger, Hyohei Nomura was perfunctorily registered by the United States Department of Commerce and Labor's Immigration Service as possessing a dark complexion, black hair, and brown eyes.

Two thousand five hundred miles across the Pacific sat Hyohei's village, Osatsu. The isolated fishing community—not until 1962, fifty-five years after Hyohei's departure, would electricity creep its way there—was known for one thing: *kachido ama*, the town's famed female divers. For three thousand years the village's women would walk across the pebbled beach, weigh themselves down with stones, gulp in as much air as their lungs allowed, and plunge beneath the ocean surface. They'd hunt for abalone and sea urchin and snails; pearls were a side benefit.

That was an ocean away now. Hyohei listed his profession as student and soon crossed into the United States, bound for San Francisco. Along the way the plan changed, and he kept traveling down past the Bay until settling in the lemon groves that would soon become Hollywood. He worked in the nursery business for four years, when he finally saved enough money to call for his wife, Ise.

Soon came a son, Minoru, in 1914, then Michiko in 1916, Miyoko in 1918, Ryohei in 1920, Takashi in 1922, and finally, in 1924, Tamotsu. The name of that youngest boy, though, didn't stick or fit quite well. Instead he'd just be known as Babe.

The earliest surviving photo of Babe hints at future promise. Dressed in shorts with knee-high socks and a baseball hat resting crooked on his head, he has his arm cocked back, clutching a ball. In the other hand, a mitt. Babe is smiling and staring directly at the camera; it's not difficult to imagine him throwing a dead strike through the lens. It wouldn't be long before the mitt was a permanent fixture on his left hand, and curiosity a fixture everywhere else. Babe and his brothers would drop cats off the landing of the stairwell in the back of the boardinghouse, just to see if the felines actually landed on their feet. Hyohei bought the boys a dilapidated Ford Model T, which the three set to restoring. In their teenage years they'd spend their nights in the car, cruising Hollywood Boulevard. At home, Babe befriended the boarders, all single men thousands of miles of ocean away from any family. He was drawn to loners and the lonely from an early age, widening his group of friends to anyone who needed it. The trait would follow him the rest of his life.

Hyohei and Ise, like most other Japanese parents, hoped their children would assimilate into American life. For the Nomura boys, the best entryway was sports. Cole Field, the baseball diamond across the street, was full nearly every day, with teams from Paramount Studios, the Screen Actors Guild, and RKO Pictures squaring off as crowds of up to 3,500 spectators cheered. The boys soon took to the game themselves.

The Japanese Athletic Union served the athletic needs of *nikkei* teens and twenty-somethings throughout California. Created in 1929 in San Francisco as a basketball league, the union soon spread across the state, eventually creating north and south divisions in communities with large concentrations of Japanese families, and expanded its sports roster to include baseball, softball, swimming, track, and weightlifting. In Los Angeles, leagues were often associated with Christian or Buddhist churches (*church* was the term used by American Buddhists as well as Christians). Games sponsored by the Young Buddhist Association served as an olive branch to parents wary of their nisei children's Americans habits. The thinking was: *If it's through a church, can it be all that bad?*

Babe dove headfirst into both leagues. By the spring of 1939, just after his fifteenth birthday, he was named a second-team all-star outfielder in the JAU by the Japanese daily *Kashu Mainichi* newspaper, often playing men ten years his senior. Two years later, while playing JAU softball against teams from across Southern California—Pasadena to Long Beach to Glendale and every Japanese neighborhood in between—he was once again named an all-star. He was a decathlete in middle school, adept as much at shot put as the mile. At fifteen he tried basketball, and was immediately picked as one of the city's best Japanese American forwards by the *Rafu Shimpo* newspaper.

These leagues, however, were isolating. As much as they introduced the young Japanese Americans to sports, they kept them sheltered, playing only within their own community. Much of this was out of their hands—most other youth leagues discouraged or outright barred their participation. Still, in order to prove himself, Babe would

need to compete against the rest of the city. He'd need to play high
school football.

Rain showers flooded the infield at Oakland's Freeman's Park as four
hundred football fans packed onto the wooden bleachers, far less than
the stadium's seven-thousand-seat capacity but still enough to bear
witness to a historic first. On the morning of January 3, 1909, the Imperials and the Fujis slid, slipped, and plowed their way across the
sodden field in what the *San Francisco Call* dubbed "the first contest of
the kind on this coast between Chinese and Japanese." *Call* reporter
T. P. Magilligan referred to one player as an "ocher youth," while the
crowd, entirely Chinese fans, featured "many pretty little maids of the
celestial empire with the soft tinkle of the orient in their voices." When
a Fuji kicked the Imperial quarterback, Magilligan referred to the
strike as "jiu jitsu tactics." In unison Imperial fans coaxed on their
team:

> *Bow wow wow*
> *Ching-a-lucka, ching-a-lucka,*
> *Buma-lucka, ching-a-lucka,*
> *Who are we?*

The Imperials won 10–0; the next morning the *Call* ran two large
photos of the game on the front page of the sports section. The game
may—or may not, depending on the veracity of Magilligan's statement—have been a first between football-playing Chinese and Japanese on the U.S. mainland, but it wouldn't be the last. The following
December the two teams renewed their rivalry, with the Fujis taking
the win under a cloud of fury. "Slit-Eye Game Ends in Riots," the Associated Press story read. Police arrived to a melee of umbrellas, sticks,
stones, and knives, with both teams fighting among the nearly one
thousand fans in attendance. One Japanese player was stabbed five

times, and another fractured his skull. Following the brawl, captains from both teams announced they would abandon the violence of football and take up rugby. The promise went unkept.

Football was growing in America, leaking out from the colleges and universities of the East, and teams of Chinese, Japanese, and soon Filipino and Korean players popped up along the West Coast. In 1919, the Asahis and Mikados—baseball rivals in Seattle—traded in their bats and took to the gridiron. Issei football leagues launched in Portland, Seattle, and the rest of the Pacific Northwest, with teams even crossing the border to compete against Vancouver squads. By 1931 the all-Chinese Yoke Choy Club played against Chinese, Japanese, and white teams, earning an invitation to the all-white McNamara Grid League in San Francisco's Golden Gate Park. The game spread to Southern California, where it flourished as nisei children rooted for USC or UCLA. Soon they took to the field themselves. In Los Angeles, Japanese American teens dotted the rosters at Poly High and Santa Monica High as early as 1920. Up the coast at Mountain View High School, in the early 1930s Toshi Hirabayashi and Harry Hamasaki paved the way for George Yoshinaga's arrival later that decade. In 1938, in Los Angeles, Phineas Banning High School quarterback James Okura and Venice High School back Izumi Itsuki were named all-league; both were described as "fast and shifty," the latter an adjective—along with "clever" and "sneaky"— that would come to define the way white journalists viewed Asian American athletes. Football, in their eyes, was a head-to-head sport, a combat to be indulged, not avoided. Any deviation around that confrontation was seen as less-than. Often undersized, nisei players "employed a variety of tactics viewed as clever by white observers," writes Asian American sports historian Joel Franks. "Called clever might be seen as a compliment but in the masculine and radicalized world of early twentieth-century sport it might be another way of accusing a team of being underhanded, of engaging in the equivalent of guerrilla warfare."

If you picked up the October 25, 1940, *Los Angeles Times*, you'd be forgiven if you missed Babe's first appearance in the metropolitan daily. The article was just two sentences and a headline—"Redshirts Win, 19–0." Squeezed among the Thursday results of the Santa Anita Open golf tournament, a column about the previous week's Tennessee-Alabama game, and the week's college football predictions, the story was nothing more than a space filler.

"A slight case of too much Nomura hit the Wilson High Class B football team yesterday as the Hollywood lighties walked off with a 19–0 victory on the Mule field. Babe Nomura registered two touchdowns, one on a 70-yard pass interception, and his brother, Tad, an end, scored another on a pass."

Tad was Tak, Takashi on his birth certificate—scan the *Times* archives from the first half of the twentieth century and you'll find a staff struggling to accurately spell the names of a variety of ethnicities. Eighteen years old and still on the Hollywood High junior varsity football team, Tak was outshined in every way by his younger brother. A week after his arrival in the *Times*, Babe appeared again, this time without Tak. The write-up was just as brief. "Sheik Lightweights Trip Marshall, 6–0," the headline read. Just one sentence followed: "A 14-yard aerial from Dick Kildy to Babe Nomura provided Hollywood High's Class B football squad with a 6–0 victory over Marshall yesterday on the Sheiks' turf."

Babe was one of the Sheiks' smallest players. The sleeves on his maroon and cream jersey would've extended to his fingers if he hadn't kept them scrunched over his elbows. He had moody eyes, and a dark mop that he flipped and styled in front, with a curl sometimes falling onto his forehead. His smile, if you could call it that, was nearly always as flat as a table. That served a purpose. For his entire life he'd be embarrassed by his teeth; pursed lips would shield them from the camera or wandering eyes.

The team was coached by Ed Warner, who had replaced Boris "Doc" Pash when Pash was called for active duty with the Army. A lumbering man, Pash was the son of a Russian Orthodox priest sent to California by the church in 1894. Pash was born in San Francisco in 1900 but moved to his father's homeland in his early teens, eventually serving as a translator for the British during the Russian Revolution. In 1924, after receiving a bachelor's degree in physical education from Springfield College in Massachusetts, he made his way to Hollywood, where he taught gym and coached football, baseball, and swimming until 1941, when he was called to the Army.

On Christmas Eve 1933, Pash traveled from Hollywood to Kezar Stadium, a fifty-thousand-seat arena in the southeast corner of San Francisco's Golden Gate Park. He visited at the request of his cousin, a local high school football coach, and he would spend his day coaching an all-star team of Japanese American players against one constructed of Chinese American players. "Orientals Set for Grid Test," the *San Francisco Examiner* proclaimed. The game was a precursor of things to come for Pash. His backs barely tipped the scales at 155 pounds, a hindrance he'd have to wrestle with in the years to come at Hollywood High as well.

After leaving Hollywood for active duty, Pash had his language and intelligence skills put to work immediately: his first assignment was investigating the rumor of a secret military base that the Japanese were building in Baja California, Mexico. Soon he was chief of counterintelligence for the Army's San Francisco–based Ninth Corps Area, which oversaw nine Western states. (In this capacity, Pash later investigated the communist sympathies of Robert Oppenheimer, the father of the atomic bomb; he recommended Oppenheimer be monitored but didn't believe he was a spy.)

Back in Hollywood, the 1940 season had stumbled out of the gates for the Sheiks in Pash's absence. In the team's first practice game, it fumbled its way to a 19–6 loss against Los Angeles High School. The following week, in a second preseason game, the team lost a tight

14–12 contest to North Hollywood High. In addition to anything re-sembling inspired play, there was another factor missing from the Hollywood eleven: Babe hadn't even touched the ball.

That changed the following week. The Sheiks eked out a 6–0 win over Lincoln in the last 15 seconds of the game, with Babe leading the rushing. Every game after—first Wilson High, then Marshall, then Belmont, then Franklin—he pounded the ball across Hollywood High's dirt field. With the Hollywood Roosevelt Hotel's twelve stories rising behind him, he led the Sheiks' junior varsity team to an unde-feated, untied, unscored-upon season.

Next to Babe's photo in his 1941 Hollywood High yearbook, a white teammate scrawled, with an arrow to Nomura's face, "The big-gest shit in Hollywood." Babe crossed out "shit" and wrote "shot."

Hollywood High School is the Los Angeles public high school that serves arguably the world's most famous neighborhood. When not busy filming, an incandescent Judy Garland would walk the halls in the late 1930s, while Jason Robards's mile time on the track team—a foot-numbing 4:18—was enough to draw interest from multiple uni-versities. In 1936, a seventeen-year-old Mickey Rooney would drive his blue Ford convertible onto the schoolyard grass, park, and pass through a throng of teenage girls on his way to class. Actors James Garner and Richard Long and Gloria Grahame, future U.S. secretary of state Warren Christopher—all called Hollywood High home with Babe.

Even the high school mascot, the Sheik, had been taken from the screen. It was borrowed from the 1921 Rudolph Valentino silent film *The Sheik*, which had shot some of its scenes less than a mile from campus. During the premiere at Grauman's Rialto theater on Broad-way, women allegedly passed out when Valentino appeared on-screen. "When an Arab sees a woman he wants, he takes her," the movie poster read. It's not unsolvable what honor high school officials believed they were bestowing upon their athletes by adopting "sheik" as their mascot.

While the school was filled with movie stars, its glory was still reserved for athletes. As far back as 1920 it was clear that football, not film, was the quickest way to the top of the social heap. "A football hero sure is he / what greater glory can there be?" wrote center Adam Walsh in the 1920 yearbook. After Walsh left Hollywood High he went on to captain Knute Rockne's legendary "Four Horsemen" teams at Notre Dame, among the most dominant teams in college football history. Before a 1924 game against Army, Walsh pulled the tape off a broken hand, then bandaged his good one as though it were the broken one. His gambit was dubiously conceived: he figured Army would try to reinjure his broken hand, knocking the star center out of the game. Army tried its best, stomping and smashing what it thought to be the broken hand the entire game. Walsh carried on, snapping the ball for every Irish down en route to a 13–7 victory.

The plan didn't pay off completely: he finished the game with two broken hands.

———————

Football is barely recognizable today from its roots, and even from the style of play through the mid-twentieth century. While the bones of the game are the same—a field, a ball, eleven men on each side of that ball—what it took to win a hundred years ago was much different from what it takes today.

For example, take the evening of August 8, 1932, at Los Angeles Memorial Stadium. Football was a demonstration sport in that summer's Olympic Games; no medals were awarded. But in an effort to expand the game to an international audience, all-star teams of college players from the East and West Coasts—Harvard, Yale, and Princeton, and Cal, Stanford, and USC, respectively—were created. It was a one-game sales pitch to the world.

"90,000 Expected to Witness Grid Battle at Olympic Stadium To-night," pronounced the morning's *San Francisco Examiner* in a head-line that spanned the entire width of the newspaper.

By the time the lights flickered off at the stadium, the Western All-Stars had defeated the East 7–6. All the points had been scored in the final quarter. The next morning's *Los Angeles Times* described the game as a "struggle." Nearly every game was like that: a grinding slog, with players mashing together in hopes that eventually one of their bodies would miraculously plop into the end zone. And Hollywood High School was no exception.

At the start of the 1941 season, Babe was promoted to varsity as the team's starting halfback. Branded with a new nickname—Twinkle-toes, after his burning speed—he was ready to pick up where his un-defeated JV team had left off the year before. He'd have to do it away from Hollywood: the school's Snyder Field was completely void of grass. Local press dubbed it the Dust Bowl, and coach Meb Schroeder refused to allow his team to risk injury on this surface. With the field's usual government-employed WPA caretakers now reassigned to con-struction projects started in preparation for a seemingly inevitable war, all games would have to be played at the opposing school.

The varsity team used an offensive scheme known as the Notre Dame Box, named after the Fighting Irish's variation on the single-wing formation. An offense based much on deception, it was often used when the team lacked a true triple-threat tailback: a player who was adept at running, passing, and kicking. (Footballers played both offense and defense in the 1940s, and true specialization was still de-cades away.) In Hollywood High's case, it was used because neither of its starting tailbacks—Babe and Jerry McClellan—tipped 160 pounds on the scale.

The first game of the season was a warm-up game against Lincoln. Babe opened the scoring with a first-quarter, 10-yard rushing touch-down, only to have the Tigers tie it up minutes later. An uninspiring second half would foreshadow the rest of the Sheiks' season; the game ended 7–7.

A week later, the speed of the Fairfax High eleven overpowered Hollywood, and the home team blazed to a 13–0 lead on two break-away runs. Fairfax and Hollywood were archrivals, sitting only a few dozen blocks from each other. Late in the game, as victory seemed to be slipping away, Babe drove the Sheiks 60 yards down the field, con-necting with McClellan for a touchdown. But it would be the final score of the game, and the Sheiks fell again, 13–6.

The rest of the season was equally dismal, with low-scoring losses to Hamilton and University High Schools, and a 20–0 thrashing by the Venice High Gondoliers. Of the fifty-five boys who dressed for the Sheiks that fall, Babe was the only Japanese American player. For the team's yearbook photo, he sat on the ground in the first row, far left, same as George Yoshinaga had, three hundred miles north in Mountain View. And just like George, Babe was almost cropped off the page.

"There is one thing I'm going to see as far as it is in my power, and that is that every boy and girl in Hollywood High School is going to know the words to 'America,' 'The Star-Spangled Banner,' and 'The Loyalty Song,'" said Hollywood principal Louis Foley, at an assembly just weeks before Pearl Harbor.

While the United States was not yet formally at war, the writing was on the wall. Since the Japanese invasion of Manchuria in 1931, that likelihood had grown year by year. Diplomatic attempts to squelch Japan's incursions into China and French Indochina had stalled, and President Roosevelt's decision to move the United States' Pacific Fleet from San Diego to Pearl Harbor had achieved none of the foreboding effect he believed it would. In a Gallup survey conducted the day be-fore Pearl Harbor, 52 percent of Americans polled expected war with the Japanese "in the near future," while only 27 percent didn't.

So, a nation prepared.

In lieu of social studies, graduating Hollywood High seniors were required to take a class entitled "National Defense," which included, among other lessons, the drawing of battlefield maps. A recruitment center was erected in the lobby of the school auditorium, biology students tended victory gardens, and art classes designed war posters. Warren Christopher, the future secretary of state, would spend his lunch period relaying the day's war news to his classmates over the loudspeakers.

The school was mostly white and middle-class, with virtually no African American or Latino students until after the war, but the school's Japanese American population was large enough by the early 1940s for a sizable student club. The numbers were still minuscule: of the 654 graduates of the class of 1940, just 26 were Japanese American.

Then, on November 26, 1941, six aircraft carriers bearing 414 airplanes departed Hittokapu Bay in the far northern reaches of Japan and pointed southeast for the ten-day journey to Hawai'i. Twelve days later, at 12:30 p.m., President Franklin Delano Roosevelt gingerly climbed the marble rostrum of the U.S. House of Representatives chamber. Gripping the podium for balance, he waited until the standing ovation of senators and representatives ebbed before speaking.

"Mr. Vice President, Mr. Speaker, Members of the Senate, and of the House of Representatives," he spoke in his prep-school drone. "Yesterday, December 7th, 1941—a date which will live in infamy— the United States of America was suddenly and deliberately attacked by naval and air forces of the Empire of Japan."

Without the aid of speechwriters, Roosevelt had dictated the address the night before to his secretary, Grace Tully. Against the advice of his secretary of state, Cordell Hull, Roosevelt kept the speech brief. (Hull advised Roosevelt to explain the diplomatic lengths to which the American government had gone to avoid war; Roosevelt overruled him in favor of "dramatic effect.") Over the next seven minutes, the president made his case for war against Japan.

"Hostilities exist," he said. "There is no blinking at the fact that our people, our territory, and our interests are in grave danger. With confidence in our armed forces, with the unbounding determination of our people, we will gain the inevitable triumph—so help us God."

Two thousand three hundred miles west, the message filtered out of the speakers at Hollywood High, trickling down hallways and snaking into locker rooms. The speech attracted the largest radio audience in American history, with 81 percent of U.S. households tuning in. Thirty-three minutes after the address, Congress declared war on Japan. Only one representative, Jeannette Rankin, the first woman ever to hold federal office, voted no. As her colleagues booed and begged her to vote "present" instead of "no," she stood her ground, eventually seeking shelter from throngs of reporters in a phone booth while waiting for Capitol Police to escort her to her office.

The Japanese club was abruptly shuttered. Soon the Japanese American faces disappeared altogether. And two days later, the *Hollywood High School News*'s lead story was "Senior Glee Clubs to Sing Yule Songs."

CHAPTER THREE

Furusato

BY THE AFTERNOON of December 8, the Federal Bureau of Investigation had detained 736 Japanese nationals on the United States mainland and in Hawai'i. Within four days that number grew to 1,370, and, eventually, to 2,192. The FBI's authority came via presidential warrant, signed by U.S. attorney general Francis Biddle. It authorized the arrest of enemy aliens considered "dangerous to the public peace and safety of the United States." The issei—shopkeepers, gardeners, farmers, dry cleaners, all charged with nothing—were loaded into police cars as their American sons and daughters looked on. In a statement two days later, Biddle halfheartedly attempted to assuage the American public—or, more specifically, the Japanese American public.

> So long as aliens in this country conduct themselves in accordance
> with law, they need fear no interference by the Department of Jus-
> tice or by any other agency of the Federal Government. They may
> be assured, indeed that every effort will be made to protect them
> from any discrimination or abuse. . . . Inevitably, there are some
> among our alien population who are disloyal. The Federal Gov-
> ernment is fully aware of the dangers presented not only by such
> persons but also by disloyal citizens. The government has control of
> the activities of these elements.

Biddle was the great-great-grandson of the first attorney general of the United States under President George Washington, and a distant relative of James Madison. His family traced its heritage in the United States to more than one hundred years prior to the country's founding. Born in Paris and raised partly in Switzerland, the Groton and Harvard Law graduate later abandoned his family's Republican roots and became a fervent Democrat, serving as head of the National Labor Relations Board under President Roosevelt. Soon came stints as a judge on the U.S. Court of Appeals (1939), as solicitor general (1940), and finally, like his great-great-grandfather 152 years earlier, attorney general. He was in office only three months before the Japanese bombed Pearl Harbor.

The seeds of the arrests Biddle oversaw had been planted years earlier. Under the shield of the Alien Enemies Act of 1798, the federal government had arrested 6,400 mostly German nationals residing in the United States during World War I. Nearly 2,400 were interned for some or all of the war. In the decades that followed, the Department of the Navy's Office of Naval Intelligence, the War Department's Military Intelligence Division, the FBI, and the State Department continued counterintelligence measures aimed at thwarting potential acts of espionage. In the 1920s and 1930s, this meant monitoring Japan's growing naval influence in the Pacific. On August 10, 1936, Roosevelt expressed his concern in a letter to his chief of naval operations.

"Every Japanese citizen or non-citizen on the Island of Oahu who meets these Japanese ships [arriving in Hawai'i] or has any connection with their officers or men should be secretly but definitely identified and his or her name be placed on a special list of those who would be the first to be placed in a concentration camp in the event of trouble," he wrote.

This surveillance was far from limited to Japanese nationals. A confidential State Department memo from late 1934 highlights some of the earliest signs of the federal government's surveillance (and hysteria) of its own Japanese American citizens.

"The Imperial Japanese Government has agents in every large city in this country and on the West Coast," the communiqué reads. "These people, who pass as civilians and laborers, are being drilled in military maneuvers. . . . When war breaks out, the entire Japanese population on the West Coast will rise and commit sabotage. They will endeavor by every means to neutralize the West Coast and render her defenseless."

By June 1940 there were so many different arms of the federal government monitoring the Japanese American community that Roosevelt had to designate the duties to avoid overlap; memos were sent to the secretaries of state, war, treasury, navy, and commerce, and to the attorney general. The Army's Military Intelligence Division handled the investigation of cases that originated in the military, including civilians employed by it. The Office of Naval Intelligence investigated cases within the Navy and its civilian employees. The FBI was responsible for all investigations of espionage, counterespionage, and sabotage involving civilians in the United States and its territories, and its duties included one other critical obligation: the discovery of fifth column activity, defined by Military Intelligence as "previous, secret, and intelligent planning . . . coordinated in time and space with those of the uniformed forces of the enemy."

Their marching orders presented, the agencies ratcheted up their efforts. As the war in Europe churned, the American defense industry readied itself. Munitions, aircraft, and warship production skyrocketed as an essential hedge in case of U.S. involvement; the FBI secured more than eleven thousand informants in the plants by the end of 1940. Convinced that, due to their racial distinctions, Japanese spies would not be able to infiltrate those factories, counterintelligence concocted a convoluted fantasy: Japan was recruiting African American workers as spies.

In a justification that would crop up again and again both before and after Pearl Harbor, intelligence officers posited that the lack of Japanese American faces in the factories *proved* that the spies were, in fact, very good. In early 1941, Military Intelligence warned of this possibility, saying "the Japanese plan to utilize American Negroes for subversion and espionage. . . . The Japanese figure that as long as the Negro is dependent upon the whites for livelihood, the political strength can be used to their advantage."

The hypothesis couldn't have been further from the truth, for one reason in particular: black Americans mostly didn't work in the defense industry. Whites sucked up the majority of these jobs, backed by the United States Employment Service, which happily filled "whites only" requests from defense contractors. State Department investigators went so far as to speculate that Japanese Americans had infiltrated A. Philip Randolph's March on Washington movement, which sought the desegregation of the armed forces and fair working practices for African Americans. In May 1941, in an effort to head off the march, Roosevelt signed Executive Order 8802, which prohibited discrimination in federal job programs and for defense companies contracting with the government; the armed forces, however, were not desegregated until 1948, three years after the war.

No corner of Japanese American life was safe from prying eyes.

Driven by special travel rates and promises of reduced hotel costs upon arrival, more than one hundred cruises had left the United States for Japan between 1938 and 1941. Intelligence officers pored over the itineraries; most involved little more than visits to parents' graves or ceremonies at Buddhist and Shinto shrines. Buddhist priests and organizations like the Young Buddhist Association were added to Naval Intelligence's list of subversive groups. The priests were disparaged for their lengthy training in Japan and for "developing Japanese spirit and for holding before their adherents Japanese ideas."

Monitoring wasn't limited to the FBI's rank-and-file. J. Edgar Hoover, then already head of the bureau for more than a decade and a half, wrote in a November 15, 1940, memo that the majority of issei would be loyal to the United States in the event of war, but that a tiny minority of "Buddhist and Shintoist priests, the Japanese-language schoolteachers, the consular agents, and a small percentage of prominent Japanese alien businessmen" may not have been inclined to do so. Two months before Pearl Harbor, in October 1941, he sent a plea to his field agents.

> *Japanese espionage activities . . . have been and are being conducted regarding various subjects whose activities have caused them to be looked upon with suspicion. Nevertheless, the practical results have been very meager. It is believed that a specific reason for this undesirable situation is the dearth of confidential informants among members of the Japanese race. Accordingly, you are instructed to take immediate steps to secure and develop confidential informants of the Japanese race.*

Hoover's instructions had a very specific effect: they splintered the Japanese community along generational lines. The FBI believed Japan was using only issei as saboteurs, not their American children, so the FBI began recruiting informants from the younger generation. The most prominent of these came from the Japanese American Citizens League, a predominantly nisei and sansei organization. While the results were limited—it's impossible to inform on a spy when no spying is actually occurring—they were *something*. "With the help of the J.A.C.L., which got to be very much on our side . . . we were able to pinpoint practically every agent that had any potential for mischief," reads one Naval Intelligence report. The boasts, however, were just that. Most FBI agents found loyal employees and, even more so, loyal Americans. In a note sent to Hoover from the FBI's San Francisco office, agents surmised that although Japanese Americans were "asked to furnish information of espionage activities, they all vehemently state that they have no information to give because the Japanese are not engaged in such activity. . . . It is my opinion that these individuals say one thing and think another, and would not cooperate if they knew of such activities." Nowhere was this misconception more evident than the docks of San Pedro Bay.

Terminal Island is a misnomer, implying a single piece of land. It is, in fact, a man-made amalgam of the former Rattlesnake and Deadman's Islands, the first named for its animal inhabitants, the second for its once human inhabitants. The first Japanese settled in the San Pedro Bay area in 1899, skimming the water of its abalone and lobster. By 1910 the men had shifted their eyes to tuna and sardines, and their homes to the newly created Terminal Island. While Filipinos, Mexicans, Portuguese, Sicilians, and Slovenians occupied the eastern part of the island, by 1930 the western stretch was indistinguishable from any fishing village in Japan. Three thousand issei called the island home, a cheap oasis from the growing prices of a booming Los Angeles. They built a labyrinthine town, with wild bamboo, rabbit pens, chicken coops, and Buddhist and Shinto temples mixing with banks, restaurants, and pool halls. A staccato blend of Japanese and English developed there, one honed in short sentences over bulging nets on the Pacific. They called the dialect *kii-shu ben*, named after the Kii district in Wakayama, the town from which many of the residents had emigrated. They came to refer affectionately to Terminal Island as *furusato*: home.

Nearly every resident was connected to the fishing industry, whether as a fisherman, a cannery worker, or a boat operator. They also, by nature of their industry, were in boats, floating alone, in the Pacific Ocean all day—excuse enough for U.S. intelligence services to monitor their daily activities. Hoover saw the fishermen as little more than sardine-scented spies. "There is a [Japanese] fishing fleet of approximately 500 boats on the Pacific Coast whose masters are more thoroughly acquainted with the waters than any other person," he wrote in an August 1941 memo to the director of Naval Intelligence. "The boats are adaptable for use as mine layers, patrol boats, and service in other capacities."

The year prior, Naval Intelligence purchased 105 acres of land along San Pedro Bay, surrounding the community. If they couldn't eliminate them, they could at least watch them.

On the day of Pearl Harbor, 40,869 Japanese nationals lived on the West Coast. By comparison, there were 51,923 Italian nationals in California alone. While the intelligence agencies spent their days monitoring every movement of Los Angeles's 8,726 Japanese nationals, 17,528 German-born residents walked the streets, virtually unharassed. Throughout the 1930s, pro-Nazi groups proliferated in the United States, with the Amerika-Deutscher Volksbund boasting members in every state save for Louisiana. Campgrounds and public parks filled with marching bands and sympathizers with their arms raised high in honor of the führer. The group's 1939 Madison Square Garden rally stands as the most visible marker of this period, but American Nazis raised swastikas in Los Angeles parks as well, hoping to draw support from the 150,000 members of Southern California's fifty German American organizations. Despite this, Roosevelt made only a glancing effort to monitor the activities of Americans of German or Italian descent. Years later John DeWitt, commanding general of the Western Defense Command, would defend that exclusion.

"You needn't worry about the Italians at all except in certain cases," he said during an April 1943 hearing before the House Naval Affairs Subcommittee. "Also, the same for the Germans except in individual cases. But we must worry about the Japanese all the time until he is wiped off the map. Sabotage and espionage will make problems as long as he is allowed in this area—problems which I don't want to have to worry about."

In October 1940, the FBI received a tip from a neighbor that a fifty-four-year-old Japanese man living in Hollywood was raising carrier pigeons. The pigeons, the tip implied, were being trained to transport messages to Japanese intelligence. Upon inspection, the FBI determined that while it was true that the man was breeding pigeons, they were used for food, not for sending clandestine messages. Feed prices had climbed so high, the man explained, that he winnowed down his usual flock of forty or so to four. Satisfied with his response, the FBI closed the investigation, and Hyohei Nomura went back to running his boardinghouse alongside his wife and five children, its front dotted with cypress trees.

Forty years into the twentieth century, Los Angeles had become the epicenter of Japanese life in the United States. "Los Angeles is to the Japanese what Harlem is to the Negro, San Francisco is to the Chinese, Stockton to the Filipino, and Hollywood to the Mid-Western girl," wrote Joe Oyama in an April 1936 edition of the *Kashu Mainichi*.

By 1930 the nikkei in America had grown to 138,834, still just 0.1 percent of the country's population. If you placed every man, woman, and child of Japanese descent into one city, that city would've been just the sixtieth-largest in America, only slightly bigger than Paterson, New Jersey. Of those a full quarter—35,000—lived in Los Angeles County. The rest were scattered mostly across the Western United States, from Seattle, Spokane, and Yakima, down through Sacramento, San Francisco, and Fresno, and finally to San Diego and southern Arizona. Though the number of Japanese and Japanese Americans was alarming to white Californians, it was the rate of growth that worried them more. From 1910 to 1930, the number of nisei spiked from 4,502 to 68,357—a fifteenfold increase.

Five years after Roosevelt's warning about Hawai'i, on December 7, 1941, the federal government had on hand a ranked list of Japanese nationals, separated into three categories. Much of the credit for the list was given in retrospect to Naval Intelligence staff officer Lieutenant Commander Kenneth Ringle, who, in March of that year, led a covert break-in of the Japanese consulate in Los Angeles. With the aid of police, the FBI, and a safecracker the group had somehow wrangled out of prison, Ringle photographed the contents of the consulate's safe, which yielded lists of agents, contacts, and codes. It also provided unexpected returns. Documents showed that the consulate viewed most issei and nisei not as potential spies, but as the opposite—traitors to Japan.

Category A comprised members of the Kokuryu Kai—a far-right, ultranationalist paramilitary group—and Sokoku Kai, which translates into "fatherland society." (The first in a long line of dubious claims by the federal government regarding the imprisonment of Japanese nationals and Japanese Americans: there is contemporary doubt whether the Kokuryu Kai or Sokoku Kai even existed in the American issei community. *Sokoku*, however, was a Japanese nationalist magazine; it's likely intelligence officials conflated the two, as anyone found on the subscription list was taken in.) The B and C categories included Shinto temple leaders, flower-arranging society members, judo experts, and Japanese-language newspaper editors. The only thing that those arrested had in common was their ancestry. In some particularly depressing instances, issei men packed their suitcases and waited to be arrested. When the FBI never showed, the men hung their heads, left wondering if they'd lost a place of importance in their communities.

The stated purpose of the list may have been to isolate Japanese nationals that the intelligence community deemed dangerous, but the reality was that it sought to exterminate every strand of Japanese culture in the United States. Leaders of both the Nippon Bunka Kyokai (the Japanese Cultural Society) and Nichibei Kinema (the Japanese American Theatrical Arts Association) were arrested. The Nippon Bunka Kyokai promoted American-Japanese relations by hosting lectures, meetings, and exhibits, introducing Japanese culture to a new American audience; the Nichibei Kinema sponsored West Coast tours of visiting Japanese movie stars and operated Japanese movie houses.

As news of the arrests traveled, Japanese nationals and Japanese Americans began to destroy any items that might be used as evidence against their loyalty. Letters, photographs, and books were burned; family heirlooms broken and discarded. One Los Angeles resident walked into his home and found his father removing two samurai swords from a dresser. One was long and needed two hands to hold, while the other was short. His father opened the inlaid cases the swords rested in and walked into the backyard. He drove the swords into the ground and buried the handles.

FBI agents fanned out across the West Coast and Hawai'i. Justice Department orders allowed for the confiscation of radio transmitters, shortwave radio receiving sets, and cameras from anyone considered suspicious. Guns were also up for removal. By the end of December the FBI had confiscated 1,458 radios, 2,114 cameras, 1,652 sticks of dynamite, 2,592 guns, and 199,000 rounds of ammunition. The agency boasted about its totals, while failing to admit that most of the guns were shotguns and hunting rifles, and most of the ammunition was purchased at sporting goods stores. The dynamite was used by farmers to blow up stubborn tree stumps.

It wasn't until months later that Biddle admitted the fallacy of the searches.

"We have not uncovered through these searches any dangerous persons that we could not otherwise know about," he wrote in a Justice Department memo. "We have not found among all the sticks of dyna-mite and gunpowder any evidence that any of it was to be used in bombs. We have not found a single machine gun nor have we found any gun in any circumstances indicating that it was to be used in a manner helpful to our enemies. We have not found a camera which we have reason to believe was for use in espionage."

Of all the people with Roosevelt's ear, his wife, Eleanor, was the most sympathetic to the plight of the nikkei. On December 3, four days before Pearl Harbor, she attempted to calm the nerves of Japanese Americans and other immigrant groups.

"I see absolutely no reason why anyone who has had a good record— that is, who has no criminal nor anti-American record—should have any anxiety about his position," she said from the dais of an immigra-tion symposium held on New York City's Upper West Side. "This is equally applicable to the Japanese who cannot become citizens but have lived here for 30 or 40 years and to those newcomers who have not yet had time to become citizens."

She went out of her way to tell the crowd that she was making this statement not only personally, but with the blessing of the departments of State and Justice.

On overnight flights west, Mrs. Roosevelt liked waking with the dawn, watching the sun paint reds and purples across the sky and exploring the shadows stretching from mountains. Two days after Pearl Harbor, she made this trip with New York mayor Fiorello La Guardia, who had just been named by her husband the first director of the Office of Civilian Defense, the office that managed blackouts, air raid wardens, sirens, and shelters in the event of an aerial attack. La Guardia and Mrs. Roosevelt landed in a rainy Burbank on Tuesday, December 9; he drove north to San Francisco, and she south to San Diego. In between civilian defense meetings, she met with groups of nisei women up and down the coast, traveling by train. When she discovered that Department of Treasury orders freezing issei bank accounts were causing irreparable harm to farmers, she immediately contacted department officials. (The orders were relaxed, allowing issei to withdraw $100 per month to pay living expenses.)

A week later, in the December 16 iteration of her nationally syndicated daily column, *My Day*, she urged unity among her readers.

Our citizens come from all the nations of the world. Some of us have said from time to time, that we were the only proof that different nationalities could live together in peace and understanding, each bringing his own contribution, different though it may be, to the final unity which is the United States. . . . Perhaps, on us today, lies the obligation to prove that such a vision may be a practical possibility. If we cannot meet the challenge of fairness to our citizens of every nationality, of really believing in the Bill of Rights and making it a reality for all loyal American citizens, regardless of race, creed or color; if we cannot keep in check anti-semitism,

*anti-racial feelings as well as anti-religious feelings, then we shall
have removed from the world, the one real hope for the future on
which all humanity must now rely.*

Despite a long-boiling animus between white Californians and their neighbors of Japanese descent, the days following Pearl Harbor were defined by cautious yet supportive editorials and headlines from the state's newspapers. On December 9, the *San Francisco Chronicle* reminded readers that "the roundup of Japanese citizens in various parts of the country . . . is not a call for volunteer spy hunters to go into action. Neither is it a reason to lift an eyebrow at a Japanese, whether American-born or not. . . . There is no excuse to wound the sensibilities of any persons in America by showing suspicion or prejudice. . . . An American-born Nazi would like nothing better than to set the dogs of prejudice on a first-class American Japanese." Rural newspapers defended their neighbors as well. In the December 8 edition of the *Brawley News*—which served a small agricultural community twenty miles north of the Mexican border—editors cautioned, "In this community we have many Japanese neighbors and citizens and nothing should occur to cause embarrassment to those whose loyalty to their adopted country remains steadfast during this time of crisis."

It didn't take long for the détente to end. Decades later, University of Chicago political scientist Morton Grodzins analyzed the editorial responses to Pearl Harbor, and, specifically, the calls for incarceration of Japanese Americans. Grodzins studied the editorials of 112 California newspapers from December 8, 1941—the day after Pearl Harbor—to March 8, 1942. During the first four weeks of the war, he found no fewer than 62.5 editorials favorable to Japanese Americans, compared to 4.5 unfavorable ones. But between January 5 and 25 editorial interest slackened, and unfavorable views begin to poke their heads through: 20.5 favorable versus 11.5 unfavorable. From January 26 on, he wrote, "favorable editorial comment was completely lost in the barrage of allegations of disloyalty, demands for a strict control program, and expressions of dissatisfaction over the government's assumption over an evacuation program."

The immediacy of the shift was most evident in the *Los Angeles Times*, the hometown newspaper of the largest nikkei community in the country. In a January 23 editorial, the paper, originally tepid in developing a response, dipped a hesitant toe: "Many of our Japanese, whether born here or not, are fully loyal and deserve sympathy over suspicion. Others, in both categories, hold to a foreign allegiance and are dangerous, at least potentially. To be sure it would sometimes stump an expert to tell which is which and mistakes, if made, should be on the side of caution."

Five days later, that call for caution was rescinded: "The rigors of war demand proper detention of Japanese and their immediate removal from the most acute danger spots."

On January 2, Hearst columnist Damon Runyon claimed incorrectly that Los Angeles health inspectors "looking over a Japanese rooming house came upon a powerful transmitter, and it is reasonable to assume that menace of a similar character must be constantly guarded against throughout the war." No transmitter was ever found in Japanese American hands. Three days after Runyon's misreport, a radio broadcaster by the name of John B. Hughes began near-daily attacks on the nikkei community, claiming that 90 percent of U.S.-born nisei were "primarily loyal to Japan." (He also presented the same dubious statistic to Attorney General Biddle in a letter later that month.) In his study of the press, Grodzins said Justice Department officials claimed Hughes's broadcasts were "responsible for arousing public opinion and flooding the California Congressional delegation with protests which had the tendency to push the government into hasty and ill-considered action."

If Hughes's broadcasts worked from the bottom up inflaming the masses, then a column by Walter Lippmann worked from the top down. A future Presidential Medal of Freedom recipient and two-time Pulitzer Prize winner, Lippmann was the country's preeminent newspaperman, with his column syndicated in 250 newspapers across the United States and twenty-five countries. His February 12, 1942, column, entitled "The Fifth Column on the Coast," laid out the most widely read argument for the incarceration of Japanese Americans, then or ever. The column was read by Roosevelt chief of staff George C. Marshall, who passed it on to Secretary of War Henry Stimson. Stimson in turn shared it with Assistant Secretary of War John Mc-Cloy; it was almost certainly read within the walls of the Oval Office.

Without ever mentioning Japanese Americans by name, Lippmann laid out his plan:

> *The Pacific Coast is in imminent danger of a combined attack from within and without. . . . I am sure I appreciate fully and understand thoroughly the unwillingness of Washington to adopt a policy of mass evacuation and mass internment of all those who are technically enemy aliens . . . [but] the Pacific Coast is officially a combat zone . . . and nobody ought to be on a battlefield who has no good reason for being there. There is plenty of room elsewhere for him to exercise his rights.*

Hearst columnist Henry McLemore made explicit what Lippmann left implicit:

> *Herd 'em up, pack 'em off and give 'em the inside room in the Badlands. Let 'em be pinched, hurt, hungry, and dead up against it. . . . Let us have no patience with the enemy or with anyone whose veins carry his blood. . . . If making one million innocent Japanese uncomfortable would prevent one scheming Japanese from costing the life of one American boy, then let the million innocents suffer.*

"Personally, I hate the Japanese," he concluded. "And that goes for all of them."

CHAPTER FOUR

How to Make It in America

THE WESTERNMOST TRACT of the North Pacific gyre is the Kuro-shio Current, known colloquially as the Black Stream. It flows along Japan's eastern seaboard, dragging warm, tropical air from the south up to subarctic regions of eastern Russia and Alaska's Aleutian Islands. There it crashes into the North Pacific Current, which tumbles down into the California Current before continuing its journey west to the Philippines and, finally, back to Japan. On the fifth day of the first month of 1841, that current dragged fourteen-year-old Manjiro into the middle of the Pacific Ocean and left him later on an island to die.

Unable to afford schooling in Japan, Manjiro had taken to the sea at thirteen, unhooking fish from their lines. On that January morning, he and four others shoved off, hoping to meet a school of sea bass arriving with the New Year's tide. They spent the next week hungry, their nets empty. A storm approached on that seventh day and the fishermen made for shore. But the water beneath them turned a deep purple, the sea bream and mackerel so plentiful that their skins darkened the water. As the storm grew, the men cast their nets, eager not to let their fortune slip away. Terror soon overpowered the prospect of profit, though, and the men rowed furiously. Five days passed before the boat ended its drift on Tori-shima Island, 450 miles from home, their only neighbors the island's albatrosses. For almost six months they survived on birds, seaweed, and shellfish. On June 27, 1841, a black dot appeared in the distance.

Manjiro tied his tattered, bleached clothes around his head and swam toward the ship. It must've seemed like a mirage: three masts laced with ten sails and jibs, crewed by more than thirty men, black and white. It was unlikely, if not impossible, that Manjiro had ever seen a man of another race. Once safely aboard, he knelt down and worshipped the strangers.

"Could not understand anything from them more than that they were hungry," William H. Whitfield, captain of the *John Howland*, wrote in the ship's logbook. "Made the latitude of the Isle 30 deg. 31 min. N,"

The *John Howland* was a whaler out of New Bedford, Massachusetts. Two days before Manjiro took to the sea in Japan, Herman Melville left New Bedford on the *Acushnet*, a nearly five-year journey that would eventually become the basis for *Moby-Dick*. The men's journeys, half a world apart, would each have historic implications. Once the five castaways had regained their strength, they took to whaling with fervor, manning the slings and tackles, cleaning the oil-smeared decks, and spotting. For six months the men traced a course south-southeast on the *Howland*, spearing fifteen whales before finally settling into a sheltered harbor the locals called Honolulu.

Upon arrival, and impressed with Manjiro's eagerness to learn, Whitfield made him an offer: *stay with me*. Having lost his own father at the age of eight, Manjiro had grown attached to the captain. Despite his hesitations—and the fact that the two men could barely communicate—he left his four comrades on Oahu and continued with the whaler. On May 7, 1843, the *Howland* passed the islands of Martha's Vineyard and Nantucket, and crossed into the calm waters of Buzzards Bay.

Thirty ships lined the docks of the Acushnet River that morning, and Manjiro watched the city's wharves, customhouses, and church steeples appear from the bulwarks. Two years and four months after pushing off from his homeland, the sixteen-year-old climbed down and stepped into America.

Though he didn't know it, Manjiro arrived in the New World 233 years after Japan's first North American colonists, who had landed in Acapulco, Mexico, in the fall of 1610, a decade before the *Mayflower* reached Plymouth Rock.

"They seem bold, not gentle and meek people, going about like eagles," Nahua historian Chimalpahin wrote of the encounter in his journal.

A second Japanese party traveled to Mexico in 1614, but the land held no interest for Japan, and, soon, neither did any people of the West. By 1623, British traders found themselves driven out of the Japanese archipelago, followed by Spaniards a year later. The Portuguese were the next to go, and by 1641, the Dutch were limited to Dejima, a man-made island so tiny it would fit inside an average Walmart. For the next two hundred years, this island in the bay of Nagasaki would serve as Japan's only window to the West.

Then, seventeen days after Leland Stanford drove the golden spike into the Transcontinental Railroad, twenty-two families landed in San Francisco. They staked their destiny on their cargo: six million tea seeds, fifty thousand mulberry trees, and an untold number of silkworm cocoons. It was twenty-six years after Manjiro's arrival when the Wakamatsu Tea and Silk Farm was founded in the summer of 1869 outside Sacramento, California, the unlikely result of a political uprising five thousand miles across the Pacific. In an effort to ward off Western imperialism, the 1868 Meiji Restoration, as the event was to become known, disassembled Japan's feudal system. Economic turmoil and a complete restructuring of the country's social order followed, effectively destroying the samurai class and driving some to leave the country altogether in search of opportunity.

The émigrés purchased a plot on a particularly American-named outcrop—Gold Hill. However, the colony was no match for the state's miners, who diverted creeks away from the Wakamatsu clan. Whether purposely or not, the miners' actions, combined with labor disputes and financial difficulties, drove the farm to collapse within two years. But the seeds of a new American immigration had been planted.

The Meiji Restoration brought with it industrialization, centralization of Japanese culture and language, and, most important to the story of the United States, emigration. Prompted by Commodore Matthew Perry's 1853 expedition to Japan and a subsequent treaty the following year, American-Japanese trade developed quickly. Direct shipping between Japan and San Francisco was established by 1855, and diplomatic relations were cemented by 1860, but the flow of people was tepid: by 1880 the Japanese population in the United States was only 148. A confluence of internal Japanese events, including industrialization's impact on farming, would change that, but there was no greater boon to Japanese emigration than the Chinese Exclusion Act of 1882.

Chinese workers had arrived in the United States a generation prior to Japanese workers; there were close to four thousand Chinese immigrants in the country by 1850, and within thirty years that number had skyrocketed to 105,000. They laid the West's railroads, gored its mines, and packed its canneries. At first the Chinese were seen as a necessary if despised minority. But following the end of the Civil War, when unemployment skyrocketed, white workers began to finger the new immigrants for their own economic misfortunes. Wall Street manipulation wasn't to blame, they reasoned; it had to be cheap "Mongolian" labor.

Chinese workers were perceived as a dual threat: they threatened the white workers both economically and racially. In 1880, the United States was predominantly a black and white society: only three-tenths of one percent of respondents to that year's census classified themselves as Hispanic, Asian, Pacific Islander, or American Indian. (The numbers are stark but don't reflect the true diversity, as Mexican respondents counted as "white" until 1930.) For years the country's Chinese population had been isolated in the West, but that was changing. Following the abolition of slavery, Chinese workers trickled into the sugarcane fields of the coastal South. Seventy-five boarded a train in San Francisco and headed to North Adams, Massachusetts, where they were hired by Calvin T. Sampson to replace striking workers at his shoemaking factory. (Some of those same men eventually moved to Boston, where they established the city's Chinatown.) Cotton fields in Arkansas, railroad lines in Tennessee—the influx of Chinese workers forced white Americans to reconsider their prejudicial hierarchies. Presented with that opportunity, most chose white supremacy.

Less than a year after Stanford drove the golden spike—literally and figuratively ending the need for Chinese workers in many white workers' eyes—anti-Chinese sentiment became one of the most dominant political issues in California. On July 8, 1870, the first anti-Asian mass meeting in America was held in San Francisco. Prior to the event, the men marched en masse to Platt's Hall, carrying lit flares. After each speech the room filled with manic applause, and the gathered men passed a resolution calling for the end of Chinese immigration.

Their sentiment soon adopted a tagline. "The Chinese Must Go!" was championed by Irish immigrant Denis Kearney, the head of the new Workingmen's Party, a group focused in theory on the rights of workers, but in practice solely on the deportation of Chinese workers. The state's Republican and Democratic parties added anti-Chinese language to their platforms, and Chinese immigrants felt the weight of the movement. On October 24, 1871, a mob of five hundred white men, women, and children descended on Los Angeles's Chinatown, beating or shooting fifteen Chinese cooks, shopkeepers, and cigar-makers before hanging their bodies. The men were hung from stagecoaches and from the gate of a lumberyard. Eight assailants were convicted of manslaughter; their convictions were later overturned on appeal.

With zero political representation or public support, Chinese residents didn't stand a chance. In 1875, President Ulysses S. Grant signed the Page Act, the first restrictive federal immigration policy in U.S. history, barring the immigration of East Asian women who had entered into contracts for "lewd and immoral purposes." Among other restrictions, the act also made it a felony to import women into the United States for purposes of prostitution. While the law now seems narrow in scope, its underlying goal was more sinister. Complete restriction of Chinese immigration was still politically untenable in 1875. But by limiting the flow of women to the country, it limited the possibility of a second generation—a generation of Chinese Americans.

Page Act enforcement led to the near-total exclusion of new Chinese women in the United States. In 1882, 39,579 Chinese immigrants entered the country; only 136 were women. During a six month span in 1878 and 1879, Kearney and his Workingmen's Party tried to commandeer the California Constitutional Convention, gathered in Sacramento to amend the organizing law of the state. Article XIX added four new provisions to the state constitution, each concerning California's Chinese population. Though each was groundbreaking in its codification of racism, the second provision was the harshest: *No corporation now existing or hereafter formed under the laws of this state shall, after adoption of this Constitution, employ, directly or indirectly, in any capacity, any Chinese or Mongolian.* The additions were paper tigers, with no means of regulation. Even so, they provided a nudge for federal politicians to revisit the issue. In 1882, the Chinese Exclusion Act was passed despite protestations by President Chester A. Arthur. He assuaged his unease with a provision that the bill would last only ten years. Ninety days later, the ban on immigration of Chinese laborers was put into effect; it would be on the books for more than sixty years.

Anti-Chinese sentiment was now approved and state-sanctioned. And, of course, after a law is passed, its consequences are not far behind. When railroad work dried up in the early 1870s, many Chinese workers in Wyoming had transitioned into coal mines, replacing striking Cornish, Irish, Swedish, and Welsh immigrants. In August 1885, notices popped up around the Wyoming mining community of Rock Springs, demanding the expulsion of those Chinese miners and other workers. On September 2, a decade of tension spilled over. Irked by a disagreement in a coal room that morning, 150 white men descended onto the Chinese camp, armed with Winchester rifles. By the end of the afternoon at least twenty-eight Chinese men would be killed— shot to death or burned alive in their own homes. Miners were scalped, decapitated, and hanged. One man, too sick to leave his home, died while the flames collapsed around him. Another's penis and testicles were cut off and later toasted and feted by the attackers as "a trophy of the hunt." Women cheered, then hustled in to rob jewelry and hand-kerchiefs from the dead. Seventy-nine homes burned to the ground. Survivors fled a hundred miles west, to Evanston. By daybreak Governor Francis Warren was in Rock Springs to survey the destruction, and within a week the federal government sent six companies of men to oversee the safe return of the survivors to the scorched camp. They returned to dogs and hogs eating the remains of the dead.

Sixteen men were arrested. A grand jury later refused to indict them, claiming "though we have examined a large number of witnesses, no one has been able to testify to a single criminal act committed by any known white person that day." The federal government made sure that no more Chinese workers would arrive in the United States; its citizens took it upon themselves to purge the land of those already here.

Within just a few years, the playbook would be pulled down from the shelf, dusted off, and opened. The names would change from Chung and Ling to Sato and Suzuki, and a new campaign would begin.

After the relaxation of Japanese emigration laws in 1868, a trickle of new arrivals appeared on the United States mainland. The first wave, mostly from elite families, headed to the universities of the East: of the 3,475 U.S.-bound passports issued by Japan between 1882 and 1890, 44 percent were for students. Those without wealth stayed in the West and found work in the sawmills, restaurants, and more lascivious trades. Japanese immigrants didn't surpass 1,000 per year until 1891, and even those numbers represent just a blip within the 560,319 immigrants who moved to the United States that year.

As Japanese immigration inched up on the mainland, arrivals in the Hawaiian Islands were exploding. The first Japanese immigrants had arrived in the current-day United States in 1868, a year before the Wakamatsu clan arrived in California, when 141 contract workers, six women, and one child boarded the HMS *Scioto* and left Yokohama for the sugarcane fields of Hawai'i. (The islands were still thirty years away from American annexation.) Of those arrivals, ninety or so stayed on the islands after the expiration of their contracts, disappearing into the populace and never forming their own community. (Due to complicated diplomatic reasons, these were the only Japanese immigrants to the islands for fifteen years.) At the same time, Hawai'i's population was dwindling, while the demand for its sugarcane was soaring. An estimated 700,000 native Hawaiians lived on the islands when Captain James Cook arrived in 1778; by 1860, measles, polio, chicken pox, and tuberculosis had scythed that number to less than 70,000. As white farmers from the United States moved onto the islands, seeking fortune in the tropical climate, they demanded more from the soil. In only thirty years, from 1837 to 1868, the sugar harvest increased 4,000 percent. The tension between declining populations and climbing production had an obvious solution: immigrant labor.

Like the mainland, the first wave came from China, and by 1884 nearly eighteen thousand Chinese contract workers lived on the islands. As those contracts expired, however, many of the Chinese eschewed the fields and built their own businesses. In Japan, rampant inflation led to high unemployment and bankruptcy. Recognizing an opportunity, the Hawaiian government subsidized the emigration of Japanese to fix their sugar production issues.

The SS *City of Tokio* was the largest ship ever constructed in the United States, and the second-biggest in world history after the British *Great Eastern*. Built in 1874 in Chester, Pennsylvania, the iron steamship stretched well beyond the length of a football field and weighed more than five thousand tons. At 9 a.m., February 8, 1885, it arrived in Honolulu with 311 men, 67 women, and 42 children from Yamaguchi Prefecture; 140 men, 43 women, and 39 children from Hiroshima prefecture; 99 people from Tokyo; and 203 more from Kanagawa, Okayama, and Wakayama Prefectures. Three days later, the group, led by Hawaiian minister to Japan Robert Walker Irwin and Japan's first consul to Hawai'i, Nakamura Jiro, hosted a reception for King Kalākaua and other Hawaiian officials. Large vats of sake lubricated the proceedings, which featured sumo wrestling and kendo demonstrations. Within days, the 944 immigrants—who would come to be known as *ikkaisen*, "first ship"—were dispersed across the islands. Ten became servants and cooks, two worked in the royal palace, and the remaining 932 found themselves in the sugar plantations of Maui, Kauai, and the Big Island of Hawai'i.

Between the *ikkaisen*'s 1885 arrival and 1894, more than 28,000 others joined them. While the majority of the new arrivals were farmers, the workload on the plantations was unimaginable. Normal contracts stipulated three-year commitments, for twenty-six days a month. If workers claimed to be sick but were found able to work by the plantation owners, they were fined; if they couldn't pay the fine, they were jailed. The fines were onerous, and applied to every possible infraction: smoking, making noise after 9 p.m., taking a single stalk of sugarcane, accidentally breaking a tool. For every ten minutes a worker was late, they were fined one-fourth of their day's pay. Foremen on horseback held whips to discourage idleness while women sang to pass the time: "*Kane wa Kachiken. Washa horehore yo. Ase to namida no. Tomokasegi.*" *My husband cuts the cane stalks and I trim their leaves. With sweat and tears we both work for our means.*

"The Hawaiian plantation was a Japanese frontier, but it was not like the great western frontier of the United States, which Americans have come to think of as synonymous with the word 'frontier,'" wrote historian F. Hilary Conroy in his 1953 book, *The Japanese Frontier in Hawaii, 1868–1898*. "It had some of the ingredients, the roughness, the crudeness, and the drabness, but none of the freedom, and little of the opportunity. The Japanese frontier was one controlled by other men."

Despite the conditions, more and more Japanese stayed beyond their three-year contracts. Of that first arrival, records suggest that 75 percent returned to Japan; by the fifteenth boat of migrants, only 25 percent chose to return. Hawai'i was becoming home.

While the relationship between the workers and plantation owners remained strained—within the first month of the *City of Tokio*'s arrival, workers on the Paia plantation refused to work when a plantation supervisor beat a Japanese laborer, and sixteen workers on the Papaikou plantation went on strike after not being paid for overtime work, disputes that foreshadowed years of labor resistance—the one place where the frustrations of the workers were permitted was the football field. The sport was introduced in the islands in 1875 by Amasa Pratt, principal at the exclusive, missionary-founded Punahou School. (A century later, future U.S. president Barack Obama would become the school's most famous graduate.) Just six years after the first intercollegiate game between Rutgers and Princeton, Pratt taught the students a rudimentary form of the sport that was then played with a rounded ball, compared to the prolate spheroid of today. Within a decade, football was popular in the streets of Honolulu and, more importantly, in the fields. Teams of native Hawaiians and Chinese and Japanese immigrants would face off against squads of *haole*, the white plantation class. The games showcased the assimilability of Asians and Pacific Islanders while also allowing the groups to physically express their anger and deny white authority. In December 1890, a Honolulu team took on a team of sailors from the USS *Charleston*, docked in Pearl Harbor. Held at the Makiki grounds at Punahou, the Navy men beat the locals 18–0 before a crowd of "many who had never seen a game before." The sailors had just returned from San Francisco, where they had transported Hawaiian king David Kalākaua, who sought medical treatment in California. He'd die there a month later, the last king of Hawai'i.

The next decade in the islands and along the West Coast would change the course of American history. By 1890, 85,716 Japanese had immigrated to Hawai'i and the United States, two entwined entities soon to become one when President William McKinley annexed the island nation during the Spanish-American War. That new political status afforded Japanese workers a new right, one of their few: the ability to travel to the mainland United States without a passport. In 1899, 2,844 Japanese had entered the mainland United States; just a year later, that number more than quadrupled to 12,635.

The first Japanese on the mainland mostly settled adjacent to established Chinatowns, and, over the next decade, built Japantowns in Sacramento and Fresno, California; Portland, Oregon; Seattle and Tacoma, Washington; and Salt Lake City. In 1890 the only city with a sizable enough Japanese population for census takers to take note of was San Francisco; that quickly changed. Hotels and boardinghouses opened to service new arrivals, and were soon operated by Japanese managers. Barbershops, restaurants, markets, and laundries followed, while Christian churches began to offer English lessons for their new neighbors. The Chinese and Japanese lived competitive but overlapping existences, and would continue to do so for decades. Chinese gambling dens up and down the coast—along with more carnal businesses—attracted issei men, and Chinese restaurants served as the first stop after many Japanese funerals. During disease outbreaks the two groups often shared the collective indignity of mandatory inoculation, no matter the cause. As the issei grew as competitors, however, that symbiosis was strained. Political tensions between the two countries jumped the ocean in 1895 following Japan's victory over China in the First Sino-Japanese War, with seven hundred of Sacramento's issei celebrating in the street. Farther south, some of San Francisco's issei ran military drills in preparation for any retaliation on the part of the city's Chinese residents. Despite their differences, a newspaper editor in

San Francisco summed up their collective foothold in America with the adage *Tusi hubei, wushang qilei*: even foxes sympathize with the deaths of rabbits as both are the prey of human beings.

Thousands of Japanese workers, freed from their contracts due to the mainland United States' ban on contract workers in 1900, moved to the Pacific Northwest, plugging a labor gap as a result of the Alaskan Gold Rush. The Great Northern Railway and the Northern Pacific Railway welcomed the new workers, then shipped them throughout the West. Five hundred Japanese men moved across desert stretches of Idaho and Wyoming rail, while up to nine hundred worked in Oregon, connecting that corner of the continent to the rest of the United States.

Often erroneously described as a people bound by passivity and deference to authority, the historical truth about Japan is more complicated. Between 1590 and 1867, more than 2,800 peasant uprisings took place in the empire; ten thousand farmers in the Chichibu area of the Kanto Plain formed a "poor people's army" in 1884, attacking the municipal officers, moneylenders, and others profiting off the industrial revolution, which was brought in to Japan during the Meiji Restoration era. While the expressions *Shikata ga nai* ("It can't be helped") and *gaman suru* ("endure") are repeated when telling the story of Japanese American incarceration, the traits those expressions embodied were promoted by the nationalist political elites in Japan, who profited off the concept of a united nation. In Hawai'i, those Japanese who remained on the islands struck for better wages and conditions, and successfully forced changes upon the plantation system, nudging incrementally toward (the admittedly still subservient) sharecropping. Between 1900 and 1906, twenty-one thousand Japanese workers struck on thirty-nine different plantations.

While economic possibilities abounded on the U.S. mainland, arrivals from Hawai'i and Japan faced a renewed effort by white politicians and labor unions to close the door there. On May 7, 1900, the labor groups of San Francisco called a meeting. The agenda was restricted to one topic: the protesting of Japanese immigrants in California. Most speakers aimed their words not at the immigrants' race, but at their economic impact—"We keep out pauper-made goods but let in the pauper," said one Stanford professor. The rally's main attraction was James Phelan, mayor of the city at the epicenter of anti-Japanese and anti-Chinese bigotry, San Francisco. Phelan was born into privilege there, the son of an Irish Catholic immigrant who found wealth as a trader and merchant during the state's gold rush. After law school Phelan spent two years traveling Europe before returning home and doubling his family's fortune through shrewd real estate investment. While in office, Phelan's San Francisco experienced unrivaled prosperity; the same forces that shifted the fortunes of Japanese immigrants— the annexation of Hawai'i, the Spanish-American War, and the Alaskan Gold Rush—were a boon to the city's business community. Phelan's political beliefs led him to corruption battles and, most famously, the fight for the beautification of San Francisco. He envisioned the growing city as a Paris or Vienna of California, modeling his plan after Pericles's beautification of Athens, which "render[ed] the citizens cheerful, content, yielding, self-sacrificing, and capable of enthusiasm."

As Phelan took to the dais, his city was under siege from the bubonic plague, the first outbreak of its kind in the continental United States. On March 6, the body of Chick Gin, a Chinese immigrant, was found dead in a basement along Dupont Street in the city's Chinatown; an autopsy revealed the plague as its cause. The Phelan administration quarantined all Chinese and Japanese immigrants, and no "Asiatics" were permitted to leave the state of California unless cleared by health officials. Police boats patrolled the harbor at night, trawling for barred residents, and Chinese and Japanese from around the state were banned from entering the city limits. White residents were free to come and go; a white San Franciscan could walk in one side of Chinatown and out the other without hassle. City officials proposed a temporary detention center for all Asian immigrants on a rocky island in Mission Bay, but the idea was killed by a federal judge who declared both it and the quarantine as racially discriminatory and too drastic. Though Phelan's remarks came a month before the judge's decision, his argument reads as a defense of his position both broadly and specifically.

"The Japanese are starting the same tide of immigration which we thought we had checked twenty years ago," Phelan said to the crowd, in a call that would become familiar to Californians over the next thirty years. "The Chinese and Japanese are not bona fide citizens. They are not the stuff of which American citizens can be made. . . . Personally we have nothing against Japanese, but as they will not assimilate with us and their social life is so different from ours, let them keep at a respectful distance."

The Chinese and Japanese, of course, were restricted from becoming citizens; that was not their choice. Their inability to "assimilate," in Phelan's words, was *due* to California's segregationist policies, which drove them from schools and forced them from their land. Their social life was different because they were, once again, not allowed to socialize with other races. These were circumstances created not by choice, but statute.

The California of 1900 was a clannish hodgepodge, an unstable, heterogeneous state populated mostly by newcomers. Despite this diversity, every wave of new outsiders was almost always viewed unfavorably. And, inasmuch as 41 percent of Japanese immigrants on the mainland United States lived in the state, that hostility led California to once again becoming ground zero for anti-Asian sentiment and action. Not that this was limited to the state: during the year's presidential race, Republican, Democratic, and Populist party platforms all specifically or ambiguously expressed anti-Japanese rhetoric. Reflecting the political alignments of the time, the Democrats, behind anti-imperialist William Jennings Bryan, supported "the continuance and strict enforcement of the Chinese exclusion law, and its application to the same classes of all Asiatic races," while the Populist Party demanded a halt to "the importation of Japanese labor." The Republican Party—seeking the reelection of William McKinley, the man responsible for annexing much of the country's Japanese population to begin with—allowed its members interpretation, stating only a desire for "a more effective restriction of the immigration of cheap labor from foreign lands."

New drives were stoked by the unexpected victory of Japan in the Russo-Japanese War of 1904 and 1905, the modern era's first major military victory of an Asian nation over a European one. In rhetoric that would echo less than forty years later, the victory stoked anti-Japanese accusations that Japanese immigrants in the United States were merely "agents of the emperor." Others surmised that Japanese peasants, tired of war and the economic hardships it placed on them, would seek aid on the eastern edge of the Pacific instead.

On February 23, 1905, the West Coast's most read and most influential newspaper, the *San Francisco Chronicle*, introduced readers to "The Japanese Invasion, the Problem of the Hour for the United States." The nine-column story, splayed across two pages, familiarized readers with the 100,000 "little brown men" poised to take over. It promised "the brown stream of immigration is likely to become an inundating torrent" following the end of the Russo-Japanese War, and then recycled the well-worn clichés of the days of the Chinese Exclusion Act.

"The Japanese is no more assimilable than the Chinese and he is no less adaptable in learning quickly how to do the white man's work and how to get the job for himself by offering his labor for less than a white man can live on," the story reads.

In the weeks and months that followed, the *Chronicle* hounded its readers with story after story. The message eventually devolved from one of labor necessities to blatant fearmongering.

Crime and Poverty Go Hand in Hand with Asiatic Labor

Japanese a Menace to American Women

The Yellow Peril—How Japanese Crowd Out the White Race

The political effect was immediate. On March 1 and 2, both houses of California's legislature unanimously passed a ten-point anti-Japanese resolution, calling on Congress to "limit and diminish the further immigration of Japanese." The resolution was stuffed with misinformation and served as a showcase for the legislators' ignorance. (It claimed that issei were transients unwilling to buy houses or land, when in fact the community was buying so many properties that, in later decades, much of the legislation in the state would be focused on banning those purchases.) The resolution lacked teeth, and no legislation was passed regarding it, but it set off a wave: for the next forty years, anti-Japanese bills were introduced in every biennial session of the California state legislature.

At the same time the legislature met in Sacramento, in San Francisco the unions formed their own response. On May 14, representatives from sixty-seven different organizations met and formed what became known as the Asiatic Exclusion League. The four leaders of the league were immigrants themselves, from Ireland, Norway, Scotland, and Sweden, but ignored their peoples' assimilability while assailing that of Chinese and Japanese arrivals. "An eternal law of nature has decreed that the white cannot assimilate the blood of another without corrupting the very springs of civilization," said one speaker.

"We have been accustomed to regard the Japanese as an inferior race, but are now suddenly aroused to our danger," said speaker Isidor Golden, a justice of the peace. "They are not window cleaners and house servants. The Japanese can think, can learn, can invent. We have suddenly awakened to the fact that they are gaining a foothold in every skilled industry in our country. They are our equal in intellect; their ability to labor is equal to ours. They are proud, valiant and courageous, but they can underlive us. . . . We are here today to prevent that very competition. . . . We cannot, we must not, we will not permit the free entry of a race that will cheapen and lower our standard of living."

The league's influence was small, its membership numbers inflated by a leadership set on proving its importance, but symbolically it was significant: just as had happened to the Chinese before them, there was now an organized movement, a specific group, dedicated to the exclusion of the Japanese.

A week before the Asiatic Exclusion League was formed, a routine decision, one likely unexpected to cause news beyond the room in which it took place, occurred at a meeting of the San Francisco school board. At the meeting, the board voted to move the district's Japanese students into one segregated school, which at that time taught only students of Chinese descent. The Asiatic Exclusion League hailed the resolution, but, perhaps reflecting the relative unimportance of the action, it sat unimplemented. So the ninety-three students, spread across twenty-three schools, continued their educations with their white peers.

Then, on April 18, 1906, the deadliest earthquake in U.S. history broke the ground under San Francisco. The initial growl was felt as far away as Oregon and central Nevada. For three days fires burned, taking whole neighborhoods with them. Three thousand San Franciscans died, and the state's largest, most prosperous city was practically destroyed. The destruction totaled between 1.3 and 1.8 percent of the country's gross national product. (The World Trade Center attacks of September 11, 2001, accounted for less than one percent.) Property owners filed more than $7 billion in insurance claims (in 2019 dollars) despite the fact that most could only recoup for fire damage, not shake damage. The claims bankrupted fourteen insurers. The rush of gold from foreign insurers to the West Coast forced European central banks to raise interest rates, pushing the United States into recession and setting the stage for the New York Stock Exchange free fall known eighteen months later as the Panic of 1907. Donations and aid poured into the region, the largest amount coming from the citizens and government of Japan, which offered to give more than $7 million in today's dollars, more than all other foreign contributions combined.

Yet any goodwill afforded California's nikkei residents by their ancestral home's financial generosity quickly evaporated. After a two-month respite, the league declared boycotts on Japanese restaurants and markets, threatening to photograph and publicize white residents seen frequenting the establishments. That fall, protesters outside Japanese restaurants handed out matchbooks emblazoned with the phrase "White men and women, patronize your own race." Business fell by at least two-thirds; the boycott was finally called off only when the restaurant owners promised to pay the league a $350 bribe.

Violence against the city's Japanese residents climbed. Later, when President Theodore Roosevelt sent his commerce and labor secretary, Victor H. Metcalf, to the city to investigate the anti-Japanese movement, nineteen separate assaults were reported by Japanese residents, ranging from eggings to mob beatings. Two incidents highlight not only the depths of violence, but the institutional hurdles the victims faced:

> *M. Sugawa, 1172a Devisadero [sic] street. I am a shoemaker. On August 17, 1906, at 8:40 p.m., as I was passing on Sutter street, near Scott, three boys, 21 or 22 years of age, attacked my person. I nearly fainted. Upon rising to my feet, they again assaulted me. This time they smashed my nose. I grabbed the coat of one of the trio, and after having my nose dressed at one of the nearby hospitals, I went home. The next day a policeman came, requesting me to give up the coat. At first I refused, but finally, upon his assuring me that it would be deposited at the police station, I gave it up. I reported the matter to the police. When the case came up for trial the youngster was dismissed on the plea of insufficiency of evidence.*

> *T. Kadono, 121 Haight street. I am a member of the Japanese Y.M.C.A. On the fifth day of August, 1906, on Laguna street, between Haight and Page streets, at 10:40 a.m., on my way to church, I was attacked by about thirty people, men ranging from fifteen to twenty-five years of age. They followed me down the street and*

beat me over the head and face with their fists. I tried to resist them,
but they were too strong for me. They made my nose bleed. I went
to St. Thomas Hospital for medical treatment. I complained to the
superintendent of the Japanese Presybterian Mission, and was ad-
vised by him not to make any complaint to the police. I was laid up
for a week on account of this attack. I have the blood-stained shirt,
which I can produce if necessary.

"Whenever newspapers attack the Japanese these roughs renew their misdeeds with redoubled energy," said one laundry owner, who was forced to hire off-duty policemen to protect his shop from near-constant barrages of eggs, rotten fruit, and rocks. Into this fray, the league renewed its demand: the exclusion of Japanese children from white San Francisco schools. On October 11, 1906, seventeen months after its initial resolution, the school board ordered all Japanese and Korean students to join the district's Chinese students on Clay Street.

The news was ignored by the press until nine days later, when poorly translated versions of the events began appearing in, of all places, Tokyo newspapers. Some reported the news correctly, but others relayed a more dire situation: that Japanese children were being excluded from the schools completely. Of the ninety-three students affected, sixty-eight were Japanese citizens, the remainder having been born in the United States. The makeup of the students added an international element to the affair, since technically the school board was discriminating not only against American children of Japanese descent, but also Japanese children, full stop.

Diplomatically, the timing couldn't have been worse. Theodore Roosevelt, eager to cut off a confrontation with a growing Pacific power that had so thoroughly dismantled the Russian navy just a year before, had sent Metcalf—an Oakland native and the lone Californian in Roosevelt's cabinet—to San Francisco to oversee what he correctly assumed a developing problem. As Metcalf worked, Roosevelt delivered his annual congressional address. Japan and its people—both abroad and in the United States—were mentioned thirty-three times in the December 3 speech, during which he made a surprising request.

> *Here and there a most unworthy feeling has manifested itself to-*
> *ward the Japanese—the feeling that has been shown in shutting*
> *them out from the common schools in San Francisco, and in mut-*
> *terings against them in one or two other places, because of their*
> *efficiency as workers. To shut them out from the public schools is a*
> *wicked absurdity. . . . I recommend to the Congress that an act be*
> *past specifically providing for the naturalization of Japanese who*
> *come here intending to become American citizens.*

Roosevelt was pummeled by the California press and congressional delegation; he never raised the possibility of naturalization publicly again. Despite his guileless reasoning for his remarks, they were vindicated by Metcalf's report, released to Congress two weeks later. Metcalf reported that the state's newspapers had purposely misrepresented the threat of Japanese students, claiming hundreds or thousands were flooding classrooms when it was only ninety-three. Newspapers called the report an "act of treachery" by Metcalf, their native son.

While public opinion—east of the Rocky Mountains, at least—sided with the students, the courts did not. Legislation made the segregation of the students legal in California. Instead, the argument would have to be made on the behalf of not the nisei students but the sixty-eight Japanese students, citing a rights-of-residence clause in the two countries' 1894 Treaty of Commerce and Navigation. The Department of Justice prepared a suit on behalf of the Japanese students, one that would skirt both the California law and *Plessy v. Ferguson*, the federal case upholding racial segregation from a decade earlier. At the same time, unbeknownst to the public, when Roosevelt wrote his address he had launched another plan that would refute much of what he delivered to Congress. The seeds of this plan had been planted the month earlier, when on November 6 Roosevelt met with the Japanese ambassador, Viscount Shuzo Aoki, the first man to hold that position. At the meeting, Roosevelt showed Aoki a draft of his congressional address, then proposed something entirely different.

"[The] only way to prevent constant friction" between the two countries, Roosevelt said, was to "prevent all immigration of Japanese laboring men."

After weeks of negotiation among the San Francisco school board, the San Francisco mayor, both houses of California's state legislature, the governor of California, the United States State Department, the United States House of Representatives, the United States Senate, the United States presidency, and the nation of Japan, Roosevelt barred Japanese immigration from Hawai'i, Mexico, and Canada. Over the next year, through correspondence involving Roosevelt, Secretary of State Elihu Root, U.S. ambassador to Japan Luke E. Wright, and Ambassador Aoki, a bigger plan came into focus. The Japanese agreed to bar passports for skilled and unskilled laborers hoping to enter the continental United States, while allowing the issuance of passports for "laborers who have already been in America, and to the parents, wives, and children of laborers already present there." (It was not uncommon for laborers to travel back to Japan during this period, a practice that complicated a precise census of Japanese immigrants in America at the time.) The agreement was hailed as a testament to diplomacy, yet the text of it was never divulged.

Japanese newspapers tracked the progress of the negotiations, including the focus on skilled and unskilled workers. So as Roosevelt and the others negotiated, Hyohei Nomura boarded the *Tosa Maru* and began his journey across the Pacific. If he wanted to move to America, this might be his last chance. Despite being a twenty-three-year-old with only an eighth-grade education, Hyohei listed "student" as his occupation, a sleight of hand that would shield him from the effects of what came to be known as the "Gentlemen's Agreement." According to the ship manifest, he was nonetheless barred by immigration officials from entering the United States, instead disembarking in Victoria, British Columbia. (Canada itself would implement its own Gentlemen's Agreement the following year, allowing only four hundred Japanese immigrants a year to enter.) From there he snaked his way into the United States, following a well-worn path of migration between the two countries. He listed his destination as San Francisco but, likely due to the destruction of the city a year earlier, continued south to the growing metropolis of Los Angeles. If he'd waited even six months he'd have likely never been allowed to board the boat.

On the other side of the Pacific, Usaburo Yoshinaga had opposite plans. He and his younger brother boarded a boat, content that their time in America was over. The economic turmoil that drove the men to leave Japan had calmed, and, as many Japanese workers at the time did, they wanted to go home. Farmland waited, as did the prospect of marriage. En route to Kumamoto the boat stopped in Honolulu. His brother continued on; Usaburo had second thoughts, and boarded the next boat back to San Francisco. He would never return to Japan.

The effects of the Gentlemen's Agreement were open to interpretation. If you were the federal governments of Japan and the United States, you considered it a success. If you were a racist Californian, you thought differently. Federal officials saw climbing emigration numbers and falling immigration ones and thought *Success!* What those numbers failed to show, though, was the reality in California.

By 1900, there were twenty-four Japanese men for every one Japanese woman in the continental United States. By 1909, the year after the Gentlemen's Agreement fully took effect, Japanese women entering the country surpassed Japanese men for the first time, a trend that was sustained for the next fifteen years. The clause that allowed for "the parents, wives, and children of laborers residing there" to immigrate to the United States spurred the picture bride industry. The effect of their arrival was immediate and to be expected. Children—Americans— were born. Californian exclusionists, unable to see past these new

Americans' skin, felt betrayed by the government's agreement. Instead of curbing the state's anti-Japanese sentiment, the Gentlemen's Agreement had, they believed, caused the opposite. While the *Chronicle* and other San Francisco newspapers toned down the rhetoric, old foes would pick up the baton and work to fix what they believed the federal government failed to remedy. And though the inflammation refused to subside, the battlefield would soon change.

———————

Forty miles northeast of San Francisco, the Vaca Valley is greeted annually by two seasons—soaking-wet winter, bone-dry summer. The valley is eight miles long, and wiggles from three to six miles in width. Snow rarely falls, and spring comes early, so the growing season runs up to 240 days a year, with fruit ripening sooner than most other corners of the market. The creek-fed trees produced small, sweet, dry fruit, perfect for canning and shipping.

In the winter of 1887, four Japanese men in San Francisco ventured east, to a plot known as Vacaville. Just like the Japanese Hawaiians who had filled the Pacific Northwest during the Alaskan Gold Rush, the men worked the orchards next to and in the stead of Chinese workers, who were arriving in dwindling numbers due to the Exclusion Act of 1882. To make their presence known, the men undercut their competitors, charging only 45 cents a day for their labors (compared to the $1-a-day Chinese workers). With that—and the exception of the short-lived Wakamatsu colony in 1869—Japanese immigrants made their first foray into the American agricultural market.

Within the next decade the community grew, and by 1906 six hundred Japanese men, women, and children lived permanently in Vacaville. By 1908 the community included four stores, three billiard parlors, one laundry, two restaurants (one serving American meals and the other Japanese meals), a barbershop, four lodging houses, four confectionary stores and ice cream parlors, three transfer companies, and a bank.

"The Japanese are ambitious and being naturally shrewd as to methods to employ have made the most of the situation, with the result that the ranchers have come to feel that they are oppressed," wrote Harry A. Millis, an economist and field investigator for the United States Immigration Commission, in the commission's exhaustive forty-one-volume study of immigration, released in 1911.

The "situation" Millis referred to was simple: the Japanese were better farmers than the ranchers. Upon arrival the men had served mostly as laborers, plucking and pruning trees and assisting with canning and drying. But starting in 1900, some of them began leasing land from their previous employers, and paid the lease with a percentage of the harvest. Soon that power dynamic shifted even further when payments changed to cash, allowing the men to make their own planting and marketing decisions and take home a larger percentage of their profits. In 1908, Japanese immigrants leased close to 75 percent of the Vaca Valley's fifteen thousand acres, and the men had purchased a small, 290-acre cluster of orchards. They would no longer be just laborers.

The industriousness of Vaca Valley spread quickly. Thirty miles southwest, George Shima, a former domestic servant in San Francisco, drained and diked a swampy, undesirable plot of the California Delta outside Stockton. Born Kinji Ushijima in the farming community of Kurume, on Japan's southern island of Kyushu, Shima left San Francisco in 1889 and toiled in the delta's fields. A prodigious potato picker, he would often compete against white laborers, speedily filling up his sack. In those moments, he realized if he could outpick the Americans, he could outgrow them as well. Prime farmland in the delta cost up to $150 an acre, but the malarial swamps could be purchased for as little as $3—even less if scooped up in large chunks. Shima recognized the value of the centuries of silt deposits and set to amassing his empire. Within two decades he was known as the "Potato King of California," and by 1913 he operated 29,000 acres. He'd cornered 85 percent of the state's potato market by 1920. Upon his death in 1926, Shima was worth nearly $250 million in 2019 dollars; he was the first Japanese millionaire in the United States.

Japanese laborers in Florin, California, southeast of Sacramento, saw the potential in old hayfields. They leveled the ground, irrigated it, and planted strawberries. When the strawberry market collapsed they switched to viticulture, planting and tending to grapevines to profit off the state's now internationally recognized wine industry. They found work in the hop yards and sugar beet fields of the Pajaro Valley, and piled their technicolor fruits at stalls in Seattle's Pike Place Market. In Oregon's Hood River Valley, they were first hired to clear logged lands. They were paid with the same land, deemed unusable by the logging companies. Berry, apple, and pear orchards sprouted soon after. The garlic industry in the San Juan Valley, the lettuce sheds of Hollister, the watermelon fields of Dinuba—all were made possible by this toil.

In the sugar beet fields of Oxnard, in Southern California's Ventura County, five hundred Japanese workers and two hundred Mexican workers created the Japanese-Mexican Labor Association to call a strike and fight against the contract labor system. Within weeks the association grew to 1,200 members, grinding 90 percent of the county's sugar beet industry to a halt. After a two-month strike, the sugar companies agreed to nearly double workers' wages and allowed the workers to negotiate directly with local farmers instead of middlemen hired by the companies. The alliance was the first major agricultural association made up of Californian minority workers, and the first to successfully strike.

Women often worked double duty, picking fruits and vegetables before dawn and then rushing home to make breakfast and tend to the children. After breakfast, the husband brought the vegetables to market while the wife and children returned to picking and watering. After dinner, she would sort the day's produce and chop tomorrow's firewood. She'd fall asleep at 1:30 a.m. and wake before the sun to begin again.

"[The Californians] had seen the Japanese convert the barren land like that at Florin and Livingston in productive and profitable fields, orchards, and vineyards, by the persistence and intelligence of their industry," said Colonel John P. Irish, president of the California Delta Association. "They had seen the hardpan and goose lands in the Sacramento Valley, gray and black with our two destructive alkalis, cursed with barrenness like the fig tree of Bethany, and not worth paying taxes on, until [K.] Ikuta, the Japanese, decided that those lands would raise rice. After years of persistent toil, enduring heartbreaking losses and disappointments, he conquered that rebellious soil and raised the first commercial crop of rice in California."

Historian Bradford Smith puts it more directly, if withholding some deserved praise:

> The issei *contribution to America was not in great men, but in the anonymous little men who made the desert spaces green with the labor of their hands, who kept the track even so that Americans could ride comfortably across the land, who tended the comfort of the well-to-do, and grew vegetables the poor could afford to buy, who sacrificed for the welfare of their children.*

By the summer of 1909, an estimated half of all adult Japanese in the United States were employed at some level of the agricultural pyramid. Three out of every four were employed in California. They built their lives on farming. So the only way to eliminate them was to eliminate their farms.

On November 5, 1912, New Jersey governor Woodrow Wilson crushed incumbent William Howard Taft and former President Theodore Roosevelt, and California's anti-Japanese contingent finally had a receptive ear in the White House. During the campaign, Wilson signed his name to a venomous statement drafted by James Phelan, who, after his years as San Francisco mayor, continued his anti-Japanese campaign from the luxury of private life. The statement, which was used to rouse support for Wilson's candidacy in California, read in part,

"We cannot make a homogenous population out of a people who do not blend with the Caucasian race. Their lower standard of living as laborers will crowd out the white agriculturist. . . . The success of free democratic institutions demands of our people education, intelligence and patriotism and the state should protect them against unjust and impossible competition." It was printed on a card; the reverse side bore Roosevelt's 1906 congressional address, quoting at length his Japanese naturalization proposal.

Soon after Wilson's election, California's legislators returned to Sacramento for the 1913 session, and within days filed Senate Bill 27: "No alien who is not eligible to citizenship under the Constitution and laws of the United States of America, and no corporation, a majority of the capital stock of which is owned by such aliens, shall acquire title to or own land or real property in the State of California." The bill was sent to committee. Two months later, at a March 19 hearing, Elk Grove farmer M. A. Mitchell stood before the committee, tears falling down his face. The Japanese had occupied his land, he said, driving white farmers away.

"We have a dead line at Elk Grove now, beyond which the brown man cannot pass," he said, referring to the line that, if passed by a prisoner, warrants his execution. "If we are denied relief from the situation that confronts us I will not be held responsible for what will surely happen."

Less than two months later, and with the tacit approval of Wilson, California's Alien Land Law of 1913 was signed into law by Governor Hiram Johnson. Issei would no longer be allowed to purchase land, and their leases would be limited to three years. The bill passed the State Senate 35 to 2, and the State Assembly 72 to 3. Meanwhile, Japanese farmers, rarely sought out for their opinions on any matter, got back to work. Some found sympathetic white farmers and attorneys willing to form corporations in their own names, while the barred farmers held a minority stake. Others bought land in their children's names, managing the properties as the children's legal guardians. World War I quieted the anti-Japanese sentiment—unwilling to differentiate between Japanese and Japanese Americans, many Californians' anxieties were allayed by Japan's position as an Allied power—and war demand led to a farming boom. In 1910, nikkei farmers owned or leased 194,797 acres; by 1920 that number had more than doubled, to 458,056. Land ownership more than quadrupled.

California held 28 million acres of agricultural land within its borders. The alien land laws had been inspired by a supposed takeover of this land by foreign influences. Yet, even at their most productive, nikkei farmers operated less than 2 percent of that land. In 1918, when Californian agriculture brought in $523 million, nikkei farms were responsible for $53 million, more than 10 percent of the receipts.

"The Japanese nation is characterized by industry and perseverance, so naturally the Japanese who are here possess the power of endurance and the habit of industry," Japanese Association of America officials wrote in a 1919 message to President Wilson. "But it appears rather strange that Americans should complain of these facts, for they themselves take pride in these very characteristics."

Just months after the end of World War I, Phelan and his band of exclusionists and racists rebooted their anti-Japanese cry. Now a U.S. senator, Phelan ran on a "Keep California White" platform, and found many willing supporters. The California Oriental Exclusion League formed from the ashes of the previous decade's Asiatic Exclusion League and launched copycat groups across the state: the Los Angeles Anti-Asiatic Association, Sacramento's Fourteen Counties Association, and the San Joaquin Valley's Americanization League. Representatives from groups as diverse as the Los Angeles Parent-Teacher Association, the Heavy Odd Contractors Association, the United Spanish War Veterans, and fraternal societies of transplants from both Michigan and Ohio joined, though much of its membership came from just four groups: farming interests, the California State Federation of Labor, the Native Sons of the Golden West, and the newly formed American Legion. (Members of the American Legion, chartered by the U.S. Congress in March 1919 to serve the veterans of World War I, were apparently unfazed by the prospect of discriminating against the hundreds of issei who joined the Army and fought for a country that withheld citizenship from them.)

The most influential of these groups was the Native Sons of the Golden West. Since its establishment in 1875 as a group dedicated to the preservation and celebration of Californian history, the Native Sons had turned ferociously anti-immigrant. (The term "native sons" did not extend to the California-born children of Chinese and Japanese immigrants who arrived since its founding.) Nearly three hundred Native Sons parlors opened across the state, including locations just blocks away from both Babe Nomura in Hollywood (Corona no. 196) and George Yoshinaga in Mountain View (Mountain View no. 215). Articles warning of the "yellow peril" appeared nearly every month in the group's *Grizzly Bear* magazine, and members relished the role they played. The group advocated for the purge of Japanese professors from Stanford and USC, and excoriated the Methodist Church as "more active in the interests of the yellow pests in California than any other agency." Future California governor and chief justice of the Supreme Court Earl Warren joined Oakland's Native Sons of the Golden West Parlor 252 on July 24, 1919. In May 1953, as vice president of the United States, member Richard Nixon welcomed the Native Sons to a ceremony at the Tomb of the Unknown Soldier; sixteen years later, they met in the Oval Office.

The new coalition set to work on fixing their obvious problem: the inadequacy of the Alien Land Law. By March 1920 the groups had drafted a law that closed the original law's loopholes, but instead of waiting until the 1921 state legislature, the group pushed a measure voted on that November's ballot. It passed in a more than three-to-one landslide.

The California Supreme Court disagreed with the voters, claiming the law had no standing to bar American citizens from holding land, even if it was managed and operated by their issei parents. The state had enacted yet another toothless law, but this one came at a higher cost. In the months leading up to the vote, the coalition and Phelan, running uphill for reelection to the U.S. Senate, threw every stereotype at voters. The American Legion produced the film *Shadows of the West*, which depicted a white woman forced to sell her farm to a Japanese man, who then kidnaps her. The woman is later saved by Legionnaires on horseback—neutered cinematic stand-ins for the Ku Klux Klan. The film was banned in some cities and rejected twice by Ohio's Board of Censorship, reflecting the film industry's reticence to feature racial and religious targets. (This was less noble than it might appear: the restriction's goal was to avoid financially ruinous boycotts from the featured groups.) It was eventually cut from eight reels to five, with the anti-Japanese propaganda minimized and the film's white knight plot intensified. The trade magazine *Moving Picture World* saw through the producers' goals:

> [The Japanese] are held up to public view in the worst light, in a way that is calculated to make them nationally hated. In fact, the evident purpose of the picture is to bring about such an overwhelming sentiment against them, and such pressure to bear on Congress, that the legislators will take some action against the Japanese to permanently keep them away from American life. . . . This is a propaganda picture first, last, and all the time.

The wave of white supremacy was not limited to California. Similar alien land laws passed in Washington, Oregon, Arizona, Idaho, and other Western states, no matter the reality: by 1920, only 4,151 residents of Japanese descent lived in Oregon, and owned just 2,185 acres. In the summer of 1920, the U.S. House Committee on Immigration and Naturalization traveled to California and Washington for a series of hearings to investigate issues involving Japanese immigration. Following the Immigration Act of 1917, Filipinos and Japanese were the only immigrants allowed from Asia—after the Spanish-American War, Filipinos were classified as U.S. nationals, and Japanese migration was still governed by the Gentlemen's Agreement. The 1917 act, vetoed twice by President Wilson before Congress overrode it, was the most sweeping attempt to limit immigration since the Chinese Exclusion Act. In addition to a wide swath of classes deemed "undesirable" by Congress—everything from "feebleminded persons," "idiots," "imbeciles," and epileptics to prostitutes, polygamists, anarchists, and contract laborers—the act created an Asiatic Barred Zone, shutting out immigrants from present-day India, most of the Middle East, Central Asia, the Caucasus, Turkey, Vietnam, Laos, Thailand, Cambodia, Nepal, Afghanistan, parts of Siberia, and all the islands between Asia and Australia, excepting the Philippines. The act also created a literacy test for immigrants over the age of sixteen, a hurdle anti-immigration advocates had been pushing for for more than twenty years. This had a new effect on immigration: it technically barred white Europeans, too. This, taken in conjunction with the Chinese Exclusion Act, effectively prevented half the world's population from boarding a boat and coming to America.

Three years later, in December 1920, Washington representative Albert Johnson introduced a bill suspending all immigration for one year. This bill, while influenced by the West Coast hearings about Japanese immigration, served a larger purpose: stemming the flow of immigrants from Eastern Europe. It passed overwhelmingly in the House but was replaced in the Senate by a different bill, which advocated a quota system weighted in favor of Northern and Western European countries. Due to the Gentlemen's Agreement and the Immigration Act of 1917, the trickling of Asian immigration was not affected. Yet the bill set the table for the next four years, which would change the ethnic makeup of the United States forever.

Takao Ozawa was born in Kanagawa, Japan, in 1875, and emigrated to San Francisco nineteen years later. There he earned a high school diploma from Berkeley High School, converted to Christianity, spoke fluent English, and became one of the first foreign students to attend the University of California, Berkeley. In 1906 he moved to Hawai'i, married, and had two children. On October 16, 1914, after spending more of his life in the United States than in Japan, he applied for naturalization.

"My honesty and industriousness are well known among my Japanese and American friends," he wrote in a legal brief after his petition was rejected. "In name Benedict Arnold was an American, but at heart he was a traitor. In name I am not an American, but at heart I am a true American."

The U.S. District Court in Hawai'i rejected his plea, and the Ninth Circuit Court of Appeals in San Francisco passed the case along to the U.S. Supreme Court. At the heart of Ozawa's case were the Nationality Acts of 1790 and 1870, which limited naturalization to either "free white persons" or "aliens of African nativity and to persons of African descent." Ozawa didn't argue the constitutionality of the acts; rather he claimed Japanese immigrants *were* "free white persons." (Despite growing up in Kanagawa, south of Tokyo, Ozawa claimed to be descended from the Ainu people of northern Japan and the desolate islands of Siberia, which he believed qualified him as Caucasian.) Seeing an opportunity to test the law, the Pacific Coast Japanese Association Deliberative Council, founded in 1914 to fight anti-Japanese legislation and rhetoric, hired former U.S. attorney general George W. Wickersham to bring the case to the U.S. Supreme Court in 1922. The results were unanimously unfavorable.

"Manifestly the test afforded by the mere color of the skin of each individual is impracticable," wrote Justice George Sutherland, himself an immigrant from England, "as that differs greatly among persons of the same race, even among Anglo-Saxons, ranging by imperceptible gradations from the fair blond to the swarthy brunette, the latter being darker than many of the lighter-hued persons of the brown or yellow races." The appellant, he added, was "clearly of a race which is not Caucasian."

The case was a devastating blow to issei rights. Permanently disenfranchised, the group was ignored by politicians, who neither sought their support nor cared for their needs. Combined with Japan's 1920 decision—nudged by the United States—to stop issuing passports to picture brides, the future of Japanese Americans in the United States was at its darkest. It would only get worse.

———

Following the 1906 San Francisco earthquake, many Japanese immigrants who didn't head to the rural farms trekked instead to a growing city 350 miles southeast. Los Angeles had more than doubled in population in just the past six years. Of its 230,000 residents, 3,000 were ethnically Japanese, living mostly on East First Street. Hamanosuke Shigeta's Kame Restaurant opened there in 1885, and the city's first Japanese neighborhood had sprouted around it. Boardinghouses, markets, and more restaurants followed. Between 1893 and 1896 the number of Japanese-operated restaurants in downtown Los Angeles grew from two to sixteen, serving workers not only traditional dishes but also beef stews and chicken dinners, with a slice of pie for dessert. The earthquake drove as many as three thousand nikkei to Los Angeles, doubling the group's population in the city. Just as in Northern California, the men quickly turned their eyes to agriculture, with special interest in the wholesale and retail flower market. By 1910, the issei population of Los Angeles had swelled to more than 7,900, a thousand more than San Francisco. Three thousand more lived in Los Angeles County. The locus of Japanese life in America had shifted, permanently, to Southern California.

Pool halls, bookstores, bathhouses, and barbershops opened to accommodate the issei laborers; the number of Little Tokyo *nomiya*—saloons that featured waitresses singing and playing the samisen—tripled in one year. The community outgrew downtown Los Angeles's Little Tokyo and spread to the fishing piers of Terminal Island, the melting pot of Boyle Heights, and a new neighborhood built on the remains of a citrus grove, Hollywood. In 1910, issei families made the two-hour trolley ride—despite Hollywood's six-mile proximity to downtown Los Angeles, the inefficiency of the Los Angeles Pacific Railroad made the trip take much longer than it should have—and bought ten tracts along Tamarind Avenue. They created a new neighborhood that would only years later include white residents. Japanese restaurants and groceries soon followed on Cahuenga Boulevard, as did boarding-houses, including the one owned by Hyohei Nomura.

The boom of Japanese families in the neighborhood reflected a general increase: between 1910 and 1919, Hollywood's population grew from 5,000 residents to 36,000, a growth rate of 720 percent. Orange and lemon trees made way for Paramount and Universal, and the modern cinema industry was created. And as the movies moved in, they expected the Japanese to move out.

Recreational indignities like banning "aliens ineligible from citizenship" from using municipal golf courses or tennis courts, as Los Angeles did in 1920 and 1921, and later adding the city's swimming pools, soon grew into economic hurdles. In late 1922, a group of Japanese homeowners proposed a development of bungalows. Prompted by angry neighbors, the city council condemned the land and turned it into a park. A few months later, after the recently organized Japanese Presbyterian Church of Hollywood bought a building to use as a sanctuary, white residents raised the perceived encroachment with the Hollywood Chamber of Commerce. "No one wants to live near them," one real estate agent said to the Chamber. "They are alright in their places, but they should be segregated. . . . The trouble with them is they worm their way into the best residential districts." By May the group had a name—the aspirational Hollywood Protective Association—and a message. Mrs. B. G. Miller, who lived across Tamarind Street from the church, hung a porch-length banner from her eave: JAPS KEEP MOVING. THIS IS A WHITE MAN'S NEIGHBORHOOD.

Her neighbor, a Mrs. Poole, was more economical in her sign choice: "You Are Not Wanted."

Five hundred placards made their way into the front windows of homes across Hollywood, informing passersby that the resident was a member of the Hollywood Protective Association. The effort spilled out of Hollywood and across the city. A new publication called *Swat the Jap* was founded, its leaflets distributed across the city. *American or Pro-Jap?* it asked in its inaugural issue, *There Is No Neutral Ground!* Copies cost 10 cents on the newsstand, and particularly enthusiastic racists were encouraged to buy a year's subscription for $5.

"Being a 100 per cent American and believing in the inferiority of the 'Yellow' race in comparison to the 'White' and favoring the expulsion of all Asiatics—American-born or otherwise—from the United States of America, I hereby order [ ] subscriptions to 'Swat the Jap,'" the order form read. Subsequent issues introduced a level of poetic ire.

> *JAPS*
> *You came to care for our lawns,*
> *we stood for it.*
> *You came to work in truck gardens,*
> *we stood for it.*
> *You sent your children to our public schools,*
> *we stood for it.*
> *You moved a few families in our midst,*
> *we stood for it.*
> *You proposed to build a church in our neighborhood, but*
> *We DIDN'T and WE WON'T STAND FOR IT*
> *You impose more on us each day*
> *until you have gone your limit.*
> *WE DON'T WANT YOU WITH US.*
> *SO GET BUSY, JAPS, AND*
> *GET OUT OF HOLLYWOOD*

Northern Californian exclusionists who had spent the recent decade spit-shining their racism into a tonier battle in the legislature and the courts were dismayed by the vulgarity of the nascent Los Angeles movement. With the Ozawa case on their side, the Northern Californians, led rhetorically and financially by Phelan and V. S. McClatchy—

a former California newspaper magnate now dedicated full-time to the cause of Japanese exclusion—took their case to Congress. In March 1924, the duo, plus California attorney general Ulysses S. Webb, traveled to Washington, focusing their efforts on the Senate Committee on Immigration. McClatchy led the charge, denouncing the perceived violation of the Gentlemen's Agreement and presenting a (patently false) astronomical birth rate for ethnic Japanese. The Japanese were only loyal to Japan, he posited, citing their creation of Japanese-language schools and the fact that many of the more well-to-do issei sent their children back to Japan to be educated. They were "more dangerous as residents in this country than any of the other peoples ineligible under our laws," he said, and "make more dangerous competitors in an economic way."

McClatchy also had a secret weapon in the chamber: his son, Leo, was a newspaper columnist and spread his father's message. Opposite McClatchy sat Reverend Sidney Gulick. Born into a family of missionaries in the Marshall Islands, the ordained Congregational minister had lived in Japan for more than a quarter century, eventually becoming one of the most notable interpreters of the country for the West. He so mastered the Japanese language that he gave sermons in it, and wrote more than a dozen books and pamphlets about the country, its culture, and its relationship to the West. He was staunchly anticolonialist, and condemned attempts to exploit the nonwhite races of the world. Upon his return to the United States in 1913, he was horrified by the treatment of Japanese immigrants in California and began studying their lives across Sacramento, Stockton, San Jose, and Los Angeles. The Federal Council of Churches of Christ in America sponsored his nationwide, thirty-city tour, where he espoused international peace and improved relations both with Japan and its citizens in the United States. He published *The American Japanese Problem* (1914) and *American Democracy and Asiatic Citizenship* (1918), both of which presented the argument that, contrary to the anti-Japanese sentiment pervasive in

California at the time, Asian immigrants were both "assimilable" and not deserving of prejudice. In an effort to stave off total exclusion, for years Gulick had proposed an immigration quota system, which he imagined would treat all countries equally.

This was naive at best. Any quota system, whether set at 2 percent, 3 percent, or 5 percent, would favor Northern European groups like the English, Irish, and German over new arrivals. Ever the internationalist, Reverend Gulick, in addition to adding Japan to any quota system, recommended the creation of a joint high commission composed of American and Japanese members, tasked with studying the immigration question and recommending a new policy. (Leo Mc-Clatchy dismissed the idea in his dispatch from the hearing: "The United States does not and should not seek the assistance or advice of other nations in determining upon what laws should or should not be enacted for the welfare of this country." He did not mention that this is exactly how the Gentlemen's Agreement was achieved.)

Gulick's testimony was listened to with half an ear; the wave was too strong. In the coming weeks Congress would pass the Immigration Act of 1924, a big-tent approach to race-based legislation. The act barred Japanese immigration altogether—the final piece needed to exclude nearly all Asian immigrants. And it created quotas for European migrants: 2 percent of a nationality's U.S. population as registered in 1890. The National Association of Manufacturers, the American Mining Congress, and the U.S. Chamber of Commerce all opposed the law; the Ku Klux Klan applauded it. That year, more Chinese, Czechs, Greeks, Hungarians, Japanese, Lithuanians, Poles, Portuguese, Romanians, Spaniards, and Yugoslavs left the United States than arrived. National origins aside, the act would also essentially slam the door on Jewish immigrants.

The U.S. ambassador to Japan and the Japanese ambassador to the United States both resigned in protest. As news reached Tokyo, scores of young men visited the Ginza Methodist Church there and demanded the deportation of its American missionaries. The same night, fifty men surrounded a vehicle idling outside a movie house and, after noticing the car's American embassy plates, threatened the Japanese chauffeur and urged him to quit. The Tokyo Imperial Hotel canceled its Saturday night American dances and hired a security guard after Japanese men broke up the previous one. On June 9, when V. S. McClatchy stepped foot off the train in San Francisco, he was greeted by the adjutant of the California state American Legion, the secretary of the California Federation of Labor, the grand secretary of the Native Sons of the Golden West, his wife, his son, and his daughter, among others. They took him out to lunch.

Ten weeks later, in Los Angeles, Hyohei and Ise Nomura welcomed their sixth and final child.

CHAPTER FIVE

9066

THE FIRST WEEKS of the war were demoralizing for the Allies. On the same day as the attack on Pearl Harbor, Japanese forces struck Hong Kong, Wake and Midway Islands, Guam, and the Malay Peninsula. Ten hours after Pearl Harbor, more than fifty Japanese twin engine Mitsubishi bombers attacked the U.S. Army's Far East Air Forces in the Philippines, destroying twelve of the force's sixteen B-17 heavy bombers and seriously damaging four more. Guam fell on December 10, and the Japanese captured Wake Island two days before Christmas.

So seventeen years after the United States ended Japanese immigration, its government set about determining what to do about those who were already here. For decades, though, Franklin Roosevelt himself had left a trail of clues as to how he might respond to an attack from Japan, and, more importantly for his constituents, signaled how he would treat the country's descendants in the United States.

Roosevelt's studies in the White House and his home in Hyde Park, New York, were filled with naval and war scenes and reportedly formed the world's largest collection of American naval prints and paintings. The surrounding drawers and shelves were stuffed with models, pamphlets, and documents highlighting the same fascination.

At age eleven he picked up Admiral Alfred Thayer Mahan's seminal *The Influence of Sea Power upon History* and read it so frequently that he nearly memorized it; for decades he would cite its importance, hoping someday to publish an updated edition. His obsession was one of projection: the closest he ever came to battle was as assistant secretary of the navy, an administrative post. Roosevelts didn't fight in the War of 1812, the Mexican War, or the Civil War; at the age of thirty-two, Roosevelt's father, James, hired a substitute to fight for him. Roosevelt's maternal grandfather, Warren Delano Jr., made his fortune in opium trading during the First Opium War. Delano bequeathed to his grandson an unusual obsession with China, one his mother, Sara, nourished with stories of her own visit to the empire in the mid-1860s and early-1870s. The family estate in Hyde Park was full of artifacts from the family's time there, including vases and a large temple bell. More than a century later, visitors to the estate will still recognize the pieces in the mansion's formal parlor.

During his Harvard years, Roosevelt cultivated lifelong friendships with Japanese classmates, but politically always favored China, perhaps due to his family's long merchant history with its people. He watched as his idol and distant cousin, Teddy, navigated Japan's growing influence after the Russo-Japanese War and his diplomacy in negotiating the Gentlemen's Agreement. In 1913 Roosevelt assumed the role of assistant secretary of the navy—a title once held by Teddy—and was almost immediately thrust into planning a possible war with Japan. California's Alien Land Act was soon to be signed into law, and Navy officials assumed the Japanese would use it as a pretext to seize the Philippines and Hawai'i. That threat didn't materialize, but it burrowed into Roosevelt's psyche, fostering a decades-long suspicion.

Into the 1920s he navigated squarely down the middle road on immigration, denouncing the literacy test created by the Immigration Act of 1917 while approving the exclusion of unhealthy and "feebleminded" immigrants. In a 1920 interview with the *Brooklyn Eagle*, during his unsuccessful run for the vice presidency, he expressed support for a model similar to Canada's, which forced new immigrants to disperse across the country. In a few decades' time, the comment would be seen as prophetic.

"Our main trouble in the past has been that we have permitted the foreign elements to segregate in colonies," he said. "They have crowded into one district and they have brought congestion and racial prejudices to our large cities. The result is that they do not easily conform to the manners and the customs and the requirements of their new home. Now, the remedy for this should be the distribution of aliens in various parts of the country. . . . Of course this could not be done by legislative enactment. It could only be done by inducement—if better financial conditions and better living conditions could be offered to the alien dwellers in the cities."

Four years later, Roosevelt would get his wish with the signing of the Immigration Act of 1924. In a column for *The Macon Telegraph* the year after that, Roosevelt doubled down, arguing that the previous reason given in most anti-Japanese waves—economics—wasn't accurate. Not only were the country's exclusionist policies valuable, he argued the law should have been *more* racial: "I know a great many cultivated, highly educated, and delightful Japanese. They have all told me that they would feel the same repugnance and objection to have thousands of Americans settle in Japan and intermarry with the Japanese as I would feel in having large numbers of Japanese come over here and intermarry with the American population. In this question then of Japanese exclusion from the United States, it is necessary only to advance the true reason—the undesirability of mixing the blood of the two peoples."

Within four years Roosevelt would become governor of New York and, another four years later, president. The Japanese American community grew parallel to Roosevelt's power, the two paths barely grazing throughout the Depression and Roosevelt's New Deal. Japanese

Americans, resigned to exclusion, began their fight for assimilation, with the nisei leading the way. And on June 8, 1933, Roosevelt sat down to write a short letter.

The parasols shone in the sun, blue, green, and pink flowers perched and spinning above the bonnets of New Bedford's women. The city was unlike anything Manjiro had ever seen, stocked with wharves and churches, ships pulling in and out of the busy harbor. Captain Whitfield guided the teenager through the bustling streets and up Johnny Oake Hill to the Seamen's Bethel. They took their seats in the church's pews, the notes from the organ enveloping the two men, and offered thanks for their safe return. Manjiro understood little, instead thinking of his mother at home, reciting the Buddhist sutra.

He helped with the chores on Whitfield's fourteen-acre farm, and for the first time in his life Manjiro attended school. One Sunday, Whitfield took the boy to his home church, sitting in the captain's private pew. After a few weeks, a deacon told Whitfield that Manjiro would need to sit in a separate pew, with the church's black congregants. Silently, Whitfield walked out and never returned. A second church rejected Manjiro and Whitfield soon after, so the pair made their way to the corner of Washington and Walnut Streets, in Fairhaven. Washington Street Christian Meeting-House, a Unitarian congregation, welcomed the peculiar new family. Every Sunday they attended the church, built twelve years earlier with the funds of the man who would sit a few pews over, Warren Delano Sr., the great-grandfather of the thirty-second president of the United States.

In that moment Manjiro couldn't have possibly foreseen what life held for him. He studied English and surveying in Fairhaven, then signed on the whaling ship *Franklin*. In October 1847 the *Franklin* docked in Honolulu, where he was reunited with the friends he had left six years earlier. He returned to New Bedford and set sail for California and the riches promised by the gold rush. His pockets lined in just a few months, he returned to Hawai'i, picked up two of his friends, and the three continued west, homeward.

As incursions from the West grew in frequency, Manjiro became a sought-after translator and was named a *hatamoto*, a samurai who directly served the shogunate. In that role he needed to select a surname; Nakahama Manjiro was born. He aided the shogunate in its negotiations with Commodore Perry and made invaluable contributions to the development of Japan's navy. He's likely the first Japanese man to ever ride a train or steamship. On June 8, 1933, three months into his presidency, Franklin Delano Roosevelt sat down to write Manjiro's eldest son a letter.

> *My dear Dr. Nakahama,*
>
> *When Viscount Ishii was here in Washington he told me you are living in Tokyo and we talked about your distinguished father.*
>
> *You may not know that I am the [great] grandson of Mr. Warren Delano of Fairhaven, who was part owner of the ship of Captain Whitfield which brought your father to Fairhaven. Your father lived, as I remember . . . directly across the street from my grandfather's house, and when I was a boy, I well remember my grandfather telling me all about the little Japanese boy who went to school in Fairhaven and who went to church from time to time with the Delano family. I myself used to visit Fairhaven, and my mother's family still own the old house.*
>
> *The name of Nakahama will always be remembered by my family, and I hope that if you or any of your family come to the United States that you will come to see us.*
>
> > *Believe me, my dear Dr. Nakahama,*
> > *Very sincerely yours, Franklin Roosevelt*

As tensions grew between Japan and the United States in the 1930s, Roosevelt instituted and championed his legion of monitors across the

Japanese American community. In 1939, the Office of Naval Intelligence's Hawaiian department studied the islands' nikkei population, determining that "except for a few who stated that they would be neutral, the majority of the citizen group stated that they would adhere to the United States." In November 1940, FBI agent Robert Shivers filed a voluminous report to Director Hoover; it once again declared the community little risk for espionage. The head of the Honolulu Police Department's espionage division, Captain John A. Burns, had grown up in a mixed neighborhood in the city, among issei and nisei. Writing under a pseudonym in the *Honolulu Star-Bulletin*, he defended the community: "They are good law-abiding citizens. The records of our police department will show this. . . . As to our Japanese aliens there is no showing that they are disloyal to the United States! That they may have some love for Japan or things Japanese may be admitted, but without that love how can we expect them to be good American aides or loyal to anything American. . . . Those units which have been investigating have not found facts which would indicate or disprove loyalty but rather the opposite."

While his intelligence agencies worked, Roosevelt created his own clandestine team in February 1941. Led by former Roosevelt speechwriter and newspaper columnist John Franklin Carter, the team consisted of secret intelligence agents tasked with informing the president on a panoply of subjects: Nazi influence in South Africa, political conditions in the French Caribbean colonies of Martinique and Guadeloupe, isolationists in Chicago. The team worked a block from the White House in room 1210 of the National Press Building, and in the months prior to Pearl Harbor was tasked with its most important assignment: the Japanese American community.

Curtis B. Munson was a DC native with a blue blood pedigree. After graduating from St. Paul's School and Yale, he joined La Fayette Escadrille, an American group of volunteers who fought for the French in World War I, before becoming an artillery officer in the U.S. Army. He moved to Alberta, Canada, following the war, where he opened a coal mine and, using the fortune provided by his contract with the Canadian National Railway, later operated a timber company and grain farm. In 1934, after one failed marriage, he wedded the best female golfer in the world, Edith Cummings. He split his time between the coalfields of Alberta and the dining clubs of Chicago, and he'd soon, for reasons and relations lost to time, determine whether Japanese Americans would spy on their own country.

Munson landed in early October in California, where he sought the advice of Kenneth Ringle, the ONI staff officer who broke into the Japanese consulate that spring. Ringle's contacts in the Japanese American community ran deep. He'd spent the previous two years virtually alone, working out of a tiny office in the San Pedro YMCA, driving an aging rumble-seat coupe, and observing the nikkei farmers, fishermen, and business owners of the Los Angeles area. He ingrained himself into the community, attending civic association meetings in civilian clothes and eating meals at Japanese American homes. On the day of Pearl Harbor, he'd be one of only twelve men in the U.S. Navy fluent in Japanese.

When the two men met, Ringle imparted to Munson everything he'd learned. One thing stuck out to the latter: while Japanese Americans may have retained many of the customs of Japan, they believed fully and completely in America, and in the prospect the country provided for immigrants and their descendants. Munson solicited help from British intelligence in California, Ringle's Naval Intelligence colleagues, and Japanese Americans in Los Angeles and San Francisco. Within two weeks, he sent a preliminary report back to Carter in Washington. It was a damning indictment of the pervading thought.

"We do not want to throw a lot of American citizens into a concentration camp of course, and especially as the almost unanimous verdict is that in case of war they will be quiet, very quiet," he wrote. "There will probably be some sabotage by paid Japanese agents and the odd fanatical Jap, but the bulk of these people will be quiet because in addition to being quite contented with the American Way of life, they know they are 'in a spot.'"

Californians, he added perhaps naively or at least optimistically, "like and trust the Jap out here far better than the East thinks they do." Carter passed the report on to Roosevelt, adding, "[Munson] has found no evidence which would indicate that there is danger of widespread anti-American activities among this population group. He feels that the Japanese are more in danger from the whites than the other way around." Fifteen days later, on November 7, Munson filed his eighteen-page final report.

"There is no Japanese 'problem' on the Coast," he wrote. "There will be no armed uprising of Japanese. . . . For the most part the local Japanese are loyal to the United States or, at worst, hope that by remaining quiet they can avoid concentration camps or irresponsible mobs. We do not believe that they would be at least any more disloyal than any other racial group in the United States with whom we went to war."

Carter copied a five-point summary of the report, attached it to the top of Munson's work, and sent it off to Roosevelt. The president hurriedly read the cover letter, focusing not on any of the elements of the report that he had asked for but rather the summary's fifth point: "[Munson] is horrified to note that dams, bridges, harbors, power stations, etc., are wholly unguarded everywhere." Due to Carter's framing, Roosevelt interpreted that point as the most dire warning in the report, making efforts immediately to quell any possible sabotage. There's no evidence he ever read Munson's full report.

California Congressional District 16 began at the Pacific Ocean and ended at the foot of the Hollywood Hills, a quarter-mile north of that neighborhood's high school. Its congressman was Leland Ford, a Republican who'd worked as a surveyor, farmer, livestock breeder, railroad worker, planning commissioner, real estate salesman, and county supervisor before being elected to Congress in 1938. A staunch antilabor and anti–New Deal Republican, Ford had voted, while serving as a Los Angeles County supervisor in 1938, against using county funds to aid a Works Progress Administration sewing project, leading to a sit-down strike outside his office. In a move decidedly the opposite of a sit-down strike, a mob of seamstresses lunged at Ford, ripping his vest and shirt open while tearing his tie off. He called the building's sergeant-at-arms to protect him. Looking back with humor two days later, the mayor presented him with a heavy canvas shirt, complete with a padlock.

After Pearl Harbor, Ford initially defended his state and district's nikkei population, citing their loyalty to the United States. However, within weeks his tone changed as his office mailbox was inundated with fervent, rambling letters calling for the removal of all ethnic Japanese. The congressman fired off a telegram to Washington demanding action: "I do not believe that we could be any too strict in our consideration of the Japanese in the face of the treacherous way in which they do things."

By mid-January Ford had fully embraced his role as lead instigator in their removal.

"If an American-born Japanese, who is a citizen, is really patriotic and wishes to make his contribution to the safety and welfare of this country, right here, is his opportunity to do so, namely, that by permitting himself to be placed in a concentration camp, he would be making his sacrifice and he should be willing to do it if he is patriotic and is working for us," he shambolically declared in a letter to the secretaries of war and the navy and to FBI director J. Edgar Hoover on January 16. "As against his sacrifice, millions of other native born citizens are willing to lay down their lives, which is a far greater sacrifice, of course, than being placed in a concentration camp."

By February his tone flew past being impatient and went directly to self-righteous.

"I phoned the Attorney General's office and told them to stop fucking around," Ford recalled in an interview seven months later. "I gave them twenty-four hours notice that unless they would issue a mass evacuation notice I would drag the whole matter out on the floor of the House and of the Senate and give the bastards everything we could with both barrels. I told them they had given us the run around long enough . . . and that if they would not take immediate action, we would clean the god damned office out in one sweep."

As Ford began his push for removal, Roosevelt released a statement drafted by Attorney General Francis Biddle, who'd spent the previous weeks attempting to calm the anxieties of Japanese Americans and nationals: "Remember the Nazi technique: 'Pit race against race, religion against religion, prejudice against prejudice. Divide and conquer!'" The statement was interpreted as an endorsement of their loyalty, even though it didn't mention them directly.

Meanwhile, Roosevelt's War Department was working on a separate plan. The week after Pearl Harbor, Western Defense Command head General John DeWitt spread rumors that a squadron of airplanes had passed over California. That twenty thousand Japanese Americans were planning an uprising in San Francisco. That Japanese Americans were signaling Japanese submarines from the windows of their homes. Stray radio signals were interpreted as secret spy transmissions and, when those signals ceased, that silence was interpreted as proof. The rumors filtered through DeWitt's office at the foot of the Golden Gate Bridge, piquing the anxiety of a man prone to bouts of it.

DeWitt was born in Nebraska, the son of a general and the brother of two generals. He abandoned Princeton in 1898 to join the Army in the Spanish-American War, the beginning of his near fifty-year military career. He moved from desk job to desk job following World War I, from supply officer to quartermaster, never rising to any degree of renown. He was a bureaucrat in the most derisive definition of the word. His indecisiveness bred paranoia and anxiety, a cluster of traits no one wants to define its military leaders, especially one in charge of the safety of Americans in eight states and the territory of Alaska. He had been described as "the creature of the last strong personality with whom he had contact." He was anxious, easily manipulated, and in way over his head.

To balance that, he succumbed to his paranoias. He couldn't accept Japanese American loyalty, ignoring Munson's report and refusing to even meet with Ringle. When presented with the absence of sabotage by the Japanese community, DeWitt viewed it as proof that "control [was] being exercised." Nine days after Pearl Harbor he floated designating a one-hundred-mile-wide strip of the West Coast as a military zone, allowing any person in that zone deemed undesirable to be removed by the military. On top of the roundup the FBI kicked off on December 7, he suggested that every German, Italian, and Japanese national over the age of fourteen be moved inland. He opposed mass removal at first, though only because he believed the removal of more than 100,000 people to be an impossible task.

Akin to DeWitt in his bigotry, Karl Bendetson was superior in his ability to transform those beliefs into action. Bendetson grew up in a Finnish neighborhood in the logging community of Aberdeen, Washington, the grandson of Lithuanian Jews and a denizen of the kind of diverse community that rarely existed outside boomtowns. Naturalization classes opened their doors to Finns, Croatians, Germans, Czechs, Poles, Italians, and Scandinavians, while Chinese railroad workers and Japanese cooks watched from outside, barred from citizenship.

A lawyer by trade, Bendetson had enlisted in the Washington National Guard at the age of fourteen, before he'd even started high school. He joined the Army's Officers Reserve Corps after graduating from Stanford Law in 1932, and was called to active duty and assigned to the Military Affairs Section of the Judge Advocate General staff in Washington, D.C., in 1940. Just thirty-two, he was the lowest-ranking officer on staff and served mostly to deal with administrative legal questions. His ascent was swift. Within a year he was promoted to major, tasked with heading up the aliens division, which oversaw issues relating to prisoners of war and the internment of enemy aliens.

In the fall of 1941, he traveled to Kilauea Military Camp in Hawai'i, where he studied military intelligence and inspected possible sites for enemy alien camps.

On December 7, Bendetson and his wife, Billie Jean, attended a luncheon in Washington, D.C. Much of the city's newspapermen and War Department officers were among the 27,000 fans at Griffith Stadium, watching the Washington Redskins and Philadelphia Eagles play the last game of the 1941 NFL season. News of the attack first reached an Associated Press reporter: "The Japanese have kicked off. War now!" the message from his editor read. The public address system began paging military and diplomatic officials, and by halftime the only journalist left was one sideline photographer. After receiving a call from his office, Bendetson dropped his wife off at their home in Bethesda, then drove his new Buick convertible downtown. His desk at the War Department's Munitions Building was stacked with plans he'd finally be able to put to use.

Long proud of his ability to work with little sleep, Bendetson spent the next forty-eight hours awake, plotting.

Bendetson was a Westerner, an attorney, and, after his stint in the War Department, well versed in enemy alien law. In the weeks after Pearl Harbor he spent his days communicating with DeWitt in San Francisco, the two men relaying their offices' needs and desires. On December 30 he climbed aboard a plane and made the journey west, to support DeWitt in his soon-to-be numerous conflicts with Francis Biddle and the Justice Department. The week before, DeWitt had once again refused the suggestion of Bendetson's boss, Major General Allen W. Gullion, to recommend the mass removal of Japanese nationals and Japanese Americans. Echoing his hesitancy from weeks before, DeWitt responded, "I'm very doubtful that it would be common sense procedure to try and intern 117,000 Japanese in this theater. . . . An American citizen after all, is an American citizen. And while they all may not be loyal, I think we can weed the disloyal out of the loyal and lock them up if necessary." That hesitancy was short-lived.

DeWitt and Bendetson never brought up the idea of mass removal during their early January meetings with the Justice Department, instead focusing on intermediary steps: registration for all nationals from enemy countries, the creation of exclusion zones, and, at Bendetson's suggestion, mass raids on issei homes. After initial conflict with Justice, Biddle and his subordinates relented. Roosevelt ordered the registration of foreign nationals on January 14, and exclusion zones were created around ports, naval bases, barracks, and airfields, including an airfield built among strawberry fields in Mountain View, California. Bendetson's influence over DeWitt, "the creature of the last strong personality with whom he had contact," was now total.

On the same day as Roosevelt's order, the Canadian government okayed the removal of all male Japanese nationals ages eighteen to forty-five from British Columbia. The order received no media attention in the United States, but to War Department officials the implication was clear: it could be done.

As Bendetson traveled back and forth from Washington, D.C., to San Francisco, both misinformation and pressure were growing in Roosevelt's cabinet. At a January 16 meeting, Agriculture Secretary Claude Wickard, without evidence, claimed that West Coast residents refused to eat produce from Japanese farmers, and, in one instance, that a gardener had confessed to putting too much arsenic in his vegetable spray. And Congressman Ford's badgering was growing to a piercing pitch, forcing Attorney General Biddle to respond. The enemy alien program had matters under control, he told Ford, and short of suspending habeas corpus there was nothing the government could do to remove Japanese Americans. Ford found a more sympathetic response in the War Department. In a letter drafted by Bendetson, Secretary of War Henry Stimson responded:

"The internment of over a hundred thousand people, and their evacuation inland, presents a very real problem. While the necessity for firm measures to insure the maximum war effort cannot be questioned, the proposal suggested by you involves many complex considerations."

That said, he continued, the War Department was prepared to take on that task and had the facilities to do so, save for one bump: the enemy alien program was under the jurisdiction of the Justice Department. *Convince them to transfer that authority*, he implied, *and maybe we can make it work.*

As Bendetson's influence spread from coast to coast, the missing piece for the incarceration of 120,000 nikkei was about to be dealt. Following Pearl Harbor, Roosevelt tasked Supreme Court justice Owen Roberts to lead a commission into the attack. While the resulting report was vague—it did not even mention the nikkei population in Hawai'i, only mentioning espionage by Japanese agents—discussions Roberts had during the investigation would influence Roosevelt. In his diary January 20, War Secretary Henry Stimson noted that Roberts told him the Japanese Americans in Hawai'i were disloyal.

"The tremendous Japanese population in the islands he regarded as a great menace," he wrote. "He did not think that the FBI had succeeded in getting under the crust of their secret thoughts at all and he believed that this great mass of Japanese, both aliens and Americanized, existed as a great potential danger in the Islands."

Newspapers and politicians pounced on the January 23 report, conflating Japanese with Japanese Americans. The *Los Angeles Times*, measured in its stance immediately after Pearl Harbor, now called for the removal of all nikkei. Seattle Mayor Earl Millikin offered the five hundred horsemen of the city's Cavalry Brigade to drive Japanese Americans out of town and across the Cascade Mountains. California attorney general Earl Warren believed the "Japanese situation" may be "the Achilles heel of the entire civilian defense effort" and bring about another Pearl Harbor. In November he'd be elected governor; twelve years after that he'd receive a lifetime appointment to the U.S. Supreme Court. Los Angeles mayor Fletcher Bowron, who just the previous year had courted Japanese American voters at campaign rallies in Little Tokyo, encouraged the community to inform on each other, and used his weekly radio program to urge their removal from the city. He conspired with newspaper editors to gin up support for the plan, and proposed a constitutional amendment that stripped away citizenship rights from Japanese Americans. Following the Los Angeles County Board of Supervisors' decision to fire all Japanese American county employees, Bowron followed in lockstep, placing all city employees of Japanese descent on an indefinite leave of absence.

The American Legion, the Native Sons of the Golden West, and the California Joint Immigration Committee—co-founded by V. S. McClatchy during his Immigration Act of 1924 victory lap—roused and joined with some of their oldest bedfellows, farmers. Reflecting the fever of the turn of the century, the California Farm Bureau Federation and newly formed groups like the White American Nurserymen of Los Angeles pushed their congressmen and state officials to take action. The stakes for mass removal were high: nikkei produce production in California alone had grown to more than $500 million in 2019 dollars. Just their share of the Los Angeles flower market was $66 million. In Los Angeles County, the pea, beet, broccoli, celery, and cauliflower markets were controlled—every single planted acre—by nikkei. Of the 39,200 acres of vegetable farms in Los Angeles County, issei and nisei farmers controlled 26,300 of them. With the war sending demand soaring, fortunes were to be made. If the farmers could not only eliminate the issei but the nisei, too, Californian agriculture would be stripped of its nikkei competition. The farmers were nothing if not honest about their intentions.

"We're charged with wanting to get rid of the Japs for selfish reasons," Salinas Vegetable Grower-Shipper Association managing secretary Austin E. Anson told *The Saturday Evening Post*. "We might as well be honest. We do. It's a question of whether the white man lives on the Pacific Coast or the brown men. They came into this valley to work, and they stayed to take over. . . . . If all the Japs were removed tomorrow, we'd never miss them in two weeks, because the white farmers can take over and produce everything the Jap grows. And we don't want them back when the war ends, either."

California governor Culbert Olson, a progressive Democrat, met with DeWitt the week after the report's release. Californians, he told DeWitt, "feel that they are living in the midst of enemies. They don't trust the Japanese, none of them." Before the meeting with DeWitt, Olson hosted two dozen nisei leaders from across the state at his office, and proposed a plan. The government would remove issei and nisei from the coast, but not get rid of them entirely. Instead they'd be transplanted to the agricultural regions of the state's interior, where they would work California's farms. It was, in effect, a California-sponsored concentration camp, holding men, women, and children, with the men forced (or allowed, depending on who was talking) to leave each day to work the fields. Some of the nisei, influenced by uncertainty, thought the plan was worth considering. Most were appalled. At the conclave, Saburo Kido and Mike Masaoka represented the Japanese American Citizens League, the organization founded in 1929 to incorporate smaller Japanese American organizations up and down the West Coast. In an effort to prove the loyalty of its members, the JACL worked with the FBI before and after Pearl Harbor to help the bureau root out any suspected disloyal issei. But this plan was too much. Kido reminded Olson that the nisei were American citizens, entitled to equal protection: "If you are so interested in our welfare, why don't you give us the necessary police protection so we can remain in our homes? I consider it the responsibility of the state to safeguard its citizens."

Olson broke up the meeting, calling the men "ungrateful" and "uncooperative." Afterward, at a chop suey café in Sacramento's Japantown, the group huddled to weigh their options. A gloom hung over the men, certain only of the fact that their governor had abandoned them.

"How much do you think you can get for your farm equipment," optometrist George Takahashi asked farmer Frank Sakata. "You'd better start unloading the stuff now."

"You'd better quit worrying about Frank," interrupted Walter Tsukamoto, an attorney and reserve officer in the U.S. Army. "And start packing your optometry equipment."

The conversation reflected the internecine conflicts that existed within the Japanese American community. Priorities of urban nikkei were different from those who lived in the farming communities. There were big, overarching differences, but also more specific ones; closing a boardinghouse is a much different proposition than allowing hundreds of acres of produce to rot. The rights of Japanese Americans, they assumed, were different from those of their issei parents. And lording over all groups were white Americans unwilling to differentiate between any of them.

In San Francisco, Kido and Masaoka weighed their options. Until that meeting the two men hadn't believed removal was truly an option; now it seemed a certainty. As generals and governors and lawyers decided their fate, the men searched the corners of their brains. If issei were removed, should the nisei stay put on constitutional grounds or, for the sake of family unity, leave as well? Would the government accept removal just from DeWitt's designated strategic zones? That desperation led to a confounding idea: the suicide battalion.

Composed of nisei volunteers, the battalion would fight in the Pacific theater, against the Japanese. As collateral of their loyalty, the volunteers' parents would be kept as hostages by the government. The idea was immediately rejected by the government, but the lengths the nisei community was prepared to go to prove its loyalty were drawn. They would die.

The same was not expected of German and Italian Americans. By 1941 there were 127,000 U.S. residents of Japanese ancestry, and almost all of them—112,000—lived in the three West Coast states. Of those, 71,000 were citizens and 41,000 were Japanese nationals denied that opportunity. In contrast, there were 52,000 Italian nationals in California alone, more than the entire issei population in the United States. In Los Angeles, the most Japanese city in America, German-born residents outnumbered Japanese nationals more than two to one. But there was no thirst for wholesale removal of German Americans or Italian Americans.

Some of this clemency may be traced to Giuseppe Paolo DiMaggio, the eighth of nine children born to a pair of Sicilian immigrants. His father, also named Giuseppe, would push off at dawn in the *Rosalie D*, combing the waters off San Francisco in the boat named for his wife. The boat was too small to venture beyond the Golden Gate Bridge—where the crabs and money waited—so Giuseppe scraped by with tiny hauls to feed his eleven-person family. The children spoke Italian at home and English outside those walls; Rosalie told the children Bible stories. Joe, as the son would be known as, held no affinity for school or the sea, only for baseball. By the beginning of 1941, Joe DiMaggio was the star of the New York Yankees and a four-time World Series champion. By the end of the year he'd be one of the most famous men in America. On May 15, 1941, DiMaggio began his record 56-game hitting streak, a mark that will likely never be broken. His face was plastered across magazine spreads and tabloids. At 6-foot-2, 193 pounds, and twenty-six years old, he was the embodiment of the American Dream. When Joe was in the minors, before walking to his boat each morning the elder Giuseppe would wake his youngest son, Dominic, to translate the box score from Joe's game the night before. Despite living in the United States for forty years, Giuseppe had never become naturalized. After Pearl Harbor, as an enemy alien, his boat was confiscated. But his loyalty was only perfunctorily challenged. No one would doubt the great Yankee Clipper's father. That, to most Americans, was beyond reason.

Likewise, while Americans had DiMaggio to smooth over any prejudice of Italians, they could also visualize and direct their anger toward Hitler and Mussolini. Japan's leaders were virtually unknown in America. So old stereotypes were happily dusted off and reapplied. Buck-toothed and bespectacled illustrations under the words "Get In Trim For Fighting Him!" soon filled shop windows and light posts. It was easy to distinguish German Americans from Nazis, and Italian

Americans from Fascists, but no such nomenclature benefited Japanese Americans. No matter how many years your family had been in the United States, you were still Japanese, not American.

As the men in Washington dithered, others took their own actions. In the cities, bricks smashed through the front windows of nisei-owned stores, while in the fields and farms vagrants attacked the homes of nikkei farmers. Restaurants posted signs claiming they poisoned "both rats and Japs." Barbershops promised "All Japanese Shaved Free: Not Responsible for Accidents." On car windshields drivers hung cards reading "Open Season for Japs." Anything even tangentially connected to Japan became a target. Chinese Americans wore "Don't shoot! I'm a Chinaman!" signs and lapel pins featuring crosses and Chinese and American flags. Both *Time* and *Life* magazines ran dubious photo spreads to help readers distinguish between their Chinese and Japanese neighbors. Teens chopped down four Japanese cherry trees along the Tidal Basin in Washington, D.C.; across town, curators at the Freer Gallery of Art removed all Japanese paintings, prints, and sculptures to prevent a similar fate. In New York City, the Parks Department placed a guard at the Flushing Meadows Japanese Pavilion, presented to the United States by the Japanese government at the conclusion of the 1939 World's Fair. After ax-wielding Queens residents threatened to invade the building, the department razed the pavilion, its salvaged lumber used to build playgrounds around the city. Japanese-made merchandise was removed from shelves and burned. In New Orleans, the members of Rising Sun Baptist Church made national news when they voted unanimously to rechristen as the Pentecost Baptist Church. The 1,500 residents of Rising Sun, Indiana, made no such decision.

The economic pressure on Japanese Americans was becoming impossible. Restrictions placed on issei following Pearl Harbor had snowballed from personal difficulty to economic crisis. With their assets frozen, business transactions were halted, and fields went unplanted. Insurance policies were canceled, leases broken. Whatever white patronage Japanese American–owned stores had enjoyed evaporated. On January 17 it was reported that most issei- and nisei-owned businesses in San Francisco would be forced "to close within a few months."

Kenesaw Mountain Landis was a lifelong Republican, but he saved particular spite for Franklin Roosevelt. The Major League Baseball commissioner and former federal judge loathed Roosevelt's domestic policies, opposed his decision to run for a third presidential term in 1940, and considered the president's war preparation inadequate at best. The feeling was mutual.

"Landis wasn't much more welcome at the White House than the Japanese ambassador," said Washington Senators owner Clark Griffith.

But Landis needed a favor: he needed the president to save baseball.

"The time is approaching when, in ordinary conditions, our teams would be heading for Spring training camps," Landis wrote in a January 14 letter. "However, inasmuch as these are not ordinary times, I venture to ask what you have in mind as to whether professional baseball should continue to operate."

Roosevelt wasted no time, and responded the next day. His reaction was front-page news across the country.

"I honestly feel that it would be best for the country to keep baseball going," Roosevelt wrote. "Baseball provides a recreation which does not last over two hours or two hours and a half, and which can be got for very little cost. And, incidentally, I hope that night games can be extended because it gives an opportunity to the day shift to see a game occasionally."

The sentiment did not trickle down to the country's Japanese communities. The previous month's issei roundup decimated the nikkei baseball leagues that thrived up and down the West Coast, while an 8 p.m. curfew and travel restrictions imposed on nikkei virtually elimi-

nated evening basketball leagues. The distraction of sports was necessary for the country's white residents, it seemed, but expendable for
others.

One day that winter, two men in dark suits walked onto a muddy
practice field at Oregon State College. The school's football team had
just won its first Pacific Coast Conference championship, earning them
a spot in the coveted Rose Bowl game. They'd take on the second-
ranked team in the country, the undefeated Duke Blue Devils. The
clash was held annually at the Rose Bowl, a ninety-thousand-spectator
stadium in Pasadena, California, but DeWitt worried the magnitude
and visibility of the game made it a prime target for a Japanese attack.
He forced the bowl's board of directors to make a decision: cancel the
game or move it inland. (In a typical bout of DeWitt pettiness, he ordered a group of Army engineers to set up camp on the field, ensuring
it would not be used for football.) After the initial disappointment—
much of the appeal of the Rose Bowl for players, coaches, and their
families was a trip to California—it was decided the game would be
played in Durham, North Carolina, at Duke. So the two teams prepared.

Crouched in a blocking drill on the muddy field was sophomore
Jack Yoshihara, one of forty-one nikkei students enrolled at Oregon
State. Jack was born in Japan in 1921, but his parents had spent time
in Oregon, working on its farms and in its canneries. With the Immigration Act of 1924 set to close the doors of America to Japanese immigrants, the family returned to Oregon with Jack, landing less than
a month before the act was signed into law. Jack grew, and grew—he
topped out at 205 pounds—and starred at Portland's Benson Polytech-
nic High School. His quickness and tenacity earned him a scholarship
to Oregon State, where by his sophomore season he'd fought his way
to backup left end.

The two men squished across the grass and handed a folder to
Jack's coach, Lon Stiner. Stiner reviewed its contents, and called Jack
over. "Son, these men from the FBI would like to have a word with

you," he said, hardly masking his disgust. The men then each grabbed an arm and escorted Jack from the field. As his teammates yelled questions at the trio, Jack looked back and could only offer a despondent glance.

Despite that fact that he'd lived in Oregon since he was three, Jack was technically a Japanese national and bound by geographic restrictions imposed after Pearl Harbor. He was released after questioning, but traveling for the game was out of the question. Protests from teammates, the student body, and even Oregon State president Francois Archibald Gilfillan went unheard. The Beavers boarded a train headed for Durham, and Jack waved goodbye from the platform.

Thirteen days later, Oregon State defeated Duke 20–16, the lone Rose Bowl victory in the school's 127-season football history.

———

After seven weeks of indecision, on January 29, DeWitt informed the War Department that he was prepared to recommend the removal of all nikkei, citizen or otherwise, from the Pacific Coast. The following day Bendetson met with a committee of West Coast congressmen and two Justice Department officials. If the Justice Department was willing to transfer authority of the alien enemy program to the War Department, he said, they'd gladly accept that mantle. Attorney General Biddle rushed to counteract DeWitt's change of heart, finally creating the military zones the general had requested weeks earlier and announcing publicly that the Justice Department was monitoring "enemy aliens." He armed himself with a new report from Naval Intelligence staff officer Ringle that argued that security issues among the Japanese American community would be best dealt with on an individual basis. There was no "Japanese problem," he reiterated.

Nevertheless, at a statehouse meeting led by Warren, the attorney general warned more than 100 California sheriffs of the looming threat of the state's nikkei population. Misinformation multiplied. At various points in the first week of February, nikkei were either communicating with Japanese submarines or plotting another Pearl Harbor, or would soon aid an Axis invasion of the West Coast. (Those three plots were floated by a governor, a mayor, and a congressman, respectively.) Letters to the White House demanding removal increased fivefold.

Biddle's staff suggested, to Bendetson's face, that he and the Western congressmen were "encouraging people to get hysterical." In a heated February 1 meeting, the line was drawn between War and Justice. "If it is a question of safety of the country [or] the Constitution of the United States, why the Constitution is just a scrap of paper to me," said Assistant Secretary of War John McCloy.

That week the first wave of photos from Pearl Harbor reached newspapers across the country. Images of the charred USS *Arizona*, guns still peeking out of the water while its hull slumped, spread. Communities that had never seen an ethnically Japanese person were now face-to-face with the wreckage. On February 9, Biddle attempted to dissuade Stimson from approving the mass removal, but the war secretary, watching victory upon victory of the Axis powers in the Pacific, couldn't shake his suspicion that the Japanese would soon invade the West Coast with the aid of Japanese Americans. Three days after the Japanese invaded Singapore, Stimson, McCloy, and deputy army chief of staff General Mark Clark wrote a memo to Roosevelt listing several items, most importantly, "Is the President willing to authorize us to move Japanese citizens as well as enemy aliens from restricted areas?" Roosevelt, consumed with frustration over the invasion and too busy to meet with the men, instead called the men in the early afternoon.

"I took up with him the West Coast matter first," Stimson wrote in his diary that night, "and told him the situation and fortunately found that he was very vigorous about it and told me to go ahead on the line that I had myself thought best."

After the call McCloy rang Bendetson at the Presidio, the U.S. Army fort looming above San Francisco.

"We have carte blanche to do what we want to as far as the President is concerned," he said, adding Roosevelt "states that there will probably be some repercussions, but it has got to be dictated by military necessity, but as he put it, 'Be as reasonable as you can.'"

While considering the fate of more than 100,000 residents, Bendetson was undergoing his own transformation. Ashamed of his Jewish heritage, he changed the spelling of his last name from the original "Bendetson" to the Nordic "Bendetsen," going so far as to create a new family tree. Instead of the progeny of Lithuanian Jews, he would now be the grandson of Benedict and Dora Robbins Bendetsen, and the great-grandson of Benedict Benediktssen, who came to the United States from Denmark in 1815.

The battle over the mass removal was over. Now the men just had to figure out how to get it done.

———————

On February 13, DeWitt and Bendetsen cowrote a six-page, single-spaced memo to Stimson outlining their recommendations. Entitled "Evacuation of Japanese and other Subversive Persons from the Pacific Coast," it served as a culmination of the racial animus and loyalty questioning that the pair had fomented over their short time together.

> *The Japanese race is an enemy race and while many second and third generation Japanese born on United States soil . . . have become "Americanized," the racial strains remain undiluted.*
>
> *. . . [I]t, therefore, follows that along the vital Pacific Coast Frontier over 112,000 potential enemies, of Japanese extraction, are at large today. There are indications that these are organized and ready for concerted action at a favorable opportunity. The very fact that no sabotage has taken place to date is a disturbing and confirming indication that such action will be taken.*

The memo requested that the president authorize and designate a combat zone along the West Coast, from which "all Japanese, all alien enemies, and all other persons suspected for any reason by the administering military authorities of being actual or potential saboteurs, espionage agents, or fifth columnists" would be allowed to be removed.

All of this—Stimson's phone call, the president's assent, DeWitt and Bendetsen's proposal—was done without the attorney general's knowledge. Six days after Stimson's conversation with Roosevelt, Biddle was still trying to convince the president of the folly of mass removal, attacking Walter Lippmann and the horde of newspaper columnists pushing the plan. "It is extremely dangerous for the columnists, acting as 'Armchair Strategists and Junior G-Men,' to suggest that an attack on the West Coast and planned sabotage is imminent," he wrote in a memo to Roosevelt. "It comes close to shouting FIRE! in the theater, and if race riots occur, these writers will bear a heavy responsibility." Roosevelt informed Biddle of his decision after receiving the memo; the attorney general's resistance evaporated.

Bendetsen got to work polishing a formal order, soon hurried to the president's desk. The next morning, on the floor of the U.S. House, the West Coast delegation, unaware of the backroom machinations, condemned Roosevelt's cabinet for dragging its feet in the removal of "all persons of Japanese lineage." In the previous weeks the group had secured the support of three firebrand Southerners well versed in racism—Senator Tom Stewart of Tennessee, Representative John Rankin of Mississippi, and Representative Martin Dies of Texas—the only members outside the West Coast to indicate any real interest in removal. Their oratorical powers were on full display that afternoon.

"They are cowardly and immoral," said Stewart. "They are different from Americans in every conceivable way, and no Japanese . . . should have the right to claim American citizenship. . . . A Jap is a Jap anywhere you find him, and his taking the oath of allegiance to this country would not help, even if he should be permitted to do so."

He later added that nisei didn't deserve citizenship just because of "the mere accident of birth on American soil." Rankin went further: "Once a Jap, always a Jap. You cannot change him. You cannot make a silk purse out of a sow's ear. . . . This is a race war. . . . The white man's civilization has come into conflict with Japanese barbarism. Christianity has come in conflict with Shintoism, atheism, and infidelity. One of them must be destroyed."

"I am for catching every Japanese in America, Alaska, and Hawai'i now and putting him in concentration camps and shipping them back to Asia as soon as possible," he said in conclusion. "If they own property in this country, after the war we can pay them for it, but we must ship them back to the Orient, where they belong. Until that is done, we will never have peace on the Pacific."

Executive Order 9066 was placed on Roosevelt's desk the next day. Using as broad language as possible—Bendetsen knew there was a chance the Supreme Court would rule the order unconstitutional, so he purposely allowed a degree of vagueness—the document laid out what the next four years of life would be like for the issei and their American descendants. In order to grant "every possible protection against espionage and against sabotage to national-defense material, national-defense premises, and national-defense utilities," the president allowed the secretary of war and his military commanders, whenever it was deemed necessary or prudent, to prescribe military areas "with respect to which, the right of any person to enter, remain in, or leave shall be subject to whatever restrictions the Secretary of War or the appropriate Military Commander may impose in his discretion."

The order was 522 words long. None of them was the word "Japanese," but everyone inside and outside the White House knew exactly for whom the order was intended.

PART

2

CHAPTER SIX

A Question of Blood

HIDEO MURATA LIVED alone in a small cottage outside San Luis Obispo, California, and had taken to his adopted country with such fervor that he fought for the American Expeditionary Forces during World War I. At one Fourth of July gala following his return, the Monterey County board of supervisors granted him a "Certificate of Honorary Citizenship." The piece of paper was Murata's most prized possession; his friends would joke that he slept with it under his pillow.

After hearing the news of Roosevelt's executive order, Murata visited the Monterey County sheriff, an old friend. *Surely this is a mistake*, he said. The sheriff informed him that it was not. Seven days after Roosevelt's signing, Murata checked into the Olson Hotel in Pismo Beach, paying for the room in advance. The next day, the cleaning crew found him dead, a bottle of strychnine next to him, with an embossed certificate in his pocket.

Monterey County presents greetings to Hideo Murata:
And in testimony of her heartfelt gratitude and appreciation presents this testimonial of her honor and respect for your loyal and splendid service to home and county in the Great World War of 1914–1919.
Our flag was assailed and you gallantly took up its defense.

You and the other sons of America pledged your all for its protection on land, on sea, in air and down under the sea. The flag, which is without dishonor and has never known defeat, was challenged and defied by its enemies, and with all those fighting freemen of our country you have returned it home again, undefiled and proudly victorious.

———

In a statement forwarded to chapters up and down the coast, JACL leaders urged cooperation with the government "in whatever action it may deem necessary for the public welfare," adding, "It is difficult for us to conceive that our government . . . would break down the equality that has always existed between its citizens."

That night, a man walked into a boardinghouse in Stockton, California, pulled out a .45 caliber pistol, and sent two bullets into the groin of Shigemasa Yoshioka, killing him. At the same time, on Ryer Island in the San Joaquin Delta, six men raided a nisei-operated asparagus farm. They robbed the sixteen workers, and then shot Uke Ukinoui three times in the leg. Between December 7 and February 15, five murders and twenty-five other serious crimes—rapes, robberies, assaults, destruction of property—were reported against nikkei in California alone.

While the Japanese American community struggled to come to terms with the president's order, California state officials had spent the previous month hastening their removal. In early February, at a conclave of California district attorneys and sheriffs, state attorney general Earl Warren had directed the crowd to conduct an end-to-end survey of all rural lands owned, operated, or resided on by ethnic Japanese. Working hand in hand with white farmers set on mass removal, law enforcement officials from thirty-five of California's fifty-eight counties sent their findings to Warren's office, where he placed color-coordinated pins in a map hung on his wall. The results showed concentrations along coastal areas, under electrical lines, straddling Southern Pacific and Western Pacific railroad tracks, near dams supplying water to San Diego, and adjacent to military bases and oil fields. In Mountain View, it found the Yoshinaga family's strawberry farm surrounding Moffett Field, now used as the West Coast's air corps training center.

"It is certainly evident that the Japanese population of California is, as a whole, ideally situated, with reference to points of strategic importance, to carry into execution a tremendous program of sabotage on a mass scale," Warren said during a congressional committee hearing. "I believe that we are just being lulled into a sense of security.... Our day of reckoning is bound to come."

There was a simpler answer: those were the only places they could live. Land along railroad tracks and under power lines was cheap, viewed as uninhabitable by the state's white residents. Coastal areas were ideal for certain crops. Alien land laws and redlining pushed rural farmers into the swamps and brambles. As for their adjacency to military bases and airports, there was an even simpler explanation.

"Even before the war there was a lot of suspicion," George Yoshinaga recalled years later. "[Military officials] used to come over and my brother would tell them 'What are you talking about? We were here before you built Moffett Field.'"

At an emergency meeting earlier that month in San Francisco, sensing the winds that were pushing for removal, the JACL presented its members with three options. The first was all-out opposition; this was rejected immediately and viewed as an impossibility. In the eyes of the JACL, outright resistance would likely lead to violence both from and against federal troops. The second was using the threat of opposition to seek a compromise, though the determination of the War Department made this impractical.

Sensing the hostility that awaited them should they choose either of the first two options and the Japanese *did* strike the West Coast—"If Japan had launched a landing, timed with the Army's preoccupation with the Japanese American resistance to evacuation, the future would not be worth considering for Japanese Americans in the United States," JACL executive director Mike Masaoka wrote in a report of the meeting—the men chose option three: "constructive cooperation."

"If in the judgment of military and federal authorities evacuation of Japanese residents from the West Coast is a primary step toward assuring the safety of this nation, we will have no hesitation in complying with the necessities implicit in that judgment," he wrote in a statement to a congressional committee deliberating their fate. "But, if, on the other hand, such evacuation is primarily a measure whose surface urgency cloaks the desires of political or other pressure groups who want us to leave merely from motives of self-interest, we feel that we have every right to protest and to demand equitable judgment on our merits as American citizens."

Even when presented with that option, the leaders of the Western Defense Command weren't satisfied.

"There are going to be a lot of Japs who are going to say, 'Oh, yes, we want to go, we're good Americans and we want to do everything you say,'" said DeWitt in a phone call, "but those are the fellows I suspect the most."

"Definitely," replied Bendetsen. "The ones who are giving you only lip service are the ones always to be suspected."

Within two weeks, DeWitt used Warren's map as a blueprint for his first phase. The western halves of California, Oregon, and Washington, as well as all of southern Arizona, were now Western Defense Command Military Area No. 1.

Removal was voluntary at first, warned the signs pasted in windows and stapled onto telephone poles. Western Defense Command officials hoped that the order would nudge most of the 107,500 Japanese Americans living in Military Area No. 1 to resettle inland, whether in the eastern portions of their states, or beyond. Their instincts were wrong.

Only 2,005 moved out of the area in the ensuing weeks, and the reasons were plain. They knew no one there. They had no jobs there. They had no houses there. They refused to move hundreds or thousands of miles for the same reason that any other American would refuse to move hundreds or thousands of miles: they couldn't.

The governor of Kansas, Payne Ratner, placed state highway patrolmen on the western edge of the state, directing them to turn back any prospective newcomers. Officials in Arizona, Nevada, Colorado, and Wyoming followed suit. Gas station owners refused to sell them gas, while one group of nikkei were so frightened by a mob of angry citizens that they fled Yerington, Nevada, and drove back to California.

Those two thousand people were far from the first nikkei removed from the West Coast. In addition to the thousands of issei rounded up in the days following Pearl Harbor—the men were sent to Justice Department prison camps across the West, many not seeing their families for the duration of the war, if ever again—the fishermen, canners, and shop owners of Terminal Island were next to go. Even before the signing of EO 9066, the Navy used the authority granted by a December executive order to oust the men of the community, which sat next to a base and airstrip. As their boats bobbed unused in the water, the men were stripped from their families, making the only residents women, children, and the elderly. On February 14, five days before Roosevelt's signing, Navy officials posted notices on the island demanding the departure of its remaining Japanese American residents by March 14. On February 25, they changed their minds: they'd have forty-eight hours to leave.

The previous two days had been hell for Southern California. A little after 7 p.m., February 23, a Japanese B1 submarine surfaced a half-mile off the California coast. Over the next twenty minutes the crew of the world's largest submarine aimed sixteen shells at an oil storage facility perched on a bluff beyond the beach. The darkness and ocean waves sent the shells out erratically; only one came within thirty yards of the tanks. Another landed more than a mile inland. The shelling did only mild damage to a pier and a pumphouse. "Their marksmanship was rotten," said Lawrence Wheeler after one of the five-inch shells flew over his roadhouse.

The bombardment, even if unfruitful from a military standpoint, was the first attack on American soil since Pearl Harbor, and thus achieved its goal of incitement. The next day's *Los Angeles Times* splashed SUBMARINE SHELLS SOUTHLAND OIL FIELD across its front page, even if the story itself called it a "hurried and nervous nuisance raid." Still, the usual tropes were trotted out. Neighbors claimed to spot nisei signaling the submarine across the night sky, while the paper opined, "There is reason to believe that this submarine attack was aided if not actually directed by signals from the shore."

Thirty hours later, at 1:45 a.m., February 25, a coastal radar picked up an unidentified object over the Pacific. One hundred twenty miles west of Los Angeles and approaching fast, the blip was soon spotted by two more radars. At 2:25 a.m. the city's air raid sirens roared awake a city already on high alert from the shelling. The entire region, from Los Angeles to the Mexican border and inland to the San Joaquin Valley, fell under a blackout. As dozens of searchlights and tracer flares lit the sky, the 37th Coast Artillery Brigade sent 1,400 antiaircraft shells into the air. Sleepy-eyed neighbors spilled out of bed and into the blackened streets, climbing on rooftops to watch the aerial display. Shrapnel knocked down telephone wires and shattered windows; rumors spread as quickly as the gunfire. A Japanese plane had been shot down and crashed into a Hollywood intersection, went one. The size of the Japanese raid varied, depending on the account, from seven planes all the way up to two hundred; one policeman claimed "they came in great dark clouds." Five Angelenos died during the havoc. As antiaircraft fire coursed above him, Henry Ayers raced a station wagon loaded with ammunition to the California State Guard station in Hollywood. Police found him slumped in his seat, dead of a heart attack, one of two caused by the night's events. The other three were killed by cars driving without headlights due to the blackout.

Fifteen Japanese Americans were arrested across Southern California the next morning. Some were suspected of having signaled the Japanese planes, while others were cited for violations as petty as leaving their market lights on during the blackout. In a pattern that would become familiar over the next four years, none of the men were convicted of espionage, sabotage, or aiding Japan in any way.

Secretary of the Navy Frank Knox addressed the incident in the morning. "As far as I know the whole raid was a false alarm and could be attributed to jittery nerves," he said. Knox's explanation was insufficient not only to the public, but to the War Department. Secretary Stimson refuted it immediately, floating two unsubstantiated theories: the Japanese had hired commercial planes and launched them from secret fields in Mexico, or the planes took off from Japanese submarines. As many as fifteen planes had plowed across the sky at speeds up to 200 miles per hour, Stimson said, tasked with finding the region's antiaircraft stores and terrifying its residents. Equally plausible was the theory, which continues to this day in some of the dustier corners of the internet, that the bright light was in fact a UFO.

All of this was wrong. No bombs had fallen from the sky. There were no planes, and certainly not two hundred. Forty years later, the U.S. Office of Air Force History made its final judgment on the night: a stray weather balloon had floated across the radar.

That morning on Terminal Island, Army jeeps filled the streets, followed by empty trucks driven by furniture dealers hoping to profit off misery. Bureaus and tables sold for pennies on the dollar. One woman, humiliated by the offers presented for her dishes, smashed each dish at the feet of the would-be buyers. Some men posed as FBI agents, warning of immediate removal. Hours later their accomplices would return to the house with a lowball offer. A Shinto priest who'd lived in the United States for forty years carried out an armload of religious materials; they were added to the mounds growing in the streets. The Japanese Fisherman's Association of Southern California sold a quarter of its fleet. The Coast Guard commandeered the rest. With nowhere to go, the families moved to Japanese-language schools inland, knowing the temporary shelter would be far from their last stop.

Six months earlier, three thousand nikkei lived on Terminal Island. By February 28, only stray dogs and cats remained. Within weeks the Navy would flatten the homes, temples, and markets, bulldozing away their lives, their *furusato*.

––––––

Twenty-five hundred miles of ocean away, the Japanese Americans of Hawai'i experienced a different fate. Nearly 155,000 Hawaiians of Japanese descent lived in the islands on December 7, making up close to 37 percent of the territory's total population. Japanese was the second-most popular language, spoken in 171 Japanese-language schools, and printed in twelve Japanese-language newspapers. The cultural influence of Japan permeated Hawai'i more than any other region in the United States.

On December 7—even before Roosevelt declared war—the entire territory was placed under martial law, where it would remain for the next three years. Barbed wire covered Waikiki Beach, while thousands of machine-gun nests popped up at intersections. Blackout enforcement extended well past house and vehicle lights, with fines levied against homeowners for too-bright kitchen stove burners, lit cigarettes, and illuminated radio dials. A Shinto priest was fined $500 for not extinguishing the eternal flame on his temple altar. All civilian courts closed, replaced by provost courts with little patience. Most trials were held on the day of arrest, and guilt was assumed. (In one of Honolulu's courts 98.4 percent of trials ended in a guilty verdict.) Wages were capped, and those who couldn't pay court fines were offered another option: they could donate blood. The rule was to give fifteen days' credit against a jail sentence and a $30 credit against any fine; the practice was only discontinued when word reached military officials that Hawaiians were referring to this as "being fined a bucket of blood."

The Army temporarily closed all Japanese-language newspapers and schools, installed curfews, and, in a first in U.S. history, registered and fingerprinted every resident save for young children. Mail was examined, and censors listened in on all transpacific telephone calls. Public conversations were required to be conducted in English. Still, there was no mass removal; instead the Army practiced a policy of "selective internment," eventually removing less than one percent of the islands' ethnic Japanese.

A multitude of factors caused this discrepancy—the logistical impossibility of removing 160,000 people from a chain of islands and the levelheaded rumor-debunking of the islands' commander among them—but the chief factor was money. While the agricultural forces of the West Coast were pushing for removal of their issei and nisei neighbors, those of Hawai'i were actively fighting against it.

For decades Hawai'i's pineapple and sugarcane fields depended on the labor of immigrants—first Chinese and Japanese, then Korean and Filipino. Much of the agricultural work on the islands was still performed by Japanese Hawaiians, as was 90 percent of the carpentry. That didn't change just because Japan attacked the islands. Seeing a ruinous economic forecast if 155,000 Japanese Hawaiians were incarcerated, the island's Army commander successfully stalled the wishes of DeWitt and Stimson on the mainland, winnowing down the number of incarcerated Hawaiians to less than two thousand.

By mid-March, as his hopes of voluntary removal dwindled, DeWitt announced the formation of the Wartime Civil Control Administration, headed by recently promoted Colonel Karl Bendetsen. DeWitt's order left no ambiguity: "To provide for the evacuation of all persons of Japanese ancestry . . . from the Pacific Coast with a minimum of economic and social dislocation, a minimum use of military personnel and maximum speed."

Fully transformed from a timid, removal-shy general, DeWitt's ultimate goal was to remove all nikkei from his entire eight-state purview—Washington, Oregon, California, Idaho, Montana, Nevada, Utah, and Arizona, plus the territory of Alaska—and then move on to the German and Italian nationals from prohibited military zones. His zealousness was overruled, but he proceeded with his plan to remove all issei and nisei from California, western Washington and Oregon, and a small portion of Arizona. (Highlighting the capriciousness of the entire process, his realm in Arizona was diminished when farmers there lobbied against removal, citing the need for labor.)

On March 26, DeWitt revoked all Japanese American travel permits, even to the eastern parts of the West Coast states. Residents who had heeded the initial warning and packed up their families, sold their property, and moved were suddenly stuck once again. One farmer who lived west of Portland, Oregon, moved his family to the state's nearly empty east. He paid $10 an acre to lease a fifty-acre ranch, and another $500 for seed. He returned home to move his mother and two sisters to the ranch, when DeWitt's new order was declared. So there he stayed, trapped, out a lifetime's worth of savings and waiting for whatever happened next.

In San Francisco, Bendetsen and DeWitt set to work on launching the largest mass removal in American history. The problem, beyond the obvious, was that there was no road map for such a task. There was no precedent and therefore no existing plan to follow. But since the men had declared these men, women, and children not only dangerous but *imminently* dangerous, *something* had to be done. It was, in a word, a debacle.

The departments tasked with carrying out the mass removal were nearly as vast as those that spent the previous decades monitoring the same community, and with similar efficiency. The Western Defense Command, Federal Reserve Bank of San Francisco, Department of Agriculture, Wartime Civil Control Administration, Department of the Interior, Federal Bureau of Investigation, local and state police forces—the list could continue ad nauseam. Chaos reigned. Big, important questions were answered on the fly.

Would Japanese Americans still be responsible for liens and debts while incarcerated, even if they no longer had jobs? (Yes.)

Would the Japanese wife of a white American citizen be required to evacuate? (No, although any children would be, as outlined in a memo with the subject line "HALF-BREEDS.")

Where was everyone to move? (To be determined.)

The same forces that pushed for exclusion, removal, and disenfranchisement for decades now saw an opportunity for profit. The Los Angeles Realty Board, after lobbying for removal during the congressional hearings, offered its services in the "liquidation of the properties" left by the removed. Competitors pounced on nikkei-owned businesses, submitting formal letters to the Western Defense Command for items as mundane as icemakers. Some letters were equal parts opportunism and desperation.

> *Dear Sir:*
>
> *I am writing you in regard to the places that have been taken from the evacuees, & I would like very much to get a place about 40 acres with a house.*
>
> *If I could help the war by raising food, I would like very much to do so. I don't have very much money to start with but I am more willing to do anything to get a place. If I could get even a job as foreman for running a place, as I have had quite a bit of experience at farming.*
>
> *If you could suggest anything I'd be very grateful to you.*
>
> *I remain Yours truly,*
> *GEORGE OLDMAN*
> *P.O. Box 1133*
> *Ajo Ariz.*

Other motives were more sinister. The Treasury Department had tasked the San Francisco Federal Reserve Bank with helping nikkei store or liquidate their property as well as mediating disputes with their creditors. JACL leaders Saburo Kido and Mike Masaoka met with Fed officials that month to discuss matters ranging from the mar-

ket effects of liquidating San Francisco's 120 nikkei-owned dry cleaners to a 500,000-hen chicken farm in Northern California. The men
met in good faith, acknowledging the position the Fed had been put in
while fighting for the financial rights of the coast's 120,000 ethnic Japanese. Behind their backs, the Fed was attempting to destroy them.

> *We have been asked by the Co-ordinator of Information to ascer-*
> *tain location of any Japanese [printing] type located on the Pacific*
> *Coast which may be offered for sale and possibly melted down for*
> *the metal content due to evacuation. The Co-ordinator is anxious*
> *to have the Type acquired by the Military. Therefore, without re-*
> *vealing the interest of the Co-ordinator, please ascertain and report*
> *to us location of such type and the possibility of acquiring either*
> *through purchase or requisition.*

The message was signed by William M. Hale, the man in charge
of the Fed's evacuee property program, and its message couldn't have
been clearer: to physically eliminate the Japanese language. Within
forty-eight hours Hale had on hand a tally of all ten Los Angeles–
based and nikkei-owned printing concerns, listing their addresses,
owners, tonnage of type, and likelihood to sell their type to their unknown bidder. It's unclear what he did with the information.

The morning of March 30 was typically raw and overcast on Bainbridge Island, a hilly, pine-covered isle in Washington's Puget Sound.
Six days earlier, a flock of GIs arrived on the island and tacked posters
up on utility poles, the ferry landing from Seattle, and the post office.
CIVILIAN EXCLUSION ORDER NO. 1, it read. For the island's 227
issei and nisei residents—mostly strawberry farmers who the previous
year had cultivated more than two million pounds of the fruit—it was
a sign, both literal and figurative: their time was up.

Bendetsen oversaw the removal personally. The first evacuation zones were selected based on their proximity to military bases; Bainbridge Island sat near the approach to Navy Yard Puget Sound, which was currently repairing five of the six surviving battleships from the Pearl Harbor attack three and a half months earlier. The fifty-four nikkei families, adhering to Army orders delivered six days earlier, took only what they could carry: clothing, linens, toiletries, plates, and utensils. To kindly white neighbors they left a lifetime of memories and keepsakes; to their Filipino neighbors they leased their fields. On the dock were classmates of the thirteen Bainbridge High School students forced to leave during the spring of their senior year.

At 11:20 a.m. the ferry *Keholoken* made an on-time departure from Bainbridge Island, bound for wherever.

If humans are judged by how they treat the most vulnerable, the case of the residents at 1841 Redcliff Street, Los Angeles, California, serves as one of its darkest examples. Every address in the removal zone that housed nikkei was assigned one police officer tasked with their extraction. Prior to their removal—and using 1940 U.S. census data—those houses were visited by said officers, and an inventory was taken. A typical inventory, in part, asked the following questions:

1. Number of evacuees in project.
2. Number of heads of families in project.
3. Number of motor vehicles taken into custody for sale to Army and number for storage.
4. Number of family units of property warehoused and space occupied (approximate cubic feet) and where stored.

The inventory form for 1841 Redcliff Street, set high in the hills of Silver Lake, read like this:

1. 43
2. 1 (school principal)
3. No motor vehicles received for sale to Army; no motor vehicles for storage.
4. No family units of property warehoused.

Eighteen forty-one Redcliff Street was Shonien, the Japanese Children's Home of Los Angeles, an orphanage. Those forty-three children, plus others from the Japanese Salvation Army Home of San Francisco and the Maryknoll Catholic Home in Los Angeles's Little Tokyo, would soon find themselves in a different institution.

Years later, when Karl Bendetsen was nominated by Harry Truman to serve as assistant secretary of the army, the U.S. Senate received a letter from Father Hugh Lavery, of the Maryknoll mission. Lavery spent his life in the city's Japanese community. During the evacuation, he had met Bendetsen and pleaded on behalf of the children.

"He showed himself a little Hitler," the letter read. "I mentioned that we had an orphanage. I told him some of these were half-Japanese, others one-fourth or less. I asked, 'Which children should we send to the relocation centers?' He replied, 'I am determined that if they have one drop of Japanese blood in them they must all go to camp.' Just as with Hitler so with him. It was a question of blood."

CHAPTER SEVEN

Japanita

THE FEDERAL GOVERNMENT created fifteen temporary detention centers, scattered mostly—with the exception of one each in Washington, Oregon, and Arizona—across California. Ninety-two thousand nikkei were removed from their homes and sent to the centers, which served as way stations before the next indignity.

They boarded buses and trains from 108 different evacuation zones stretching from the arid flats of Santa Cruz County, Arizona, to the glaciers of Washington's Cascade Mountains. Each zone represented roughly one thousand nikkei. Some, like Los Angeles's Little Tokyo, spanned only a few blocks. In southern Arizona, Evacuation Zone 38 covered close to fifty thousand square miles, an area large enough to hold Connecticut, Rhode Island, Massachusetts, Vermont, and New Hampshire, plus New Jersey and Delaware.

The Nomuras lived in Exclusion Area 10; the Yoshinagas Area 96. In the weeks after Army officials nailed the Civilian Exclusion Order to light posts and pasted it into bakery windows, a member of each family would've walked to their Civil Control Station to pick up their family's tags: one per person, one per bag. In that last week of April, each member of the Nomura family hung their #09725 tag from their lapels. The Yoshinagas were family #03772. For the rest of his life, if you asked George his Social Security number, he'd have to find the card. If you asked his camp number, he'd rattle it off immediately.

The months since Pearl Harbor had been kind to neither of the teens. Babe's name slipped from the box scores and headlines of the *Times*, his prowess on the football field, baseball diamond, and basketball court shelved indefinitely. Patriotism flooded the halls of Hollywood High as buglers played "To the Color" each morning during the flag-raising ceremony. Once a week the school orchestra would gather beneath the flagpole and perform the national anthem, drawing passersby to stop and salute. Los Angeles County school superintendent Vierling Kersey ordered a physical examination of each student, vowing to make the county's students "the most health-adequate youth in America," while encouraging students to raise livestock in their backyards. By spring the district's students were tending to nearly ten thousand rabbits and chickens, and one thousand pigs.

A National Defense Dance was held to raise money for the war effort, and students purchased war bonds by the tens of thousands. To streamline the process, the Army set up its district recruitment office in the lobby of the high school's auditorium. Every Saturday night nine hundred mattresses filled the gym floor to accommodate servicemen who spent their leave attempting to catch a glimpse of Hollywood royalty; for a quarter the next morning they'd get a meal and a smile from one of the eighty high school girls serving breakfast. In an editorial entitled "Japs or Jalopies?" the student newspaper implored students to stop driving to school: "Is a broken-down jalopy really of more value than the rights of liberty and democracy? Oil up your knee joints and start walking!" In the six months after Pearl Harbor, the future and plight of the school's nisei students were never mentioned in the paper.

If the spring of 1942 for Babe was marked by numb anticipation, George's was the opposite. Three FBI agents visited the family home, taking away his older brother's rifles, a cruelty to any farmer hoping to defend his berry crop from nibbling pests. One day, while walking home from school, George passed a schoolmate.

"Hey, it's a Jap," the boy yelled. "I'm going to shoot you."

Unfazed and now accustomed to the taunts, George kept walking. But once the boy returned from his house with a .22 rifle, George broke into a sprint. The bullet struck him in the lower back, slowed only by the weight of his leather jacket. That night, his mother and sister eased the slug out of his skin with a butter knife.

The Nomuras left the keys to the boardinghouse with Marion Binder, a widow. Binder had emigrated to the United States in 1913 from Yokohama, one of the first ports in Japan to open to foreign trade. Binder, née Culty, was the daughter of a French merchant and a Japanese woman. As such, she lived in both worlds; family lore claims the emperor, interested in Western culture despite centuries of self-imposed exclusion, would send Marion to Europe to learn about fashion and etiquette. In Yokohama she met Edward Binder, a German tailor and the son of Nicolaus Binder, a philanthropist and the first mayor of Hamburg. At the start of World War I the couple and their children fled Japan as enemy aliens, spending time in Seattle and San Francisco before settling in Los Angeles. Edward died in 1925, and with him any trace of Marion's Japanese heritage: on census forms and marriage licenses in the intervening decades Marion listed her heritage as either French or German, and alternated her place of birth between France and Germany. Japan evaporated from her life story. After Edward's death she became a maid, lived with her daughter and son-in-law, and kept her true heritage concealed, a clear-eyed decision that saved her from the same fate as the owners of the building she was tasked with caring for.

Had Edward stayed alive it's likely that Marion would've avoided removal even if her true ethnicity was known. Nisei women were allowed to stay on the West Coast under one condition: if they were married to a white man.

With the cypress trees at their backs, the Nomuras took the twenty-minute walk to 1127 North La Brea Avenue, past the studio where Charlie Chaplin shot his silent classics *The Kid* and *The Gold Rush* decades earlier. A month later and four hundred miles north, the Yoshinagas left their fifty-acre farm next to Moffett Field and met close to a thousand others at the men's gymnasium of San Jose State College. That week, George's friends gathered at his house. They divvied up his bicycles and sporting equipment, and said their goodbyes. His brother sold the strawberry farm for $400 an acre, a little over $6,000 in 2019 prices. Today, the plots surrounding Moffett Field are home to the headquarters of Yahoo, Google, and LinkedIn, among dozens of other Silicon Valley firms. The land is assessed at more than $3 million an acre.

The Nomuras boarded a bus, the Yoshinagas a train, and the two families headed to the prettiest horse track in the world.

On Christmas Day 1934, a brown mare named Las Palmas crossed the finish line at Santa Anita Park, the first horse in twenty-five years to win a race in California.

Forty thousand visitors left their stockings on the chimney and packed the tiered grandstand for the park's grand opening. Crowds one-hundred-deep waited to feed their coins into the totalizator, a new machine tasked with collecting bets, determining odds, and then broadcasting the victories and defeats to the wager-holding crowd. A $100,000 electronic camera-timer was installed for the opening. Accurate to one-thousandth of a second, the machine emitted a light beam that, when crossed by the first horse out of the gate, triggered a camera. Pictures were again taken at the furlong mark, and at the finish. In a feat of modernity, those photos were then developed within three minutes. With that, the photo finish—a now ubiquitous event and expression—was born.

Despite the winter sun driving temperatures into the mid-70s, women beneath the cantilevered roof donned fox-trimmed coats and magenta-dyed ostrich-feather blouses. Another draped a knee-length cape trimmed with gray caracal atop her wool suit; a hunter green hat with fresh orchids rested on her head. Pelts of leopard and golden ermine roosted across the women's shoulders, while thousands of Alpine sports hats topped the men. "The women's feathers were brighter, longer, and much more saucy, tilting into the air," *Los Angeles Times* fashion editor Sylvia Weaver reported. Oliver Hardy and Will Rogers were two of the hundreds of Hollywood stars on hand. Ignoring the depths of the Great Depression, bettors that day wagered $259,000, close to $5 million today.

Built in an architectural combination of staid Colonial Revival and the aerodynamic curves of the Streamline Moderne style of Art Deco, the park offered the first six-figure prize in horse-racing history, and its stables could house one thousand horses. On that first Christmas, $5 million worth of horses stood on the premises. No expense was spared; it was rumored that funds were so low on opening day that there was no money left to make change at the concession stands.

Stars like Bing Crosby and Al Jolson were part-owners, while the park's proximity to Hollywood—it sat less than twenty miles east of the boulevard—assured that silver screen icons like Cary Grant, Betty Grable, Lana Turner, and Jane Russell also became regulars later in the decade. The grandstand faced a panorama of the dusty green San Gabriel Mountains, powdered with a topping of snow. From there the physics seemed impossible: miles of flat, undeveloped California land abruptly changing course and turning six, eight, ten thousand feet toward the sky. The vista would travel the world on postcards.

On March 27, 1942, Santa Anita Assembly Center welcomed its first prisoner. Field artillery battalions weighed heavy with full belts of live ammunition met them at the gate. Some prisoners wept; others, too dazed to comprehend their fate, just walked by the troops, bewildered. Of the fifteen racetracks, fairgrounds, and expo centers the U.S. government used as temporary camps, Santa Anita squeezed nearly twice as many people—nearly nineteen thousand—into its stables, barracks, and grandstands as the next-largest center.

"For some it is a vacation, filled with recreational pursuits and splashed with gay exchanges of visits to neighboring barracks," wrote the *Los Angeles Examiner*, "to others it is an idle period, spent in stolid contemplation of the future. This is Japanita."

They were greeted by a bronze statue of the legendary horse Seabiscuit, and reminders of the track's previous and future lives were hard to miss. The driveway in front of the camp's showers was named after champion two-miler Malicious, the bridle path after Triple Crown winner Gallant Fox, and the service barracks fronted on Seabiscuit Lane. The alphabetical avenues ran from Azucar to Your Honor; some incarcerees had the distinction of living on Man o' War Avenue, named after the twentieth-century's top thoroughbred.

While the names and statues served as a reminder of their new location, there was another, more pervasive reminder: the smell. The first 7,182 incarcerees were herded into stables, the next 11,411 into the five hundred barracks constructed on the track's parking lot. The stables, which had held horses just weeks before, were bleached, the equine smell mixing with ammonia in the spring sun. Workers removed and replaced fourteen inches of dirt from each stable, but it was little help. Eight years of horse urine and feces soaked into the wood, scenting the makeshift rooms. Each person was handed a mattress cover and pointed toward a pile of straw with which to stuff their bedding. In an effort to raise the mood, everyone who lived in the stables claimed to occupy the stall that housed Seabiscuit.

Evacuees lined up as early as 6:30 a.m. for breakfast, standing in line for anywhere from ten to ninety minutes. Because of limited resources, every dish had to be used and washed three times for each meal, driving up wait times. Sugar rationing across the country began on April 27, with each American allotted a half-pound per week, a fifth of the usual consumption rate. At Santa Anita evacuees were limited to a teaspoon a day, or less than a quarter-pound per month. By early June, a shortage of toilet paper led to its removal from the latrines. Instead, each apartment, which served a minimum of four incarcerees, was given a roll to use. After a week, they'd be granted a new roll.

The Wartime Civil Control Administration (WCCA), the agency

created by DeWitt and the Western Defense Command to oversee removal, was granted a food allowance of 50 cents per day per person, the same allotment as the Army. The temporary detention centers spent only an average of 39 cents, and calls from the public demanded that costs be cut even more. The quantity and quality of the food, according to one resident, was "deplorable." Others considered it palatable though odd in a very specific way: accustomed to eating rice in a bowl with chopsticks, the meal was instead served on a plate with a fork. Police were called in late May when the chief steward of one mess hall attempted to serve hot dogs that had been left out for three days. Fifty incarcerees refused the meal and demanded new food.

"The goddamn sons of bitches had a chance to eat and wouldn't," the steward yelled, "and now they can all go to hell."

Attempting to quell the growing tension, a group of Japanese cooks offered to prepare chop suey for the group. Before they could serve the meal, the head of kitchens, Chauncey Brewster, cut them off.

"The goddamn sons of bitches are always complaining," he said, echoing his steward's language, "and they are better fed and housed than they ever were before in their lives."

Five doctors serviced the nearly 19,000 residents, or about one doctor per 3,800 people. Outside the barbed wire the rate was closer to one per every 800 Americans. Despite the fact that they made up only 39 percent of Santa Anita's population, residents of the horse stables accounted for 75 percent of the illnesses treated at the hospital. For the first three months, only 150 showers were available for the 19,000. Like their homes, the showers were intended for horses—communal, partitionless. Lines formed as early as 5:30 a.m. just to try and beat the crowds. By the time you reached the front of the line, it was almost time to join the breakfast line. Much of life in Santa Anita was just waiting: waiting to bathe, waiting to eat, waiting to learn your fate. Waiting, waiting, waiting.

Roll call was taken at 6 a.m. and 9:30 p.m.; lights-out was 10 sharp.

To call schooling an afterthought would imply it was considered at all. The Army made no effort to create a formal education system, forcing inmate volunteers to teach elementary school, middle school, and high school. All classes were held under the grandstands, in a hall so large that teachers had to shout to the point of becoming hoarse. Textbooks were donated from area schools. Carey McWilliams—a journalist and left-wing political activist who at the time served as the head of California's Division of Immigration and Housing—surmised in a report that, due to the lack of education or entertainment, "the birth rate is going to go to spectacular proportions."

Almost six miles of clothesline snaked through the barracks and stables. Thirty-five hundred letters arrived each day; 5,500 departed. Due to a lack of barbershops, amateur barbers clipped hair on nearly every street, with customers sitting astride overturned produce crates.

Santa Anita was twice-guarded: once from the inside and once from the outside. Army police patrolled the exterior and monitored the entrances and exits, while internal police officers were deputized to uphold local and state law. (The FBI was technically a third law enforcement branch, keeping a close eye, as they did outside the camp, on "suspected subversive activities" and violations of federal law.) The Army officers rarely intervened with life within Santa Anita but still had a profound effect on the newly incarcerated residents.

"The high fences and the presence of the military police definitely signify the loss of freedom and independence," reads a Red Cross inspection report. "Although there is general group acceptance or rather compliance with evacuation, many individuals reject it."

Some of that cynicism was rooted in the gulf between the residents and camp management. There was virtually no communication between the two groups, a silence highlighted by the management's first-come, first-served employment policy. Other than the hospital, which was staffed with certified doctors, every other position was simply given to the first man through the door. Lack any culinary skills but want to work in the kitchen? Here's a cutting board. Haven't picked up a broom in your life? Welcome to the maintenance staff.

Wages hadn't cleared for some workers, even some who'd worked in the camp for more than two months. DeWitt had established a wage schedule that could charitably be described as Dickensian: $8 a month for unskilled labor, $12 a month for skilled labor, and $16 a month for professional and technical work. (The median income for an American man in the early 1940s was $80 a month.)

Babe and George were both spared the stables, instead meeting among the rows and rows of identical barracks. It was impossible to tell the difference from block to block—lost children became so common that camp officials alerted new incarcerees to the inevitability—and in that disheartening sameness the two boys found each other. The majority of the camp's residents were from Los Angeles, with a smattering of families from Santa Clara, San Diego, and San Francisco Counties. While Babe lived among friends and competitors, George was left alone. The Los Angeles teens were the stylish product of their environment and the times, with pompadoured hair and letterman jackets, the white undersides of their Levis cuffed skyward. Mountain View teens were anything but; George was tagged as a "farm boy" and "prune picker." Babe must've seen the same thing he saw in the dozens of men who passed through his family's boardinghouse: someone in need of a friend. The two began a relationship that would outlast a war and six decades.

On the afternoon of March 10, Milton Eisenhower walked into the Oval Office and was greeted by a tired, cold Franklin Roosevelt. The men exchanged no pleasantries.

"Milton, your war job, starting immediately, is to set up a War Relocation Authority to move the Japanese Americans off the Pacific Coast," he said. "I have signed an executive order which will give you full authority to do what is essential. The Attorney General will give you the necessary legal assistance and the Secretary of War will help you with the physical arrangements. [Budget Director] Harold [Smith] will fill you in on the details of the problem."

Roosevelt returned to the paper he was reading. Without looking up, he continued.

"And Milton, the greatest possible speed is imperative."

Eisenhower was born in the waning months of the nineteenth century, the seventh of seven Eisenhower brothers; the third would become the thirty-fourth president of the United States. A sickly child, Milton favored academia over his brother's military urges, graduating from Kansas State with an industrial journalism degree. After a stint in the Foreign Service he served as director of information for the Agriculture Department from 1928 to 1941, where he spent the Great Depression acting as a spokesman for Roosevelt's New Deal. In the months leading up to Pearl Harbor he was tasked by Roosevelt to study all the war-related informational services of the federal government, should the need arise: how to keep the American people informed of the war, how to disseminate accurate information to the Allies, and how to counteract Axis propaganda. Eisenhower recommended the creation of an Office of War Information, and stressed honesty above all else.

"Our real strength lay in telling the truth, sticking to the facts, and presenting a full and accurate explanation of our war purposes," he told Roosevelt.

Leaving the Oval Office that next March, the forty-two-year-old Eisenhower had been placed in a position created by just the opposite. He knew next to nothing about the 120,000 people he was tasked to oversee, nor the rationale for their removal in the first place. Once arriving on the West Coast he saw the challenge would be even greater than his own illiteracy on the subject. The racism of DeWitt and Bendetsen was overshadowed only by the lack of planning. Tens of thousands of nikkei were flooding racetracks and fairgrounds, with no plan for what came next. On April 1, after less than three weeks on the job, he wrote to his former boss, Agriculture Secretary Claude Wickard: "I feel most deeply that when the war is over . . . we as Americans are going to regret the avoidable injustices that may have been done."

On April 7, Eisenhower flew from San Francisco to Salt Lake City to meet with the governors or their representatives of ten Western states. Bendetsen kicked off the meeting, dryly describing the Western Defense Command's reasoning for removal by tilting that defense in a new direction: the removal would not only quelch any espionage activity, it would also *protect* Japanese Americans in the event of a Japanese invasion. White Americans wouldn't be able to discern Japanese from Japanese Americans, he reasoned, putting their lives at risk.

Eisenhower then pitched a plan loosely based on the Civilian Conservation Corps, the New Deal program he'd spent the previous decade touting for Roosevelt. After reminding the gathered politicos that none of the nikkei had been convicted of espionage or sabotage, he laid out his idea: fifty to seventy-five locations, all inland, all in areas of agricultural or manufacturing need. Eisenhower knew that thousands of acres of sugar beets in Wyoming, Montana, and Utah were rotting and overrun with weeds due to a lack of labor, and he based his pitch around that. Some would work in the camps—in a bout of euphemism that would become all too common in the WRA, he referred to them as "relocation centers" and the removed were called "evacuees"—while others would work in the private sector. The camps would more closely resemble staging areas, he envisioned, than prisons.

Prisons, though, sounded pretty good to the governors. Governor Herbert Maw of Utah thought the WRA was too concerned with the constitutional rights of Japanese Americans, and suggested changing the document. Idaho governor Chase Clark said "the Japs live like rats, breed like rats, and act like rats." The only way he'd let them into his state was "in concentration camps, under armed guards."

Colorado governor Ralph Carr, who bounced around the state as a child as his father chased gold, grew up around Chinese immigrants. A conservative, anti–New Deal Republican, he spoke fluent Spanish and socialized with the small issei community in the town of La Jara, refusing to believe the men were used as tools of Japan. He idolized

Abraham Lincoln and shared with him the belief that American liberty and democracy were what separated the country from other nations. In a radio address three days after Pearl Harbor, he reminded Coloradans of the country's heritage.

"From every nation of the globe people have come to the United States who sought to live as free men here under our plan of government," he said. "We cannot test the degree of a man's affections for his fellow or his devotion to his country by the birthplace of his grandfathers."

Colorado, he said, would open its doors. "If Colorado's part in the war is to take 100,000 of them, then Colorado will take care of them," he told the surprised room.

Months later as a mob confronted the first trainloads of nikkei to the southeast corner of the state, he challenged the protesters, saying, "If you harm them you must harm me. I was brought up in a small town where I knew the shame and dishonor of race hatred." Pointing at the men, he added, "I grew to despise it because it threatened the happiness of you, and you, and you." Voters rewarded him by voting for his opponent, Roosevelt loyalist Edwin C. Johnson, in his run for U.S. Senate that fall.

Not wanting to be outshone by the invective of Maw or Clark, Wyoming governor Nels Smith explained that Wyomingites "have a dislike of any Orientals" and "simply will not stand for being California's dumping ground." Unsatisfied, he sought out Eisenhower during a break. In the WRA director's memoir, published three decades later, he claims Smith "shook his fist in my face, and growled through clenched teeth, 'If you bring the Japanese into my state, I promise you they will be hanging from every tree.'"

Eisenhower's plan was dead on arrival. Dejected, he concluded the meeting.

"The whole picture is much worse than anyone can imagine," he wrote in a letter to Attorney General Biddle the next day. "We are going to have to fight every step of the way to do a decent job."

While the removal was peaceful, it was in some cases carried out in quiet resistance. Issei veterans of World War I wore their U.S. Navy uniforms and decorations on the day of removal, while others were more active in their defiance. Gordon Hirabayashi was a twenty-three-year-old University of Washington senior on the day of Pearl Harbor. A Quaker and registered conscientious objector, he quit school after the attack to volunteer with the American Friends Service Committee. The group had spent the previous decade on a mission to ease racial tensions, and following Pearl Harbor that meant aiding nikkei in relocation or storing their belongings. Hirabayashi ignored DeWitt's curfew command, walking the streets of Seattle hours past the 8 p.m. deadline. When volunteer relocation turned to mandatory removal, he refused to register at his neighborhood civic control station. He instead turned himself in to the FBI, and was convicted and sentenced to three months imprisonment. The case achieved what Hirabayashi intended, as its appeals wound their way to the Supreme Court.

Minoru Yasui was the first Japanese American graduate of the University of Oregon's law school, the possessor of a legal mind so bright he would years later have the highest bar exam score in the state of Colorado. Timing, though, was not on his side. He graduated in 1939, as tension with Japan was ratcheting up, and legal work eluded him. Instead he took a job as a speechwriter and translator at the Japanese consulate in Chicago. After Pearl Harbor he quit and moved back to Oregon, where he was commissioned a second lieutenant in the Army Reserve. He reported for active duty only to be denied nine times. He instead helped fellow nikkei get their legal affairs in order before removal; he was the only Japanese American attorney in Oregon.

As his issei father languished in Justice Department and Army camps, Yasui's ire grew. Unable to serve his country and unable to see his father, he, too, fought DeWitt's curfew. One night he approached a

Portland police officer and demanded to be arrested; the officer refused. Yasui then walked to the closest police precinct, whose employees happily obliged him. Out on bail, he purposely violated DeWitt's
travel restriction order, visiting his family's fruit farm in Hood River,
Oregon. Like Hirabayashi, Yasui's case wended its way through the
courts, though it faced a nearly insurmountable hurdle: during one of
his trials the court found that, due to his work for the Japanese consulate, he was no longer an American citizen, nor afforded the protective
rights that come with that citizenship. While the Supreme Court disagreed and restored his citizenship, Yasui was convicted and served
nine months. Once released from prison he was sent to a prison camp.

Like Yasui, Fred Korematsu's first plan after Pearl Harbor was to
enlist. After being turned away by the National Guard and the Coast
Guard, he became a welder in Oakland; he was quickly fired, part of
the wave of anti-nikkei firings that spread through the West Coast in
early 1942. After the removal notices were posted he changed his
name, bleached his hair until it was chestnut brown, and paid a sur-
geon to alter the contours of his eyes and nose in an attempt to look less
Japanese. The ploy—the only such attempt, at least documented by the
press—didn't work. "Clyde Sarah," of Spanish and Hawaiian descent,
was arrested May 30 in San Leandro. While awaiting trial, he was
visited by the director of the San Francisco office of the American Civil
Liberties Union. *Would you*, he asked, *be interested in becoming a test
case to challenge Japanese American imprisonment?* Korematsu agreed.
Freed on bail, he was sent to Tanforan Assembly Center, a retrofitted
horse track in San Bruno just like Santa Anita. He was convicted and,
like Yasui, sent to camp. *Korematsu v. United States*, though, would
soon have much wider implications.

––––––––––

The incarcerees of Santa Anita eked out a life, thanks largely in part
to their own ingenuity and the center's recreation department. Marble
contests, glee club concerts, model airplane competitions, and talent

shows battled wartime ennui, but the spotlight shone brightest on Anita Chiquita, the recreation field. Hundreds of spectators would gather daily before and after work to watch the exploits of the ad hoc sports leagues. Sumo wrestling and basketball drew fans, and softball teams played across three leagues. A golf driving range was built later in the summer, and incarcerees founded an all-female judo team. Crippled by a lack of funds and equipment, friends on the outside would pass cash and sports equipment over the fence. Babe picked up a bat and made his way onto one of the astounding seventy different softball teams; George spent his mornings running laps on the mile-long track. Dozens or hundreds of miles from their homes, their lives were stuck in the unknown.

For many, especially the teenagers, their only commonality was the country of their parents' ancestry. Multiple nights a week, the Starlight Serenaders orchestra—using instruments they had brought from home—entertained up to two thousand dancers in front of the grandstand. The tongue-in-cheek Sayonara Balls hosted more dancers than all but the largest Los Angeles ballrooms. George didn't know how to jitterbug or swing, so he taught himself on the spot.

Everything was going peacefully if dully until June 16. One of the largest enterprises in the camp was a camouflage netting factory. Large nets would hang from the roof of the grandstand while incarcerees weaved dyed burlap strips through the pattern. The net was gradually raised until six-story sections of the stands were hidden from view. The nets varied in size from 22 x 22 feet all the way up to 36 x 60 feet, almost half the size of a professional basketball court. Established by the Army but under private contract, the enterprise employed 1,200 nisei and built more than 250 nets each day. (Due to a Geneva Convention stipulation, issei were not allowed to work for the United States in what amounted to a military operation.)

In the early weeks of June, volunteering for the factory flagged, forcing officials to threaten inmates with what one inmate called "the blacklist." The list would limit the inmates' ability to seek other work in camp, among other things. The conditions were nothing short of inmate labor—dusty, under the summer sun, with workers' hands left green from the dye.

"The greatest irony is that we are told, 'Here is a chance to show your patriotism,'" wrote one incarceree. "There is nothing wrong with the statement really, except that for a 17-year-old city girl to work 44 hours a week under unfavorable working conditions isn't very consistent with the American Way."

On June 16, handbills made their way across camp, calling for higher wages, better living conditions, and a doubling of food rations. The handbills also stated that "there is no democracy for the Japanese in the United States" and that disease awaited the net makers after their work was done. The strike was brief, and the next day all the workers returned under the promise that WCCA officials would raise their wages from $8 to $12 per month.

If the WCCA thought it had dodged a bullet with the camouflage strike, they were mistaken.

On June 18, after the morning head count, Santa Anita police chief Clyde Dawson met with police inspector F. H. Arrowood and center manager H. Russell Amory in Amory's office. The topic of conversation was one that had been weighing on Amory's mind: theft. Silverware, china, padlocks, towels, and other equipment had gone missing from the mess halls, Amory said, and he wanted Dawson and Arrowood to find them. A thorough search of all barracks in this center, he offered, would be the best solution.

According to the WCCA's operations manual—issued by order of Karl Bendetsen—that search was within the agency's purview. Still, Amory suggested a ruse. Incarcerees would be notified, in the twice-weekly, incarceree-run *Santa Anita Pacemaker*, of an additional head count, and instructed to be at their barracks at the appointed time. Instead of the head count, interior police officers would search each apartment for stolen items and other contraband. Alcohol and weapons were prohibited, but so were mundane items like literature written in Japanese, and perishable foods other than fruit. Hot plates, prone to overloading the camp's weak electrical system, were allowed only with special permission from the center's medical staff, and only to be used for heating baby formula.

The three men left with a plan, but no timeline. A month later, on July 22, Dawson received a teletype from Western Defense Command, ordering the search and confiscation of all Japanese phonograph records. Literature printed in Japanese was already banned, but De-Witt and his men were determined to eliminate whatever traces of the language remained in the centers. (Incarcerees were also barred from holding meetings in Japanese.)

––––––––––

Two hours after sunrise on Tuesday, August 4, fifty-four officers of the interior police department assembled. Their usual shift ran from midnight to 8 a.m.; by the time the day ended, most had worked more than twenty hours straight. Joined by Pomona Assembly Center officers brought in specially for the search, the seventy-two men stood as Amory and Dawson addressed the group.

Dawson's skepticism regarding the search was evident. In the weeks prior, he'd told Amory as much, saying it would drag the camp's morale down even further. That morning he gave his men brief instructions: the search was to be conducted as quietly and diplomatically as possible, and the officers were to be especially careful not to cause any incidents that might ignite trouble. Should they encounter any issues, he and other commanding officers would be available for questions. Amory then read a list of items subject to confiscation. In a decision that would later prove fateful, he included in that list all hot plates "whether or not they had a permit."

After seeing the officers off to their assigned areas, Amory and Dawson left the center and enjoyed breakfast at a local café.

At 9:30 a.m. the officers began their rounds. They worked in pairs inspecting each barrack, while others guarded against incarcerees moving contraband from barrack to barrack to avoid confiscation. Everything started smoothly, if gruffly. One woman, in a letter to her brother-in-law, described the officers emptying her boxes of tampons and pads in their search. She considered asking the men to Lysol their hands, but refrained. "I was afraid I might antagonize them and they would even trample on my sterilized goods," she wrote.

The strife grew in the bachelor quarters, where thousands of single young men lived. Reports of houses being broken down, hundreds of dollars stolen during a ransacking, $8 taken from an elderly woman: rumor soon mixed with truth—the unexpected removal of hot plates drew immediate resentment from mothers—and the camp's tense if peaceful nature was ready to be tested. Every inspection was now monitored by a roving audience. Officers squeezed through gaps in the crowd, patience thinning on both sides.

At 1:30 p.m., as news of the inspections drifted to the Santa Anita grandstands, camouflage work was suspended so the workers could return home to monitor their belongings. Twelve hundred men spilled into the dusty August streets. Gardeners working across the track from the grandstands noticed that the camouflage nets had all been lowered at the exact same time. Sensing an issue, the men put down their clippers, abandoned the oleanders, and ran the half-mile to the other side of the track.

A description of an officer accused of theft—white, black hair, no hat—spread and was vague enough that many on the camp's police force became suspects. (Over the course of the day the description matured slightly to include "fat" and "curly-haired.") The group grew from dozens to hundreds. By 2:50 p.m. the throng reached Orange mess hall; more than two thousand men had joined, surrounding an officer.

Rocks flew from the crowd as he was punched in the back of the head and smashed with a glass soda bottle. He forced his way into the mess hall. Undaunted, the crowd followed, picking up china cups from the tables and pitching them at him. They soon reached the same steward who months earlier called them goddamn sons of bitches for refusing to eat spoiled hot dogs. The officer hid himself in the mess hall's office, frantically calling for backup. When it arrived the officers surrounded the steward, the crowd ceasing to push only when one pulled his gun.

Inspector Arrowood arrived to calm the crowd, but was met by dozens of men who rocked his car from side to side, attempting to flip it. (It was later reported by the assistant police chief that during this incident the crowd was shouting "Kill the white sons of bitches" and "Get the lousy white trash," though out of the more than a dozen interviews filed by the FBI on the incident, only one is from a nikkei.) The crowd drove Arrowood and the other officers to the Pass Gate, which separated the center from the military police zone on the other side of the fence. While hurling rocks, fruit, and milk bottles the incarcerees demanded Arrowood turn over the officer responsible for the theft. The crowd now filled the avenues from house to house; the din could be heard blocks away. Police backup arrived, sirens on full blare. They were drowned out by the chants. Men smashed the police cars' windows, slashed the tires, and climbed atop the hoods. As the police fled the scene they looked back and saw one of their own, alone. But it was too dangerous to turn back. With officers hanging from the running boards, the cars sped off.

Arrowood reached the gate and called the center's police station; FBI special agent Edmund Mason answered the phone. The station, he said, was also surrounded.

At 3:45 a.m., on April 29, Santa Anita welcomed its first newborn. The father of the boy, Roy Yoshida, was initially disappointed when he saw his son: he already had two boys and hoped to be able to name a daughter "Anita."

Since the boy's arrival, dozens of other mothers gave birth while incarcerated at Santa Anita. Add to that the number of newborns and infants brought to camp, and it quickly added up to hundreds of hungry children. And while the mess halls served older children and adults, everyone else would need to be served at home, whether by breast or bottle.

Each barrack was assigned one electrical outlet, which hung from the ceiling. Early arrivals to the camp wrote to friends and family members on the outside, informing them that, if they could spare one, an extension cord would be helpful. As the barracks filled up, center officials realized they had yet another concern to add to the pile: the track's electrical system wasn't designed to handle that many users. Fuses would blow and whole sections of camp would go dark; incarcerees used pennies in place of the fuses, a dangerous fix in dry Los Angeles.

When the Western Defense Command insisted on the confiscation of Japanese records, though, it gave Santa Anita officials a cover for removing the center's biggest electrical hazard: hot plates. Used by mothers warming formula and food for newborns and infants, the appliances had spread across camp into the barracks of incarcerees who simply grew tired of standing in line to eat. On August 4, as officers moved door to door, hot plates were confiscated blindly, with no regard for the occupant's permit. Alcohol, butcher knife, Japanese record, hot plate—it didn't matter. All went into the pile of items growing at the edge of each barrack district. As word trickled out of the confiscation, the new mothers formed their own mob. They first demanded answers at the center hospital, then, unsatisfied with the response, closed in on the police station.

Looking up from her desk at the front of the station, the police secretary saw the group, four hundred strong, walking toward the building. She informed police chief Dawson, who upon opening the door was beset with a torrent of questions. The noise grew; no one in back could hear Dawson's responses, and no one in the front could hear the questions from the back. Five women and one man were picked to channel the group's questions to Dawson. That boiled down to just one: *Why?* Dawson—who had been skeptical of the confiscation for months—called in Amory, the center manager. The group wore Amory down. He agreed to accompany them to where the hot plates were stored, at the hospital; they were permitted to have their hot plates returned. The women dispersed. The break would be brief.

At 4:15 p.m. Arrowood and the other officers fled the gate by car, with the crowd trailing. Part of the mob met them at the police station nearly simultaneously, demanding the officer responsible for the theft be turned over to them, while a group of two hundred men split off. Rocks and light bulbs flew overhead, breaking windows and hitting officers inside. Prisoners inside the station were removed and secreted to Amory's office for the duration of the uprising.

The men who'd split from the group beelined for Barrack 9. It was home to an old woman with a poor heart and another woman named Jeanette Shimizu, the common-law wife of Harry Kawaguchi. Shimizu watched from a mess hall two barracks down as the group, satisfied that Kawaguchi wasn't in the barrack, moved on.

Kawaguchi's friendliness with the center's police department was common knowledge; in an FBI report released a month after the riot, he identified himself as a police informant. Though police reports from the day never address why Kawaguchi was attacked on August 4 specifically, it can be surmised that, in the throes of an uprising, all scores were to be settled.

Word reached the group that Kawaguchi was sequestered in an office. Climbing through the windows and doors, they forced Kawaguchi out of hiding, striking him first with an inkwell, then with a fist. From his knees Kawaguchi begged as the first typewriter dropped on his head. Now unconscious, he was struck with more typewriters and piled with every piece of furniture in the room: desks, tables, chairs. The center's personnel director pleaded with the group, running from window to window trying to stop the flow of men into the room. Only when he yelled that Kawaguchi would be killed if the beating continued did the men stop. Kawaguchi was pulled from under the pile and sped to the hospital in the bed of a pickup.

Outnumbered, center officials played their last card: they called in the military police. Within minutes, two hundred men stormed the camp, bayonets fixed. George watched the men as they flowed off the trucks, machine guns mounted to the roofs. He'd spent the afternoon flitting around the edges the mob, watching as it pulsed down Man o' War Avenue until it finally found Kawaguchi. It was the first time he'd witnessed the growing resentment in the camp, the first time he'd noticed anything other than the inconvenience of it all.

Despite their rifles and bayonets, the military men shook; the mob laughed and taunted them, touching the tips of their bayonets.

"Is it sharp, mister?"

Four days later, the WCCA released a statement about the events of August 4.

> After being stationed within the Japanese Assembly Center at Santa Anita for three days, the result of a disturbance accented by an assault upon an evacuee of Japanese and Korean ancestry, the military police were withdrawn Friday evening.
>
> The assault upon the evacuee occurred during the routine inspection by the interior police. Suspected of being an informer, the evacuee was set upon by several hundred other evacuees.
>
> A milling crowd of about 2,000 Japanese gathered almost at once. The military police were summoned. Some 200 were ordered in. The beaten evacuee, badly but not serious hurt, was rescued by the soldiers and removed to a hospital.

*The Santa Anita center contains a total population of almost
19,000 evacuees, evacuated from Military Area No. 1 of the Pacific
Coast.*

Nineteen Santa Anita police officers were fired or resigned over
their roles in the events of August 4, with some expressing their reluc-
tance to patrol the camp at night. Center manager Russell Amory, who
had set the day's events in motion with his desire to recover stolen
camp items, was replaced.

"The camp is now proceeding with normal routine on a quiet
basis," reads the final sentence of the FBI's incident report.

No incarcerees were arrested for their roles in the riot, but that
didn't mean there weren't consequences. An unsigned note to Edward
J. Ennis, the director of the Department of Justice's Alien Enemy Control Unit—the group responsible for apprehending allegedly dangerous
U.S. residents from Japan, Germany, and Italy—lays out the effects:

> *I suppose riots at Japanese centers are not really our problem but
> the problem of the War Relocation Authority. It does affect us in-
> directly however in that it builds up a pressure to compel us to be
> harsher in our treatment of the Japanese. If these riots are caused
> by Japanese sympathizers, these Japanese sympathizers should be
> apprehended and interned. I suggest that we write to [the] War
> Relocation Authority and ask it if it can furnish us the names of the
> persons responsible for causing the disturbance as well as the names
> of those who were heard to yell "get the white s. of b.'s." If these
> individuals were apprehended and interned, I am sure it would
> have a very salutary effect upon maintaining discipline and putting
> the quietus on potential agitators.*

Every morning when George woke up, he'd leave his barrack and
head to the track. As the sun rose and the camouflage mill churned on

the grandstands above, he'd lace up his sneakers and circle the infield, following the one-mile track lap after lap.

"What do you think you are," onlookers would shout, "some kind of horse?"

Though his time at Santa Anita was short, George took something with him from those three months, something that would stay with him until the day he died. For the next seventy-three years, he'd be known by a new name. He was now Horse.

———

Santa Anita closed as shoddily as it opened. Though technically open from March 27 to October 27, most of the incarcerees were gone by the middle of September. The first left on August 26.

One day in late August, an internal police officer walked into the Yoshinaga family's barrack and told them to pack up. Horse looked around; it wouldn't take much packing. The issue, though, was that no one knew where they were headed. Despite their removal from their homes, and the months-long stay at Santa Anita, the handling of their lives was so poorly communicated by the WCCA and the WRA that rumors swirled that not only were they not going home, they weren't staying *in America*. Repatriation to Japan—a place most of those at Santa Anita had never even visited—was a very real fear.

It wasn't until he stepped on the train that he learned of his new home. He overheard a group talking, and the destination leaked out. Horse thought for a moment.

Where in the heck is Wyoming?

CHAPTER EIGHT

58 Minutes

FORTY-EIGHT MILLION YEARS ago, as the inland seas of North America began their retreats to the oceans and crocodiles swam in the warm waters above the Arctic Circle, the earth underneath southern Montana shook and shoved forth a five-hundred-square-mile slab of dolomite and limestone. That piece of carbonate scraped and ground its way twenty-five miles into Wyoming, traveling at more than 100 miles an hour, lurching into its final resting place just thirty minutes later.

The cause of the event—the largest surface rockslide in the history of the planet—is still unknown. Most scientists believe a volcanic or steam explosion set the earth in motion, its movement aided by either hydrothermal fluids from a nearby volcano or the creation of a gas from the heating of the limestone. In this second scenario, the gas would have supported the slide in the same way a hoverboard floats over a surface.

Over the next 48 million years erosion swept away much of the slide. What was left is an 8,100-foot-tall lump of carbonate unlike any other 8,100-foot lump of carbonate in the world, and it's the first thing you see when you step off the train in Vocation, Wyoming, a made-up town created to jail eleven thousand human beings. What you see is Heart Mountain, a geological anomaly rising above a human ignominy.

After being shouted out of his own meeting in Salt Lake City, Milton Eisenhower launched his backup plan, abandoning the idea of resettlement for one of confinement.

"If the active racism of the West Coast was the initial catalyst for evacuation and the more passive racist climate of the nation as a whole the precondition for its acceptance, the racism of the interior western states was the final determinant of WRA policy," according to historian Roger Daniels.

Ten sites would be needed to house the close to 120,000 men and women currently residing in racetracks and fairgrounds across the West Coast. The requirements were convoluted. The camps needed to be situated on federal land that could be used for large-scale agricultural projects. (Eisenhower had not given up hope on this portion of his plan.) The sites also needed to be located a safe distance from "strategic installations," a definition that covered everything from naval bases and manufacturing plants to reservoirs and power lines, the latter two a contradiction when considering services needed to ensure the well-being of 120,000 people. The requirement for hundreds of acres all but demanded that the camps be built in the most inhospitable corners of the country, lands passed over by even the most desperate of pioneers.

To call the sites unattractive would be an overstatement. Gila River, in central Arizona, was built on an Akimel O'otham and Maricopa Indian reservation; construction began before the tribes approved the deal. Temperatures that summer reached 105°F or hotter on twenty-five of July's thirty-one days. At Minidoka, in Idaho, dust storms would whip the volcanic-ash-rich soil into barracks. Rohwer and Jerome were built atop drained swampland in southeastern Arkansas; both parcels had been abandoned by landowners too daunted by the landscape. They flooded regularly and with little warning, washing poisonous snakes into the camps. Sometimes the snakes made it onto the menu. (Snakes aside, the state was governed by Homer Adkins, who began his political career twenty years earlier by winning the Pulaski County sheriff's race with the backing of the Ku Klux Klan.) Topaz, in Utah, was covered in greasewood, and Granada—better known by its postal designation, Amache—was built in a corner of southeastern Colorado's high prairie that still sat slumped from the Dust Bowl and Great Depression. Tule Lake rested on the ancestral home of the Modoc tribe, who had been ripped from their homes seventy years earlier and sent to Oklahoma. (Two—Manzanar and Poston, in California and Arizona—were selected by the Army before the WRA was even created.)

Heart Mountain sat in the Bighorn Basin of northwest Wyoming, a part of the state so physically removed from the rest of the state that during the nineteenth-century demarcation of the Western United States, some surveyors suggested it be attached to Montana instead. Surrounded for millennia by mountain ranges, the basin was circled by Crow, Sioux, and Shoshoni Indians following the Indian treaties of 1868. Fur trappers explored the region in the early nineteenth century but abandoned the idea of settlement when the yield from the rivers was outweighed by the prospect of being mauled to death by a mountain lion or grizzly bear. A cattle boom in the 1880s was quickly extinguished by overgrazing and numbing winters.

An altitude of four thousand feet meant little precipitation—less than six inches of rain a year, and less than twenty inches of snow—but wild temperature swings. Winters could bring nighttime to 30 degrees below zero, while in the summer the basin was the hottest patch of Wyoming. In both winter and summer, as the sun warmed the ground it lifted warm air upward, which in turn drew cool air out from the west. That process produced gusts of wind that could knock an unsuspecting person down, often topping 60 miles an hour. Those same winds could take a meager snowfall and convert it into a blizzard, whipping the flakes from the ground; whole homes were buried. By the late nineteenth century the basin's permanent residents consisted of only a few cowboys and ranchers.

The closest town that could provide supplies was a two-day wagon ride away, across state lines into southern Montana. Into that gap stepped Colonel William "Buffalo Bill" Cody. Buffalo Bill was the most recognizable American in the world at the turn of the twentieth century, a six-foot stunner with brown hair flowing across his shoulders and a Vandyke beard framing his lips. The bronco-riding, wagon-train-driving, bison-slaughtering showman was the epitome of the American West, and Buffalo Bill's Wild West show toured North America and Europe showcasing the sharpshooters, Indians, and cowboys of the lawless region. He performed for Queen Victoria, Kaiser Wilhelm II, and Pope Leo XIII; he sold 2.5 million tickets to Londoners alone over the course of just ten months. He became very, very rich, and, as very, very rich men often do, he bought a ton of land.

Staring west from the top of Bighorn Peak one day in 1894, he marveled at the land, then one of the last unsettled stretches of America. He joined the effort of a group of Sheridan, Wyoming, businessmen already plotting a new community. Out of that he carved a town, and named it after himself. A few miles up the road, he laid out plans for a sixty-thousand-acre irrigation project, one that would provide water and fertile farmland for a burgeoning frontier empire. Despite the sandy soil, Cody envisioned miles of irrigation ditches supplying water to thousands of acres of farms. Fruit and nut farms would dot the land, granting farmers a respite from the price deflation of wheat and corn in the Midwest. Every drop of water would line his pockets, and allow him to retire. Soon, the Shoshone Irrigation Project—so named for the nearby Shoshone River, recently renamed from "Stinking Water" due to its overwhelming sulphur content—was advertising in the Wild West show program.

"The settler's cabin and the stockman's ranch house and corrals" had replaced the "cone-shaped tepees of the region," an article in the program said. "But the air that fills men's lungs with health, their brains with noble thoughts, and their veins with new life, still remains." Cody went on to describe the air as "so pure, so sweet and bracing, that it intoxicated when poor, weak, cramped, decayed, smoke-shrivelled lungs are distended by it."

Even a shrewd businessman, though, couldn't tame the Bighorn Basin. An initial canal was dug, but cost overruns made investment money evaporate. The Chicago, Burlington and Quincy Railroad, getting word of Cody's new enterprise, proposed a spur from Montana. Railroad officials then strong-armed Cody, threatening to end the railroad miles outside the town unless given half of the new plots. Cody relented, further diminishing his potential windfall. Still, Cody believed. He constructed a lavish granite hotel and named it after his daughter, Irma. He tried to lure residents, reaching out to various emigrant societies and even Social Democratic Party leader Eugene Debs; Debs ignored the invitation. Cody begged the Wyoming Board of Land Commissioners to petition the federal government to purchase back the land. The Interior Department took over. And decades later, the planned project sat, stalled and fallow, until the federal government began looking for a home for eleven thousand people.

Even before the camp was announced, *The Cody Enterprise* began its fear-mongering: a February 25, 1942, story mentioned that someone had spotted "about 400 Japanese men, all blindfolded, being marched up the [Shoshone River's] Northfork under guard." A popular conspiracy theory was that, on orders from Japan, the incarcerees would blow up the area's dams. "One stick of explosive in the Corbett Tunnel would destroy the water supply for the irrigation of about 60,000 acres," Park County commissioner Henry Attebery wrote in a letter to Wyoming senator Joseph C. O'Mahoney.

On May 27, the news was announced with a seven-columns-wide, front-page headline: 10,000 JAPS TO BE INTERNED HERE. Tucked at the bottom of the front page was a regular feature of the *Enterprise*, "War Rumblings and Local Defense News." It was usually dedicated to young Cody residents sent to war, or bond announcements. This time, though, editor Jack Richard turned his pen to the impending camp. "Certainly we are not crazy about the idea, but it is far better to have these 10,000 Japanese on the broad plains of Wyoming than in the industry-packed west coast," he wrote. "The Japanese (many, probably most of them, are good loyal Americans) must be removed from the coastal areas. . . . There should be no organized complaints filed with state or federal officials. There should be no loose talk about 'open season' on the internees. There should be no crabbing and no crying." What the town was being asked to endure, he concluded, was "our duty, just as much as if we were in uniform."

By mid-June Milton Eisenhower had grown weary to the point of insomnia. He hadn't slept well in months, his nights racked with anxiety. In between meetings he assuaged his guilt by calling university presidents across the country, hoping one, any, would be willing to accept nisei student transfers. He spent hours on the phone with officials at Princeton, MIT, and Duke, to no avail. They claimed that war research was being done on campus, or that the students could not receive appropriate background checks, a preposterous educational requirement at the time. His doggedness bore fruit eventually—with the help of the American Friends Service Committee's cajoling, 4,300 nisei students left camps over the next three years for colleges across the Midwest and on the East Coast—but it was cold comfort.

Usually boisterous, with a wide smile, Eisenhower was miserable. He'd spent the previous three months complaining and commiserating about the position with his former Agriculture Department colleague Dillon Myer on their morning carpools, and one night found himself at a dinner party at the Myers'. After serenading the guests on the piano all evening, Eisenhower waited until the party cleared to talk with Myer. Eisenhower relayed that Roosevelt was relieving him of the role—would Myer be interested? The men talked for hours. Myer's decision boiled down to one thing, he wrote in his autobiography: "I was sure I could sleep."

On June 18, before packing his desk for a return to the Office of War Information, Eisenhower wrote a long memo to Roosevelt. He was blunt: "Life in a relocation center cannot be pleasant . . . [T]hey have suffered heavily." He saved his harshest criticism for Americans themselves.

The future of the program will doubtless be governed largely by the temper of American public opinion. . . . I cannot help expressing the hope that the American people will grow toward a broader appreciation of the essential Americanism of a great majority of the evacuees and of the difficult sacrifice they are making. Only when the prevailing attitudes of unreasoning bitterness have been replaced by tolerance and understanding will it be possible to carry forward a genuinely satisfactory relocation program and to plan intelligently for the reassimiliation of the evacuees into American life when the war is over.

Eisenhower spent much of the rest of his life as a college president, first at his alma mater, Kansas State, then at Penn State and Johns Hopkins. He helped write his brother Dwight's 1961 farewell address, warning Americans of the creeping influence of the military-industrial complex. For years he cherished a desk-size bonsai tree given to him by JACL national secretary Mike Masaoka in recognition of Eisenhower's attempts to ameliorate the effects of the executive order. Eisenhower's failure to halt the construction of the camps lingered with him for the rest of his life.

"I have brooded about this episode on and off for the past three decades, for it is illustrative of how an entire society can somehow plunge off-course," he wrote in his 1974 memoir. "The evacuation of the Japanese-Americans need not have happened."

Sometimes the route took three days, sometimes a week. Some trains sped through the desert in pitch darkness, curtains drawn tight, while others leaked light, allowing children to peek through, hoping to spot a cowboy. There were no beds, no pillows. Spoiled pea soup coursed through stomachs, an inconvenience at home but a public health calamity on a train with few bathrooms. Pregnant women sat on the unforgiving wooden seats, praying that their child wouldn't arrive before their final destination, wherever that was.

One man with a heart ailment was pulled from a Los Angeles hospital and loaded onto the train. From there he traveled up and over the Continental Divide, his heart fighting more than seven thousand feet of altitude change. At a stop in Cheyenne he was taken to a hotel and given medical treatment, then loaded once again. WRA officials allowed him to finally disembark in Deaver, Wyoming, where a car drove him the final stretch of the trip. He was able to lie down for the first time in days; later, in his diary, a camp official called the episode little more than "premeditated murder." Trains were sidetracked for hours as freight and passenger trains passed by. Horse's train was greeted in Salt Lake City by dozens of protesters. For five hours the passengers sat, waiting, as the protesters, men and women, cursed and threw slurs. His mother, slowly dying of diabetes though she didn't know it, sat with him and his sister.

Just after midnight on August 12, 1942, the first train slumped to a stop on a patch of cleared sagebrush. The commotion was terrible. Hundreds got off, their luggage and scant household items tossed onto the backs of waiting trucks. From the depot the community didn't look like much: a half-dozen or so Army barracks, a dozen more for the camp's white civilian employees, an administration building. In the distance to the northeast, a chimney puffed, signaling the location of the camp hospital. Through tears, silence, anger, or resignation, the men, women, and children began the quarter-mile walk up a hill, and their fate came into focus. An endless army of 459 barracks extended beyond the limits of anyone's vision, divided tidily into twenty blocks, each with two mess halls, unpartitioned toilet and shower buildings, and a recreation building. Each block housed twenty-four 20-foot-by-120-foot barracks, and each barrack contained six single-room apartments. Families of six were crammed into a 20-foot-by-24-foot room with no walls. There were no ceilings, so voices traveled the 120 feet before echoing back. Each room had a coal stove, one light bulb dangling in the center, and an Army cot and mattress. A bucket of water sat outside the door of each apartment in case of fire. The barracks were constructed in sixty days by three thousand eager workers, lured from across Wyoming, Montana, and Nebraska by the promise of good pay. Each barrack was built in fifty-eight minutes.

In the haste of planning, the WRA acquired green wood, which meant that the barracks were shrinking before they were even completed. Dust covered the rooms, and incarcerees would later be forced to plug pages from Sears, Roebuck catalogues into the growing gaps. Construction crews left messages on the walls. Sometimes it would just be a name—Willie Frederick, Dominic McMahon, "Rick Beck Was Here"; sometimes it was a small, pencil-drawn penis. Other times it was more direct: "A SLAP FOR THE JAPS."

Each camp was called not a concentration camp, or an internment camp, or a prison, but instead a "relocation center." Its occupants were not prisoners, or internees, or incarcerees, but "colonists," according to the WRA. On August 25, the camp put out a bulletin welcoming the new residents; it served as a precursor to the *Heart Mountain Sentinel*, a weekly newspaper that would soon launch. Bill Hosokawa, a newspaperman from Seattle, was appointed to run the weekly, and he wrote the camp introduction.

"The entire nation will be looking on these camps as mighty experiments," he said. "The records that we establish here will, no doubt, play a great part in the manner in which we will return to civilian life after we have won this war. We are starting a new chapter in our lives here in the free, clear air of the West under fortunate and favorable circumstances. An able, sympathetic and co-operative Caucasian staff is here to help us. The rest lies in our hands."

Within a month, the camp swelled to 6,281 incarcerees. By October it was the third-largest city in Wyoming, its 10,000-plus denizens forming a community dwarfed only by Casper and Cheyenne.

"Our city really looks like something at night," WRA administrative officer John Nelson wrote in his diary the night of September 11. "Row on row of lights and from a distance it looks like a real city. It gives one a sort of queer feeling tho to look out over the area at night with all the lights on and then realize that the city houses a race of people who because of their race have been isolated from society under very trying and difficult conditions, and many of whom may never return again to their original home and property.

"War is a cruel thing," he continued. "Seems that man with his brilliant mind could find a human substitute for war. Am afraid tho that as long as there are nations there will be war."

Horse disembarked, grabbed his bag, and walked to apartment A in the tenth building of the twenty-fourth block, his home for however long the federal government decided it would be.

Further bulletins spelled out the inadequacy of the camp plainly. Incarcerees were encouraged to build a protective bank of dirt around the outsides of their barracks to block soon-to-arrive winter winds. Just four days after the camp opened, they were warned that it would be overcrowded. Military police were not to be spoken to. The camp was so big that the administration recommended putting ID tags on children so when—not if—they were lost they'd be able to be pointed home correctly. When men began to collect scrap lumber to build furniture, the head of security scolded them, claiming the act was theft. Medical officers gave rattlesnake bite tutorials.

In mid-September, shipments of cots and blankets couldn't keep up with the five-hundred-person trainloads, forcing Heart Mountain administrators to open a wing of the hospital for women and children to sleep in. The men spent the night wandering the streets of their new home and steeling themselves against the first snowflakes of winter and, for many, the first snowflakes of their lives. Other families huddled together for warmth in coal-less apartments. When the coal was delivered, the stoves blasted out so much heat that it could be dangerous in such a confined space. In the predawn darkness of September 26, Horse scorched his right pinkie toe so badly that doctors diagnosed it as a third-degree burn. Even after healing, it would swell through December.

Other basic functions were similarly ignored. Food delivery shifted wildly, with some mess halls serving just hot dogs for three straight days while others ran out of food altogether. Still others served spoiled food, hospitalizing large numbers.

Medical care was just as haphazard. Sterilization was often done over Sterno cans, cots lay sheetless, and water unusable. The hospital opened without towels, washcloths, or soap. Despite U.S. Public Health Service recommendations of one nurse per every two hundred residents, the total number of registered nurses at camp never topped ten, or just one per every one thousand residents. The war siphoned off nurses nationwide, making recruitment, especially to a prison camp in nowhere Wyoming, near impossible. Once, while transporting an incarceree to an eye specialist in Billings, Montana, a Heart Mountain doctor and nurse stopped at both Billings Deaconess and St. Vincent's Hospitals, begging nurses to join them. There were no volunteers. Only the resourcefulness of the camp staff kept the situation from reeling out of control.

The first of 552 babies born in camp arrived September 4; the first of the camp's 183 deaths was on August 28. Christians were buried in a small cemetery on the outskirts of camp, while the bodies of Buddhists were placed, alone, on a train and shipped four hundred miles to the closest crematorium, in Great Falls, Montana.

Despite the circumstances, signs of life began to reveal themselves. West of Block 5, where an elementary school was originally planned, cactus and sagebrush and rattlesnakes were scraped from the ground, replaced by a baseball diamond. Basketball and volleyball courts were laid out, as were horseshoe pits. The industrious residents of Block 22, Barrack 26, cleared the pebbles and stones and built sumo pits to showcase the talent lumbering in from the Portland, Pomona, and Santa Anita temporary detention centers. And on September 26 the first football game was played, a six-man match between residents of Santa Clara and San Jose. If there was any glimmer of hope in that first autumn at Heart Mountain, it was illuminated by athletics, one of the most consistent distractions over the next three years.

Just as at Santa Anita, Heart Mountain's educational system was an afterthought. Nearly a quarter of the camp's 10,767 incarcerees were school-aged, and since this would be their home for indeterminate weeks or months or years, accommodations would need to be arranged. It was easy for the government to dismiss educational concerns at Santa Anita; it was *temporary*, they argued. But now education would be insisted upon.

Like everything else, schooling stumbled out of the gate. Housing adjustments delayed school construction, so all classes were held in barracks, which meant clearing the barracks of their residents and jamming them into a recreation hall. The first school opened at 8:30 a.m., September 30, 1942. More than two hundred elementary school students waited outside the barrack as carpenters scurried to complete the makeshift benches and tables, the only adornment in most rooms. Margaret Jones, a fifth-grade teacher from New Jersey, covered her walls with maps and photos of Wyoming, and brightened her desktop with pine cones, dried vegetation, and colorful coral formations. For the school's forty first-graders, their first-ever day of school was in a concentration camp.

The high school filled six barracks composed of thirty-four classrooms, one storeroom, and one office. The classrooms were just as spartan as the housing barracks: a coal stove, benches, and a piece of plywood painted black to mimic a chalkboard. Desks didn't arrive until January 1943. Textbooks were limited, forcing four or five students to share a book. Paper and pencils were scarce. The coal stove blasted so high that students crammed near it would peel down to T-shirts, while students in the back of the uninsulated rooms would sit shivering in hats and wool coats. Sometimes the stove would belch its smoke in reverse, filling the fifty-student classroom. Just as in their apartments, the classrooms lacked ceilings, dropping the sound of algebra lessons atop history lessons, history lessons atop Latin lessons. On the first day of classes, a teacher sprinted between barracks blowing a police whistle to signal the end of a period.

Even more so than the nuts and bolts of building schools and minds, bureaucratic issues proved to be the toughest for the administration to navigate. Most of the students came from large public high schools in California, which were forced to have multiple school sessions: one that began in the fall, and another that began midyear. Combined with their forced removal from their classrooms in the spring, many students didn't know where they fell, grade-wise. A student that began his or her sophomore year of high school midyear, and then was pulled in April and sent to Santa Anita, for instance, only took a few weeks of sophomore year classes. Some students were skipped ahead, while others kept back. Transcripts from Los Angeles and Mountain View and Seattle arrived weeks and months later, making verification of both grades and grade levels all but impossible. The most difficult question was existential: *How do you teach American students about civics when they've been unjustly imprisoned by their own government?*

Heart Mountain project director C. E. Rachford hired a school superintendent, Clifford Carter, and a principal, John Corbett. Both men had spent decades in Wyoming education, but neither in a district that came close to the scope of what Heart Mountain's population demanded. Corbett was the principal of Lingle High School, fifteen miles from the Nebraska border, in the southeast corner of the state. The town of Lingle was home to 428 residents, a third of the population of Heart Mountain High School alone. The pair set about hiring teachers and principals, luring them mostly from Wyoming and Nebraska schools with good salaries, overtime for working Saturdays, and, as war service appointments, a promise that they were helping the war effort at the same time. Instructors were paid $2,000 a year, and senior teachers $2,600 a year, salaries that drew criticism from districts around the state that couldn't afford the rates. Those hired from outside the camp were all white. A handful of incarcerees were hired as well, including one with a master's degree in biology from USC and another with a chemistry degree from Berkeley. Each was paid $228 a year, the maximum allowed by the federal government, and just under the pay for an Army private. "Valid Only at Heart Mountain" was handwritten on their teaching certificates.

None of the teachers had any experience teaching Japanese American children, and some—perhaps most—believed the children deserved to be in the camp. "Well, at first I had a little prejudice, but I will never have that prejudice now," said home economics teacher Clarissa Corbett, John Corbett's wife, years later.

Compounding the issues facing the students, teachers, and administrators was pressure from camp administration. While the nearly eleven thousand incarcerees of Heart Mountain were under twenty-four-hour guard, they were allowed, even encouraged, to leave the camp for one thing: work. In Wyoming, that mostly meant harvesting sugar beets. Sugar supplies from the Philippines and Java, now under Japanese control, had dried up, and conversion of sugar to industrial alcohol for use in synthetic rubber was skyrocketing because of the war. All federal planting restrictions were lifted, allowing sugar beet farmers to expand their acreage by 25 percent. But the draft and the promise of better-paying, less labor-intensive defense industry jobs sapped the fields of their workers.

So, two days after the high school opened, Project Director Rachford implored his students to do their part.

"Here is a real opportunity . . . to be of outstanding service to the nation, and at the same time to earn some spending money for the long winter months ahead," he wrote in the campwide bulletin. "Special arrangements will be made to help these students make up their school work upon return to Heart Mountain at the conclusion of the harvest in four or five weeks."

George and Babe dismissed the call; George found work in a mess hall, while Babe joined the camp's garbage crew. But with the promise of real wages, and having only attended two days of high school since April, dozens of boys loaded into trucks and went out to the fields. Stan Igawa, a slight East Hollywood boy with a half-inch scar on his upper lip, climbed into the back of a pickup and headed north for the fields of Montana.

CHAPTER NINE

Kannon-sama Is Crying

ON DECEMBER 22, 1934, Amelia Earhart left Los Angeles. She climbed aboard the SS *Lurline*, ratcheted her Lockheed Vega plane onto the aft tennis deck, and set sail for Honolulu. The five-day trip was in preparation for a solo flight from Honolulu to Oakland, the first of its kind. After two weeks of preparations, Earhart strapped into the plane, gunned the engine down a muddy runway, and nosed the six-thousand-pound bird into the sky. The *Lurline* churned below, hauling its 715 passengers and 359 crew members across the Pacific and back to Los Angeles.

Fifteen months later, *Lurline* passengers Stan Igawa, nine, and his brother George, seven, put on brand-new brown suits and nervously debated what to call their father. *Dad? Pop? Papa? Father* seemed too formal, but when you're seeing the man for the first time in your short memory, formality may be the simplest path. The two eventually settled on *Dad*. They stepped off the ship and into a new life.

The Daifukuji Sōtō Mission sits on a broad, pleasant hill, fifty yards off Māmalahoa Highway, the belt road that circumnavigates the island of Hawai'i. Built in 1918, the brick-red Zen Buddhist temple with the bleached-white hip-and-gable rooftop stood in quick contrast to the jungle of green immediately behind it, and even starker contrast to a tiny house in that jungle.

Eizo and Kinu Igawa led a taut life. Eizo immigrated to Hawai'i from Japan in 1896; like many before him, he found the work in the coffee fields unbearable. He deserted the plantation and fled as far as he could, clear across the island, from 'Ōla'a to Kona. He became a fish peddler, but was too lenient with his customers, bartering with them for a chicken or allowing them to build mounting charge accounts. To make ends meet, Kinu baked and sold *senbei*, Japanese rice crackers. The *senbei* crackled as she heated them in an outdoor fire pit, rattling as they flipped in their cast-iron molds. During breaks she'd steal a pinch of tobacco from its container and roll a cigarette one-handed.

Outside their kitchen window was a fishpond, and next to that a pig trough, where Eizo would drop extra papayas and avocados from the trees that surrounded the house. A two-seat outhouse sat seventy-five yards back, near a stand of coffee trees. They had children, and one of those daughters, Kimiko, had two sons of her own. Three months before Stan's fourth birthday, in July 1930, Kimiko and the boys' father, Toshio, left Hawai'i to join his brother in the city of Los Angeles, in a growing neighborhood called Hollywood. Stan and George stayed, in the little house behind the big temple. They wouldn't see their parents for the next six years.

The temple became their family, its broad yard hosting not only games of marbles, hide-and-seek, and tops but the Buddhist celebrations the Japanese immigrants brought to the island. They'd annually celebrate the Buddha's birthday with a flower festival, honor their ancestors with *bon* dancing every summer, and compete in judo and kendo. The boys threw pebbles at the temple's large mango tree, willing the fruit to fall, and raced to the top of a house stuffed with Filipino coffee-pickers whenever the occasional airplane would fly overhead. They walked three miles each way to elementary school. The Igawa boys were, Stan would say years later, "country jacks."

When the *Lurline* pulled into Los Angeles on April 11, 1936, that all changed. The boys moved into 4629½ Fountain Street, the ½ indicating the two-bedroom house behind the home owned by an elderly man named Mr. Morin. The Igawas' conversion from country jacks to city kids was immediate. Mr. Morin's grandsons lived in the front house, and the four boys became inseparable. The Igawas learned about Yom Kippur and Jewish delicacies, while the Angelenos took lessons in aloha. The four boys dented Morin's garage door with baseballs every afternoon; on the off chance of rain they retired inside for checkers or chess instead. No longer bound by the dirt roads of Kona, Stan and George would roller-skate two miles down Sunset Boulevard just to get a haircut. They'd climb aboard the bright red, double-decker buses, sitting among tourists on the open-air roof only to get off at Selma Avenue Elementary School for class.

School was unlike anything the boys had ever encountered. Every morning, before the opening bell, each class would line up in military formation. After inspecting the students, the principal would cue a drummer, who tapped out a cadence on his snare. *Brrrrap rap rap . . . brrrrap rap rap.* Beginning with the younger grades, the students would march to the drumbeat into their classrooms, where they'd stand at attention and recite the Pledge of Allegiance.

Some of Stan's country tendencies had lingered. Upon his arrival in California, Stan was placed in fourth grade. The rosy-cheeked Mrs. Hess was friendly—early that fall, she happily instructed her new Hawaiian pupil that the state flower of California was an incandescent bloom known as the golden poppy, and then helped him paint one. One morning, Stan heard a noise overhead and bolted from his desk to see. Craning his neck, he stared into the sky and spotted the rare sight. His classmates turned; Mrs. Hess asked why he had run to the window. From his perch a block off Hollywood Boulevard, Stan responded, "I wanted to see the airplanes."

Those rural eccentricities soon faded, and Stan's group of friends expanded. Salvatore, Hyman, Jacque—like Babe Nomura a few blocks away and a few years older, Stan's taste in friendship wasn't limited to his fellow nikkei children. He played softball every chance he could, and by junior high was a sprinter and high jumper. At barely five feet, he was not an outstanding leaper.

In the fall of 1941, Stan entered ninth grade at John Marshall High School, a Gothic cathedral of a school set high atop a pine-covered hill in Los Angeles's Los Feliz neighborhood. That fall, ha-zel-eyed Marshall student Rosemary LaPlanche would be named Miss America, one year after being named first runner-up. She was so thoroughly *American*, the judges concluded, that they were willing to overlook the fact that she had falsified her age. She was only sev-enteen and thus ineligible to compete. In the decades to come, the building would be viewed as so quintessentially American that it would be used as the fictional high school for dozens of movies and TV shows, including *Grease*, *A Nightmare on Elm Street*, and *Pretty in Pink* and the TV shows *The Wonder Years* and *Boy Meets World*. (In a less wholesome but equally noteworthy history, it was also featured in the music video for Van Halen's "Hot for Teacher.") Stan ran JV track and earned a spot on the "C" basketball team. He sang in the chorus and took long bus rides to Japanese classes forced on him by his parents. He climbed atop the rumble seat of a friend's hot rod en route to the Rose Bowl, where he'd watched the Marshall Barristers football team take on Franklin High School, or traveled west to Hol-lywood High, where the Sheiks were led by an escape artist named Nomura.

On December 7, 1941, Stan and his friend Beep spent the morning at Polar Palace, a cavernous ice rink wedged between Paramount Stu-dios and the Hollywood Cemetery. After a free skate, the boys strad-dled their bikes and pointed them home. On the way, with radios blaring out of every car and home, the news of the day became clear. Unlike most Americans, though, Stan knew exactly where Pearl Har-bor was.

The first thing the U.S. government did after Pearl Harbor was arrest Hawai'i's Buddhist priests. As community leaders, the men were viewed by both military and civilian officials as a national security threat, an unfounded suspicion that would foreshadow the treatment of American Muslim communities sixty years later in September 2001. Called "heathens" and "pagans," their religion was viewed warily and was seen as incompatible with American life. As martial law set in, the territory's Buddhist temples were seized by the military. Daifukuji, where Stan spent his childhood shooting marbles and hurling stones at mangoes, wasn't spared.

"The temple was filled with soldiers," remembers one of its members. "At night there were blackouts so the soldiers had to use candles and were afraid of ghosts. My mother used to say to me 'Kannon-sama [the bodhisattva Kannon] is crying' because there were only soldiers in the temple."

Stan wasn't spared, either. As he got off the bus at the corner of Vermont Avenue and Fountain Street one day, a woman approached him. "You goddamn Jap," she said to the fifteen-year-old. He was furious. Unlike Babe and Horse, Stan was a sansei, third-generation. His family hadn't been in Japan for nearly fifty years. He restrained himself, content with muttering under his breath and shooting her a dirty look. But the encounter affected him deeply, and he carried it with him for decades.

While Horse and Babe were sent to Santa Anita, Stan and his family were bused to Pomona Assembly Center, built atop a fairground thirty miles east of downtown L.A. Stan worked in the mess hall, washing hundreds of pots and pans, utensils, and dishes for $12 a month. To fend off boredom, his friends from Marshall High created a softball team, the Devil Dogs. Like many families, Pomona had broken up the Igawas; they ate almost every meal at separate tables.

In August, the four of them began the train journey to Heart

Mountain. One wheel of their car kept clicking, over and over, across California and Nevada. *Click clack*. Arizona and Utah. *Click clack click clack*. Colorado and finally Wyoming. *Click*. As the sound of the wheel kept the whole car from sleeping, the soot from the engine billowed in through open windows, blackening the passengers' faces and clothes. With no washrooms they sat, dirty, in the infernal car.

The Igawas were assigned Block 2, Barrack 18, Apartment B. The showers and latrines were forty yards away; the first blasts of winter froze Stan's hair to his head as he left the shower and walked home. Six weeks after his family arrived, Stan's high school principal suggested he move to a sugar beet field, and, with nothing else to do, he did just that.

On June 26, 1876, Lieutenant Colonel George Custer was shot once through the left temple and once right under his heart. Following his failed and final stand, an arrow was rammed through his penis, and then his body and that of his brother Tom were wrapped in blankets, buried in shallow graves, and marked only with a travois weighed down with rocks. Within a year animals had picked over and scattered most of the bones of the country's most notorious Indian slaughterer, and sixty-six years later Stanley Igawa hunched nearby, pulling sugar beets out of the frozen soil, weeks away from his sixteenth birthday.

The sugar beet fields of Montana straddled the Bighorn and Yellowstone Rivers, a boon to a corner of the country still climbing out of the depths of the Great Depression. In 1937, the Holly Sugar company opened a 23,000-square-foot processing plant and a 10,000-square-foot warehouse in Hardin, a small town that sat on the northern edge of what remained of the Crow Reservation. The event was so momentous for the 1,500-person town that 3,500 people attended the plant's grand opening. As World War II began, the demand for sugar and lack of labor led the company and its rival, Great Western Sugar, to seek new workers. German prisoners of war and Mexican migrant workers helped plug that gap, so much that labor training manuals were translated into German and Spanish. But they needed more.

Nikkei offered the sugar companies something their former white, mostly Northern European employees didn't: shortness. In a business where workers spent their entire shifts hunched over tilled ground, every inch of height—or its opposite—mattered. Protein-heavy diets of meat, eggs, and dairy hadn't infiltrated Japan before the issei wave of emigration, a reality reflected in the stature of its people. The average American man in 1910 was 5'8"; the average Japanese man the same year was 5'3". (Due to similar factors, the average Japanese citizen grew more than 10 percent taller in the twentieth century, a rate only surpassed by South Koreans. Americans grew barely 3 percent taller.) After a beet field was plowed, workers would straddle a tilled row, squatting so they didn't have to bend their backs. The workers would pull beets, at least two per hand, then knock the brown balls together to remove the dirt. ("Don't lift beets any higher than necessary to knock dirt off," reminded the labor training manual.) Then, without standing, they'd toss the beets into a pile and continue down the row.

Each man was handed a knife, a foot-long cross between a machete and a butcher knife with a three-inch hook at the end. The hook was used to spear a single beet from the pile, and then, while placing his right hand beneath the beet to protect his fingers, the worker would use the blade to lop the beet greens from the root. The greens would fall to the ground, the worker's left hand would toss the beet into a pile, and the right would spear another beet. At the end of the day, six men would form a line on either side of a truck bed, lifting three or four beets in each hand and placing them in the truck. For every two thousand pounds of pulled, piled, topped, and loaded beets, each man would make $1.25.

In Hardin, Montana, Stan slept in an adobe shack, his hands numb from the monotonous work. The crew soon left Hardin and drove two hundred miles northeast, to Savage. October snow fell around the boys and their Mexican compatriots, two groups of men unfamiliar with the cold, never mind one that set in in late September and wouldn't leave until May. As the temperature dropped, the beets froze, making topping nearly impossible. One day, as Stan squatted over his row, tops trailing behind him, he swung and swung at a beet, the knife barely sinking into the flesh. With a final swing he cleaned the beet and lodged the knife hook into his right calf. He returned to work the next day.

Despite helping to save the local economies—in some communities the nikkei laborers harvested as much as 25 percent of the season's crop—the boys weren't welcome in the towns' restaurants or barbershops. Movie theaters would rarely open their doors for the workers, only hosting special matinees on Sundays "for Japs only." Sugar company representatives coerced and intimidated them, threatening the men with jail for insubordination and blacklisting those who demanded better working conditions. After attacks from locals, the Army enlisted county sheriffs to protect the men, who were required to carry travel permits and identification cards at all times.

The boys headed farther north to a shack in Sidney, Montana, where the fields straddled the North Dakota border. Better suited for tools than humans, snow swept through cracks in the walls of the shack, the old cast-iron stove little help against nature. Stan suffered frostbite on his feet, and at night, as the wind creaked and the snow filled the room, the men slept with their right hands clenched in pain.

CHAPTER TEN

"Trapped Like Rats in a Wired Cage"

BABE WAS GETTING fat. You could see it in his cheeks and his chin, and in the way his shirts cinched a little tighter than before. He'd ballooned, packing thirty pounds onto his previously lanky frame.

They all had, the teens. After months of inaction and a diet that consisted mostly of potatoes and hot dogs, everyone was feeling the effects of Santa Anita and Heart Mountain, physically as much as emotionally. Intramural sports were picking up—six-man football leagues, ad hoc softball tournaments on cleared lots—but nothing could replace the competition of interscholastic sports. There was one major obstacle to this, of course: they were a high school in a prison camp.

If Heart Mountain High School wanted to compete against outside schools, it needed to persuade the Wyoming High School Athletic Association, which corralled the ninety member schools and arranged state championship tournaments. Luckily, on its board sat John Corbett, the principal of a small school near the Nebraska border, the one who'd recently resigned that position, packed up his wife, Clarissa, and moved clear across the state to an eleven-thousand-person concentration camp. On November 27, 1942, Heart Mountain High School was officially voted a member of the Wyoming High School Athletic Association.

Extracurricular activities were slim the first fall, but one thing the camp valued above almost everything else was news. Before camp, newspapers like the *Rafu Shimpo, Kashu Mainichi, Nichibei Shimbun,* and *Shin Sekai Asahi* delivered daily accounts of Japanese American life to readers' doorsteps in Los Angeles and San Francisco. After removal, the staffs were spread across the West—their journalistic talents only slowed, not snuffed. At Santa Anita, the incarceree-led *Pacemaker* was overseen (and heavily censored) by camp officials but ran its circulation up to five thousand; institutions including the Library of Congress and the New York Public Library requested twice-weekly copies. Each of the fourteen other temporary detention centers produced papers as well, a trend that continued at every camp. That hunger for news trickled down to even the high schools.

At a time when absences were common simply because students lacked appropriate clothing to take on the Wyoming fall, Heart Mountain High School had already released two issues of *Echoes,* the student newspaper. By late November the twice-monthly mimeographed paper had a staff of five editors, including a sports editor from Mountain View who finagled a short profile of his new best friend from Hollywood, a story entitled "Meet the Champ":

> *Tamotsu Nomura, husky speed burner, hails from Hollywood High, one of the finest schools in southern California, according to loyal Hollywood followers.*
>
> *Standing 5'10" in height and weighing about 185, "Babe" is one of those superman-like athletes having excelled in every department of sports of Hollywood High.*
>
> *Last year though only a junior he made first string varsity halfback, under coach Schroeder, Hollywood's pigskin professor. "Babe" was expected to be all-conference material when his brilliant career was brought to an abrupt end by evacuation.*
>
> *Playing for the Hollywood "Huskies," Japanese basketball club, he was the leading scorer in the league and his sharp shooting accounted for many of his team's victories.*
>
> *In the good old American sport of baseball, Tamotsu was first*

*string varsity shortstop for Hollywood High, where it was said that
he could make the hardest stop look easy with his superb ability.*

Babe's skills, on sabbatical since the spring, had a new audience.
But first he needed to get in shape.

———————

On their first Thanksgiving behind barbed wire, the residents of Heart
Mountain Relocation Center ate 7,500 pounds of Army-surplus turkey, then watched a few football games.

By late November 1942, the sport had taken over the camp. Six-
man teams, teams for each of the camp's five separate Boy Scout troops,
teams made up entirely of men who had met at Santa Anita or grown
up in Santa Clara County, a whole league just for sixth graders. The
sports section of the *Sentinel* was packed, week-to-week, with results.

On Thanksgiving Day, the Santa Anita Jackrabbits met the Valley
Sportsmen. As their names predicted, the Jackrabbit eleven had met at
Santa Anita; the Sportsmen's players all originated in the San Gabriel
Valley, east of Los Angeles. The Jackrabbits had Babe—but the Sports-
men had Toshio Asano.

Tosh was a 160-pound bullet packed into less than five and a half
feet of man. He grew up in Monrovia, California, where his dominance
on even the junior varsity football team was covered by the *Los Angeles
Times*. With legs like compressed coils, in the spring of junior year he
long-jumped 21 feet, 6 inches, a stunning distance for someone of his
height. And that wasn't even his best event. On May 18, 1940, before
6,500 fans at the Los Angeles Coliseum, Tosh tore down the cinder runway, a bamboo pole steadily bouncing between his two hands. At the end
of the runway he jabbed the pole into the ground, flinging himself up
and over the bar. Twelve feet and a victory lap later, he was crowned the
lightweight pole vault champion of Southern California for 1940.

His high school accomplishments would pale in comparison to
what he achieved in college. In the 1940s, every junior college in South-

ern California not only funded athletic departments, they fielded football teams, too. Junior colleges in Bakersfield, Los Angeles, Pomona,
Santa Monica, Riverside, San Bernardino—they all fielded teams. The
colleges would play not only against each other but against freshman
teams from four-year universities as well as teams of inmates from
area prison farms. Tosh chose Citrus Junior College, just seven miles
east of his high school. In the fall of 1941, he was one of the best junior
college players in the country.

Five games into the season, Tosh had scored 74 of Citrus's 123
points, grinding into the end zone from his position at right half, then
coolly booting the extra point. A week later, in a game against El Cen-
tro, he scored three touchdowns and tallied 5 extra points. Tosh was a
5-foot-5, 160-pound, nineteen-year-old nisei, and he was the leading
junior college scorer in the United States. After Citrus's run cooled—
the team only scored 14 points in its final three games—Tosh slipped
to fourth in the country when the season ended. Due in part to Citrus's
middling 5–4 record, he was only named to the all-Southern California Board of Football's second team at the end of the season, but he
didn't go unnoticed. While at Citrus he got a call from Red Strader,
the coach at Saint Mary's College, then one of the West Coast's most
dominant football programs. The team was interested in his services,
Strader said, if Tosh was willing to make the move four hundred miles
up the coast for the next season.

Citrus played its last game of the 1941 season on November 14, a
14–6 loss to San Diego State's freshman team. Tosh went scoreless, the
Japanese bombed Pearl Harbor three weeks later, and he would never
play another down of college football.

The results of that Thanksgiving game aren't what's important.
(The Jackrabbits won 13–6; Babe and Tosh each scored a touchdown.)
What matters is that it jump-started a rivalry that would last the en-
tirety of the two men's stays in camp. The unofficial title of the best
athlete of Heart Mountain was on the line every day, and neither man,
one five days shy of his twentieth birthday and the other a high school

junior, wanted to lose. It gave the two men, stripped of their futures, something to fight for.

On December 22, a combined Boy Scout drum and bugle corps assembled outside Principal Corbett's office and led the gathered crowd in "To the Color" as the Stars and Stripes was raised. A group of high school seniors had fundraised and coordinated to move a flagpole from an old Civilian Conservation Corps camp so the ramshackle high school could have a place to fly the flag. Corbett was nervous, wondering whether the students would want to salute the flag of a country that had stolen them from their homes and dropped them onto this wind-whipped patch of earth. Ted Fujioka, the student responsible for the purchase, reassured him. Shortly after the ceremony, a poem was anonymously sent to the *Sentinel* office:

> *A thrill pulsated through my heart*
> *At the sight once more of our grand ole flag.*
> *Fluttering smartly in the breeze, Its stars and stripes in full galore,*
> *The bleakness in my heart was melted away,*
> *The thrill I felt was no whit, no less*
> *No matter what, it is my flag.*

Two days later, on Christmas Eve, the United States government asked them to sign up for the draft.

Unbeknownst to most in the camp, War Department officials had been toying with the idea of reinstating Japanese Americans into the Selective Service, after having reclassified all eligible men as 4-C, "an alien ineligible for military duty," back in June. The purpose of reinstatement was unambiguous. "Resumption of conscription alone should produce a total of an additional 16,800 which, with the approximately 4,000 now in service . . . would be ample to provide and sustain a division," wrote Colonel M. W. Pettigrew, chief of the Military Intelligence

Service's Far Eastern Group, to Assistant Secretary of War John McCloy in November. If the purpose was clear, the explanation was counter-intuitive. The war couldn't be won with nikkei living on the West Coast, the government reasoned, but it also couldn't be won without the enlistment of Japanese Americans. It wasn't known at the time, but that contradiction would change the lives of every family at Heart Mountain, and set the stage for one of the biggest draft-resistance movements of World War II. But first they needed to celebrate Christmas.

Evergreens filled each mess hall, decorated with ornaments donated by the kindly owner of a Woolworth's in Rapid City, South Dakota. As Bing Crosby's "White Christmas" sat atop the *Billboard* charts for eleven straight weeks, the *Sentinel* suggested do-it-yourself Christmas gifts: rag rugs braided from scraps of old clothing, necklaces strung with seeds, cardboard boxes partitioned into storage for socks, handkerchiefs, and jewelry. To aid parents struggling on the WRA's measly salaries, Santa delivered presents donated by the American Friends Service Committee to the camp's 3,500 children. On Christmas Eve, tenor saxophonist George Igawa and his orchestra—a collection of musicians who refused to leave their instruments behind—performed hits by Glenn Miller and Tommy Dorsey alongside traditional Japanese melodies to a dancing crowd. Children caroled from bed to bed at the hospital, then paused at the guard tower and sang there as well. For the first time in many of the incarcerees' lives, it snowed on Christmas.

A high school student, Miyuki Aoyama, summed up much of the camp's feelings in a poem in the *Sentinel*.

> *Snow upon the rooftop,*
> *Snow upon the coal;*
> *Winter in Wyoming—*
> *Winter in my soul.*

On Christmas Day, as the temperature hovered in the teens, Tosh and Babe battled again, this time to a 6–6 tie.

As the Christmas spirit waned and the calendar revealed a second year in the camp, the political fire of Heart Mountain was stoked. Camp officials had first felt a jolt of unrest in October when thirty-two children were detained by military police for sledding on a hill just outside camp. News spread through the camp as the children, ages seven to eleven, sat in the police station waiting for their parents, holding the sleds their fathers had built out of scrap lumber. The cruelty of the act belied the WRA's position that the police were present to protect the incarcerees. Later that month, camp officials began erecting a barbed wire fence on the pretext of keeping grazing cattle at bay. The incarcerees saw through the shabby lie, and any hope the WRA had of volunteer assistance in the fence's construction evaporated. Following a meeting between the incarcerees and camp administrators, a petition was sent directly to WRA head Dillon Myer, reading in part, "If the WRA sanctions and approves such erection of fence and maintenance of towers, it seems that our status will become similar to that of internees or prisoners of war in a concentration camp. . . . Said fence and the towers are ridiculous in every respect, an insult to any free human being, a barrier to a full understanding between the administration and the residents." The fence and guard towers were completed shortly thereafter. The third-largest city in Wyoming was a prison camp.

In the first week of January an anonymous poem began circulating not only at Heart Mountain but throughout Minidoka, Poston, Tule Lake, and the other camps. It landed in the mailbox of the *Sentinel* on January 7, signed only from "The Mad Mongolian." In the decades that followed the author never revealed his or her identity, an act of defiance and selflessness that only added to the poem's power.

THAT DAMNED FENCE

They've sunk the posts deep into the ground
They've strung out wires all the way around.
With machine gun nests just over there,
And sentries and soldiers everywhere.

We're trapped like rats in a wired cage,
To fret and fume with impotent rage;
Yonder whispers the lure of the night,
But that DAMNED FENCE assails our sight.

We seek the softness of the midnight air,
But that DAMNED FENCE in the floodlight glare
Awakens unrest in our nocturnal quest,
And mockingly laughs with vicious jest.

With nowhere to go and nothing to do,
We feel terrible, lonesome, and blue:
That DAMNED FENCE is driving us crazy,
Destroying our youth and making us lazy.

Imprisoned in here for a long, long time,
We know we're punished—though we've committed no crime,
Our thoughts are gloomy and enthusiasm damp,
To be locked up in a concentration camp.

Loyalty we know, and patriotism we feel,
To sacrifice our utmost was our ideal,
To fight for our country, and die, perhaps;
But we're here because we happen to be Japs.

We all love life, and our country best,
Our misfortune to be here in the west,
To keep us penned behind that DAMNED FENCE,
Is someone's notion of NATIONAL DEFENCE!

As Heart Mountain teetered on the edge of the unknown, Babe's mind wandered to a different place, one that he'd missed for almost a year. He laced up his sneakers. Basketball season was about to start.

CHAPTER ELEVEN

Everything Is Going Along Fine

FOR THE FIRST seventeen years of Babe Nomura's life, the temperature had never dropped below freezing. In his first winter away in Wyoming, the mercury fell as far as –28°F. For eleven days in mid-January 1942 the thermometer didn't climb above –9°F. The recreation department flooded twenty-two blocks to create ice-skating rinks, which soon filled with hundreds of shaky first-time skaters and served as a popular place for high schoolers to play hooky. The barracks, finally insulated, provided scant protection for the sunny Californians. Students skipped school to escape the frostbite that awaited them on the walk there, or hid beneath newly purchased wool coats and Army surplus blankets before sprinting to the latrines. Some families opted for a metal pail first, instead of facing the cold that knifed its way along the dirt streets at night.

For a community lacking an indoor basketball court, the weather made the idea of basketball practice unrealistic. Still, the camp's recreation department had somehow managed to arrange a series of games with outside teams willing to play a team of imprisoned Japanese Americans. The mayor of Lovell, a town thirty-five miles east of Heart Mountain, had come to know the incarcerees through their work in the town's sugar beet fields and extended an invitation. So, on the afternoon of February 6, Babe and a dozen teammates piled into a truck and drove the thirty-five miles east to meet the Lovell West Ward Indians. They breathed free air, watched the camp disappear behind them, and then suffered one of the most polite demolitions anyone could possibly expect on a basketball court.

Lovell had been a town for twelve years before the Mormons arrived, and it didn't take long for the group to completely subsume the non-Mormon population. The town, along with the other Mormon communities of Byron and Cowley, represented the only other permanent white settlers in the Bighorn Basin upon Buffalo Bill Cody's arrival. There was maybe one thing the Mormons of Lovell prided themselves on equally with religious devotion, and that was basketball.

Every year, the Church of Jesus Christ of Latter-day Saints held the Mutual Improvement Association Basketball Conference championship games—pitting ten thousand teens and twenty-somethings from Mormon communities around the United States, Mexico, and Canada against one another in what the church called the largest basketball tournament in the world. Teams would square off in regional tournaments, then 2,500 spectators would pile into Salt Lake City's sweltering, musty Deseret Gymnasium every March for the finals. In 1940 and 1942, the last team standing on its polished maple floor was the Indians from Lovell, Wyoming's West Ward LDS church. Three of the team's starting five were named to the tournament's all-star team, including the sharpshooting Doerr brothers, whose accuracy was credited to their underhand shots. Defeating the Lovell West Ward Indians would've been a tall task for the Heart Mountain team. It became an impossibility with its latest addition.

Charles Roberts was new to the Bighorn Basin, a football and basketball coach at nearby Burlington High School. But there was more to him than met the eye. "Charlie" Roberts had grown up in Lehi, Utah, won divisional basketball crowns there, then went to Brigham Young University, where he lettered in basketball, football, and track, and played intramural tennis when he grew bored with dominating the other three sports. He was an all-American in football by his sophomore year, and named the most valuable athlete at BYU at the end of his senior year. In 1981 he was inducted into the BYU Athletic Hall of Fame, but on the night of February 6, 1943, at a March of Dimes fundraiser in a high school gymnasium in Lovell, Wyoming, he spent his evening beating the hell out of a team of prisoners.

The game was never close. The Indians' fast-break offense and swarming zone defense sank Heart Mountain's All-Stars into a 23–11 hole at halftime, and they never took their foot off the gas. Roberts and Norman Doerr scored a dozen apiece, good enough to beat Heart Mountain by themselves. Babe tallied only 4 points in the 45–22 thrashing. The town's mayor treated both teams to malted milkshakes after the final whistle. The crowd raised $154 for the March of Dimes, a charity founded by the president who had signed away the opposing team's freedom almost exactly a year earlier.

So, after more than a year on the sidelines, Babe's first game against outside competition was a complete dud, and it wouldn't get much better. The following Monday, the outfit sweated out a win over Byron High School, 40–37, an effort despite suiting up a player from Stanford University's freshman team and Art Kaihatsu, a Hollywood High graduate named to all-league status in Los Angeles. The camp team's lack of practice—not to mention working out on an indoor court—weighed on any potential successes, but something less avoidable was also at play: the Heart Mountain team was much shorter than their opponents. Any speed advantage was immediately negated by their opponents' heights, basketballers towering five or six inches above the All-Stars on average. Babe, just 5-foot-10, played off-position as the starting center.

Three weeks after the drubbing at the hands of the Lovell West Ward Indians, Heart Mountain returned to Lovell High for the first interscholastic game in the camp's history. (During the winter the school competed in a free-throw contest with high schools from across both Montana and Wyoming; the results were mailed in to the *Billings Gazette* each week. Heart Mountain came in second in its division.)

Babe, finally competing against players his own age, shot out of the gate, scoring 9 points and leading his team to a 21–16 advantage at halftime. It wouldn't last. "Lovell Drubs Prep Cagers," the *Sentinel* headline read the following week. The final score was 50–27. Heart Mountain was outscored 34 to 6 in the second half; Babe didn't score another point.

The junior varsity team fared just as poorly. Led by an East Hollywood-by-way-of-Hawai'i sophomore named Stan Igawa and a promising, quiet teen named Keiichi Ikeda, Lovell nearly tripled up the team 41–14. The only highlight of the trip was when Lovell fed the teams a steak dinner before the game and then another one afterward.

Life in camp was in no way reminiscent of home, but small concessions by the WRA staff helped. Two movie theaters, the Dawn and the Pagoda, opened, drawing sellout crowds. Between October 1942 and the close of camp, attendance for film screenings topped 600,000, good enough for every incarceree to have seen nearly sixty movies. The first audience watched *Freckles Comes Home*, a sixty-three-minute action-comedy shot two blocks from Stan's middle school in Los Angeles. Tickets cost 10 cents for adults and 5 cents for kids six and up. With few other options to distract moviegoers, over the next three years the theaters took in more than $770,000 in 2019 dollars.

After four flailing months camp administrators recognized that recreational programming was best left to the incarcerees themselves. Officials arranged the acquisition of three former CCC buildings, plopped them in the middle of camp, and the Heart Mountain recreation center was established. Soon the recreation center and mess halls were stuffed with activities. Incarcerees taught sewing, knitting, embroidery, shorthand, bookkeeping, flower arrangement, bridge, drama, and sixteen other subjects. Classes for Go, a board game, were offered for twelve hours every day, in two separate blocks. *Shodo*, the calligraphic depiction of the Japanese language, was offered Tuesday through Friday, from 7 to 9 p.m. If you walked by Barrack 9-25-N at seven on any night but Sunday you'd be greeted by the wafting chants of *shigin*, Japanese poetry. Sixty-person kabuki performances drew five hundred spectators.

Wood carving classes led to handmade signs for the front doors of each apartment. The Nomuras hung a 16-by-8-inch depiction of Hyohei's voyage to America, Mount Fuji looming as a boat set off across the Pacific. On the back was a small map of the city of Heart Mountain's thirty blocks, the small piece of wood a depiction of his entire life's journey. Six thousand of the camp's nearly eleven thousand inhabitants participated in at least one of the classes. Not that the WRA would let them have complete free rein.

"It was general policy to discourage Japanese type[s] of entertainment," wrote community activities supervisor T. J. O'Mara in his 1945 final report. "American sports were emphasized. Some Japanese entertainment, while not sponsored, was permitted, but it was always previewed and censored before permits were issued."

Buddhist, Protestant, and Catholic churches, Boy Scout and Girl Scout troops, five post offices, five child-care facilities, three community stores, a library, a courthouse—despite the guns and the cold and the barbed wire, they were going to try their damnedest to make this place home.

Heart Mountain headed back to the community of Byron on March 12. In an effort to buoy the spirits of not only the team but the student body, the school administration held a pep rally, and that night it hosted the Sink Byron Benefit Dance. Tickets cost 10 cents, which would go to defray the transportation for the team. (The WRA was increasingly okay with the students leaving for games, but that leniency did not come with a budget.) Open only to couples, the dance's main draw was a quarter-by-quarter update of the game, live via telephone. The announcer would be Horse.

While Babe and Stan were busy getting whipped on the basketball court, Horse was equally thrashed that month in a bid for class
president. Hoping to cash in on his popularity and his experience as
class president at Mountain View, he ran against Ted Fujioka, a
classmate of Babe's in Hollywood, and the student who brought the
flagpole to Heart Mountain High School. Horse was crushed. "He
got 350 votes and I must have got ten," he later recalled. (The actual
tally wasn't nearly as dire, but was certainly a landslide: Ted 885,
Horse 454.)

Licking his wounds, he accompanied the team to Byron. That
night, the only thing to dampen the mood of George Igawa's orchestra
lilting to seventy-five dancing couples was Horse's reports. Byron beat
Heart Mountain almost as badly as Lovell had, 42–20. The team then
finished out its winless season with a 37–32 loss to Cowley. Babe
scored nearly 40 percent of the team's points, but it wasn't close to
enough.

Despite their athletic misfortunes, in March the school held a vote
for its colors and mascot. No longer content with being anonymous,
the student body took to the polls.

"Swooping down out of the brilliant blue of the sky, swift and true
in flight, the eagle, high-flying symbol of the American Republic, has
been chosen as the symbol for Heart Mt. High School," according to
the March 17 *Echoes*. "Matching their colors to the natural habitat of
the eagles, the students chose the blue of the air he travels in and the
white of the mountain peaks he frequents."

When Lieutenant Ray McDaniels and his Army recruitment team arrived at Heart Mountain on February 6, they expected a model camp.
The 10,700 incarcerees had been presented that way to the Army by
the WRA, a product of omission and sleight of hand on the part of new
camp project director Guy Robertson. Any disturbance—over a barbed
wire fence or the arrest of children for sledding, say—was minimized,

its sharpness dulled by camp officials' reports back to Washington. That practice would soon be impossible to continue.

In late January, the War Department—in coordination with and approval of both the WRA and the Japanese American Citizens League—announced plans to create a segregated, all-nisei combat unit. Service would be voluntary, and draw from across the mainland and the Hawaiian Islands, including WRA camps. The JACL actually fought in favor of *drafting* nisei, opposing the War Department's voluntary tack. Their belief, however misguided, was that nisei men should be treated like any other Americans despite their present imprisoned status.

In allowing Japanese American men to fight, the Army would gain much-needed soldiers; out of 10,000 eligible men, it hoped 3,600 would volunteer. Part of this was precedent. There were already Japanese Americans serving in the armed forces: on the day of the Pearl Harbor attacks, nearly 5,000 nisei were enlisted as soldiers. But the attacks changed everything. Their weapons and ammunition were confiscated. They drilled with wooden rifles, toy soldiers among live ones. They cleaned latrines and performed other menial tasks. In less than three months, on Easter Sunday 1943, Franklin D. Roosevelt would visit Fort Riley, inspecting the Kansas facility's war preparations. As Roosevelt listened to an Army band concert, his Scottish terrier, Fala, on his lap, forty-two nisei soldiers were driven ten miles away to spend the morning mending fences and digging holes. Another 120 of the base's nisei marched in single file into an airplane hangar and wedged onto temporary bleachers, guarded by their fellow soldiers' .30-caliber machine guns. After sitting in silence for four hours, trailed by drawn pistol even to the latrines, the men were released to their barracks. One soldier complained in a letter to the War Department. The note was intercepted; he was demoted.

While the new combat unit would provide the Army with men, it granted the Office of War Information an important piece of propaganda: an all-nisei unit would counter Japanese propaganda that the war was a racial one, waged to defend the Far East against "Caucasian imperialism."

"It is the inherent right of every faithful citizen, regardless of ancestry, to bear arms in the nation's fight," said War Secretary Henry Stimson, who less than twelve months earlier demanded the imprisonment of the same faithful citizens. "When obstacles to the free expression of that right are imposed by emergency consideration, those barriers should be removed as soon as humanly possible. Loyalty to a country is a voice that must be heard, and I am glad that I am now able to give active proof that this basic American belief is not a casualty of war."

The *Sentinel*, whose editor, Bill Hosokawa, was long derided by some of the more politically minded incarcerees as little more than a mouthpiece for the WRA, proved its opponents right with an editorial supporting Stimson's plan. Entitled "Vindication," it called Stimson's plan an "epic milestone in the long uphill battle to re-establish our positions as Americans" and praised the secretary's statement, saying it "may well become a classic quotation in the history of democracy."

The prisoners of Heart Mountain were stunned. A year ago they weren't loyal enough to live on the West Coast, but today they were loyal enough to fight in the Army? The confusion was compounded by the distribution of Selective Service Form 304A. Formally it was entitled "Statement of United States Citizen of Japanese Ancestry." Informally it became known simply as the loyalty questionnaire. Versions of the form had been in use by the WRA to determine whether an incarceree should be cleared for outside work or resettlement. (Though nikkei were forbidden from returning to the West Coast, the WRA encouraged and even cajoled them to move to other parts of the country.) The questionnaire was deceptively bland, especially when taken in concert with the Army's announcement.

The vast majority of the questions pertained to basic information: family members, past residences, educational levels, language skills, religion, recreational activities, affiliations with associations, even reading materials. Unbeknownst to the incarcerees, though, was a point system designed by Census Bureau statistician Calvin Dedrick to help determine the loyalty of each respondent. Take question 16, for example: "Religion." Those who answered Christian were granted two points. Those who answered Buddhist were deducted a point. Any who answered Shinto were immediately denied clearance. Respondents were similarly rejected outright if they admitted to traveling to Japan three or more times, made substantial contributions to organizations connected to the Japanese armed forces, or ever applied for repatriation to Japan. The last two questions, though, drew the most attention.

> **Question 27:** *Are you willing to serve in the armed forces of the United States on combat duty, wherever ordered?*
>
> **Question 28:** *Will you swear unqualified allegiance to the United States of America and faithfully defend the United States from any and all attacks by foreign and domestic forces, and forswear any form of allegiance or obedience to the Japanese Emperor, or any other foreign government, power, or organization?*

When taken in conjunction with Stimson's announcement, to nisei men Question 27 seemed little more than an invitation to the front lines. It also raised a more philosophical question: *Am I willing to defend the country that imprisoned, and continues to imprison, my family?* Question 28 was a slap in the face to not just nisei men, but all issei and nisei. For issei the question was impossible to answer without becoming, in a sense, stateless. Since issei were barred from U.S. citizenship, what did "yes" actually mean? And if they said "no," would they be deported? Nisei resented being asked to renounce their loyalty to an emperor they'd never served, from a country that many had never even visited.

Confusion reigned, and into that confusion stepped Lieutenant Ray McDaniels, whose only job was to spend the next ten days convincing American teenagers to fight for a government that put them behind barbed wire. He gave a series of informational speeches, promising, with little basis in the truth, that "your government would not take these steps unless it intended in going further in restoring you to a normal place in the life of the country, with the privileges and obligations of other American citizens." His messages back to Washington were optimistic. "Everything is going along fine," he wrote. "There is a lot of enthusiasm."

On the morning of registration, five hundred incarcerees calmly approached McDaniels and his team. They asked the lieutenant to delay registration until the questions of loyalty were answered and politely threatened to kick over the team's table if they did not comply. Stunned and hesitant to escalate the situation, McDaniels relented. He met with the men, repeating Stimson's and Roosevelt's platitudes on the subjects of loyalty, honor, and citizenship. The crowd, crammed into a mess hall, wasn't buying it. UCLA senior Frank Inouye stood and read his own list of grievances, needling McDaniels on the hypocrisy of the government imprisoning 120,000 Japanese Americans only to ask them a year later to pick up a gun and die for that same government. He demanded the government acknowledge his rights as a citizen. McDaniels attempted to stammer out a rebuttal but was drowned out by the crowd. The plan disintegrated in front of his eyes.

To channel their grievances, the men formed the Heart Mountain Congress of American Citizens, and set to work derailing what meager hope remained in the War Department's plan. They whittled their complaints down to four subjects:

— clarification of nisei citizenship status
— publicizing that clarification to the American public, by Roosevelt, Stimson, and Attorney General Biddle
— postponement of registration until clarification is achieved
— implied consent of the nisei to serve in the armed forces upon clarification of their citizenship status

The final point was contentious. For obvious personal and political reasons, many didn't want to serve in the Army. At the same time, they didn't want to lose their citizenship. After debate, the Congress decided a qualified response to Question 27 was the most effective means to bargaining. Many disagreed. Frank Emi, a twenty-six-year-old produce stand owner from Los Angeles, hand-printed his responses to Questions 27 and 28 and tacked them up in the camp's latrines and mess halls. "Under the present conditions and circumstances," he wrote. "I am unable to answer these questions." Kiyoshi Okamoto, a cursing, ACLU-donating soil engineer, tore the registration process to the ground, citing the Constitution and Bill of Rights in another mess hall meeting. The government trampled their rights the minute they opened the camps, he argued; it shouldn't be rewarded with appeasement. The crowd was impressed and surprised by the deep legal knowledge of this crass soil expert.

McDaniels's recruitment—and virtually all activities in camp—came to a standstill.

By February 18, Project Director Robertson was weary. He denied the Congress's request to telephone representatives in the nine other camps, and strong-armed the *Sentinel* into avoiding coverage of the debacle. Then, in a camp-wide note, he threatened the incarcerees:

> *Any willful interference, threat, intimidation, or false rumor is a violation of the Espionage and Sedition laws of the United States and carries a penalty of a $10,000 fine or imprisonment for not more than 20 years, or both. It is the duty of every citizen to report any such violation. Citizens should answer an unqualified "yes" or "no" to question 28.*

A week passed. Little changed.

"Let me again bring to the attention of the people of Heart Mountain that your response to the present registration will have an important bearing on your future," he wrote on February 25. "The eyes of the nation are upon you. Your loyalty to this country will be judged by your answers."

By early March he was livid. In a memo to Heart Mountain community leaders, he chided them for their registration efforts and questioned their loyalty: "Whether the parents realize that life-long stigma will be borne by the children who fail to assume their responsibility in a democratic government will reflect upon your often-mentioned desire to continue to live as good citizens."

Behind the scenes, things were falling apart for Robertson. In a memo from February 6, just before McDaniels arrived, Robertson suggested that two hundred men had expressed interest in volunteering but "the figure will undoubtedly increase." On February 13 he told WRA director Dillon Myer that the Heart Mountain Congress was "not so boisterous as they were. . . . I feel today that the situation is gradually easing up." By March 6, while expressing indignation publicly, he was cowed by Myer.

"For the past 30 days I have been trying, through the group leaders in the camp, to work up an enthusiastic response to the combat unit," he wrote. "However, the results speak pretty plainly."

In his final note on the subject, Robertson groveled.

"I am very sorry that I was not able to develop any favorable leadership in either the issei or nisei group during the progress of registration."

The War Department eventually caved to the Heart Mountain Congress's demands and allowed conditional responses to Questions 27 and 28. For some, it was too late. Faced with the choice of swearing allegiance to a country that wouldn't allow them to become citizens, 151 issei instead elected for repatriation to Japan, to return to a country they'd left decades earlier. Faced with the choice of fighting a war for a country that had stripped them of their rights, 329 nisei elected for expatriation, to move to a country of their ancestors—a country in which none of them had been born.

Babe filled out the form in pencil, in a quiet, stylish cursive that would bring him pride for the rest of his life. He told the War Department that he read *Life* magazine and the *Los Angeles Times*, and classified his Japanese reading, writing, and speaking skills as "poor." He donated 10 cents to the March of Dimes in Hollywood and another 30 cents at Heart Mountain. The Red Cross received a dollar. When asked whether he was willing to serve in the armed forces, he told the United States "no, until all branch of service is open." He swore unqualified allegiance to the United States, then signed his name. Indicative of his personality, Horse filled out his form entirely in capital letters, save for his i's. He worked as a valet at a Stanford University parking lot and as a fruit canner and ranch hand for a Mountain View neighbor named Richard Woffle. He was a Buddhist, swore unqualified allegiance to the United States, and was unwilling to serve in the armed forces until his citizenship status was clarified.

Lieutenant Ray McDaniels arrived at Heart Mountain Relocation Center with 1,700 possible volunteers before him. He left with thirty-eight. Only nineteen were inducted into the Army.

CHAPTER TWELVE

A Determined Effort to See the Job Through

On the morning of April 13, 1943, Harold Brest, James Boarman, Floyd Hamilton, and Fred Hunter trussed and gagged two armed guards, stripped to their underwear, smeared themselves with industrial grease, slid out of a workshop window, stumbled down a cliff, scaled a barbed wire fence, and broke out of Alcatraz.

Boarman was shot first, knocked unconscious by rifle fire. Brest held on to his limp body and the two men bobbed in San Francisco Bay, the grease doing little to fight the icy water. As a prison launch approached the men, Boarman slipped from Brest's grasp, sinking, never to be found. Prison officials captured Brest and soon found Hunter hiding in a cave. They filled the cave with tear gas and he surrendered without a fight. Hamilton was presumed dead until he was found two days later, under a pile of materials in a prison storeroom. After witnessing the gunfire and the tear gas and the hypothermia, he snuck back in through the window he had climbed out of, hoping his absence wasn't noticed. Warden James Johnston called it the most sensational escape attempt in the penitentiary's history. As it unfolded, in the offices of the Western Defense Command high above San Francisco Bay, General John DeWitt prepared for his testimony before the House Naval Affairs Committee.

He'd spent the prior weeks scoffing at the War Department's loyalty questionnaire, unwavering in the necessity and appropriateness of the camps. While much of the War Department recognized the rapidly decreasing likelihood of a Japanese attack on the West Coast and was actively discussing how and when to ease restrictions on nikkei or allow their new volunteer nisei unit to move freely back to the coast, DeWitt was adamant. He called the questionnaire a "sign of weakness" and "an admission of an original mistake." At the same time, his plan was wending its way to the U.S. Supreme Court, after the Ninth Circuit Court of Appeals pushed up the cases of Gordon Hirabayashi and Minoru Yasui—convicted of refusing to report to a temporary detention center and purposely violating curfew restrictions, respectively. So, during the House committee meeting, a brief, fifteen-minute session on the effects of large military bases on local communities, DeWitt unloaded.

"There is a false sentiment on the part of certain individuals and some organizations to get the Japanese back on the West Coast," he said. "I don't want any of them here. They are a dangerous element. There is no way to determine their loyalty. . . . There is a feeling developing, I think, in certain sections of the country, that the Japanese should be allowed to return. I am opposing it with every proper means at my disposal."

The next day, seemingly unsated with having raked his superiors in just a congressional setting, DeWitt held an off-the-record meeting with reporters. It quickly leaked.

"As I told the War Department, the Japanese government finding out we are bringing these men in, it is the ideal place to infiltrate men in uniform," he said. "A Jap is a Jap. The War Department says a Jap-American soldier is not a Jap; he is American. Well, all right. I said, I have the Jap situation to take care of and I'm going to do it."

The comments ran on the front page of the *Sentinel* and other camp newspapers. Stimson and the rest of the War Department in Washington were furious. Combined with the failed recruitment efforts of McDaniels and his colleagues, relations between the department, the WRA, and the incarcerees were fraying. DeWitt still had one supporter, though. In a statement that ran in newspapers across California, Native Sons of the Golden West grand president Lloyd Cosgrove applauded his actions, saying, "No one should have his testimony given more serious consideration than a person who is on the scene and who has studied California's Japanese emergency problem, and that man is General John L. DeWitt."

Despite DeWitt's comments, the WRA pressed on with a more liberal leave stance, allowing individual camp project directors instead of Washington officials to approve indefinite leave—moving to any part of the United States save the West Coast. Realizing it was cheaper to pay the incarcerees to leave than to continue to provide them with food, shelter, and an education, the WRA promised a coach train ticket and $8 a day for meals en route to their new home, plus a no-strings-attached $100 if the applicant could prove that he or she lacked the funds to move.

Ads flooded the *Sentinel*.

Housemaid and chauffeur in home of doctor. Man must be 38 years or older and draft exempt. Wages—if experienced $100 per month with meals; if inexperienced $75 per month with meals. Denver, Colo.

Ten or twelve girls to operate power sewing machines on piecework basis. Wages minimum 40 cents per hour; possible to earn 80 cents to $1 if highly skilled. Hours 8 a.m.–4:30 p.m. Rockford Ill.

Four automobile mechanics, Milwaukee, Wisconsin.

Couple to work on small farm, Overland Park, Kansas.

Five steam cleaners, Cleveland, Ohio.

The jobs piled up until dozens and then hundreds of opportunities sat on the other side of the fence. Families split up, fathers

heading to Indiana or Utah or Michigan and making ten times the
$16-a-month wages paid by the WRA and sending the extra back to
their wives and children in the camp. Jobs were the easy part; housing was a different story. Cities were crammed with men and women
moving in to work in the defense industry, straining the housing
market. Racism only compounded that difficulty, for both Japanese
Americans and African Americans arriving from the South. For
those leaving the camps, the process was aided by two dozen hostels
opened in cities from Minneapolis to Boston. Usually just a few
rooms, the boardinghouses were sponsored by Quaker, Baptist, Lutheran, Unitarian, and other Christian communities. Demand was
high: in one Cincinnati hostel, 777 nikkei passed through the twenty-
four beds in less than three years. The churches hosted teas and
Christmas parties, and welcomed the new arrivals to not only their
congregations but their cities.

On April 1, Babe submitted his first leave request. Even though
he hadn't graduated yet, school was an afterthought. His grades had
never been stellar—As and Bs in gym and woodshop, Cs, Ds, and an
occasional F in the remainder of his classes—and he was placed on
the vocational track at Heart Mountain High School. He muddled
through with Bs and Cs in mechanical drawing and general art
classes, but knew school only as a means to play sports. His leave request was for Hartford, Connecticut, and the promise of a job serving
tables at a sandwich shop. While he waited, he took out his baseball
glove.

Wyoming's winter had finally broken, the blitzes that would freeze
icicles horizontal against the wind now a memory in the 60-degree
sun. Incarcerees cleared and leveled 1,100 acres and dug a mile-long
canal to fulfill Buffalo Bill Cody's dream of an irrigated desert. Farmers from Washington's Yakima Valley recognized the harsh planting
conditions from home and built a system of small greenhouses to pro-

tect fledgling broccoli, cabbage, cauliflower, pepper, and tomato plants from any late frosts. Once planted, each seedling received a small wax-paper "hot cap" to protect it from the wind. Farmers planted forty-five different crops, including traditional Japanese produce like daikon radish, burdock root, *shirouri* melon, and *shungiku* greens. Mess halls replaced tinny canned vegetables with not only fresh vegetables but ones that were actually part of the Japanese American diet. That year's harvest reaped 2.1 million pounds of produce, so much that the camp shipped some to other WRA camps. Like their neighbors back home, incarcerees planted small victory gardens. Industrious groups scoured the base of Heart Mountain for wild black mustard grass, filling sacks and bandanas with the young greens before pickling them into *tsuke-mono*. Two thousand five hundred trees and shrubs were planted, soon to blossom and provide at least a nodding defense against the dust storms that made just spotting a barrack across the street an impossibility.

Gone were the green outfields of Southern California, though, replaced by a dusty, pebble-filled softball field in the shadow of the WRA administration building. Babe crouched in the dust between second and third base waiting for something, anything, to happen. His presence at shortstop was an anomaly. The position was nearly always manned by right-handers, who wouldn't have to contort their bodies to make the throw to first base. But Babe's talent and athleticism were too great to hide in the outfield. So he bent his knees, shifted back and forth, and waited. Five thousand fans stared back, a number that would've made the crowd the sixth-largest city in Wyoming.

That April afternoon the Lovell High School Bulldogs' visit to the softball diamond marked the first interscholastic game played in the Heart Mountain Relocation Center, and the newly named Eagles were ready to return the beating from the winter's basketball contest. Instead of on the court, Charlie Roberts was now coaching, leaving his athletic prowess on the sidelines. The physical advantage of the Bulldogs that was so evident on the basketball court was erased on the softball field, and the Eagles took advantage, plating 11 runs in the second inning alone. The Bulldogs managed only two hits the whole afternoon, and Heart Mountain High School won its first game ever.

It would be the last interscholastic softball game played at the school. A return game the following week was canceled for unknown reasons, and a home-and-home series with Worland High never materialized. As the school year came to a close, so did the window on Babe's high school playing career. Never again would he sprint down the basketball court, shedding defenders along the way. Never again would he drop a perfectly weighted touchdown pass into his receiver's arms, or turn a double play. He'd achieve all of these again, maybe, but never in a high school uniform. He was a month away from high school graduation, and light-years away from his dreams.

The same day, eight hundred miles away in southern Arizona, Eleanor Roosevelt walked into her first concentration camp.

Since the signing of Executive Order 9066 the previous winter, the first couple's relationship had been strained. Eleanor Roosevelt was blindsided by the order, which she viewed as "a violation of everything she understood about her husband's commitment to law and justice, and everything she believed represented America," wrote biographer Blanche Wiesen Cook. Her anger was personal, but also political. If he could issue an executive order *imprisoning* Japanese Americans, what was stopping him from issuing one that did the opposite: allowing the rescue, removal, and entry of Jews across Europe? Once his closest confidant, Eleanor was now sidelined, unaware of even her husband's gravest decisions.

In February, Mrs. Roosevelt received a letter from a Seattle woman named E. Harriet Gipson. The contents of the letter are lost to time, but they prompted the first lady to forward the note to Congressman John Tolan. His response stunned the first lady, who was evidently unaware of the exact details behind the War Department's decision the year earlier. Tolan explained that no instances of sabotage by Japanese Americans had ever been discovered, and the rumors of nikkei involvement in Pearl Harbor were equally baseless.

"The evacuation itself and subsequent developments to date have not tended to clear up the confusion and doubt in the public mind concerning loyalty of the Japanese-Americans," he wrote.

So Mrs. Roosevelt set to clearing up that confusion. She wrote to WRA head Dillon Myer and eventually convinced her husband to allow her to visit one of the camps. (Her suggestion that, as an indication of their loyalty, a Japanese American family move into the White House was rejected.) After a state dinner with Mexican president Manuel Ávila Camacho in Monterrey, Nuevo León, the Roosevelts inspected a naval air station in Corpus Christi, Texas, then the two parted, with Eleanor boarding a train for Phoenix. She spent the night at the Hotel Westward Ho, the tallest building in Arizona, and then drove forty miles south, past the two-story saguaro cactuses, to the thirteen-thousand-incarceree Gila River Relocation Center, "desert country which flowers only when water is brought to it," she wrote in her *My Day* column. She met alone with six members of the camp's community council; all they asked for was a cooler for the hospital, which "would be much appreciated by the tuberculosis patients." She toured the mess halls, declared the milk spoiled, and looked out over the seven thousand acres of produce planted by the incarcerees.

Though some of her words came across as mixed messages—in a comment that some interpreted as victim-blaming, she encouraged the incarcerees to spread out and assimilate after the war instead of retrenching in Japanese American communities—an interview at the *Los Angeles Times* three days later spelled out what seemed to be her true feelings.

"'A Japanese is always a Japanese' is an easily accepted phrase and it has taken hold quite naturally on the West Coast because of fear, but it leads nowhere and solves nothing," she said.

A Japanese-American may be no more Japanese than a German-American is German, or an Italian-American is Italian, or of any other national background. All of these people, including the Japanese Americans, have men who are fighting today for the preservation of the democratic way of life and the ideas around which our nation was built.

We have no common race in this country, but we have an ideal to which all of us are loyal: we cannot progress if we look down upon any group of people amongst us because of race or religion. Every citizen in this country has a right to our basic freedoms, to justice and to equality of opportunity. We retain the right to lead our individual lives as we please, but we can only do so if we grant to others the freedoms that we wish for ourselves.

The Japanese American community gained a quick ally in Mrs. Roosevelt. In her most public opposition of the war, she advocated for the closure of the camps, saying, "The sooner we get the young Japanese out of the camps, the better. Otherwise if we don't look out we will create another Indian problem." She convinced her husband to meet with Myer, something Franklin Roosevelt had not done in the year of Myer's service. She dedicated her next two *My Day* columns to the camps, and wrote an article for *Collier's* magazine in which she penned perhaps the most succinct description of anti-Japanese sentiment ever written: "This happened because, in one part of our country, they were feared as competitors, and the rest of our country knew them so little and cared so little about them that they did not even think about the principle that we in this country believe in: that of equal rights for all human beings."

Roosevelt's impression stood in stark contrast to a series of stories that ran the next day in *The Denver Post*. Written by sportswriter Jack Carberry and entitled "Hostile Group Is Pampered at Wyoming Camp," it was a total takedown of Heart Mountain. Carberry claimed the camp's cooks were hiding food in the attics, that incarcerees were trading food caches for whiskey, and that high-end tractors were being used not for tilling the earth, but for races. His source was Earl Best, a disgruntled assistant steward who had resigned his position earlier in the month and was, as the facts would bear out, a prolific liar. Carberry spent parts of two days at the camp, but the majority of his time in Wyoming was at the bar at the Hotel Irma in downtown Cody. Camp director Guy Robertson fired back, though in doing so he inadvertently proved the miserable conditions he perpetuated: the camp spent 36.8 cents on food per person, per day, he told the Associated Press, though the WRA allowed him to spend up to 45 cents.

Angry letters flooded the offices of Wyoming's senators. The incarcerees were called a "lazy and shiftless lot," and one letter suggested the camp "be segregated by sex because we don't need more little Japs." The town councils of Cody and Powell met in a joint session that week, both passing petitions that called for increased security at the camp and a guarantee the incarcerees would be moved out of Wyoming after the war. (State officials had already protected the Equality State's political interests by passing a blatantly unconstitutional bill that February barring anyone "brought into . . . Wyoming by the WRA" and "interned in a relocation center or concentration camp" from voting in any election in the state.) The story quickly earned the attention of Wyoming's junior senator, E. V. Robertson. In office just four months, the Cody resident—and Welsh immigrant—took to the Senate floor and accused the WRA of "petting and pampering" the incarcerees, many of whom "profess loyalty to Hirohito and his war regime." He urged the WRA to return control of the camps to the Army, and implied that incarcerees who passed a dam on the way to the camp's sawmill might sabotage the installation. There was nothing to stop incarcerees out on work details from purchasing firearms, he said, possibly forgetting the near impossibility that any Wyoming firearm dealer would sell a gun to them.

Upon his next visit home, the camp's block leaders sent a telegram to the Cody resident, asking him to visit. He signed for the telegram but never responded. When approached by a WRA employee at a Cody restaurant and invited to the camp, which sat a fifteen-minute drive away, Robertson refused. He was "too busy." He never visited the camp.

Later that fall, the source of the conflict, Earl Best, was arrested for forgery in Los Angeles. After his conviction he was deported to Canada, his home country, and from where he'd snuck into the United States at least two times. The instigator of all the lies was an unlawful resident.

On June 10, Ernest J. Goppert, a Cody attorney and the Wyoming state commander of the American Legion, took to the stage and addressed the first graduating class of Heart Mountain High School: "To all those of you who are good loyal American citizens, there is given the job of so living and conducting yourselves—that your fellow citizens who are hoping to see restored to you your privileges and rights of American citizenship, are not embarrassed by your failure, be it ever so slight, of your duties and obligations as Americans."

No one recognized, or at least vocalized, the disrespect of allowing a state commander of an organization partly responsible for the removal of 120,000 nikkei from the West Coast to address an auditorium full of those very people.

As the girls' glee club sang "I Hear America Singing," Babe sat in the audience, though he shouldn't have been there. He had failed English. Well, to be more accurate, Babe *had been failing* English on April 15, 1942, when his family was removed from their home and sent to live at a horse track. So by the spring of 1943, when school officials at Heart Mountain were finally working their way out from the landslide of transcripts that come with thousands of students, they realized that Tamotsu Nomura would be one credit shy of graduating on time.

Nevertheless, school officials allowed him to graduate, stipulating he'd need to complete one last class to receive his diploma. The next morning, instead of waiting for summer school to begin, he packed a bag, boarded a train, and headed to eastern Washington.

The Northern Pacific Railroad Company is seeking two crews of 80 men each for work in Western Montana, Idaho and Eastern Washington.

O. H. Underwood, representative, revealed that wages have been raised from 52 cents to 56 cents an hour for eight hours a day and time and a half after nine hours. Each worker will be charged $8.75 per week for subsistence.

—Heart Mountain Sentinel *supplement, March 23, 1943*

With little but boredom to fill his time, Babe joined 140 other men from Heart Mountain and took off for Hatton, Washington. Hatton was a town in name only, a forty-person dot on an arid patch of Washington so scoured by cataclysmic floods that planetary scientists believe it is perhaps the best analog on earth of Mars's outflow channels. Temporary leave permit in hand, and following in the footsteps of the thousands of issei who built the railroads a generation earlier, Babe set to work. He wasn't alone.

In the year since arriving at Heart Mountain, the camp had sprouted a dozen social clubs: the Kiowas, the Alpha Victory Club, the Hi-Jinx, the Herculites, the Starlettes, the Double Cs. Babe and Horse were Jackrabbits, a group comprising eighteen mostly Los Angeles and Hollywood boys, with Horse wedged in. They wore dark letterman jackets with white and black striped cuffs. Their logo, an impish embroidered jackrabbit, sat on the left chest, right above their names. Babe served as athletic manager for the club the first year; Horse took the reins the second year. They'd find a kind mess hall cook willing to let them use their building, push the wooden picnic tables to the side, and host monthly dances with names like Moonlight Mood and April

Showers and Blue Champagne. They'd find some bootleg liquor made from fermented raisins and add it to some fruit punch and *bang*— "super punch." When the lights came on at the end of this night and the railroad called a little bit later, most of the graduating Jackrabbits headed to Hatton. The morning after graduation, Babe and Omar Kaihatsu were the first to leave.

The conditions in their new destination were brutal. Ninety-degree temperatures, under a sky that gifted only a quarter-inch of rain a month. Babe worked a stretch between Lind and Ellensburg, the latter a six-thousand-person town that passed as a metropolis as far as that segment of rail was concerned. Even for athletes, the work was relentless. Hauling and laying track, clearing brush, setting ties; nothing on the softball or football fields could prepare you for it. Less than three weeks after leaving Heart Mountain, on June 27, Babe sent a handwritten note to Frank A. Brown, a relocation officer in the WRA's employment division a hundred miles away in Spokane.

> *Dear Sir,*
>
> *Resigning from Extra Gang #2, I, Tamotsu Babe Nomura, would like to obtain a traveling permit to Wyoming + also would like to ask you whether if it is permissible for me to stay at Spokane for a few days on my way back.*
>
> *I intend to return to Heart Mountain, Wyoming, leaving here July sixth, nineteen hundred + forty three to relocate myself to continue school. Would appreciate your prompt reply.*
>
> *Respectfully Yours,*
> *Tamotsu Babe Nomura*

The WRA's position at the time was to try and relocate as many incarcerees as possible. Brown's response reflected that push.

"Although you may find the work rather strenuous during your breaking-in period, we feel that you should take pride in working for the railroad during this emergency," he said. "Maintenance of the

The Nomura family in 1925, outside their Hollywood boardinghouse. *(Babe Nomura Family Photo Collection)*

Babe was athletically inclined from a young age. He dominated Japanese American basketball and baseball leagues before taking up football. *(Babe Nomura Family Photo Collection)*

The Yoshinagas. As strawberry farmers, George and his family moved frequently across Northern California before Pearl Harbor. *(Courtesy of Yoshinaga family)*

Babe, in a 1941 game for Hollywood High School. The famed Hollywood Roosevelt Hotel is in the background. *(Babe Nomura Family Photo Collection)*

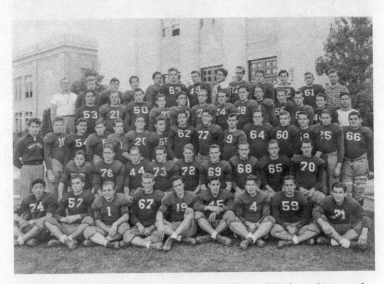

In 1941 the Japanese American population at Hollywood High was big enough to have its own student organization, but Babe *(bottom left)* was the only nisei member of the school football team. *(Babe Nomura Family Photo Collection)*

The promise of good pay and steady work brought workers from across the West to construct the barracks at Heart Mountain. *(San José State University Special Collections and Archives)*

In the fall of 1942, one of the first improvements incarcerees made at Heart Mountain was the construction of a baseball diamond. The field was a welcome distraction for the next three years. *(Japanese American National Museum [Gift of Mori Shimada, 92.10.2BI])*

Heart Mountain, at night. *(National Archives photo no. 210-G-E98)*

Babe, Horse, and Keiichi Ikeda pose during the 1943 football season. *(Babe Nomura Family Photo Collection)*

With only limited entertainment options, football fans lined the field for every game, no matter the temperature. *(National Archives photo no. 210-G-G213)*

Babe, Horse, and the Jackrabbits social club take on a camp All-Star team on Thanksgiving Day 1943. *(National Archives photo no. 210-G-G234)*

Babe (*second from left*) helps force Tosh Asano (*right*) out of bounds during the 1943 Thanksgiving game. The two battled for years for the title of Heart Mountain's best athlete. *(National Archives photo no. 210-G-G198)*

More than a dozen social clubs sprouted in camp, and the groups often held fundraising dances. *(National Archives photo no. 210-G-G224)*

Babe and Horse (*top row, third and fourth from right*) pose with the Jackrabbits social club. Most of the Jackrabbits were from Los Angeles; they made an exception for Horse. (*Babe Nomura Family Photo Collection*)

Meals were served cafeteria-style, a stress on families attempting to maintain their prewar family traditions. (*National Archives photo no. 210-G-E134*)

Fire was a constant worry in camp, as quickly constructed barracks were combined with poorly insulated stoves. The camp's all-volunteer fire department was the top-rated department in Wyoming. (*Japanese American National Museum [Gift of Mori Shimada, 92.10.2BY])*

Paul Nakadate, one of the leaders of the Heart Mountain Fair Play Committee, with his son, Tomio. (*National Archives photo no. 210-G-E715*)

The 1944 Heart Mountain All-Star baseball team, with Tosh Asano (*top row, left*), Babe Nomura (*top row, fourth from left*), and fellow Eagle Bill Shundo (*top row, second from right*). The team played visitors from Gila River Relocation Center. *(Japanese American National Museum [Gift of Mori Shimada, 92.10.2B])*

Yoichi Hosozawa bats down a Worland pass during a September 1944 game. Brothers Shuzo and Poly Sumii provide backup. *(Heart Mountain Wyoming Foundation Collection)*

Shiro Teramoto snags a touchdown during the Eagles 60–0 blowout of Carbon County in October 1944. The 60 points were the most scored by a Wyoming high school in nearly four years. *(Heart Mountain Wyoming Foundation Collection)*

George "Crazy Legs" Yahiro breaks free for a long run against Worland. He scored the only touchdown in the Eagles' 7–0 victory. *(Heart Mountain Wyoming Foundation Collection)*

The 1944 Heart Mountain Eagles, coached by Babe Nomura (*middle row, far right*).
(*Heart Mountain Wyoming Foundation Collection*)

Mas Ogimachi attempts to tackle all-state Natrona County fullback LeRoy Pearce as Poly Sumii sprints in to assist. The game would be the last high school football contest played in camp. (*Heart Mountain Wyoming Foundation Collection*)

Heart Mountain project director Guy Robertson (*left*) and Dillon Myer during a March 1945 visit from the War Relocation Authority director. *(National Archives photo no. 210-G-G819)*

After saying goodbye to friends and family moving back to the West Coast in May 1945, incarcerees make the long walk back to the barracks from the train station. *(Japanese American National Museum [Gift of Mori Shimada, 92.10.2D])*

By July 1945, five trainloads of incarcerees were leaving Heart Mountain every week. The train would stop in Billings, Montana, where passengers would board mainliners for the West Coast, or new homes in Chicago and elsewhere. *(National Archives photo no. 210-G-G945)*

Horse in the Army. *(Courtesy of Yoshinaga family)*

Back in California, Babe teamed up with former Hollywood High teammate Barry Brown at Los Angeles City College. This photo ran in the team's game-day programs; the middle finger was removed. *(Babe Nomura Family Photo Collection)*

Babe (*top row, right*) with fellow Eagles Yoichi Hosozawa, Mas Ogimachi, Jack Funo, and Bozo Nomura, and others, on the front steps of his parents' boardinghouse after the war. Many of the players would remain friends for the rest of their lives. (*Courtesy of Yoshinaga family*)

railroad rights-of-way is of vital importance and through your work you are making an important contribution to the war effort. No finer indication of your unswerving loyalty to this country could be evidenced than by determined effort to see the job through."

Brown urged Babe and fellow Jackrabbit Aki Shiraishi, who wrote a similar letter, to stick it out until school started, then politely reminded the teens that contractually Northern Pacific wasn't required to pay for their train rides back to Wyoming unless they stayed on for sixty days. Babe pushed again on July 14.

> *Dear Sir,*
>
> *Previously I have written a letter and a application stating the reason why I wish a travel permit to return to Heart Mountain. The reasons were I wish to attend school this coming fall. As I know this place will be a ideal place to save money but it will take time to get information from various schools. I realize that railroad is vital essentially but I believe that education at the present would be important. If it isn't too much to ask of you I would like most soon as possible or by this week. Thank you.*
>
> > *Sincerely,*
> > *Tamotsu Babe Nomura*

Neither man could've predicted what awaited Babe back at Heart Mountain.

PART

3

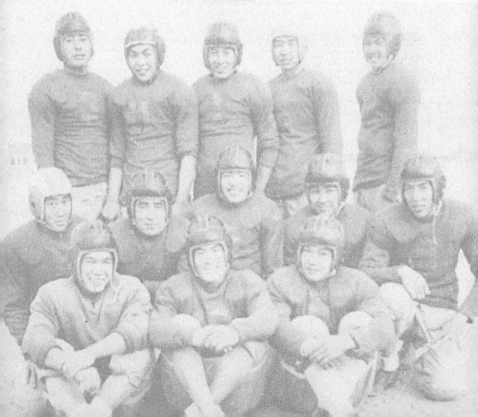

CHAPTER THIRTEEN

13 Days

TOYOSHI KAWASAKI WAS 5 feet 6 inches and 190 pounds, so everyone decided it would just be easier to call him "Tubby."

His days of athletic dominance were behind him, left in the early 1930s when he toured California with Los Angeles's famed Olivers baseball club, competing against the best teams the nikkei farming communities could throw at them. At Lincoln High his size lent strength at center for the varsity football team, and he manned second base on the city-champion baseball team. On December 9, 1933, in front of five thousand fans, he played tackle for the Los Angeles Junior College Cubs in the Southern California Junior College Conference championship, a grinding 7–6 loss to the Santa Ana Junior College Dons. He didn't start for the Cubs, instead usually subbing in when the first-stringers tired. His place on the sidelines granted him a unique perspective—he was able to watch both the coaches and the players. He saw what failed the Cubs in the championship game, but also glimpsed the future of the sport a week earlier, when the team used an air-raid offense to drop 32 points on the Taft Junior College Terriers, the most points the school had ever scored in a football game. After his playing days he returned to coach the Oliver clubs, leading the team to titles throughout the 1930s.

In December 1941, he earned $30 a week working at a produce stand in Los Angeles's Grand Central Market. He spent his days washing fruit, working the register, and stocking the shelves. On his loyalty questionnaire he was to list two items under skills and hobbies: poster making and coaching football.

In the first week of September, Heart Mountain High School's administration made a decision that would affect not only the school's students, but the entire camp. Athletes of high school age would no longer be allowed to play intramural camp sports, said John Corbett, recently promoted from high school principal to district superintendent. The goal was not just to adhere to Wyoming regulations—the high school was technically an "unofficial" member of the state's athletic association and should live up to its regulations, Corbett argued—but to build school spirit. There was one problem: there were no interscholastic games scheduled. The shoddiness of the previous year's basketball and softball schedules lent little hope that the new rule would actually benefit the students, especially those who had played community football the previous fall. A hire from neighboring Cody High School would make all the difference.

Ray and Wedge Thompson were a two-man demolition crew for Wyoming's Thermopolis High School in the mid-1920s. The boys lived in Gebo, a coal mining community eleven miles outside the city, and spent each morning and afternoon running the railroad tracks to and from school. In the state track championships of 1923, the Thompson brothers scored more points than the rest of the competitors combined: Wedge took home titles in the 50- and 100-yard dashes, javelin, discus, and broad jump, while Ray won the high and low hurdles and the relay. The event was Ray's first-ever track meet. During a 1924 meet, two stopwatches clocked him in at a cinder-melting 24.6 seconds in the 220-yard low hurdles, shattering the world interscholastic record and bettering the college records of the nearby Missouri Valley and Rocky Mountain conferences. No one believed that a kid from a future ghost town in the middle of nowhere Wyoming could have possibly run that fast, and the record was never recognized.

Ray became a two-sport star at the University of Wyoming, spending four years on the football team and three on the track team. After college,

Thompson spent middling seasons coaching at Ten Sleep High School in the Bighorn Basin and University Prep, in Laramie, before landing at nearby Cody High School as head basketball coach and an assistant football coach. The results at every school were disappointing. Thompson had once-in-a-generation physical gifts, ones lusted after by coaches and competitors alike, but couldn't convert those into coaching success.

In the early spring of 1943, Ray Thompson left the security of Cody High and trekked fourteen miles up U.S. Route 14 each morning for work. He was thirty-seven, his previously lanky 5'11" frame now filling out with the first signs of middle age. His hairline ran for the rear. He was hired as a dual agriculture–phys ed teacher, and spent most of that spring erecting playground equipment in the Wyoming sun. But he had one attribute that no one else in the camp had: he was revered in Wyoming athletics.

Thompson cashed in those chips, and scheduled that first intermittent basketball season. When school administrators ruled that students would no longer be allowed to play in the center's community leagues in early September, his job shifted. He'd not only need to schedule an entire football season, he'd need to figure out who would coach it as well. There was only one logical choice.

Working on the railroad was good for one thing: getting into shape. Babe returned to Heart Mountain, his muscles toned, and on September 7 headed back to school, needing only to finish one class to graduate. Despite his quiet manner, he elected for dramatics, which he hoped would make up for the F he had received in advanced composition while still at Hollywood High. The class would perform a one-act play at the end of the semester, and Babe could walk away with a diploma. Horse, a more natural fit for a class as aptly named as "dramatics," joined him.

Less than a week after classes started, word spread: Thompson had booked a football game.

Worland High School was the powerhouse of the Bighorn Basin, coached by Carl Dir. Dir was revered nearly as much as Thompson in the region, having starred at halfback for the Worland Warriors from 1926 to 1928 and led the team to the latter two of four straight state championships. He joined the University of Wyoming after Thompson's departure and led the Broncos to their only winning season between 1925 and 1949. The Associated Press named him second-team all-conference. Worland was a juggernaut, returning seven from the previous year's starting eleven. Heart Mountain had only three boys who'd ever played high school football.

On the morning of September 18, Thompson and forty teenage boys met on the rocky field behind the new school's auditorium. Football was the only sport offered at Heart Mountain High School in the fall, so the first practice drew any boy with an ounce of athletic talent. Babe, Horse, and a stocky tackle from south L.A. named Lomo Shinji were the three who'd played at the high school level. Shinji grew up blocks from Terminal Island, and was the only nisei player on the Phineas Banning High varsity football team. He weighed in at 175 pounds, the heaviest player at tryouts. (The student newspaper said of Lomo, "Food, of course, is of much importance to him; give him some nice baked ham, and he'll play football all day.") To call the rest of the team scrawny would be polite; at 125 pounds Yoichi Hosozawa would nearly disappear if someone turned him sideways.

There was Mas Ogimachi, the straight-A son of a fisherman; Mas longed to become an accountant. There was Tayzo Matsumoto, who spoke English, Japanese, and Spanish, and collected stamps. He grew up in an apartment behind his parents' laundry off Skid Row; Tayzo and his brother Akira would help out after school, translating for their parents. In the spring, Tayzo was named the top athlete in the tenth grade. Two years later, in an interview with the Department of Justice, his parents would say Tayzo was "very disturbed about the evacuation" and that he loved his brother very much. There was Stan Igawa, who decided to forgo another season of sugar beet harvesting and stay in school. There were thirty-three other boys, and then there was Keiichi.

Keiichi Ikeda was five years old when he spent the morning with his father watching the world's fastest humans swim at Griffith Park.

In 1932, the Xth Olympiad had come to Los Angeles, and the city's nikkei community rolled out the red carpet for the visiting Japanese athletes. Issei and nisei jammed the stadiums, natatoriums, and grandstands of the Games, lined the marathon course, and peered through the fence at practices. Their cheering was so raucous that they were eventually barred from training sessions, but it didn't matter. They instead spent an estimated $2 million (in today's dollars) on tickets. Those who couldn't afford tickets flooded into Little Tokyo to hear live radio broadcasts of the events. The Los Angeles nikkei even created a slogan and logo for the Games: Japanese and American flags framing the Olympic rings. The slogan was *"Nihon wo kataseyo,"* "Make Japan Win." Nowhere was this slogan more relevant than at the swimming pool.

At the 1928 Olympics in Amsterdam, something unprecedented happened. A little-known Japanese railroad worker named Yoshiyuki Tsuruta defeated world record holder Erich Rademacher in the 200-meter breaststroke, besting him by nearly two seconds and setting a new Olympic record. The victory set off an explosion of the sport in Japan, which went from having only two competition-size swimming pools in the entire country to, on the eve of the Los Angeles Olympics four years later, one of the most dominant swim teams in the world. Japanese sports scientists studied body movement by placing cameras underwater, then radicalized the sport by suggesting swimmers roll their shoulders in and out of the water instead of remaining square-shouldered, the accepted wisdom. When the Japanese Olympic team set sail for Los Angeles, 200,000 of their countrymen cheered them off at the dock.

Mimicking the anti-Japanese slander of previous decades, newspapers mocked the athletes as "little brown men," then watched as the team dominated the pool. The Japanese team won gold in five of the six men's events, and snagged eleven of the sport's possible eighteen medals. During the medal ceremony for the 100-meter backstroke, every spot on the podium was taken by a Japanese swimmer.

Autograph seekers hounded the team. On the final night of the Games the nikkei community held a farewell banquet for the team at downtown Los Angeles's Biltmore Hotel. Massive Japanese and American flags were draped side by side in the hall, and the next morning five thousand fans wished the team goodbye from the dock in San Pedro.

Due to space constraints at the Olympic swimming stadium, swim teams were sent to various city pools around Los Angeles for training. Keiichi and his father, a laborer at a tofu factory in Little Tokyo, left their house on Folsom Street in Boyle Heights one summer morning and began the seven-mile journey to Griffith Park. For the first time Keiichi watched athletes who looked like him, men who twisted and twitched their frames to eke out one more inch where it seemed impossible, men whose size should've relegated them to other sports, men who just a decade ago would've been laughed out of the pool. He watched them lap after lap and thought, *This is it.*

From that moment on, you couldn't break him away from sports. Baseball, basketball, track, everything. When his family moved from Boyle Heights to Hollywood five years later to open a grocery store, he befriended an older nisei. His name was Tamotsu, but everyone just called him Babe. When signs for JV baseball tryouts went up in February 1942, Keiichi walked the four blocks down Cahuenga Boulevard to the Nomuras'. He didn't have a glove, so Babe pointed to a cardboard box and told him to pick whichever one he wanted. He made the team, but the federal government ensured he'd never play an inning for Hollywood High. Keiichi took that glove to a horse track, then took it on a train ride to Wyoming. When he heard his camp high school was fielding a football team, he didn't think twice that he'd never played football. He walked out of the first apartment of the third barrack of the twenty-ninth block, and down to a piece of dirt with a set of wooden goalposts.

They had thirteen days.

CHAPTER FOURTEEN

Warriors

THE CITY OF Kent, Washington, held its first annual lettuce festival in 1934. Twenty-five thousand people visited the self-proclaimed Lettuce Capital of the World to honor the crop, which filled thousands of acres of the White River Valley with its green and red leaves. Lettuce floats circled the town, and the Lettuce Queen and her attendants posed for photographs with fans. Her court was half-white, half-nisei, the former in gowns, the latter kimonos. Festivities capped off with a salad that fed five thousand people, made with two tons of local lettuce and barrels of Nalley's mayonnaise.

The harvest was the work of the area's nikkei community, which grew 70 percent of the produce consumed in western Washington. The man at the top of that industry was Ernest Kyozo Saito. Saito owned the White River Packing Company, and he realized that the lettuce, cauliflower, and peas of Kent could fetch higher prices if he shipped them to the East Coast. In the process he became the richest nikkei in the small city, buying a two-story home once dubbed "the showplace of Kent." It still stands today, and houses the Kent Historical Society.

Every summer, the company sponsored a picnic for its suppliers at a park overlooking Puget Sound. Families brought *bento* boxes stuffed with teriyaki chicken, *maki* rolls packed with broiled eel, spinach, soy-sauce-fried egg, and julienned Japanese squash. Even in the depths of the Great Depression the picnic would go on, with Saito and his partner, Mr. Hanada, filling a truck bed with watermelon, ice cream, and soda water. Saito also owned the Saito Trading Company, a Seattle concern that took him back to Japan on at least six different trips.

On December 7, 1941, Saito ran two prosperous companies, owned a 3,500-square-foot home, and employed ninety-five workers. On December 8, he was detained and interrogated by the Federal Bureau of Investigation, and on May 6, 1942, he, his white wife, Augusta, his stepdaughter (and 1935 Lettuce Queen), Thelma, and his son, Ray, traveled to the Lonely Acres Skating Rink. From there they rode by bus to the darkly nicknamed Camp Harmony, formally known as the Puyallup Assembly Center. The Hanada family avoided removal by moving to Worland, Wyoming, and, before the War Department ended voluntary relocation, the Saitos left Puyallup and followed the Hanadas eastward.

Which is how in the early afternoon of October 1, 1943, Ray Saito, a sixteen-year-old nisei from Exclusion Zone 39, found himself standing outside a concentration camp, waiting to play a football game.

High school students spent the previous week moonlighting as ticket salesmen: 10 cents for students, 20 cents for general admission. Each ticket was hand-typed:

FOOTBALL
WORLAND VS. HEART MOUNTAIN
FRIDAY, OCT. 1, 1943
ADMIT ONE
ADULT SCHOOL

Four thousand fans, more than a third of all the incarcerees at Heart Mountain, bought tickets. They lined the grassless field five-, six-, eight-deep. During gym class that week, Thompson made the students walk the field picking up any rocks and stones they discovered. There were no grandstands.

Worland arrived at the camp fresh off a listless, scoreless tie against Sheridan High. Heart Mountain arrived having just experienced the repercussions of the previous spring's loyalty questionnaire controversy. In July, Congress, the WRA, and the Japanese American Citizens League came to an agreement: they'd segregate all the incarcerees deemed "disloyal" by the questionnaire. The result was a second forced removal of twelve thousand nikkei—more than 10 percent of the total camp population. They'd be sent to Tule Lake, and 6,500 "loyal" Tule Lake incarcerees would be spread among six other camps. Tule Lake became nothing less than a maximum-security prison. More barbed wire was piled atop the fence, and an eight-foot-high double "man-proof" fence was added. The number of guard towers rose from six to twenty-eight, manned by an additional one thousand military police in armored cars and trucks.

At 5 a.m., September twenty-first, 428 bleary-eyed Tuleans deboarded the train and were greeted with breakfast and a welcome from Heart Mountain's Boy Scout drum and bugle corps. By 1 p.m., a group of nearly one thousand had gathered to say goodbye to the 434 Heart Mountain incarcerees now deemed too dangerous to live in a prison camp in Wyoming; they boarded the idling train that had arrived eight hours earlier, and began the same journey as the Tuleans' in reverse. Ten days later, the new arrivals were part of the first high school football game held in an American concentration camp.

Babe quarterbacked, with his Hollywood neighbor Keiichi starting at left halfback. Horse held down left tackle, while Mas Ogimachi and Mas Yoshiyama filled out the backfield behind Babe. Despite only weighing 125 pounds, Yoichi Hosozawa started at center. Anchored by all-state third-team selections Saito and left halfback Jack Troseth, the Worland Warriors came into camp with seven starters returning from the Bighorn Basin title runners-up in 1942 and the expectation of avenging that title-game loss. They averaged 170 pounds a man.

Troseth grew up in a house that demanded athletic excellence. His father, Oscar, played football as early as 1919 in Richmond, Utah, a tiny Mormon town near the Idaho border. After moving to Wyoming, he took over managerial duties of the semi-pro Worland Indians baseball team in 1924, a role he held for the better part of forty years, until his death. He coached while climbing the corporate ladder at the Holly Sugar beet company, which hired much of its labor from the camp during the war. He was known in Worland simply as "Mr. Baseball."

The Warriors employed a bruising running game, a style reflected in their lack of scoring. Despite their 5-1-1 record from the previous season they topped 20 points only once, against lowly Lander High, a team that didn't score a single point in four of its five games. So Ray Thompson and Tubby Kawasaki held the Eagles' playbook tightly to their chests, hinting only that they hoped to take advantage of the team's speed.

As the crowd jittered nervously in the warm air, yell leader Dempsey Maruyama egged them on.

Go back, go back
Go back to the woods
You haven't, you haven't
You haven't got the goods
You haven't got the yell
You haven't got the team
You haven't got the pep
That the Eagles have

With a Suzy Q
And a truckin' on down
Come on Eagles
Mow 'em down

E-A-G
L-E-S

eagles

Eagles

EAGLES

Over the past two weeks Babe, Horse, and Lomo must've spent as much time coaching as playing. There's a difference between thinking you know how to play football and actually knowing how to play football. There are formations and penalties and time-outs and that pesky clock tick-ticking down. There are defensive reads and offensive reads and dozens of minor adjustments every time the ball is snapped. There's rhythm and pace, false starts and late starts, first downs and fourth downs. Trap blocks, pull blocks, screen blocks, double-team blocks. The Eagles took the field in white jerseys with gold pants. In lieu of thigh pads, they wrapped their legs with cardboard, pulled up their pants, and cinched them into place with athletic tape. In just thirteen days they'd gone from two dozen teenagers to a team, and from the first whistle, the crowd could see that this was going to be a very different kind of team at that.

The Eagles, using an unbalanced offensive line and switching between single and double wingback formations, made their speed apparent. After a few meaningless three-and-outs, the Eagles found themselves on their own 47-yard line. The snap from Yoichi shot into Babe's hands. As Yoichi held off the Worland giant barreling through the line, Babe flicked the ball to Keiichi, sprinting from the left half on a reverse. With nothing but open field before him, he broke free for a 50-yard gain before finally being tackled on the Warriors' 3. On first down, fullback Mas Yoshiyama slammed up the middle for no gain; on second down Babe wriggled down to the 1½ yard line. The Eagles lost a yard on third down, setting up a fourth-and-goal from inside the 3-yard line. On a handoff from Babe, Keiichi slammed into the Warriors' line, pushing, hoping to find the goal line.

He fell a yard short, and the Warriors took over on downs. But something important had happened—everyone realized they could *play*.

The first half teetered back and forth mindlessly, with Saito's booming 40-yard punts serving as the only entertainment. The third quarter was equally dull. Early in the fourth, Worland drove 53 yards, and found themselves on the Heart Mountain 10. For the Eagles, their experience lay in defense. Horse and Lomo, the team's two biggest players, were both more comfortable on the defensive side of the ball, and it showed. The team held on downs and took over on their own 10. Instead of running an offensive play, Babe attempted to punt the ball out of danger, a decision rarely used in today's game. Worland jumped off the line, slapping the ball out of the air and recovering on the Eagles' 3. After nearly three quarters of plodding football, the crowd was finally seeing some action. And with the clock nearing its end, the Eagles knew they'd need a stop if they wanted any chance of winning the game.

Troseth, who would become the starting running back at the University of Wyoming after graduation, took Saito's handoff and sprinted toward the right end. All 5 feet, 6 inches of Jack Funo met Troseth 4 yards behind the line and dropped him to the dirt. Saito threw incompletions on the next three passes, and the Eagles took over on their own 7.

With time slipping away, the Eagles had 93 yards to go. They also had one advantage. In his time in junior college, Tubby's coach experimented with a no-huddle offense, speeding up the game so much that it confused and winded their opponents. It was unusually hot for the first week of October, a sunny 80 degrees at kickoff. In football, being smaller is rarely an advantage. But it's also not usually 80 degrees in October in Wyoming. So Tubby decided to pull a page from his old coach. With the Warriors dragging down the field, Babe zipped off three quick first downs, nearly doubling the team's total from the entire first half. On the Worland 40, he shot a 30-yard pass to Keiichi, the second-longest play of the game after his 50-yard reverse. Suddenly on their heels and their own 10-yard line, the Warriors called time-out. The only problem was they had none left.

After the penalty, the Eagles twice jammed the ball unsuccessfully toward the goal line, gaining nothing. With four minutes left to play, and no particular hope that either team would have a chance to score if they didn't score *right now*, the Eagles called up a pass play. Babe took the snap and, as the Warriors were distracted by the Eagles' two halfbacks, bulleted a pass to Mas Yoshiyama in the end zone.

After the six points, Babe booted the extra point: 7–0 Eagles. The final whistle blew. Two hours earlier, only three of the Eagles had ever played a high school football game. Now they were 1–0.

After the game, the Worland Warriors walked to the high school auditorium, where they were greeted with a reception by the Heart Mountain High School pep club. Dinner soon followed, not at a mess hall with the players but rather the administration dining hall.

In the early evening, the twenty-five members of the Worland Warriors began the hundred-mile journey home. Twenty-four of them had just spent their first day in a concentration camp. The last was free, but still trapped.

CHAPTER FIFTEEN

Coyotes

THE 27TH OF February 1943 was a Saturday, which means the seventy-seven men in the Smith Mine were getting paid time-and-a-half.

For decades in the early twentieth century, the coal mines that give Carbon County its name drew thousands of Finns, Italians, Scots, Russians, Serbians, Germans, Norwegians, Croats, and Greeks, creating an international boomtown in the mountains of southern Montana. By 1910, three-quarters of the county's population were either immigrants or the children of immigrants, working tirelessly in the mines of Red Lodge, Bear Creek, and Washoe. The Great Depression mortally wounded the industry in Carbon County, leaving only Smith Mine open by the beginning of World War II. As the need for coal picked up again with war, Smith Mine jolted from its sleep. Desperate for coal to fuel their factories, gun, ammunition, and tank producers single-handedly revived the coal industry. Men filled Smith Mine, digging two miles into the earth to sate the war machine.

A little before 10 a.m., the normally short, serene whistle of the mine switched to a longer, more frantic pitch. *An accident*, it translated. Smoke followed, billowing out of the mouth of the pit. A spark from an ignition charge or cigarette combined with trapped methane gas; the result was the deadliest mine disaster in Montana history. Seventy-seven men climbed down into Smith Mine that morning. Over the next nine days, seventy-four bodies would be pulled out.

Coffins were shipped in from across the West to accommodate the dead. Many had died instantly from the coal dust explosion, while others waited, trapped, as the carbon monoxide slowly ate away at the oxygen from their red blood cells. In their final moments of consciousness they scrawled notes to their families on the subbituminous walls.

It's 5 min pass 11 o'cock, dear Agnes and children I'm sorry we had to go this God Bless you all. Emil with lots kiss.

Good bye wifes and daughters. We died an easy death. Love from us both. Be good.

Seven months later, the coach of the Carbon County Coyotes looked at his football team, and wasn't quite sure what to make of them. The disaster had rattled the whole county, itself less than eleven thousand residents. Now the war was taking its own toll. Already a Class B school due to its smaller size, the Coyotes' ranks shrank when two starters quit in the middle of the 1942 season to join the Navy. The following spring, three more starters joined them. Only two starters returned to school for the 1943–44 school year. In the first week of practice, Coach L. E. Hallsted told the *Billings Gazette,* "A few promising freshmen and sophomores may be added to the team," seemingly trying to convince himself of their promise.

The first game of the season snapped that promise back into reality. Carbon County ground out a 0–0 tie with Charlie Roberts's Lovell team, with both teams employing the simplest of football plays, the straight-line buck. The quarterback takes the snap and hands off to the tailback, who runs straight ahead. It's football at its plainest, and most boring.

Using the same game plan the following week, they lost by two touchdowns to Cody High.

While the Coyotes nursed their losses, the Eagles were flying high. They'd beaten the best team in the Bighorn Basin, stealing a win in the last five minutes of the game. And they'd done it by playing their own brand of lightning football. Tubby spent the week devising a new set of plays to utilize that weapon, plays that would make the straight-line buck look even more simple by comparison. They'd alternate between single and double wingback formations, utilizing Babe's and Keiichi's quickness. Laterals, sweeps, and reverses intrigued Tubby, so he drew up some diversions. One of the ideas was for kickoffs.

The 1,100-person student body filled the sidelines once again. If the Worland game was expected to be a blowout in favor of the visitors, the fans, coaches, and players had no idea what to expect from the team from Red Lodge. The county's location on the state line meant the Coyotes split their games: half Montana teams, half Wyoming teams. No one at Heart Mountain knew anything about the Smith Mine disaster, or the fact that most of the Coyotes were off in the South Pacific aboard a Navy ship. All they knew was that the team had lost to Cody the previous week, which didn't stop the *Sentinel*'s sports editor from confidently announcing, "With Babe Nomura leading the attack from his tailback position, the Heart Mountain eleven is favored to take the Red Lodge prepsters by a three-touchdown margin."

The teams lined up under a 78°F sky, and the Carbon County kicker sent the ball deep. Keiichi took the ball at the 10-yard line and ran diagonally across the field, heading to the left sideline. Babe faked as a blocker, then sprinted toward Keiichi. The pitch was flawless. Babe cradled the ball, looked downfield, and saw nothing but open dirt.

Arms pumping as the dust kicked up beneath him, he was gone. Gone from that field, gone from camp, gone from Wyoming. Remove the barracks and the barbed wire and the military police. Add some bleachers, and sketch in the Hollywood Roosevelt Hotel looming over the field. Replace the stones with grass, color in the green of the palm trees and the white of the wobbly HOLLYWOOD sign watching from Mount Lee. Replace all the bad with all the good and for those seconds he can be just a boy doing what he loves most.

Babe strode into the end zone, untouched.

Out of either pity or kindness, Tubby and Thompson pulled the first team. In went Tayzo and Stan and the others, second- and third-stringers determined to fight their way into the starting lineup. Their baptism was beset by penalties—holding, clipping, offsides, spending too much time in the huddle. The first two were the result of careless-ness, but the latter two were more understandable: eleven teens who'd never played the sport before, on a stage in front of four thousand of their peers and neighbors. The anxiety and indecisiveness could be forgiven. Despite their nerves, in the second quarter backup quarter-back Billy Shundo marched the Eagles down the field. The drive ended on a 20-yard strike to a wide-open Mas Uchida in the end zone.

The first-stringers returned for the second half and kicked off to the Coyotes. It didn't take long for the ball to be back in Babe's hands. Standing on the Coyote 47, he called a play for himself. Horse cleared the way at left tackle. Babe cut back to the middle and went untouched again through the back of the end zone. Up 19–0, Tubby decided to try another one of his new plays on the Eagles' next offensive possession.

At 5 feet 11 inches, Horse was the tallest player on the Eagles. On a team mainly of teenage boys between 5 feet 5 inches and 5 feet 8 inches, this should have meant that he'd play either quarterback or another position where his height could be used in passing or catching situations. But Horse lacked one thing: any real ability with his hands. He couldn't throw or even catch. He couldn't shoot a basketball par-ticularly well, nor hurl a baseball. The only thing he could do well with his hands was throw a punch. On the football field he could block, and that was about it.

Still, Tubby saw a chance to use Horse's size. On their next offen-sive possession, Yoichi snapped the ball to Babe, who faked a run up the middle. Babe wheeled around, pitching the ball to Horse, who'd peeled off from left tackle and was breaking downfield with a head of steam. As the Coyotes collapsed on him, he lateraled to Mas Ogimachi, drifting wide right. The 20-yard gain was nullified by a penalty, but the message was clear: We're going to play *our* style of football.

In the waning minutes of the third quarter, the Coyotes punted from deep in their own territory. Keiichi ran it back 38 yards for the fourth and final touchdown. The Eagles' starters took the field for only six plays the entire afternoon. They walked off with a 25–0 win.

After the game, Babe was interviewed by the high school newspaper. When asked about his prowess not only on the football field but the basketball court and the baseball diamond, he would only say that he knew "a little bit about ping pong."

————

While the Heart Mountain teens had been in camp, the jitterbug had exploded. Once confined to black clubs, the swing dance was now popular across the world, exported to Europe and the Pacific by American GIs. The one place it hadn't caught on was Heart Mountain. During the postgame Pep Club dance, the Coyotes' players showcased their moves, feet gliding and hips swiveling. The Eagles' lack of prowess on the dance floor prompted the school newspaper to beg the student body to catch up.

"While the hep cats are flying high to the music of 'Anvil Chorus I and II,' Heart Mountain High still seems contented with 'Moonlight Serenade,'" read a story under the headline "Wanted: Jitterbugs." "Come on, students, rheumatism or lumbago haven't set in yet. Get hep and les' jibe! Waltzes and Fox Trots for the elders, yes, but as for the teeners, its definitely out."

Now 2–0, the coaching staff faced an unexpected but welcome situation: the possibility of making the playoffs. In order to be invited to the tournament, though, they'd have to play more games. The most logical opponent was Cody High, Thompson's former team. And the Eagles had reason to be optimistic about that game.

"Your team is much faster, shiftier, and better all-around," said Carbon County coach L. E. Hallsted when asked to compare the Eagles and the Broncs by the *Sentinel*'s sports editor. "I should think that you would beat them by the same score as you beat us."

As Thompson reached out to schools hoping to find a team with a free Friday or Saturday afternoon and the desire to play in a concentration camp, he received some information that would change the course of the season.

CHAPTER SIXTEEN

Bulldogs

LOIS RUNDEN'S STUDENTS chose two one-act plays to perform as the final project for the fall semester dramatics class. The first was *The Calf That Laid the Golden Egg*, a farce written by Babette Hughes, and the second was *A Night at an Inn*, a simple play purported to have been written by Anglo-Irish fantasy author Lord Dunsany one afternoon between his lunch and afternoon tea. In *A Night at an Inn*, a trio of sailors steal a ruby from an idol in an Indian temple, then return to England and their patron, an enigmatic man known only as The Toff. They're soon tracked by the temple's priests, who are subsequently killed by the sailors. At the risk of spoiling a little-known, century-old, one-act play, it does not end well for the sailors or The Toff, either.

The roles were perfectly cast. Horse would be The Toff—"We're all in together in this," he waxes. "If one hangs, we all hang; but they won't outwit me." Babe would be known simply as "First Priest." Horse was allowed to star, while all Babe had to do was walk across a stage and pretend to be stabbed. All that was standing between Babe and a high school diploma was his ability to collapse onto an auditorium floor.

The class lacked props, costumes, and makeup, but rehearsals were underway. The performance was scheduled for Thanksgiving Day.

In 1943, the eligibility requirements for the Wyoming Athletic Association were straightforward:

1. No player shall participate in more than four fall and spring semesters in a particular sport.
2. Players must have passing grades in three subjects during the week previous to each game.
3. Transfers must be living with parents at the time or have been in school one semester to be eligible.
4. Players cannot be over twenty years of age.
5. Players who cut classes on day of games are ineligible to play.

When the Bighorn Basin conference admitted Heart Mountain High School in September, the school agreed to adhere to those rules. Rule one was moot: none of the Eagles had even been in Wyoming for more than fourteen months. Rule three was equally gratuitous—everyone lived in the same *room* as their parents. No one on the team was twenty, and as far as Rule 5 was concerned, *where would they go?*

Rule two, however, was different. And Babe was only taking one class. The *Sentinel* broke the news with an October 23 headline:

Nomura's Loss Big Blow; Backfield Reshuffled for Today's Grid Game

Babe was the only Eagle whose eligibility was questioned; Horse sneaked by, taking three classes in his final semester. The team was gutted. The playoffs, an impossibility at the beginning of the season but a glimmer the week before, now seemed unattainable. Babe was the rock, the anchor leg of the relay, the escape hatch. Babe was a kicking-blocking-running-passing Swiss Army knife that scored seemingly at will. Babe was it.

He handed the team captainship over to Horse. With nothing else to do, Babe joined the ash crew, going door-to-door, emptying pails of coal ash from the barracks, mess halls, schools, and the hospital. It was necessary but mindless work. Over the next month he worked 192 hours and was paid $19.

Tubby went back to the drawing board. Thompson was unsuccessful in scheduling a game with Cody, but called on Charles Roberts in Lovell again. As the team prepared for life without Babe, they'd have to do it under the worst conditions of the season. Temperatures fell from a balmy 75 on Sunday to a sleeting 34 by Tuesday, preventing outdoor practice. The high school closed after the camp ran out of coal. The empty coal furnace, which was usually fed two thousand pounds of coal a day in the winter, dropped temperatures inside the classrooms to 40 degrees.

Outside of the football team, the camp experienced one of its most harrowing moments. On the morning of October 16, five Heart Mountain teenagers walked along U.S. Route 14, the two-lane highway that ran outside the camp. They were walking to the farm of Jim Hart, where the boys were employed doing seasonal harvest work, when an oil worker by the name of A. H. Petrich pointed his truck at them. All five leapt into the barrow pit, narrowly avoiding Petrich's front fender. He pulled over, threatened to come back and kill them, and drove off.

Minutes later he returned with a friend, a loaded gun, and a drained bottle of whiskey. Hart noticed the commotion and knocked Petrich unconscious. The second man, Dale Wirth, swung the empty whiskey bottle at the men before being overpowered and taken to the ground by Hart. Petrich was charged with felonious assault with intent to kill. It was the first time any incarcerees had been threatened physically outside camp, but it was hardly an unforeseen possibility. While Park County farmers were happy to accept nikkei labor, the shop owners of Cody were less welcoming. When student and scout groups would take trips to the Buffalo Bill Museum, or the *Sentinel* staff went into town to produce the weekly edition, storefront windows were lined with "No Japs Allowed" signs. The region's creameries and merchants and farms welcomed the WRA purchasing contracts, but to actually see the incarcerees? To watch them walk into your shop? To cut their hair or sell them an ice cream cone?

The Heart Mountain High School band gave its first performance on Friday, October 22. The sounds of ten trumpets, five trombones, four clarinets, three drums, two alto horns, and one flute filled the air of the crowded gymnasium. The acoustics of the gymnasium were terrible. Horse introduced the team, Tubby thanked the students for their support, and the all-female Pep Club performed a skit that introduced the rules and elements of football to the audience, peculiarly from the make-believe perspective of kindergartners.

The Eagles were familiar with Lovell's baseball and basketball teams, but were blind when it came to their football squad. Odd for a town of just more than two thousand residents, virtually none of the star players of the three sports overlapped. If the Eagles were unfamiliar with the players, they certainly knew Coach Roberts. But despite his pedigree, he hadn't brought success to the Bulldogs. A 3-2-1 season in 1942, Roberts's first as head coach, was a disappointing debut for the BYU standout. The 1943 season kicked off with a 0–0 tie against Carbon County, whom the Eagles had rolled 25–0 earlier in the month.

Bill Shundo would take over for Babe, a move driven by desperation more than talent. Bill delivered one touchdown against Carbon County, but spent most of the afternoon missing wide-open receivers and completing only 4 of his 17 pass attempts. The team would have to rely on Keiichi's quickness and punt returning if it stood any chance. Once again thousands filled the sidelines. Boy Scouts wandered the crowd selling bottled soda.

The first quarter got off to a shaky start for both teams, with neither pushing the ball into dangerous territory. The second quarter did not provide much optimism, either. Instead of lofting the ball to his receivers, Bill fired it at them, or, more accurately, at the ground. It was hard to blame him. A month earlier he'd never played a down of high school football; a week earlier he'd never started a high school football game, never mind helm a team. Then, late in the second quarter, he spotted his man, Tayzo Matsumoto, standing on the goal line, with no defenders nearby. He lofted the pass, watched it fall to Tayzo's hands . . . and then hit the ground.

The first break for the Eagles came minutes later, when a Lovell punt from deep in their own territory trickled out to just the 29-yard line. After no gain on first down, Bill smashed through the line and roared 17 yards for a first down. He lost 4 on the next play, then dropped the snap and pounced on it to avoid the turnover. An incompletion to Keiichi ended the half, with the Eagles frantically trying to get something, anything, going without Babe. For the first time all season, the team was exhausted. The two Mases spent the whole first half blocking Lovell's monster left tackle and left end, Don Ash and Cal Asay. If they were going to win this game, they were going to need to give Bill and Keiichi time. They were also going to need to get a little lucky.

As the third quarter kicked off, Kaza Marumoto found a pinch of that luck, landing on top of a Bulldog fumble on the Eagle 36. Mas Yoshiyama dropped Don Ash for an 11-yard gain, Bill ran for a short gain of 3, and Mas galloped for another 9. Finally something was working.

On the next play Bill pitched the ball to Keiichi on a reverse. He sped upfield, waiting for a block at the 6 before sliding across the goal line. The celebration was short-lived. A clipping penalty was called on the block, and the Eagles turned it over on downs soon after. The Eagles were racking up yards—they outpaced the Bulldogs 227 to 67—but their lack of experience showed. Combining that inexperience with nerves, penalties, and a lack of concentration and it was a recipe for disappointment.

With four minutes left, a Lovell penalty gifted the ball to the desperate Eagles on the Bulldogs' 19. As the clock slipped away, three crunches toward the line netted only 6 yards. On fourth down, Tubby called a reverse to Keiichi. After the game ended he'd go to the camp doctor, who'd diagnose a pulled muscle in his left leg. He'd spend the next two and a half weeks navigating the dirt streets on crutches. But in this moment, exhausted from getting his 125-pound frame pummeled all day and dragging around a useless leg, he swept to the 5-yard line for a first down. On the next play, after a day of blocking, Mas Yoshiyama grabbed the handoff and plunged the final 5 yards into the end zone. The Bulldogs fumbled the kickoff, and the Eagles limped away victors, 6–0.

In the following week's *Sentinel*, sports editor Jack Kunitomi raked the teens and Tubby, who had supplanted Thompson as head coach in all but title. Setting aside the loss of Babe and seemingly forgetting that the majority of the Eagles had never played high school football two months earlier, Kunitomi didn't mince words.

"An obvious error in calling signals was evident during the early stages of the game."

"Failure to complete any of the eleven passes attempted is a sorry performance, especially for the winning team."

"The only logical explanation for the poor passing attack is the failure of the passers and receivers to concentrate during their practice sessions. Some of the players who have been chosen on the squad fail to heed the advice that 'practice makes perfect.' In practice only can one perfect the art of throwing and catching passes. It is no wonder that players tighten up in games."

While praising Keiichi and the Mases, the column made one thing clear: Kunitomi and the rest of the incarcerees of Heart Mountain not only expected the Eagles to win; they expected them to dominate. Heart Mountain High School had gone from no football team to expecting perfection in just three games.

But there would be no more high school games. A road matchup against Red Lodge fell through due to a lack of funding and administrative support, and invitations to play Cody went unfulfilled. (Though never articulated, the town's antipathy toward the camp and its residents likely played a role in this.) A radio announcer for KPOW, an AM radio station in nearby Powell, declared the high school's Panthers' "the only undefeated team in the Bighorn Basin," irking the

Eagles. Thompson had unsuccessfully tried to schedule a game against Powell, a team that had beaten Lovell and Worland by one touchdown just like the Eagles. But it wasn't to be.

There would be one more game of the 1943 season, though it wouldn't be against an outside school. Tosh Asano called the Eagles' number, and the high schoolers answered.

———

On Halloween afternoon 1943, Asano and Babe wrote another chapter of their rivalry. While Wyoming Athletic Association rules prohibited players from competing in local leagues outside of interscholastic competition, they didn't bar them from one-off all-star games. So it was decided that, in lieu of finding any high schools willing to play the Eagles, Tosh Asano would assemble a squad to challenge the undefeated, unscored-upon high schoolers.

Just as Tubby and Thompson had done two months earlier, Tosh and coach Ronnie Sugiyama set to building a team. They found Jan Kurahara, a recent arrival from Tule Lake and a Sacramento-area junior college track star, and slotted him in opposite Tosh at right half. Kaz Sugiyama was named first-team all-Marine League by the All-Southern California Board of Football in 1939, and voted top all-around athlete by the graduating seniors of Phineas Banning High. A champion pole-vaulter like Tosh, he played right guard. Two-hundred-pound Aki Washiro filled out the backfield at fullback, spelled by speedy Dick Miyakawa. Thirty-eight-year-old George Kishi filled in at right tackle. Steady-handed Lloyd Kinoshita would wait on the other side of Tosh's passes. (Athletic prowess aside, Kinoshita [as Lloyd Kino] later went on to a nearly fifty-year career as a Hollywood character actor, guest-starring on *McHale's Navy*, *Magnum P.I.*, and *M*A*S*H*, along with films including *The Cable Guy*, *Mortal Kombat*, and *Godzilla*.)

Because the game wasn't governed by the state athletic board, Babe returned. But the player who'd performed so capably in his stead would not. Keiichi spent the day on crutches. In his place was a little-used second-stringer for the Eagles: Stan Igawa. The *Sentinel* sold the game as a battle of "youth and speed versus experience and weight," but everyone watching knew it was a battle between Babe and Tosh. The usually bland walls of the camp's seven mess halls were decorated with ghosts, black cats, witches, and jack o'lanterns as children bobbed for apples and told stories in the dark. Outside, the thermometer climbed only to the mid-30s, with a wind that could easily stop or sail a football depending on the direction it flew. The conditions thinned the crowd from the usual thousands to just three hundred.

After fielding the opening kickoff, the Eagles failed to move the ball and were forced to punt. Babe boomed the kick, grabbing a tailwind that then pushed the ball. The return man misjudged its trajectory. Eagles right guard Kaz Marumoto jumped on the ball, gifting the Eagles a first-and-10 from the All-Star 20. On first down Babe hit the tackle for a gain of 2, and a reverse by Stan was sniffed out and fizzled for no gain. After an incompletion, the Eagles sat at 4th-and-8 from the 18. Stan performed his best Keiichi impression, sprinting from his right halfback position to the end zone. Babe floated a pass over the All-Star defense, hitting Stan on the goal line for the first strike. His kick for the conversion was good: 7–0 Eagles before the All-Stars even got the ball.

The rest of the half wouldn't go as smoothly. The conditions were brutal, with the winds and temperature making the dirt feel like asphalt after every tackle. Passes fluttered and fell; Babe completed only six out of sixteen attempts in all the game, and Tosh failed to connect on any of his eight tries. Frozen hands led to five fumbles for the All-Stars, who outgained the Eagles the entire game but couldn't overcome their turnovers. Babe snagged one fumble in the second quarter, taking off from his own 25. His blockers tired, though, and the All-Stars caught him before he could score.

If Tosh wanted to score, he was going to have to do it himself. In the middle of the third quarter, he smashed through the line and—in a *Sentinel* description too specific to omit—"snake-hipped" his way 48 yards down the field. From the Eagles' one yard, he wriggled over for the touchdown. The wind drove his dropkick for the extra point wide, leaving a valuable point off the board. The rest of the afternoon found the two teams fumbling and dropping passes, forcing both teams to nearly abandon the forward pass altogether.

Late in the fourth quarter, the Eagles marched to the All-Star 21. Hoping to score one last time to put Tosh away, Babe called a spread formation, damning the wind and betting on his arm. Stan broke free, turned, and spotted the ball coming his way. Wide-open, he waited for the ball, the wind and his myopic astigmatism forcing him to squint to find it in the dry desert air. As the ball landed in his arms in the end zone he was rocked by a tackle, jarring loose the score. The All-Stars flooded Babe, breaking through the smaller Eagle line and sacking him on the next two plays. Time expired as the All-Stars desperately tried to flee their own end. Once again, the crown was passed to Babe over Tosh.

———————

In November, Cheyenne's *Wyoming Eagle* newspaper named its annual all-state football team. Worland tackle Bob Kitch and end Jack Heron were named first team; Ray Saito was voted to the third team, honored as one of the best quarterbacks in the state. Later in the month, Saito, Kitch, Heron, and guard Clinton Putnam were named first-team all-conference for the Bighorn Basin. They were joined by four players from undefeated Powell High, and a player apiece from Greybull, Thermopolis, Cody, and Riverton High Schools, four schools with a combined record of 11 wins and 18 losses.

On December 10, the Eagles met in the Block 15 recreation hall. The tables were topped with miniature goalposts, the walls with pennants emblazoned with each player's name. Principal Ralph Forsythe, Tubby, and Thompson presented each player with his varsity letter: a seven-inch-tall blue block M with a small white H in the center.

In another month Babe and George would graduate, finally receiving the diplomas they should have been given a year earlier and nearly a thousand miles away. The production of *A Night at an Inn* was a success; George earned a B and Babe a C. They'd spent their waning days of high school coaching the Block 7 elementary school football team, holding practice every day after school. They'd taught the boys the fundamentals of the sport just like they'd taught their classmates four months earlier. When asked by the school newspaper what his goal was, Horse said simply: "To give them a chance to play, to keep them busy during their leisure time, and to give them a swell time."

Of course, neither Babe nor George knew what the future held. Returning to the West Coast was an impossibility and it was unlikely any East Coast college would take a chance on a player like Babe, despite his ability. Football season soon gave way to basketball season, the frozen dirt replaced by a brand-new maple floor. The gym lacked the only thing that a basketball court truly needs—baskets—so the team spent two hours after school every day passing, dribbling, and practicing weave drills. Forty-five boys tried out for the twelve-man squad. Keiichi supplanted Babe at the top of the roster.

On December 22, eighty-five teenagers pulled on their long underwear and covered themselves in wool coats, scarves, and mittens. They caroled outside the hospital, singing as children smushed their noses against the cold glass. They walked to the front gate, where the sentry allowed them past the barbed wire. Out of their barracks wandered the military police, encouraging more songs and requesting "White Christmas." The group wound its way to the teachers' dormitory, where they were treated with Christmas chocolates. They linked arms and sang from barrack to barrack, stopping only to dance. They ate cookies and filled their hot chocolate with marshmallows sent from a friend in Chicago.

It would be the last Christmas in camp for many of the Eagles. Some would relocate, accepting the government's offer of $25 and a train ticket east. Others would find themselves in the Army, or working on a broken stretch of railroad. And one would be out on bail, awaiting a federal trial and wondering how much more of his life would be spent behind barbed wire.

CHAPTER SEVENTEEN

4-F

ON JANUARY 20, 1944, the War Department reinstated the draft for nisei. Since the disappointing volunteer numbers of the year before, Secretary of War Henry Stimson had been trying to find ways to boost troop totals, discussing reinstatement of the Selective Service as early as May 1943.

True to form, the announcement was blunt, masking all the controversy and hypocrisy it contained: "Japanese Americans considered acceptable for military service will be reclassified by the selective service boards on the same basis as other citizens, and called for induction if physically qualified and not deferred."

The *Sentinel*, soon to become a major participant in the story of this debate, presented the announcement positively, running a front-page story under the headline "Selective Service Open for Nisei." WRA director Dillon Myer—who didn't learn about the decision until it was already finalized—called it "another significant step forward for the American citizens of Japanese descent." The War Department's announcement came on the heels of a Stimson report on the heroics of the 100th Infantry Battalion, made up mostly of Japanese Hawaiians. (The battalion's self-selected motto was "Remember Pearl Harbor.") After pleading with the War Department to send them to battle—and refused by North African campaign commander General Dwight D.

Eisenhower—the battalion landed in Algeria in early fall 1943, tasked with guarding German POWs. Unhappy with their assignment, Colonel Farrant Turner demanded his men be allowed to join Allied troops in a succeeding campaign, pushing the Germans out of the heel of Italy. On September 22, the 1,300 men walked onto the beaches of Salerno. By the War Department announcement four months later, 96 of the men would be dead, 221 would be wounded, and 17 would be missing.

The likelihood of a large contingent of nisei soldiers fighting in the Pacific theater was nil. In a March 4 letter, War Department executive assistant Lieutenant Colonel Harrison Gerhardt wrote: "If a Japanese American unit were present in combat in the Pacific it would be possible for the enemy Japanese to secure American uniforms from dead soldiers and mingle with American Japanese units, thereby causing considerable confusion and increasing hazards of enemy infiltration." Gerhardt's letter did not address German Americans fighting in Germany, Italian Americans fighting in Italy, or his inability to conceive of a situation where Japanese American soldiers would be able to discern a Japanese soldier in their unit.

The fate of the 100th Battalion was a less-than-ringing endorsement for the draft. The men of Heart Mountain quickly understood that, as Japanese Americans in a segregated Army, they'd more than likely fill the ranks of those lost on the front lines. Kiyoshi Okamoto, whose Heart Mountain Congress of American Citizens had hibernated after the loyalty questionnaire debacle a year prior, jolted awake.

Okamoto had spent the past year fighting for quality-of-life improvements in the camp: garnering better, healthier food, broadcasting abuses within the internal police, and railing against the WRA. By late 1943, Okamoto, Paul Nakadate, Frank Emi, and a small group of others were meeting regularly to discuss the constitutionality of incarceration. Okamoto was a fiery speaker, later derided as an "intellectual hobo" and "latrine lawyer" by his critics. Nakadate was bookish, an insurance salesman and married father of one, who taught at the camp's night school. Emi ran a family produce market in Los Angeles before the war; he sold it for just $1,500, months after investing $25,000 in upgrades.

On February 8, the newly christened Fair Play Committee held a meeting for sixty men in one of the mess halls. Their message was nearly identical to the one Okamoto pushed a year earlier: Restore all Japanese Americans' rights as citizens and we'll gladly serve. The Selective Service, they argued, was morally corrupt and legally indefensible otherwise.

Hundreds of men soon joined the nightly meetings, which moved to different barracks around camp. Two hundred seventy-five men paid the $2 dues to join the FPC, with another 125 regularly filling out the standing-room-only crowds. Cigarette smoke poured out of the windows as Okamoto and Nakadate condemned the WRA and the War Department. The draft affected everyone in camp, they argued— not only the camp's two thousand draft-eligible men, but the parents and families they'd leave behind barbed wire. Emi and his brother bought a mimeograph machine and tacked the committee's messages around camp. They'd walk door-to-door, urging parents of nisei boys to consider all their options. Guntaro Kubota translated the proceedings from English into Japanese for issei parents. The requirements to join the Fair Play Committee were plain. First, you needed to be a loyal American. And second, you needed to be willing to serve in the military if your rights were restored. That was it. When Emi learned that Horse was considering registering, he met with Horse's mother to convince her to try to get him to change his mind. She was unmoved.

"She always had that philosophy that we're Americans and we're Americans first," Horse said years later. "That's one thing that I learned from [my parents] . . . even though I'm Japanese I'm really an American."

As the draft controversy grew, Babe and his two brothers took seasonal clearance and moved to Hardin, Montana, just as Stan had done eighteen months earlier. They spent their days working for sugar beet farmers, and their nights taking on members of the Crow Agency in basketball games.

Tayzo spent the previous fall relegated to so little playing time on the football field that when the Eagles received their varsity letters in December, he wasn't even invited to the ceremony. Five days after the War Department reinstated the Selective Service for nisei men, he turned eighteen. He went to one Fair Play Committee meeting and decided immediately: No. He didn't discuss it with his brother, Akira, or his parents. He was convinced.

"When your constitutional rights are deprived," he said, decades later, "that was reason enough."

———————————

The movement spread quickly at Heart Mountain, and similar resistance popped up independently at other camps. At Poston, in southern Arizona, twenty-nine-year-old George Fujii was arrested and charged with sedition after posting a somehow equally idealistic and militaristic list of demands around camp. Among them:

— A personal apology from General DeWitt for his "A Jap is a Jap" comment, and DeWitt's resignation.
— The removal of "No Jap," "You Rat," "No Oriental or Colored Admitted," and similar signs across the United States.
— Racially diverse Army units.

At Amache, in Colorado, the FBI held five nisei after they failed to report for their induction physicals. At Minidoka, a group of issei mothers met in secret, drafting a petition to President Roosevelt. The two-page, typewritten letter echoed the argument made by the Fair Play Committee and was signed by more than one hundred issei mothers. (The petition was actually a rewrite of one penned by Min Yasui, a new Minidoka arrival following his prison stay for violating curfew restrictions. The women read the mealymouthed letter as "too weak" and wrote their own.)

Both Fujii's arrest and the detention of the men at Amache were reported in the *Sentinel*, the message from Project Director Robertson clear: *Stop*. Instead, to cover their actions legally as well as spread the word about the Heart Mountain Fair Play Committee, Okamoto contacted an attorney, Samuel Menin, and the editor of the bilingual *Rocky Shimpo*, Jimmie Omura, both in Denver.

Robertson resorted to the same tactics of fear and intimidation that he unsuccessfully attempted the year before. Just two days after the founding of the Fair Play Committee, he called out the group. "Nisei men, in accepting advice of older people in regard to the draft, should exercise care so as not to violate selective service laws," Robertson told the *Sentinel*. He then reminded the men that any violation was subject to up to five years in prison, a fine of $10,000, or both. He spent weeks trying to cultivate spies within the meetings, hoping to gather enough information to banish Okamoto to Tule Lake, the camp used to imprison "disloyal" incarcerees. No one budged. In coordination with the high school, he pushed lessons on Selective Service laws. He urged church groups to discuss the draft, and hosted community meetings intended to counteract the Fair Play Committee. He was willing to try anything to avoid another embarrassment like the loyalty questionnaire, even meeting with an FBI special agent to try and build a sedition case against Okamoto.

The committee was not only unfazed, but invigorated. On February 25, Okamoto wrote a letter to the community entitled "We Should Know." His public rhetoric transferred to the written word with no diminution.

> *Under these conditions, what are we? Are we American citizens? Are we Enemy Aliens? Or, are we . . . what? This absence of clarification of our status and rights is the keystone of our indecision towards any proper orientation of attitude towards the draft.*

*If we are Enemy Aliens then, we owe no obligation to bear
arms for a Country that is not Ours.*

*If we are nothing but oriental monkeys as have been
attributed to us at times then, propositions and offers of
compensation should be advance [sic] for the ruination of
health and the uncertainties of Fate on foreign battlefields or, to
compensate for the loss of life valuable to dependents and loved
ones.*

*If we are Americans by right of birth and Constitutional grant
then, why our wholesale pauperization; why our evacuation, why
the denial to us of the due process of law, why the deportation into
another state by threat of military force, why the concentration,
why the detention and why the denial to us of justice, freedom security and the other guarantees of the Constitution and the Bill of
Rights?*

On February 28, the Fair Play Committee sent a letter to President
Roosevelt pleading their case. After almost two years behind barbed
wire, they argued, they deserved a clarification of their citizenship
status. The petition outlined a list of requests similar to Fujii's list at
the Poston camp: full restoration of civil rights, the right to return
home, the ability to join any branch of the armed forces. The president
did not respond.

Using the mimeograph machine bought with committee dues,
Okamoto and Emi crafted their message and posted it across camp.
Under the banner "one for all—all for one," the notices cited the Fifth
Amendment of the Bill of Rights and Abraham Lincoln.

"If what we are voicing is wrong, if what we ask is disloyal, if what
we think is unpatriotic, then Abraham Lincoln, one of our greatest
American Presidents, was also guilty as such, for he said 'If by the mere
force of numbers a majority should deprive a minority of any Constitutional right, it might in a moral point of view justify a revolution.'"

In the first week of March, the Fair Play Committee voted unanimously to refuse Selective Service induction and to skip the Army's physical examination until their rights were restored. The flyer was direct:

"We are not being disloyal. We are not evading the draft. We are all loyal Americans fighting for JUSTICE AND DEMOCRACY RIGHT HERE AT HOME."

The chrome bumper of the Burlington Trailways bus nudges out of Heart Mountain Relocation Center before the sun rises. It's March 7, and the passengers include sixteen nisei men: nine single, seven married, five with children, two with children born in the last ten days. The other passengers assume the men are seasonal workers, commuting to the sugar beet fields of Worland or some rail yard in Montana. "I hope I can get in the medical corps," says one. "I want to save lives, not kill people." He's quiet. It's hard to imagine him killing anyone.

Lunch is in Worland, supper in Casper. As the sun falls below the prairie and the moonglow takes its place, the cherry-red bus continues along U.S. 87 until it stops, 450 miles later, at the CB&Q Burlington Bus & Railroad Depot, in Cheyenne. The depot is bright despite the clock sitting at 1 a.m., the bus lights shimmering off the sandstone walls. Thirty-four other Heart Mountain draftees greet the recently arrived sixteen on the platform, and Babe and his fifteen compatriots, sleepy and anxious, make their way to the outskirts of town, to Fort Francis E. Warren.

Fort Warren began its life in 1867 as Fort D. A. Russell, a military installation tasked with protecting Union Pacific workers from Native American tribes. By the beginning of World War I it was one of the largest military bases in the country; fifteen years after World War II it would become the first fully operational Air Force intercontinental ballistic missile base, with SM-65D Atlas missiles cradled in aboveground launchers. On this day, as Babe steps onto base, it's home to five thousand men, the largest quartermaster depot in the Western United States. Five hundred German prisoners of war fill out the barracks, performing KP and other chores.

When the boys finally arrive at the fort at 2 a.m. they pile atop benches and tables. They roll up towels for pillows and drape jackets as blankets. They drift off for minutes, or maybe an hour or two, and at 5 a.m. a corporal barks everyone awake. They line up three abreast and march to the mess hall. There, POWs teach American sergeants German, while the sergeants attempt to impart a few English words. Within minutes the boys are finished, out the door, and on to their physicals, where they are prodded, x-rayed, measured, squeezed, elec-trocardiogrammed. *Are you between sixty and seventy-eight inches tall? (Yes? Good.) Do you have a venereal disease? (Yes?* Acceptable, as long as the "local capacity for treatment provided no disabling complica-tions.") Each body part is graded.

"You'll be sorry! You'll be sorry!" a soldier sings out as he passes the boys, some smoking furiously and all waiting in the induction hall to see whose life will be upended once again and who will go back to their makeshift homes. An hour passes before a man in blue appears in the doorway. He reads the names of twelve rejectees, then turns around and disappears again. A half hour creeps by. The man in blue returns and reads off the names of the dozen who've passed. "Jen-sen . . .Tomlieh . . . Anderson . . ." He pauses, cocks his head, examin-ing the letters like a bird trying to figure out how to open its cage. "I'm not even going to try this one. H-I-G-A-H-I-G-U-C-H-I."

They're back at the Cheyenne bus depot by late afternoon, breaking up into small groups to shop or eat or see a movie, luxuries that would've seemed like minor decisions two years ago. At 3 a.m., twenty-four hours after they pulled into Fort Warren, they're back on the road again, driv-ing under a second moon. Of the sixteen Heart Mountain boys, six pass, nine are rejected, and one is held over for further examination.

As the prairie glides by, the boys stare out the bus, its blinds high and open, allowing them to take in the sagebrush. Under the moonlight Babe sits, labeled 4-F by the United States Army: "below minimum standards for induction." The best athlete in Heart Mountain has flat feet.

CHAPTER EIGHTEEN

Letter from Laramie County Jail

By MARCH 11, the *Sentinel* had lost any sense of serving its readers. That week's front page featured eight stories, seven of which were either about the draft or the bravery of nisei troops. An editorial entitled "Our Cards on the Table" did just that, demanding the arrest of any man who failed to report to his preinduction physical.

"The so-called Fair Play Committee . . . was conceived in the mind of one of the center's most persistent and clever trouble-makers," it read. "It would be well for all center youths to remember that this chief agitator and his not-so-clever followers who drew the unsuspecting into a tangle of intrigue during registration were too deceptive to answer honestly the question of loyalty. . . . We feel assured that his group will soon be broken and dispersed on the solid rocks of reason and law."

The following week, committee members were branded "Janus-faced" and "rat-like," "lacking both moral and physical courage." Then a counterstrike came from an unlikely source. Emi had kept Jimmie Omura, the Denver newspaper editor, abreast of all the Fair Play Committee's actions; his *Rocky Shimpo* was widely read in camp. Omura blasted the *Sentinel*, saying the staff "had purchased a seat in the great gallery of bigots, racist demagogues, autocrats, and fascist-minded. . . . [The *Sentinel* had] deserted justice, fair play, equal rights, and all that are revered in our constitution and the government of our United States."

Editorials from Nakadate and Emi followed: long, defiant screeds against the paper and the policies it supported.

"The editors of the *Sentinel* said in today's issue, that 'we should be men among men and not whimpering weaklings who are afraid to prove themselves,'" Emi wrote on March 19. "If these persons feel that what they say is right, that what they write is being loyal, why do they not volunteer their services to the combat unit? Why do they not back up their convictions with parallel action? To sit in an office and write bold words does not take courage. You do not have to be a man among men to utter such words behind an office desk."

As Emi and Nakadate, the *Sentinel* staff, and Project Director Robertson threw words at each other, Fair Play Committee crowds were spilling over their spaces in the barracks, with boys and their families even trying to follow the proceedings through the windows. Then the first men took action. On March 6, two refused to board the bus to Cheyenne. On the seventh, three more. The following day, eight. Heart Mountain staffers questioned the men, then, lacking the authority to charge them with any crime, returned them to their barracks. Robertson was furious. He called Wyoming U.S. attorney Carl Sackett and attempted to convince him to arrest the resisters immediately. His concern that their actions would spread was ultimately prophetic. But Sackett said his hands were tied; his sparsely populated district didn't require another grand jury to be called until early May. Since the men weren't a flight risk—the men were *already* in a prison, so why just move them to another one?—Sackett waited.

Sackett was born in 1876 in a sod house in southwestern Nebraska, though his upbringing belied his lineage. His father traced his blood to the same line as George Washington, while another distant relative was allegedly the first white child born in Cambridge, Massachusetts. His father chased buffalo across the Black Hills of South Dakota, eventually settling into a log cabin along a branch of Wyoming's Hanna

Creek, up and over the Bighorn Mountains from Cody, Worland, and Heart Mountain. As a child, Carl would climb to the top of Sackett Hill and watch as Plains Indian tribes arranged their tepees on his father's homestead. He'd spend hours watching the men perform their maneuvers in silence, eagle feathers bouncing from their horses' tails. He rose from early schooling in a dirt-floor trapper's cabin to two terms as city attorney for nearby Sheridan and a seat in the Wyoming House of Representatives. One of the first actions Franklin D. Roosevelt took following his inauguration in 1933 was the appointment of Sackett as U.S. attorney for the district of Wyoming.

While Sackett had the luxury of time, Robertson did not. He circumvented the U.S. attorney, funneling his concerns to WRA director Dillon Myer. Myer in turn convinced the Justice Department to skirt its own rules. On the morning of March 25, a phalanx of wide black automobiles pulled onto the streets of Heart Mountain Relocation Center. U.S. marshals walked door-to-door collecting the first twelve men and serving them with warrants for failure to report. The arrests made national news, splashed across newspapers from Hawai'i to Maryland, from California to New Jersey.

To Robertson's surprise and consternation, the arrests had the opposite effect, as twenty-five more men soon refused. Four days later, Emi and a Fair Play Committee colleague, Minoru Tamesa, walked from their barracks to the front gate of the camp. If the group was going to challenge the constitutionality of the draft, they figured they'd need some evidence. The two men attempted to walk out the front gate, only to be stopped by the military police.

We are American citizens and imprisoned without charges, Emi explained. *We're going into town to do some shopping.*

"If you want to get shot, go ahead," the guard replied.

During an uprising at Manzanar in December 1942, military police lobbed tear- and vomit-gas grenades into a crowd, and then, when the crowd rushed toward the men to escape, they pumped three bursts of submachine gunfire and three shotgun blasts into the fog. Two men were killed; one eyewitness remembers a sergeant barking "Remember Pearl Harbor! Hold your line!" as the crowd lurched forward. In April 1943, at Topaz, a military police sentry shot and killed sixty-five-year-old James Wakasa after he allegedly refused the sentry's order to step away from the camp's western fence. An investigation revealed that Wakasa was five feet inside the fence and facing the sentry, with a wind at his back that would've made hearing the sentry's order "highly improbable." The sentry was acquitted on manslaughter charges by an Army court-martial. Kanesaburo Oshima was fifty-eight when, mad with anxiety over business debts and separation from his family, he climbed the fence at the Fort Sill, Oklahoma, detention center. His fellow incarcerees tried to pull him down and yelled at a guard, "Don't shoot! He is insane." A guard shot him through the head, and he died between the camp's inner and outer fences. Toshio Kobata and Hirota Isomura were killed with a 12-gauge shotgun blast at the hands of Private Clarence A. Burleson. Their crime was walking too far off the road on the way to the Lordsburg, New Mexico, detention facility. Burleson testified the two men were running away. It was later learned that Kobata was suffering from the after-effects of tuberculosis. Isomura had a spinal column injury. Neither men could walk for much time without needing to rest. Burleson was acquitted. Shoichi Okamoto was shot at Tule Lake after allegedly refusing to show a sentry his ID. The sentry—whose name has never been released—was acquitted, though fined a dollar: the cost of a bullet fired in an "unauthorized use of government property."

The killings sat in Emi's and Tamesa's minds as they turned away from the fence, and submitted to arrest. They spent the night in the brig and "enjoyed good food for a change," Emi wrote, and were released. Later in the week they were summoned to Robertson's office for a hearing. As the men walked into the room they were stunned by the crowd. Fanned out behind the project director's desk were Robertson, the chief of internal security, the project attorney, a representative from the military police, and a second internal security officer. Even more curious was the presence of Nobu Kawai, the *Sentinel*'s associate editor and author of the more vile of the paper's anti–Fair Play Committee editorials. If there was any doubt remaining that Robertson and the *Sentinel* were working together to thwart the Fair Play Committee's influence, it evaporated.

Behind the men hung a schematic drawing of the camp, along with two posters. One featured a drawing of a U.S. Navy battleship, the other the barrel of an artillery gun, pointed right at the viewer.

Let ME Do The Talking! read the top line of the poster.

Serve In Silence, read the bottom.

Robertson, a former coal executive with a droopy right eye, questioned the men for more than two hours before eventually dismissing the charges after the men agreed not to try leaving camp again. Despite his ire, Robertson must have known the consequences of convicting Emi and Tamesa. The fuse was burning, but slowly—there was still time to limit the damage. The last thing he needed to do was pour gasoline on it. Instead, he'd simply snip the fuse.

He first summoned Okamoto for a leave clearance hearing, despite Okamoto never asking for one. He denied the clearance, declared him "disloyal," and shipped him to Tule Lake. In protest of Okamoto's banishment, Sam Horino attempted to walk out the front gate; he was arrested and soon joined Okamoto. With Okamoto and Horino gone, and Emi and Tamesa cowed by their agreement with Robertson, the WRA had one target left.

A year earlier, Nakadate had answered "yes" to Questions 27 and 28 of the loyalty questionnaire, saying, "Democracy is sharing of equal responsibilities and equal rights." In the intervening year, however, those equal rights had been abandoned. In another sham leave clearance hearing with Robertson, he carefully stated he wasn't sure if he would refuse his induction physical. (He had not yet been called.) Despite having committed no overt act, Nakadate joined Okamoto and Horino at Tule Lake.

No Wyoming jail was large enough to hold the sixty-three men arrested at Heart Mountain, so resisters found themselves in Cody, Rawlins, and Casper, among other cities. In Casper they were so trusted that the sheriff not only left the cells unlocked, but allowed the men to cook dinner for themselves, the sheriff, and his wife. Most found themselves at the Laramie County Jail, a two-story building so dark and claustrophobic that it would be the subject of multiple federal lawsuits in the decades to come. ("Its sinister architecture makes it comparable to that of an inverted tomb," wrote one litigant.) Windows ran along one wall; the view was the exterior of another building. For a few hours each day, sunlight would reflect off the neighboring building and trickle into the cells, the only light available beyond the three or four light bulbs the dozens of inmates shared. Built in 1911, the walls were sixteen inches thick.

The mattresses and blankets were so vile and soaked with the urine and vomit of former residents that the men tried not to roll their faces into them. Due to overcrowding, the jail lacked any public space, so the men played bridge feet away from their cellmates on the toilet. Because previous inmates had burned books to reheat their coffee, they were allowed no reading materials other than letters. Candy and fruit were available for purchase. The men were held on $2,000 bail; the $200 bond would've been difficult for many of the men to gather under normal circumstances, never mind when only making $12 or $16 a month in camp. To distract themselves as they waited for the grand jury to convene, they wrote letters to Emi.

"We are eagerly and determinedly awaiting the day knowing deep within our hearts and minds that no matter how the trial ends we are right," wrote George Ishikawa, who at twenty-eight was one of the oldest resisters. "Our conscience and our heart shall be clear knowing that we have had the courage to fight for a fundamental principle. We may lose the verdict, but the verdict shall be man made and with the passing of time, eternal truth and right will come to light; that is my firm belief. . . . The violent propaganda of race hatred and race baiting now being so glibly expounded by these self-styled super patriots can warp and poison the minds of the uninformed and unthinking."

By the end of April, Sackett had refused all visitors, save two. After dinner on April 28, Joe Grant Masaoka and Min Yasui arrived at the jail and, with Sackett's permission, interviewed six of the seventeen resisters held there. Masaoka was a regional representative for the JACL from Denver and brother of JACL executive secretary Mike Masaoka. (Mike Masaoka, for his role in acquiescing to incarceration in 1942, was nicknamed "Moses" Masaoka: he led his people out of California.) Yasui's complicated legacy—from jailed curfew-breaker to JACL spy to civil rights leader after the war—is hard to square.

The men were brought in one at a time, prison pallor "already becoming evident on their faces and hands," Masaoka and Yasui wrote in their report. One after another, the men echoed each other nearly word for word. *We are fighting to assure court action in order to clarify our citizenship rights and status. If we serve in the Army and when this war is over, we'll be sent back to our homes—it'll be behind barbed wire fences in the Heart Mountain Center.*

All were willing to enter the Army if their citizenship and equality concerns were answered to their satisfaction. Nevertheless, Masaoka and Yasui concluded that "it was apparent that these boys [were] wavering in their faith in America." Which could have been viewed as true, if America had been viewed solely as their jailer. But viewed more universally, it was laughably incorrect. It was their exact faith in America—its Constitution and rights—that had made them willing to fight for it in the first place. The decision to do so wasn't easy. To be identified as a criminal or, perhaps worse, a coward could bring shame not only to the man but to his family. Everyone understood the repercussions of their decision. Despite the profundity of the resisters' actions, Masaoka and Yasui concluded that "some are too young and immature to formulate any profound convictions of their own."

In an effort to break the resolve of the group, the JACL representatives made a surprising, though ultimately unheeded suggestion: solitary confinement. "It would supplant individual decision for group pressure." The interviews concluded at 10 p.m. Without exception, every person stated that the decision to refuse to report was his own personal decision.

Within a month, the report made its way from Cheyenne to the Denver field office of the FBI to Washington, D.C., where it landed on the desk of J. Edgar Hoover. Earlier in the week, WRA head Dillon Myer wrote to Hoover and thanked him for investigating "the difficulties which have developed [at Heart Mountain] during the last month or so incident to the re-institution of Selective Service for American citizens of Japanese ancestry." The boys had the attention of not only Heart Mountain, not only the WRA, but the head of the FBI. If they were confident about their rights before, that confidence was sucked out of the room without their even knowing.

On May 8, the grand jury that Robertson so desperately wanted finally met in Cheyenne, and indicted the sixty-three men. The formal charge was a violation of Section 311, Title 50, of the U.S.C.A. Selective Service and Training Act of 1940: "failure to report to the local draft board."

Through funds raised by family members and Heart Mountain residents, the unincarcerated, unbanished members of the Fair Play Committee hired Samuel Menin, the Denver attorney they had previously contacted and who had a reputation as a fighter. He fought against the distribution of Bibles in Denver's public schools, brought civil rights cases on behalf of the city's black and Mexican residents, and in 1942 defended a Jehovah's Witness minister on draft evasion charges. He was also a literal fighter: during a 1940 trial, he punched an opposing attorney so hard he broke his left hand. If the resisters stood a chance in hell of beating the federal charge, they'd need a man like Menin in their corner.

Presiding over the case was T. Blake Kennedy, only the second federal judge in the history of the state. Decades earlier Kennedy had endorsed placing educational requirements on voting, saying any such law would "practically place so high an educational qualification upon the voter that the rank and file of negros are thereby disenfranchised." Blacks in America couldn't progress as steadily as whites, he argued, because their "natural laziness is too preeminent to ensure thrift." He supported interracial marriage bans, and believed Northern Europeans assimilated easier into the United States than any other group. On Monday, June 12, the first day of the trial, he referred to the sixty-three defendants not by name but as "you Jap boys" before quickly correcting himself. He was one of the worst federal judges a group of sixty-three Japanese Americans could imagine finding themselves against, and he was the only one in all 97,818 square miles of Wyoming.

The sixty-three resisters sat in the Cheyenne courtroom, forming not only what was likely the largest group of nikkei anyone in the courthouse had ever seen, but the largest federal trial in Wyoming history. They sat in four rows: sixteen men, sixteen men, sixteen men, and fifteen men. Some slouched, some sat upright. They nearly all wore wide-collar shirts, collars flaring out to the shoulders like model airplanes. Some were in sweaters, others jackets. Almost none wore suit coats. When a photographer snapped a picture of the sixty-three, they appeared different from most defendants. They looked *confident*. They looked the way anyone would look if you stripped them of their rights, shipped them to the middle of the desert, broke apart their basic ways of life, sacrificed those good people to the gods of military preparedness, and said *We gave you a chance to prove your loyalty and this is how you repay us?*

They looked ready.

As the sixty-three resisters languished in prison, federal officials were debating what to do about the 120,000 other nikkei in camps or relocated outside the West Coast. Any drop of military necessity—no matter how convoluted—had evaporated. It was no longer a matter of if the camps would close, but when. There was another matter to consider, though, one beyond the military's purview: the 1944 presidential election.

Rumors of declining health put a target on Roosevelt's back, with contenders as varied as governors Thomas Dewey of New York and John Bricker of Ohio to General Douglas MacArthur, whose campaigning was hampered by the pesky fact that he was still leading Allied forces in the South West Pacific theater. California governor Earl Warren, who years earlier had paved the way for incarceration, won the California primary but was a nonfactor at the nominating convention. Roosevelt faced no primary opposition, and as a wartime incumbent was the clear favorite to win in November. Despite that, his staff worked to stack the deck in his favor.

During a May 26 cabinet meeting, Secretary of War Stimson raised the possibility of canceling the exclusion order. Stimson, Attorney General Biddle, and Interior Secretary Harold Ickes, whose department had absorbed the WRA in recent months, agreed that, militarily, the camps were no longer necessary, but "doubted the wisdom of doing it at this time before the election." On June 8, two days after 156,000 Allied soldiers invaded the beaches of Normandy, Ickes pleaded with Roosevelt.

"It is my understanding that Secretary Stimson believes that there is no longer any military necessity for excluding these persons from the state of California and portions of the states of Washington, Oregon and Arizona," he wrote in a letter. "Accordingly, there is no basis in law or in equity for the perpetuation of the ban. . . . The continued exclusion of American citizens of Japanese ancestry from the affected areas is clearly unconstitutional in the present circumstances. . . . The continued retention of these innocent people in the relocation centers would be a blot upon the history of this country."

Four days later, as the federal draft-resistance trial opened in Wyoming, Roosevelt responded: "The more I think of this problem of suddenly ending the orders excluding the Japanese Americans from the West Coast, the more I think it would be a mistake to do anything drastic or sudden."

So it was decided that Americans of Japanese descent would remain behind barbed wire, in perpetuity, for no reason other than the political expediency of a sitting president.

———————

The hailstones fell from the sky as if they were mad at the ground. Pea-sized, then walnut-sized, then plum-sized, they grew and grew until they were bigger than baseballs, smashing through the lights and signs and people of downtown Cheyenne. One stone sliced through the head of a railroad worker, while a separate barrage knocked a woman to the ground. The hail tore through the soft-tops of convertibles and beat storefronts until the glass gave way. The next morning, attorneys and reporters navigated around the leafy boughs of spring trees and shattered glass, passed under the federal courthouse's limestone frieze emblazoned with THE UNITED STATES OF AMERICA, and the largest mass trial in Wyoming history gaveled open.

Save for the defendants, the courtroom was nearly empty. A few family members sat in attendance, alongside curious soldiers passing through Cheyenne on their way to or from Fort Warren. The men agreed to a joint trial and waived their rights to a jury. Sackett's goal was to keep the scope of the trial narrow: the men had defied an order and deserved to be punished like any other man who did the same. The politics of the act were irrelevant. Menin took the opposite tack. He needled, prodded, and filibustered. Under the misguided assumption that Kennedy would or could not tell the difference between his nisei clients, he convinced some of the men to shave their heads and refuse to respond unless addressed specifically by name. The judge was less than amused; the tactic failed before it even left the ground.

As the trial began, the *Sentinel* might as well have sat at the prosecutor's table. "Loyal Japanese Americans as a whole condemn the Fair Play Committee and the action of the 63 defendants as being as serious an attack on the integrity of all nisei as the sneak attack on Pearl Harbor, the treatment of Allied prisoners on Bataan, and other acts which have placed all persons of Japanese ancestry under suspicion," the staff wrote in an editorial.

The trial lasted six days, but from the outset it wasn't hard to tell how Kennedy would rule. Menin argued for a motion to dismiss due to insufficient evidence, and that the evidence presented "lacked intention and malice." Kennedy denied the motion. Menin countered that the acts and conduct of the defendants didn't warrant conviction because of a lack of felonious intent. Kennedy denied the motion. During cross-examination by Menin, FBI agents testified that during their interviews forty-five of the men indicated not only a loyalty to the United States, but a desire to join the Army after their constitutional rights were restored.

With the trial set to close, Menin threw his last bomb. Placing American citizens in camps, he said, was "something Hitler would do." Sackett exploded.

"The defense counsel has compared the system of relocation to something Hitler would do," he said, swinging his right arm overhead as he yelled. "I resent that. These men and their families have been housed, clothed, fed, and schooled by the federal government, perhaps better than the court when he was a young man and, I know, better than I was. When the Jews were kicked out of Germany they were left to shift for themselves, but our government cared for these men and their relatives."

Ten days after closing arguments, Kennedy announced his decision. Heart Mountain's community division received a Western Union telegram at 3:12 p.m. on June 26 from the Hotel Albany in Cheyenne:

VERDICT READ HALF HOUR CONSOLIDATED INTO ONE GROUP
THREE YEARS SENTENCES AWAITING ATTORNEY GENERALS
DESTINATION OF PLACE

All sixty-three were found guilty. Kennedy found that they had "willfully and intentionally neglected and refused to obey the order." As for the clarification of their citizenship rights, he contended that the moment the federal government shifted their draft status back to 1-A "their pure American citizenship was established beyond question."

"This Court feels that the defendants have made a serious mistake in arriving at their conclusions which brought about these criminal prosecutions," he wrote. "If they are truly loyal American citizens they should, at least when they have become recognized as such, embrace the opportunity to discharge the duties of citizens by offering themselves in the cause of our National defense."

The older defendants awaited removal to the United States Penitentiary, Leavenworth, the largest maximum-security prison in the country since its opening in Kansas in 1903. The younger defendants awaited removal to McNeil Island Federal Penitentiary, in Washington State.

On July 3, Kennedy walked back into his courtroom. Before him was a group of immigrants awaiting naturalization. Ordinarily during these ceremonies Kennedy would give remarks about the duties and privileges of citizenship. Instead, he told the crowd, he would speak about patriotism.

"If discouraging problems arise in our government or other institutions which at times threaten to shatter our faith, we must work within ourselves to accomplish needed reforms, instead of adhering to the enemy and becoming disloyal," he said. "Let not the privileges which you will thereby enjoy overshadow your loyalty to the Country of which you are now a part. Stand up for the United States of America and proclaim without stint her manifold virtues."

They all recited the Pledge of Allegiance, and the ceremony was adjourned. On a highway east of Cheyenne, a bulletproof Justice Department bus ticked along, spending hours in Nebraska before briefly dipping into Iowa and Missouri. The bus and its thirty prisoners came to rest at the United States Penitentiary, Leavenworth. It would not be the last time a bus with nisei men made the trip.

CHAPTER NINETEEN

Boys of Summer

THE HEART MOUNTAIN High School class of 1944 gathered in the auditorium. After performances by the orchestra and glee club and a speech by Lovell mayor Frank H. Brown, valedictorian Paul Mayekawa took the stage. He did not mince words.

"What are we, you and I?" he asked his peers. "Are we Japs, simply in a sense as General DeWitt declared 'A Jap is a Jap'? Certainly I admire him for his courage in declaring so plainly an apparently undeniable fact regarding us, but I deplore him for his lack of wisdom and his complete disregard for Abraham Lincoln's anthem of 'goodwill towards all and malice towards none,' which even grade school children know by heart and cherish as an ideal for all human beings everywhere in the world."

In the senior will, Babe bequeathed his flat feet "for further Heart Mountain victories," and Stan willed his position on the team "to an ardent fan."

Babe, Horse, Stan, and Tayzo walked across the stage, shook Robertson's hand, and stepped into adulthood.

Tayzo's induction physical was scheduled for June 5. He was instructed to report with the forty-three other inductees at the administration building at 8:45 a.m. sharp. They'd then be driven to Powell, and from there they'd take the train to Denver. Once in Denver they'd take another train to Fort Logan, eight miles outside the city.

Instead of the administration building and Powell and Denver and Fort Logan, Tayzo walked to the baseball field. He started in center field that summer for the Shamrocks, roaming the dirt and batting .572, winning the junior batting title by nearly 100 points. He and twenty-two others were arrested that summer and fall, and taken to the same jail in Cheyenne as the original sixty-three. Unlike the others, though, he was bailed out. He never learned who paid the $200, but he was free until the trial, whenever that would be. Putting to use his prewar skills as a repairman, he was hired in the camp's auto shop. Then he waited.

The summer of 1944 was a season of change for not only Tayzo, but the entire camp. As induction notices changed to active duty notices, the camp's population slowly dwindled, only to be replaced when the first of the WRA's concentration camps, Jerome, closed on June 30. Five hundred of its residents moved from Arkansas to Heart Mountain, their third camp in as many years. Tosh Asano left on June 8, destined to better whichever softball, football, or basketball team recruited him at Fort Shelby in Mississippi. Lomo Shinji, the only player other than Babe or Horse with any football experience prior to the previous season, enlisted in July.

Northern Pacific Railway's Extra Gang #6 was looking for men, so Stan boarded a train and arrived in Lignite, a minuscule community buried in the forests of far northern Idaho. The labor made beet-pulling look easy, but he got to work with his father, who was already on the crew. Stan was hired as a jack man, shimmying and hoisting the steel rails so that rotten and cracked ties could be replaced underneath. The entire crew was Japanese American, save for the foreman and the two spikers—burly Italians who sledgehammered spikes through the new hardwood ties. He worked with Honolulu (who was from Hawai'i), Tojo (who looked like Japanese prime minister Hideki

Tojo), and Copenhagen (who favored that brand of chewing tobacco). The work was more than backbreaking—it was dangerous. Freight and passenger trains passed frequently, charging to Spokane or Helena or Yakima loaded with tanks and jeeps and munitions or hewn timber from the surrounding hills. The only way to warn the jack men of an incoming train was to set a charge on the rails a quarter-mile up-track, which would detonate as the train passed over. The explosion would give Stan and Honolulu and Tojo and Copenhagen a few seconds to scatter far enough to avoid not only death, but the toilet paper, urine, and excrement the train spat out.

If they had survived the trains and the shit, they were eaten alive by the bedbugs, which hid in the sheets and blankets and mattresses, sparing no one. On weekends Stan and his father would buy flannel shirts at the Montgomery Ward in nearby Sandpoint, the town's lumberjacks click-clacking their way down the sidewalk in their spiked caulk boots. Or they'd visit the department stores of Spokane, Washington, scouring the city for an ivory mahjong set. Whenever they'd pass the city of Coeur d'Alene, Stan would stare out the window at the sign and think about how beautiful it sounded to his ears. *Coeur d'Alene.*

Extra Gang #6 was named the best, fastest gang in all of Northern Pacific's 8,600 miles, setting records for the most rails and ties laid over specific times and distances. When Stan applied for a Social Security number that summer, the first number came back as 7, a designation granted only to railroad workers. It was a point of pride for the rest of his life.

As Stan fought bedbugs and rails in Idaho, Horse embarked on his own new career. He was driving a coal truck when he first approached the *Sentinel* editor, hoping to put his high school writing skills to work. "Well, what's your expertise?" the editor asked. Horse paused, and thought on it.

"What does 'expertise' mean?"

The editor sent Horse to find a dictionary to learn what "expertise" meant. He returned a few weeks later with a small addition to his vocabulary and a proposition. *I'm interested in sports*, he said, *Why don't I write about that?* The editor had an idea, one that would shift the course of Horse's life forever: "Why don't you write a sports column?"

For a teenager blessed even by teenage standards with a rash of opinions, it was a perfect fit. His first column was nothing much, just a piece on how the summer baseball ranks would be thin due to relocation or active duty, but it was *something*. Before the *Sentinel* hired him, he had worked as an office boy, a truck driver, a guard, a maintenance worker, and helped in a mess hall. Now he had a new title: reporter.

So he wrote. He wrote and wrote and wrote. He used phrases like "cloudy, windswept day" and "struck pay dirt." He stretched his vocabulary further and called players sparkplugs and gridmen and pigskinners. And a few months later, when asked his occupation by the United States Army, he'd respond by checking the box for "authors, editors, and reporters."

———————

On July 20, the FBI arrived at Tule Lake with arrest warrants for Kiyoshi Okamoto and Sam Horino. Frank Emi, Paul Nakadate, and Guntaro Kubota were taken away from Heart Mountain. Agents walked into Leavenworth and dragged out Ben Wakaye and Minoru Tamesa, both serving three-year bids for their draft evasion conviction just weeks earlier. And in Denver, FBI agents and U.S. marshals swarmed *Rocky Shimpo* editor Jimmie Omura's house.

Omura's arrest confused everyone. The Fair Play Committee had forwarded press releases to him, and he had championed their cause, but no one had ever even spoken to him, either in person or by phone. Some in the group were so unfamiliar with him that they thought he was Irish—Jimmie O'Mura. But the FBI and the U.S. Attorney's Office saw his role differently. By the spring of 1944, the bilingual *Rocky Shimpo*'s subscriber base had stretched far beyond the Japanese American community of Denver, its ten thousand subscribers dotting not only Colorado but every WRA camp. Every week, 1,200 copies of the *Rocky Shimpo* were delivered to Heart Mountain alone. After he began his series of editorials about the draft resistance movements not only at Heart Mountain but Amache and other camps, the paper was deluged with letters.

All eight men were charged with conspiracy to violate the Selective Service Act and urging others to resist the draft. They found themselves in the same dingy Cheyenne jail as the sixty-three resisters; Wakaye and Tamesa were only gone for a month.

After the arrests, the reality of the stakes of the Fair Play Committee's goals was fully realized. The July 29 issue of the *Sentinel* brought news of the deaths of Corporal Yoshiharu Aoyama and Lieutenant Kei Tanahashi, the first two soldiers from Heart Mountain to die in battle. The two had known each other since childhood, both as members of Boy Scout Troop 379 in Los Angeles and graduates of UCLA. While working as a forward observer for the 442's Cannon Company, Aoyama rushed to save a wounded soldier. Both of his legs were blown off by an 88mm shell, but he refused medical attention, demanding the doctors tend to others first. He died the next day. Tanahashi spoke four languages. Before volunteering, he was working on a master's degree in economics and finance from the University of Nebraska. He had been married for three months when, serving with Company G, 2nd Battalion, of the nearly all-nisei 442nd Regimental Combat Team outside Castellina, Italy, he was killed by machine-pistol fire. It was the Fourth of July. Both men were posthumously awarded the Silver Star, and Aoyama's actions were memorialized in issue #34 of *Heroic Comics*. The January 1946 story was entitled "G.I. Jap—American Hero."

Two funerals were held behind barbed wire, Aoyama's in a Buddhist church, Tanahashi's at a mess hall.

The Gila River All-Stars arrived in camp just as the calendar was flipping from August to September. The team from the only camp visited by a member of the first family was stacked and well conditioned, the result of Kenichi Zenimura, who, upon his death twenty-five years later, would be christened "the Father of Japanese American Baseball."

Zenimura was in his mid-forties, a Hiroshima native who'd lived in the United States most of his life. A switch-hitter who could play all nine positions, he had made his name in the 1920s and 1930s as both a player and promoter. He led barnstorming tours of Japan and was an integral part of the negotiations that led to Babe Ruth and Lou Gehrig's tour of the country in 1934. In 1927, spotting an opportunity for two groups of baseball clubs excluded from the upper echelon of American pro ball, he teamed up with Negro league legend Lonnie Goodwin. Zenimura's Fresno Athletic Club and Goodwin's band of black all-stars, dubbed the Philadelphia Royal Giants, traveled to Japan for a "goodwill tour," and were so thoroughly welcomed by the Japanese that Emperor Hirohito presented the Royal Giants with a trophy.

So it only made sense that once incarcerated at Gila River, Zenimura would attempt to make a world-class baseball community out in the middle of the Sonoran Desert.

Zenimura began clearing sagebrush, and soon the lot was full of men and children with shovels, digging out the brush, piling it, and burning it. Zenimura somehow procured a bulldozer to level the field, then flooded it to even out the dirt. By the summer of 1943 he'd planted Bermuda grass in the outfield, and had convinced a camp plumber to cut into the laundry room's water line and extend the pipe two hundred feet to the pitcher's mound so he could condition the infield. He persuaded the camp's fire department to hold its drills in the outfield so the excess water would feed the grass. His teenage sons dragged the infield to catch any stray rocks.

What began on a whim grew into a thirty-two-team league, with different age divisions, and open invitations to outside teams to challenge the ones in Gila River. That summer, Babe and a team from Heart Mountain convinced the WRA that the competition would be good for morale, and took the 2,300-mile round-trip from Wyoming.

The team was mostly a re-creation of the prewar San Jose Asahis, plus Babe and Tosh Asano. Stepping off the bus into 120-degree heat, the Heart Mountain team wilted. Injuries felled multiple players, a nightmare considering only thirteen men made the trip. Games were played after dinner nearly every night for two straight weeks, with temperatures still sitting over 100 degrees. Pitchers split the skin on their hands throwing in the hot air, which was 40 to 50 degrees higher than the temperature at Heart Mountain that week. Only five players were able to play in all thirteen games. With his teammates sidelined, Babe filled in around the infield, even pitching one game. Outside the baseball diamond, Tosh pitched two softball exhibitions, using his rising fastball to such a degree that he no-hit his opponents. Despite the circumstances, the Heart Mountain team took eight of thirteen games, drawing crowds so large that they took home nearly enough money to pay for the journey.

In the last days of summer in 1944, Zenimura's Gila River team made the reverse trip. The team they met in Heart Mountain had been decimated by the draft and relocation. George Hinaga, who batted .400 in the 1943 series, was gone, and Babe had just returned from six months working in Montana. The rust showed. The Gileans took nine of the thirteen games, one of the losses an embarrassing 8–0 shellacking in the finale.

With baseball season over, Babe sat in camp, unsure of his next move. His permanent leave had yet to be approved. The Jackrabbits, his club stuffed with his best friends, had disbanded in late August, active duty and induction plucking a boy at a time. Football, once the most important thing in his life, was a distant memory. There was nothing left to do but wait and hope the barbed wire would soon come down.

CHAPTER TWENTY

Chasing Perfection

RAY THOMPSON RESIGNED a week before classes started. It wasn't uncommon, this resignation. Heart Mountain High School's teachers never stuck around for more than a semester or two, with some picking up and leaving in the middle of the semester, if not the school week. When classes opened on September 4, twelve of the thirty-nine white teachers were new.

Thompson was more than just the head of the school's physical education department and football coach, though. He was the conduit to the outside. His connections with the Wyoming Athletic Association had greased the Eagles' entry the year before, and his renown around the state helped build the football schedule, meager as it was. But if Thompson had a hard time convincing Wyoming high schools to play in a concentration camp, his successor would have trouble for an entirely new reason: no one wanted to *lose* to a team from a concentration camp.

The man tasked with trying was Talbot Rudolph. Rudolph and his wife, Mona, moved into camp from Big Piney, a two-hundred-person Wyoming town so cold its nickname was the Ice Box of the Nation. (The record low is –50°F.) Talbot was an agriculture instructor, so the Rudolphs had spent the past two decades bouncing from state to state—Colorado, Nevada, back to Colorado—before moving to Wyoming in 1941 for a teaching gig in Pine Bluffs, the last town you pass through before leaving southeastern Wyoming. In both Big Piney and Pine Bluffs, Rudolph led the schools' basketball and football teams, to varying degrees of success. He was undefeated as a football coach, though there was one catch: he'd only ever coached six-man teams. Six-man football was developed during the Great Depression as a way for smaller high schools to still field teams. The games are high-scoring, with scores in the 60s and 70s not uncommon. While the rules are much the same as eleven-man football, stylistically it's a much different game. But Heart Mountain was desperate. Not only had Thompson left the team, but so had Tubby. He spent that fall not coaching, but delivering the camp's mail.

Jack Sakamoto was a twenty-one-year-old Jackrabbit who'd spent the previous year working as a waiter in New York City, squeezed into a tiny apartment in Morningside Heights. Before that he worked in a chrome plating plant in Cleveland. His family was stretched thin. His younger sister couldn't work due to what doctors called "a twisted spine." His older brother, James, had moved to Cleveland and worked as a dental technician, and was joined soon after by the youngest Sakamoto, who attended school. Caring for two, James couldn't afford to send any money to his parents in Heart Mountain, who had sold all their possessions for $150 after Pearl Harbor. Jack would regularly send all the money he could back to his parents: $10 a month. Meanwhile, at Heart Mountain he'd made $16 a month, with no housing or food costs. He decided to go back to camp, where there happened to be an opening for an assistant football coach.

The Eagles might still have won with new coaches. New players would be another story. Gone was every player with any football experience—Babe, Horse, Lomo—along with starting fullback Mas Yoshiyama, who was now attending his third high school in as many years after his family relocated to El Paso, Texas. The same was true for guard Shoichi "Bozo" Nomura, in Libertyville, Illinois. Both became starters on their new teams. Second-stringers like Stan now spent their days in the hard corners of the West; Tayzo was out on bail and expecting the next three years of his life to take place far from any football fields.

On an early September afternoon, forty-five Heart Mountain high schoolers met their new coaches, and they set to figuring out who among them would soon be called Eagles. Nine lettermen returned, including four starters: starting backs Keiichi Ikeda and Mas Ogimachi, end Jack Funo, and center Yoichi Hosozawa. As the players practiced passing drills and light punting, two transfers from the Jerome camp, Norman Yasui and Ed Wasuda, navigated the social structures of the tryout. Yasui had started at left tackle for the Jerome High School team the previous season, which played two games against outside competition. Both games were against Louisiana Training Institute, an all-white reform school eighty miles south in Monroe, Louisiana. One ended in a 54–0 thrashing by the Jerome team.

Beyond the players, there were more changes that boded well for the Eagles. The camp bought new shoulder pads and helmets for the team, and the student body raised enough money to buy a set of tackling dummies. The team also had the *Sentinel* on its side. Through a bit of ethical gymnastics the reporter assigned to cover the Eagles' season was its former starting left tackle, Horse Yoshinaga.

As the season began, Rudolph and Sakamoto added Yuk Kimura to the staff to coach the linemen. With little eleven-man coaching experience between the three of them, though, they'd need another coach to help on offense. Lucky for them there was someone available. On September 14, Babe climbed out of his limbo and onto the coaching staff. Once again, he was an Eagle.

———

The schedule was shaping up. Games against Worland, Carbon County, Cody, and Columbus, Montana, were on the books, with a maybe from Powell. Even if the Eagles played just the games already scheduled, they'd surpass the 1943 season. To test both teams, the Cody

Broncs made the thirteen-mile journey to camp to scrimmage on September 20. The Eagles were unsure of their chances. In addition to being outweighed by thirty pounds a man, they'd lost nearly their entire second string to the potato harvest, forcing the starters to drill just among themselves. Cody was never a football power—their last season above .500 was 1938—but the societal strain between the two communities made for a scrimmage that had been years in the making.

Weeks earlier, in a letter to Cody mayor Raymond Howe and published in the *Sentinel*, Dr. E. W. J. Schmitt, the pastor of a church in suburban Philadelphia, Pennsylvania, took the town to task for its racism. Schmitt had visited Cody six years earlier on his honeymoon, and returned as a member of the Citizen's Cooperating Committee, a Philadelphia group dedicated to helping Japanese Americans get on their feet after relocating from the camps. He expected a pleasant visit to the city that "exemplified the freedom and hospitality of the West," but within five minutes of his arrival he was searching for a way to leave. As he walked down the street, he saw a huge, crudely drawn sign hung in a barbershop window: *NO JAPS*.

"There is no reason under the sun why any of the evacuees would want to patronize a Cody barbershop unless it would be to maintain contact with the outside world," Schmitt wrote. "Obviously, then, the purpose of the barbershop sign must be to tell a passerby who is Japanese, or American of Japanese ancestry (I doubt if our friend the barber would draw any distinction) that he is not wanted. Would it not be better if the signs read: 'We are prejudiced, the proprietor of this shop does not believe in the principles of democracy—stay out!'"

Schmitt continued that once he'd made his way to camp, he learned that a similar sign hung in the Hotel Irma, Buffalo Bill Cody's lavish granite monument to his daughter. Later, upon his return home, two nisei in Philadelphia told him they were asked to leave the Range Restaurant in Cody because "we can't have Japs mixing with the others."

"I sincerely hope that you can do something so that other fellow Americans will not come to the conclusion that Cody has joined the ranks of those who stir up dissention among Americans of different racial strains and is thus destroying the principle for which our brave boys are fighting," he concluded.

The contents of Schmitt's letter were damning, but they weren't news to Heart Mountain incarcerees. For the past two years the towns of Powell and Cody had been passing ordinances banning issei and nisei from the towns, only to rescind them when farmers argued that their absence would hamper the harvest. Once, while walking down the street in Cody, an incarceree was punched in the face by a military police officer and suffered a broken jaw. No action was taken against the soldier. Even if viewed as the actions of a minority, they clouded the views of Cody in the eyes of every incarceree.

The rules of the scrimmage were laid out plainly: 90 minutes, with the ball placed at the 50-yard line after each score, no extra points. On the first play, the Eagles lined up in an I formation and called a cross buck. With the second-stringers starting the scrimmage, quarterback Shuzo Sumii—rail thin and with a hedgehog for a haircut—took the snap, faked to the fullback, then handed it off to reserve halfback Isamu Ito. The line held and Ito was off, evading a safety and finding himself in the end zone. Within seconds the Eagles were up 6–0, and they accelerated from there. Keiichi scored twice on end sweeps and threw for another touchdown. The closest George Yahiro got to the football team the prior year was when he played his trombone at a team pep rally. Today he was lined up at right halfback and found himself adding six points to the scoreboard more than once.

The Broncs were baffled by the Eagles' speed. If the Eagles' line held and their backs made it into the secondary, they were gone, untouched. New guard Evan Oyakawa caused havoc all afternoon, worming through the Cody line and stopping their backs dead in the dirt.

"How much do you weigh?" asked Cody coach Hank Walleren.

"A hundred thirty pounds," Evan replied.

Walleren looked over at his players, exhausted from the fight. "Well take it easy on my guard, he only weighs 170."

After the scrimmage's ninety minutes the Eagles had scored eight touchdowns. Cody made it once to the 25-yard line. The final score was 48–0. In the weeks to follow, the Heart Mountain coaching staff would try to pin down the date for the official Cody game they had been promised before the scrimmage. The game would never happen.

The Eagles had no time to rest on their victory. Two days later they were scheduled to play Worland, whom they'd narrowly escaped the season before, 7–0, after a last-second pass from Babe to Mas Yoshiyama. While the stars of 1943's Worland team were gone, there was a new threat. Captain Chuck Harkins was a barrel of a boy, squared at the shoulders and with thighs that could pass for Spanish hams. He'd bulldoze across the line from the fullback slot, churning his legs that would be so prized as a semipro catcher in Wyoming, Texas, North Carolina, and California in the years after high school.

The coaches reviewed the scrimmage. The line held up better than they expected, a marked improvement over the fledgling group who showed up at the beginning of practice. Left halfback George Iseri stunned not only the Broncs but the coaches, using his speed and drive for big gains. This team might have been less experienced, but they were faster and lighter than the 1943 team. Now all they had to do was weaponize those differences.

As with Ray Thompson the season before, Talbot Rudolph was quickly overshadowed by his assistants. In yearbook photos the following spring, he's not even in the team photos, instead featured just with the six-man team; the reason may have been familial, because Rudolph's son, Bob, on the six-man team, was the only white player on any Eagles team. (Made up of freshmen and sophomores, the team went on to outscore its opponents 167–6 over the course of the four-game season.) In Rudolph's stead, Sakamoto and Babe installed an I-formation offense, a switch from the previous year's single- and double-wing variations. They took Norman Yasui, who played left tackle at Jerome

High, and moved him to fullback, utilizing his size to clear the way for the smaller, faster halfbacks.

Babe and Jack also had to deal with a reality that had not faced their predecessors: induction into the military. The all-nisei 442nd Infantry Regiment had adopted the motto "Go for broke"—Hawaiian gambling slang for betting everything on a single dice roll—and had spent the past months taking heavy losses in Italy. In just one forty-mile stretch of the campaign the regiment suffered casualties of 1,271, including 239 deaths. In a few weeks they'd be sent to fight dense fog, trench foot, and German soldiers in an effort to rescue an American battalion trapped high on a French hill. They succeeded, their heroism enshrined forever in movies, books, and a painting that still hangs in the Pentagon. But the cost was high, and the war still wasn't over. They'd need more men. During the week, right tackle Ed Yasuda traveled to Fort Logan for his Army physical; he returned as right tackle Private Ed Yasuda. Babe and Jack would have to plan for every game wondering if their players would even still be in camp by kickoff.

And right now, that plan was failing. After an opening 35-yard drive down to the Worland 34, all inklings of consistency vanished. The I formation was a disaster; there was no movement, no flow. A team that had spent the past year confusing and exasperating defenses had morphed into a predictable bore. Luckily, its defense was shining. Yoichi, Evan, and guard Rabbit Shiraki swarmed through the Warriors' line, gang-tackling Harkins whenever he touched the ball. Harkins would boom punts deep into the Eagles' half, and battles in the trenches would be renewed. The whole game moved like that—feet here, inches there. The Worland offense was performing so poorly that the Eagles consistently went for it on fourth down, only to fail to convert again and again.

With only three minutes to go and the Eagles stuck on the 50, Jack and Babe abandoned both the I and the team's starters. Keiichi and Mas Ogimachi were pulled from the backfield, replaced by Shuzo Sumii at quarterback and George Yahiro at right half. The I was replaced by the spread, about as different a formation as can be conjured on the football field. (In an I formation three backs line up directly behind the center, like the letter I. A spread formation moves those same players—save for the quarterback—out wide, thereby spreading out both the offense and the defense.) It was immediately as if an entirely different high school were playing. Shuzo connected with George and Shiro Teramoto on three straight passes, flinging the ball 41 yards. *Tick tick tick.* With 35 seconds to go, Shuzo subbed out for third-stringer Babe Fujioka. A mindless penalty—Fujioka failed to report to the ref—pushed the Eagles back to 14. *Tick tick.* First down fell incomplete. *Tick.* With 14 yards to go, Fujioka stood in the shotgun, spread his backs across the line of scrimmage, took the snap, and faded. Shiro headed left, George right. Fujioka stepped into his pass and delivered a strike to George, waiting in the end zone.

The Eagles lined up to kick the extra point. Keiichi took the snap, and instead of teeing it up, peeled off and around for the conversion. The Eagles may have played poorly all day, but they were still going to win their way. The clock expired before Worland could try a desperation play, and—in almost identical fashion to their 1943 win over the Warriors—the Eagles escaped 7–0.

Four games, four wins, zero points allowed.

The next week, Evan Oyakawa nursed a broken collarbone. Guard Rabbit Shiraki left the team for seasonal work. His classmates and teammates filled the fields and drove the tractors of the camp, harvesting thousands of pounds of daikon, potatoes, and carrots across 187 acres. Thirteen draft resisters returned to the camp, free on bail. And Coach Sakamoto packed his bag, took his $25 from the WRA and his 1–0 record with the Eagles, and boarded a train for Cleveland. There he'd live with his two brothers while awaiting a call from the Army, the three sending back as much money as they could to their parents and sister. With Rudolph training the six-man team and Sakamoto bound for Ohio, there was only one natural fit for head coach.

Babe's coaching résumé included two lines. One: teaching elementary school students the basics of football. Two: co-coaching the Lil' Yokums, the 1943 Heart Mountain intramural girls' basketball champions. But familiarity, skill, and drive mattered more than experience. So, ten days after being hired, Babe Nomura became the fifth head coach of the Heart Mountain Eagles. Carbon County would be there in two weeks.

The team from Red Lodge was experiencing its own similar brand of turmoil. Coach L. E. Hallsted, who'd led the team the past three seasons, was inducted into the Army in August, leaving the Coyotes coachless. It was an epidemic around the state. "Coaches are getting as scarce as new jalopies," wrote the *Billings Gazette*. By early September the school lacked an athletic director, making the mere scheduling of any games a miracle for the small, 180-student school. Of the thirty-five players who tried out for the team, only five had made the trip to Heart Mountain the previous year.

The district hired Frank Ward as athletic director and football coach, but their prospects when they reached the Heart Mountain gate were not rosy. Saddling the memory of last season's 25–0 loss to the Eagles were a pair of losses in their opening games, a 33–6 beatdown at the hands of the Cody Broncs and a more respectable 19–12 loss to the Lovell Bulldogs.

Babe switched to a T formation and moved Keiichi from quarterback to left half, prioritizing his speed over his arm. That opened up space for Poly Sumii (Shuzo's brother) in the backfield. Resembling General Patton with his helmet on, Poly was the fastest Eagle, clocking the 100-meter dash at near 10 seconds on the Wyoming dirt. With a stiff-arm that could daze a bull, Poly could be used either as a runner or blocker, racing ahead to free Keiichi or George out of the T. Speed was of the essence this week especially, with Evan and Rabbit sidelined by injuries and work. Filling in on the line was untested 125-pound

Taka Katsuma. Finding ways *around* the Coyotes would be more important than finding ways through them.

"Eagle Gridders Ruin Coyotes" was how the *Sentinel* would later describe the afternoon. It took the Eagles only five plays from kickoff to land on the Coyotes' 10, an opening drive that capped off with a left-end sweep from George for the touchdown. Two minutes later, Coyotes captain and quarterback Ray Sandin found himself pinned on his own 5 and punting out of danger. What went unsaid when Yoichi Hosozawa's weight was mentioned was the fact that this made him virtually unblockable. With a quick first step or a deliberate jab-step, he'd be through his opponents' offensive line, eyes trained on the ball. Yoichi's hand hit the ball at the same time as Sandin's boot, and quickly made its way into the arms of tackle Sus Terazawa, who walked in for the second score.

The next quarter and a half was a blur. Forty-five-yard touchdown passes, 30-yard runs, 15-yard losses on blown laterals—even when the Eagles were failing, they were doing it spectacularly: 6–0 ballooned to 19–0, then ran to 40–0 by halftime. The Coyotes' first real chance of the game came in the third quarter, after the Eagles failed to convert a fourth down from their own 45. Hoping to catch the Eagles on their heels, Sandin launched a quick-strike passing attack, finding fullback Louis Jordan and end Leo Spogen for a combined 20 yards. The Eagles held Sandin to just 5 yards over the next three plays, and a fourth-down heave fell incomplete. In an otherwise penalty-light game, the Eagles blundered and, instead of taking over on downs, lost 15 yards after roughing the passer.

The Eagles' defense tightened. With four downs and 10 yards to go, victory was no longer in doubt, but pride was. Over four and a half interscholastic games they'd scored 85 points and surrendered none. Add in the Cody scrimmage, and the Eagles had scored a blinding 133 points against their high school peers. Sandin took the snap and pushed the Eagles' line for 6 yards; Jordan added another on second down, and the Eagles held on third.

Sandin called his own number on fourth-and-goal from the 3. He took the snap and sprinted to the right, attempting to skirt the end. He met a wall of Eagles, fighting to keep the scoreboard blank. Heart Mountain took over on downs, Keiichi punted them out of trouble, and the final score was 60–0.

Five games, five wins, zero points allowed.

After tinkering with his lineups and formations, Babe's Eagles were clicking. The 60–0 victory was the most points scored by a Wyoming varsity eleven since Powell dropped 66 on Basin High School in November 1940, almost four years earlier. Whether due to politics or fear, the team from just up the road refused to play Heart Mountain despite invitations from both Rudolph and Thompson. The Bighorn Basin League, of which Powell was the most dominant school, refused to schedule the Eagles for league games despite their acceptance into the Wyoming Athletic Association. Of the nine teams in the state's Northwest Division, the Eagles' 1943 record outshined seven, bested only by Powell's 9–0 season; no other team lost fewer than three games. Powell went so far as to declare itself state champions in 1943, claiming the crown as the only undefeated and untied team in Wyoming. This, of course, overlooked the high school that sat closer to Powell than any other one in the state.

With games against Cody and Columbus (Montana) falling through, the Eagles called on their steadiest of rivals.

Football was in Fred Winterholler's blood. His uncle, Johnny Winterholler, was the greatest athlete in Wyoming during the 1930s, an All-American at the University of Wyoming in baseball, football, and basketball. After graduating in 1940—the Winterholler family was fourteen children deep; the tail end of the children were closer in age to their nieces and nephews than their oldest siblings—Johnny forwent a professional baseball tryout and instead shipped off to Marine officer training school. As Fred walked onto the field at Heart Mountain, his uncle sat in a Japanese POW camp, forty-five pounds under-weight and paralyzed from the waist down following a spontaneous blood-vessel rupture in his spine. Following the war, Johnny would go on to become a member of the Rolling Devils, the first wheelchair basketball team. In 1964, *Sports Illustrated* named him to its Silver Anniversary football team. The gymnasium in Lovell still bears his name today.

To make it out of Heart Mountain with a win, Fred would need some of his uncle's spirit. Gone was his burly left side, its line swelled by Don Ash and Cal Asay, which had held the Eagles to just six points the season before. He'd need to rely on new talent. Leland Fillerup would try to take some of the pressure off Fred from left half. Six weeks after the game his mother would receive a sixth star for her service flag, as Leland enlisted and joined his five older brothers in the Army.

Just like against Red Lodge, the Eagles flew out the gate. Four plays after kickoff, right end Jack Funo took an end-around to the house, hanging six points on the scoreboard before anyone even broke a sweat. Keiichi's kickoff pinned the Bulldogs on their own 10, but Winterholler, Fillerup, and right half Ed Horsley picked up two quick first downs, equaling Worland's total for the entire September game. Lovell lost most of its offensive line; it made up for it with flashy new backs. The defense needed a stop, and it came on time. The Bulldogs' opening drive was squelched, but the Eagles could see that stopping Lovell would be more difficult than they'd planned.

In one play that all changed. After a snappy 22-yard drive to the Lovell 48, George took the handoff from Keiichi, and slashed to his left. Forty-eight yards later, the Eagles were up 12. Unused to having to defend such sustained drives, Babe swapped out his first-stringers. No matter. On the first play, Winterholler dropped back to pass, only to hit Ham Miyamoto instead of his receiver. The ensuing touchdown run and extra point put the Eagles up 19–0 as the first quarter ticked to a close.

Sitting in a three-touchdown hole, Winterholler seemed determined to claw the Bulldogs back into the game. Babe was substituting freely at this point, rotating Keiichi, Shuzo, and Babe Fujioka at will into the quarterback slot. With the Eagles threatening on the 10-yard line, Winterholler jumped a pass from Fujioka, intercepting it and sprinting 50 yards before an Eagle could tear him down. Then a first down. Fillerup gained eight more on a center buck, and the Bulldogs were marching, finding themselves on the Eagles' goal line, with three downs to put the ball over the line. Yoichi and Sus Terazawa ensured that did not occur, exploding through the Lovell line and stopping their backs dead.

Lovell could intercept a pass and high-step down the field at will, but the Eagles would not let them cross the line.

Midway through the third, Shuzo passed for two straight first downs, finding himself on the Lovell 24 and with a chance to put the game away. Winterholler refused. Stationed on the 5-yard line, he plucked Shuzo's next pass out of the air, turned upfield, and saw no one: 5 yards, then 10; 20, then 30. His teammates crowded around him, a flock protecting its leader. With a sure touchdown in his sights, he passed the 40 before he felt a tug. Shuzo had sprinted back the whole 40 yards, weaved between the blockers, and dragged Winterholler to the dirt. *You. Will. Not. Score.* The Bulldogs punted soon after.

The Eagles went into the spread, and Keiichi found Poly Sumii, who romped 50 yards for the touchdown. With less than four minutes to go, Norman Yasui, the lineman turned fullback, barged into the end zone for the final score: 32–0, Eagles.

Six games, six wins, zero points allowed.

As the wins piled up, the Eagles' frustrations also grew. Horse took up their cause.

"The local prep gridsters should have every right to the Big Horn Basin title," he wrote in his column. "Since the defending champion Powell Panthers refuse to meet the local outfit, the Eagles can claim the championship on the basis of their performance against the teams that the Panthers have also played."

Horse argued that the Heart Mountain victories over Lovell and in the Cody scrimmage were more impressive than Powell's wins over the two teams, and he had a point. Heart Mountain beat Lovell 32–0; Powell beat them 26–0. And while it was just a scrimmage, the Eagles allowed no points to Cody; the Powell Panthers won 40–13. The column was a sign of things to come for Horse's entire life: expressing views he knew would rattle and consternate readers. As Horse and the Eagles debated Powell's dodge, the rest of the camp turned its eyes to Cheyenne.

On January 24, 1934, Abraham Lincoln Wirin found himself blindfolded and bound, alone in the desert eighteen miles outside Brawley, California. After walking nine miles to the nearest town, he telegrammed President Roosevelt:

OUTBREAK OF ARMED VIOLENCE AND UNCONTROLLED MOB
ACTION IN IMPERIAL VALLEY DEMANDS YOUR ATTENTION. A. L.
WIRIN, ATTORNEY UPHOLDING CONSTITUTIONAL GUARANTEES
KIDNAPED, BEATEN AND THREATENED WITH DEATH LAST NIGHT.
PROMINENT CITIZENS SENT TO INVESTIGATE CONDITIONS HELD
UP AND RUN OUT OF COUNTY BY ARMED LEGIONNAIRES. ALL
RIGHTS OF LABOR UNDER NRA SUPPRESSED. STATE OF TERROR
EXISTS.

Wirin was born in Russia and as a child moved to Boston. There his parents learned about and grew fond of Abraham Lincoln, gifting the name to their son, who would loathe it his whole life. Wirin's career in civil liberties began early; as a child he was arrested and fined $5 for protesting assaults perpetrated by sailors during a peace march. His interest in protecting the rights of the underserved only grew from there. Following law school he joined the Southern California ACLU, which is how he wound up kidnapped and abandoned in the Colorado Desert in California. (Wirin was in town to address the area's lettuce pickers, a group of Mexican migrants who were attempting to unionize.) After Roosevelt signed Executive Order 9066, Wirin testified before Congress in support of the Japanese American community. He wrote columns about the progress of Japanese American civil rights cases for the *Pacific Citizen* and the Southern California ACLU's *Open Forum*. During the war he worked as counsel for the JACL, then, in spite of that relationship, found himself in Cheyenne, Wyoming, trying to keep eight nikkei men out of federal prison.

In April, ACLU founder and executive director Roger Baldwin dismissed any support of the Fair Play Committee, writing to Kiyoshi Okamoto and saying, "The men who have refused to accept military drafts are within their rights, but they of course must take the consequences. They doubtless have a moral case, but no legal case at all." He warned the committee leaders to "expect severe treatment." Because of this, Wirin represented the men privately.

With Judge T. Blake Kennedy on vacation, Judge Eugene Rice was called to Cheyenne from his usual perch atop the federal bench in Muskogee, Oklahoma. Wirin was honest with the men from the outset: the prospects weren't good. They would likely lose the district court case but, because of the constitutional questions involved, might have a better shot in appeal. Omura requested and was granted a separate trial; after the sixty-three resisters' luck with Kennedy, the seven remaining defendants opted for a jury trial.

No stranger to major constitutional cases, Wirin set about building a much different defense from the one employed in the June trial. In that case, U.S. Attorney Sackett simply had to prove the men had failed to show up for their physicals. This case was more complicated, the First Amendment rights of the defendants commingling with the draft-evasion conspiracy. Wirin built the case with appeal in mind, railing against the judge's refusal to accept it as a test case and the lack of

Japanese Americans on the grand jury. (This wasn't as preposterous a point as it seems. Heart Mountain's thousands of Japanese Americans, combined with small Japanese American communities across the state, accounted for more than 5 percent of Wyoming's 1944 population.)

Each of the defendants took the stand and admitted to his role in the Fair Play Committee. One day, a neighbor of Frank Emi's took the stand. Jack Nishimoto was in his late thirties, and Frank had done some small favors for the man in camp. On the stand Nishimoto lied repeatedly about the defendants; they were baffled by his testimony. *Why is he lying?* Emi wondered. At the time, the men only referred to him as an *inu*, the Japanese word for dog that had come to represent a slew of invictives in camp: informer, rat, snitch, conspirator. Years later, after requesting his declassified FBI file, Emi learned the answer—Nishimoto was an FBI informant. He'd befriended Emi at the behest of FBI agent Harry McMillen, who worked with Heart Mountain community analyst Asael Hansen, a WRA employee. After the FBI's fruitless interrogations of Emi, Nishimoto saw an opportunity to fill in the gaps, no matter how untruthful.

"The man's duplicity was unbelievable," Frank would write decades later.

The trial lasted almost two weeks. On Wednesday, November 1, 1944, Rice submitted the case to the jury. As it began its deliberations, a bulletin came across the Associated Press wire:

HEART MOUNTAIN, Wyo., Nov. 1—The Heart Mountain high school football team has scheduled a game with Casper high school for Heart Mountain next Saturday, C. D. [Clifford] Carter, superintendent of school at the northwestern Wyoming Japanese-American relocation center, announced today.

Carter said the Heart Mountain team has not been scored on for two years and has run up a total of 99 points against opponents so far this year.

CHAPTER TWENTY-ONE

November 4, 1944

JOE SCHWARTZ COULDN'T find enough cars. The coach of the Natrona Mustangs made call after call that Thursday night, only to get the same answer each time. *Sorry, no.* So by the time Friday afternoon rolled around, he piled as many of his players as he could into the few cars he could commandeer, and twenty-two of his Mustangs were on their way.

The drive from Casper to Heart Mountain is 230 miles of Wyoming loneliness. It requires only three turns—one in Shoshoni, one in Thermopolis, and one in Cody—and spends thirteen of its miles slicing through Wind River Canyon, a snaking gap of tectonic-molded rock that climbs to heights of more than 2,500 feet. The route is dotted with sagebrush, greasewood, and saltbush, hearty plants that have adapted to the state's scorched summers and winter winds.

As the Eagles languished with their shortened schedule, so, too, did the Natrona Mustangs. Due to injuries and war-bred roster depletion, Schwartz's team would play its fewest games since 1921. The team was scheduled to play Riverton on November 4, but Riverton canceled due to a lack of healthy players. Which is how a gap on November 4 ended up on their calendar, and twenty-two teenagers from Casper, Natrona County, Wyoming, found themselves driving into an American concentration camp.

Natrona consistently fielded one of the state's most dominant squads, winning the state title in two of the previous six seasons, and seeding the all-state teams with its players. The team's last losing season was 1926, the year before most of the team was born. The school was the largest in the state, a terra-cotta Collegiate Gothic–style masterpiece funded with 1920s oil boom cash. It housed the first indoor swimming pool in Wyoming; seventy years after its construction it was named to the National Register of Historic Places. Despite all their history and resources, the Mustangs pulled into Heart Mountain sitting at only 2-2-1, the victim of one out-of-state loss to Montana's Billings High and another to Cheyenne Central, the undisputed king of Wyoming football. (The school was named state champion in 1941, 1943, 1944, and 1945.) Natrona had one thing, though, that no other school in the state could claim: LeRoy Pearce.

LeRoy was a 210-pound mortar round of a teen. The previous spring, at the state track championships, he won the broad jump and the low hurdles. Five minutes after winning the hurdling title, he lined up for the final of the 220-yard dash; he took second. He was edged at the line in the 100-yard dash, though many bystanders thought he won. To finish the day, he led the Natrona relay to a gold medal. If LeRoy was his own high school, that school would've had the second-best track team in Wyoming in 1944.

Charles Edwin LeRoy Pearce was the son of Herbert and Lucile Pearce, an English immigrant and a Michigander fourteen years her husband's junior. Lucile was also a devout Seventh-day Adventist. After the season, LeRoy would be named first-team all-state, along with his center and right tackle. (His right end was second-team.) Working behind the best offensive line in the state, he bruised his way through the season, eventually becoming the starting tailback for the University of Wyoming. He parlayed his playing success into a decades-long coaching career that took him from Wyoming to the University of Arkansas, the University of Tennessee, Iowa State University, the University of Nebraska, and the University of Georgia, before finishing his coaching career at the University of Miami. Because of his mother's strict adherence to Seventh-day Adventist principles, she believed in no activities outside the home from Friday sundown until Saturday sundown. Before each home game, LeRoy would make himself a fried egg sandwich because his mother refused to cook him dinner. She never saw her son—one of the best athletes in the history of Wyoming, a man whose name still draws wonder when mentioned in the state today—play a single down of football.

As LeRoy and the rest of the Mustangs pulled into the camp, four thousand fans encircled the field. Their arrival was the day's second-biggest news.

The jury's decision was swift, and punishing. All members of the Fair Play Committee were found guilty. Jimmie Omura was spared and found not guilty; the prosecution's case against the newspaperman was spotty at best. The seven others received either two- or four-year sentences at Leavenworth. Wirin urged Judge Rice to release the men on bail while he appealed the case; Rice not only denied the request but called the men agitators and claimed "their own people are probably better off without them." The *Sentinel* was practically gleeful in its coverage, emblazoning "7 Fair Play Leaders Convicted" above the November 4 masthead.

As they awaited appeal, the men moved to Kansas, where they reunited with many of the sixty-three men convicted in June. They lived among the murderers and drug dealers common in high-security prisons, but also a collection of war-related inmates. On one end of that spectrum were the thirty members of the German American Bund who, while guarding a POW camp, helped German prisoners escape. On the other end were eight nisei solders from the 1800th Engineer General Service Battalion, a collection of soldiers from Japanese, Italian, and German descent. The men were all deemed to need additional surveillance by the federal government; in the nisei men's cases it was because they protested their treatment by the Army, which stripped them of their weapons and forced them onto latrine duty. The men petitioned to be treated like equals, like their white countrymen. Only they wrote the petition in Japanese, and signed it in their own blood. For the act of trying to serve their country they were dishonorably discharged, tried, convicted, and sentenced to fifteen years in Leavenworth.

To while away the time, Emi and the rest of the Fair Play Committee put on judo demonstrations, choreographing the routines so the smaller men would throw their larger compatriots. None of the other inmates ever bothered them after that.

The day was a picturesque, built-in-a-lab day for football. Fifty-six degrees and clear, warm enough to soften the dirt but not hot enough to slow down the players. The Mustangs' bright orange uniforms gleamed against the sun, their sleeves capped with black and white stripes. It would be hyperbole to call the Eagles' uniforms rags, but not by much. The team's pants sagged and drooped, and players' thighs were bound with tape to keep the makeshift cardboard pads in place. Their white jerseys, recycled and reworn game after game, practice after practice, weren't much more than pinnies with blue numbers stenciled on the back.

The Eagles elected to receive the opening kickoff. Within two plays they'd fumbled it away, gifting the Mustangs and their fifteen returning lettermen the ball just 35 yards from the end zone. The Mustangs' offense was like most at the time: grind until you hit the end zone. LeRoy and quarterback Jack Afferbach did just that, smashing the smaller Eagles, alternating carries up the Heart Mountain dirt, and shredding the defense, left gasping after just a few minutes. The Eagles were always the faster team. With LeRoy on the other side of the ball that was no longer true.

Sitting on the Eagle 11-yard line, Afferbach lateraled to Pearce, streaking around the left end. Two defenders stood between him and six points. He easily dismissed both and walked into the end zone. After six games, a scrimmage, an all-star game, hundreds of hours of practice, and surviving the fact that almost none of them had ever played a down of football in their lives until fifteen months earlier, the Eagles surrendered their first points. On their next set of downs, deep in their own territory, the Mustangs bulldozed 52 yards. Afferbach called the same play—a left-end sweep—from the Eagle 40. Pearce was off. Using his all-state speed, he left the Eagles panting, and walked into the end zone once again.

At the end of the first quarter the Eagles trailed 12–0. They went from undefeated and unscored-upon to the cusp of being run off their own field in just 12 minutes.

Already clipped by injuries, the Eagles fell victim to more, as the all-white refereeing unit allowed the Mustangs to have their way. Tripping, holding, shoving after the play was whistled dead—virtually everything was allowed. In the following week's *Sentinel*, columnist Youngren Mishima wrote "time and again the local officiating body failed to call penalties, resulting in an unnecessarily rough game." He then referred to the matchup, with tongue firmly in cheek, as an "up and at em affair."

As the game clock slid to the second quarter, though, the Eagles woke up. Co-captain Mas Ogimachi returned a kickoff to his own 35, and Babe called on what had worked for the past six games: speed and rotation. Keiichi, Shuzo, and Babe Fujioka swapped in and out at quarterback as the Eagles marched into Mustangs territory. On their 34, Shuzo pitched the ball to George Yahiro, who tiptoed down the sideline to the Mustangs' 2. On the next play, George lined up at right half. As Yoichi snapped the ball to Shuzo, George snagged it out of the air. In the Heart Mountain High School yearbook the following spring, every senior Eagle received a laudatory three- or four-sentence write-up. "Once in the open he was unstoppable," Yahiro's read. "He was full of guts and his opponents have learned to respect him on the field." Sprinting for the hole created by left guard Kow Miyahata—a six-man player called up just for this game—George bounded into the end zone for six. A Shuzo-to-George pass for the conversion was good, and the Eagles found themselves down just 12–7. If the Eagles could just get a stop on defense, get some yards, get a breath, get *anything*, they'd not only be back in the game, they'd be on top.

Minutes later, Afferbach fielded an Eagles punt at the home team's 43-yard line. Racing up the field, the quarterback flicked a lateral to Mustangs backup quarterback Jim Hult. Fresh legs beneath him, and dealing with an Eagles defense that had been dragged up and down the field by LeRoy and Afferbach all afternoon, Hult sprinted the rest of the way, added a QB sneak for the extra point, and put the Mustangs up 19–7. The rest of the half was a dispiriting slog; any hope the Eagles had drawn from George's touchdown waned.

With 30 seconds left in the half, the Eagles and their fans resigned themselves to the clock and hoped the second half would be better. The Mustangs weren't content. They wanted to put away this team, this team that thought it could beat the Mustangs, this team that talked a lot of shit about being undefeated. *But who had they played? Had they played Cheyenne Central? Had they played Billings?* No. They'd played Worland and Lovell and *Carbon County*, for chrissake.

So as the clock ticked to zero Afferbach dropped back and, instead of handing it off to LeRoy, soared a pass downfield. *Put them away*, the ball yelled over their heads. At the Eagles' 40, Rabbit Shiraki quieted the ball, snapping it out of the air. Even with the Eagles' pace, there wouldn't be enough time to get off more than one or two attempts at the end zone. So Rabbit did the second-best thing rabbits do: he ran as fast as he could. He ran past his own stunned teammates. Then he ran past Afferbach. Then he ran past the best athlete in the state. He ran 60 yards, and when he was done, the Eagles were heading into halftime down just 19–13.

The play was invigorating. After halftime the Eagles soared onto the field, dominating what quickly switched from an offensive fire sale to a defensive clinic. The Eagles tightened up and showed why they hadn't given up a point before today. Then they took control. From their own 30, the Eagles drove to the Mustangs' 10-yard. On first, second, and third downs, they made little headway, chipping away inches instead of yards. But they weren't going to come this far without scoring. On fourth down, Keiichi, the stalwart of the Eagles' offense all year but bottled up by the collapsing Mustangs defense, took the snap and faded from his line. He waited, and waited. With the defense swarming the backfield, George leaked out to the right corner of the end zone. As the Mustangs collapsed around Keiichi, he spotted George and lofted a pass. The ball hit George in the hands, and bounced to the right, then left. Bounce, bounce.

Once in the open he was unstoppable. He was full of guts and his opponents have learned to respect him on the field.

The next day, Babe Nomura would board a train bound for a sandwich shop in Hartford, Connecticut. In two days, former student body president Ted Fujioka would be killed as the 442 fought in France; the flag atop the flagpole he worked so diligently to erect would be flown at half-mast. In three days, Franklin Delano Roosevelt would win his fourth term as president of the United States. Horse wrote his final *Sentinel* column under the byline "Pvt. George Yoshinaga" that week, signing off, "Well there it is, the final 'bits by yours truly. Thanks for bearing with me and until we meet again. . . . Adios!" On the morning of Roosevelt's victory, Horse would pack his bags and board a different train from Babe's and head for Fort Leavenworth. His mother and sister would walk him to the front gate, where his mother would whisper "Take care" as he boarded the train, neither of them knowing it would be the last words she ever spoke to him.

The ball bounced between George's hands and everyone held their breath, not knowing what might happen next.

CHAPTER TWENTY-TWO

Going About Like Eagles

PRESIDENT ROOSEVELT KNEW he needed to get out in front of the Supreme Court. Since October he had monitored the Court's progress on two separate cases: *Korematsu v. United States* and *Ex parte Mitsuye Endo*.

Endo was a twenty-two-year-old clerk for the California Department of Motor Vehicles on December 7, 1941, who was summarily fired soon after. She was sent to Tule Lake, where she was introduced by letter to James Purcell, a California attorney seeking a nisei for a test case to challenge the federal government's treatment of Japanese Americans. Endo was perfect in their opinion: she was a Christian, had a brother in the Army, had never traveled to Japan, and could neither speak nor read Japanese. In the summer of 1942 Purcell filed a habeas corpus petition on her behalf, arguing that the government's actions amounted to little more than "undeclared martial law" and claiming her incarceration could only last as long as it took to determine her loyalty.

The Supreme Court heard both cases on October 16, 1944, and was prepared to announce its decision on December 4. Political machinations from the Roosevelt cabinet delayed the announcement just long enough to blunt its impact.

"Favorable progress of the war in the Pacific, as well as other developments, had resulted in a determination by the commanding general of the Western Defense Command, with the approval of the War Department, that the continued mass exclusion from the West Coast of persons of Japanese ancestry is no longer a matter of military necessity," the War Department announced in a December 17 press release. "For this reason, mass exclusion orders under which persons of Japanese ancestry were evacuated from the Pacific Coast area in 1942 were revoked today."

It wasn't difficult to parse why the War Department made its decision. Following the ascendance to the bench of Roosevelt nominees Hugo Black, William O. Douglas, and Frank Murphy, the Supreme Court had sprinted to the left. This was beneficial to most of Roosevelt's domestic policies, save for one. On December 18, the Supreme Court ruled unanimously in favor of Endo, ruling not on the constitutionality of incarceration, but writing "whatever power the War Relocation Authority may have to detail other classes of citizens, it has no authority to subject citizens who are concededly loyal to its leave procedure." The Court ruled 6–3 against Korematsu, however, deciding the removal itself legal.

Justice Frank Murphy, who spent his court recesses as a lieutenant colonel in the Army Reserve and once appeared in court not in his robe but his uniform, wrote in dissent:

> *I dissent, therefore, from this legalization of racism. Racial discrimination in any form and in any degree has no justifiable part whatever in our democratic way of life. It is unattractive in any setting but it is utterly revolting among a free people who have embraced the principles set forth in the Constitution of the United States. All residents of this nation are kin in some way by blood or culture to a foreign land. Yet they are primarily and necessarily a part of the new and distinct civilization of the United States. They must accordingly be treated at all times as the heirs of the American experiment and as entitled to all the rights and freedoms guaranteed by the Constitution.*

In the 155-year history of the Court it was the first time the word "racism" was used in an opinion.

Politicians and professional bigots along the West Coast were furious over the announcement. U.S. representative Harry Sheppard, chairman of the California delegation's "committee on Japanese problems," warned that giving freedom to issei would be a "grievous error," adding, "I trust the military people who are handling the destiny of the West Coast have not made a mistake they will later regret." The founder of a Southern California group named the Ban the Japs Committee warned that the return would place an "unnecessary load on our short-handed peace officers' organizations," while the president of Kent, Washington's Remember Pearl Harbor League vowed that his five hundred members would not sell, lease, or rent farmland, homes, or storefronts to returning nikkei.

Even before Roosevelt's announcement, communities were preparing. In previous years, Pearl Harbor remembrances consisted mostly of moments of silence and the occasional bizarre act of patriotism. In 1942, for instance, Angelenos were treated to a reenactment of the attack. A full-scale model of a Hawaiian village was built outside Los Angeles City Hall and then leveled with explosives. The exhibition was followed by a one-minute moment of silence. But on December 7, 1944, as the likelihood of the camps' closure increased, an estimated seven thousand residents of Imperial County, California, met on the football field of Brawley High School. The community whose newspaper editors had cautioned against harming its nikkei neighbors three years earlier was now vehemently opposed to their return, claiming they posed a risk to nearby military installations. The forces that so actively fought for removal—the American Legion, farmers—awakened. At the annual California Farm Bureau Federation convention, attendees unanimously adopted a resolution declaring that "no Japanese, whether native born or alien, should be allowed during the period of the war to reside in California except under military surveillance."

The announcement should've been a moment of celebration at Heart Mountain, an exhale of relief, a return to normalcy. Instead, one question occupied everyone's minds: *Now what?*

_____

The letter floated into the *Sentinel* office two weeks after the ball and the Eagles' perfect record slipped through George's fingers.

In the intervening weeks the Eagles, emboldened by their showing against the Natrona team, invited the Powell Panthers to camp one last time to prove once and for all who was the best team in the Bighorn Basin. After two years of ignoring the Eagles' challenges, Powell finally accepted. The Panthers were 6–1, with the one loss coming in its 12–7 squeaker of an opener against Sheridan. Since then they'd outscored their opponents 232–13. The game was scheduled, and then, two days before kickoff, Talbot Rudolph received a call from Panthers head coach L. A. Kohnke. *My players*, he said, *have voted against the game.*

Rudolph, a mild-mannered man who spent much of the season not even coaching the team, was resolute. As the Eagles turned in their uniforms, he made an executive decision: if Powell wasn't going to play them, he was going to declare his Eagles the Bighorn Basin champions.

"There aren't any more teams to beat around here," he told the boys. "We've beaten all the teams that would play us in the area, and I think we've proven our superiority."

Under the banner "Big Horn Basin Champions," the *Sentinel* ran a three-column-wide picture of the team, one of the rare times it used a photo on the sports page. The declaration didn't sit well with one Powell resident.

Sports Editor
Ht. Mt. Paper
Ht. Mt. Wyo.

    Ht. Mountain isn't in the same class with Powell—
    Ht. Mountain isn't a full member of the Big Horn Basin
Conference—
    Ht. Mountain must play four conference games in B.H.B in

order to be in championship. You win Basin Championship and
don't claim it—
    Who to hell do you and your coach think you are fooling
besides a few people in Mont.?
    The comparative scores with Worland, Thermop, Ht.
Mountain and Powell give you some idea.
    Let not be so foolish and claim or even mention such a claim—
Your out stating yourself. Take it up with Basin officials.

It was signed "a fan." On November 17, Cheyenne's *Wyoming State Tribune* named its top five teams in the state. Cheyenne Central was first, followed by Powell, Natrona, Sheridan, and Lusk, which was defeated later that same day 47–0 by Powell. When the paper announced its all-state team, it was much the same as the previous year. Natrona placed three players on first team, one on the second team, and one honorable mention. Cody, whose line had been manhandled by the Eagles, placed its left tackle on the second team. The first-string quarterback was from Lusk, a team that couldn't put one point on the board against Powell.

There was no George Yahiro, who scored five touchdowns and three extra-point conversions over just four games. There was no Yoichi Hosozawa, who shimmied through the line to block eight punts. There was no Keiichi Ikeda, the pilot of a Wyoming offense that hung the most points on an opponent in years. There was no Ham Miyamoto or Shuzo Sumii or Rabbit Shiraki. For two years the Heart Mountain Eagles had assembled a winning percentage unlikely ever to be touched in the state of Wyoming, and now it was as if they had never played a down.

The Office of the Provost General prohibited Babe from working in plants or facilities "important to the war effort"—he was flagged because he was Buddhist, among other, similarly petty reasons—so instead he found himself on the floor of the S&N Three-Decker Sandwich Shop in Hartford, Connecticut. "Bigger and Better" was the shop's motto, an ode to their towering creations. S&N was widely known for its Asian employees, so much so that when Hartford police performed "a routine check on Orientals in the city" in April 1943 they knew to stop there as part of the sweep. Babe's boss was named Mrs. Nakaoka. On his WRA leave application he listed his prospective occupation as "waiter" but wound up washing dishes.

There may have been another reason he chose Connecticut, though.

"The biggest kick of all was the lesson in democracy that was being enacted out there," read a *Hartford Courant* sports column on October 26, 1944. "In the starting Connecticut backfield was fullback Nakaoka, a Japanese boy. The boy's origins didn't mean a thing to players or spectators, for he got the biggest hand of the day, from both sides of the field."

Kiyoto "Ken" Nakaoka was joined on the team by Kay Kiyokawa, a 4-feet 11-inch back that the paper described as "probably the world's smallest football player" and "of Japanese origins but a good American." Both found their place on the University of Connecticut roster after the school became one of 143 colleges and universities east of the Mississippi to welcome nisei students out of camp. University president Albert Jorgensen saw how German universities kowtowed to Hitler's demands—dismissing Jewish professors as well as those who disagreed with his beliefs—and vowed to be different. When at the behest of former WRA head Milton Eisenhower the American Friends Service Committee began trying to place nisei students in universities, Jorgensen accepted the call as an opportunity to highlight the value of democratic inclusivity. Eighteen nisei moved to the nearly all-white campus in 1943 and 1944.

Babe never joined the team or visited campus. In fact, the most Babe ever told his family about his time in Hartford was that he washed dishes. His stay in the state would be short, wending his way west again in March. But there had to be something gnawing at him.

Horse was sitting among the palmettos and pines when someone got the mistaken notion he could speak Japanese. After leaving Heart Mountain, he passed through Fort Leavenworth on his way to Camp Blanding, a gargantuan ten-thousand-building infantry replacement training center in North Florida. A week before basic training was over, a group from Fort Snelling in Minnesota visited Camp Blanding. Fort Snelling was home to the Military Intelligence Service Language School, which would train Japanese-language interpreters, interrogators, and other personnel, then send them to the Pacific theater.

The instructors tested all the nisei soldiers at Camp Blanding; Horse failed spectacularly. Since childhood his Japanese skills had been virtually zero.

"Who are you trying to kid?" the instructor asked. "No Japanese American can be so illiterate in Japanese."

Horse shrugged. Five weeks later, his commanding officer asked twenty men to step forward. *Yoshinaga*, he called. Instead of shipping off to France, his commanding officer said, he'd be moving someplace just as exotic: southeast Baltimore. Confused by the new assignment, Horse asked why.

"All you guys are proficient in Japanese."

"No, I'm not."

"Well," his CO responded, "the instructor said you were faking it so you wouldn't have to go to the Pacific war."

Camp Holabird was a steep, muddy patch of Maryland turf, perfect for test-driving—and refining—the indestructibility of jeeps and other military vehicles. Thousands of men filtered in the camp for vehicle training, then out of it, taking their auto repair tools around the world in the service of the U.S. military. In 1945, the camp's mission expanded in a new direction: counterintelligence.

Horse was assigned to the 60th Counter Intelligence Corps; his first exam was a Japanese aptitude test. Just like every other Japanese-language test he'd taken in his life, he flunked. His CO was stunned. *Well*, he said, *do you know how to drive?* Soon Horse could be found wading and rooting around the ex-marshland that Camp Holabird was built on as his CO's personal jeep driver.

After months of driving—and learning the ins and outs of becoming an intelligence agent—Horse and the 60th Counter Intelligence Corps shoved off for Northern Luzon, in the Philippines. It was summertime when the SS *Pennant* steamed across the Pacific. The Danish ship known as the *Grete Maersk* was seized by the United States after the German declaration of war, and hastily renamed and converted into a troop transport vessel. Bunks were stacked five high. Senior personnel were gifted the top bunks; in rough seas the bottom bunks would be drenched with vomit.

Horse's unit's plans changed on August 6. With victory secured in Europe three months earlier, the war in the Pacific was coming to a close as well. The *Pennant* was in the middle of the Pacific when the *Enola Gay* dropped Little Boy on Hiroshima, and when the *Bockscar* dropped Fat Man on Nagasaki three days later. When Horse first heard the news, he was confused. *What's new about that?* he asked when a friend told him about bombing Japan. Then he learned of the gravity, the hundreds of thousands of dead. Two months later, the *Pennant* pulled into Yokohama, the same port the first 148 Japanese immigrants to the United States had left seventy-seven years earlier.

Horse looked down at Japan for the first time in his life. *I finally made it*, he thought to himself. *I'm finally going to set foot on Japanese soil.* As he looked out, a white GI spit on the dockworkers below. "*Baka-yarou!*," the man yelled back. Horse knew little Japanese, but he understood that phrase: *You stupid idiot.* The workers looked farther up the ship and saw Horse. The looks on their faces stayed with him for the rest of his life: *Is he Japanese?*

Horse and twelve other nisei CIC members left the pier in the back of a truck, watching men, women, and children wander along the roads, the bombed-out husk of Yokohama fading over the horizon.

They bounced from rain-soaked tents at Camp Zama to Japanese military houses in Okayama. From there, he hunted Japanese war criminals, capturing a high-ranking naval officer who was alleged to have been part of the Pearl Harbor attack. In the subway stations of Tokyo he'd see people dying of starvation. In Hiroshima he watched as people fought to stay alive, consumed by their own survival while ignoring the corpses rotting in the street.

He was asked over and over again as he moved around Japan that fall: *Anata wa Nihonjin desu ka?* Are you really Japanese? Through broken Japanese (some of the lessons finally took) he would explain— "My parents emigrated to America and I was born there, therefore I [am] classified as an American." The most common response was puzzlement, followed by befuddled comprehension. Because of his height and complexion his own unit called him "Blanket Ass," a slur they usually reserved for Eskimos and Native Americans.

Jazz was always on the record player at the Dayton, Ohio, boardinghouse—Duke Ellington, Erskine Hawkins, the velvety tones of Sarah Vaughan and Billie Holiday. On Sunday afternoons, the tenants all ate lunch together, a break from the monotony of their daily lives, suddenly lurched into gear after years in camp.

Stan moved to the boardinghouse that winter, tired of spending the coldest months of the year in shacks across the West. More than 150 nikkei moved to Dayton between 1943 and 1946, practically the first ever to do so—only two residents of the 210,000-resident city had marked "Japanese" on the 1940 census. Unlike more popular relocation destinations like Chicago and Denver, Dayton built its ethnic Japanese community from scratch, with the help of the city's 140 churches. The city throbbed with the war effort. General Motors' aeroproducts division churned out revolvers and propellers for the B-17 and B-29 bombers. Delco pressed shock absorbers for tanks and trucks. National Cash Register produced bombsights and code-breaking machines used by Naval Intelligence. Frigidaire converted its refrigerator and air-conditioning business into a propeller parts and 50-caliber aircraft machine gun business.

Guiding the new residents was Robert Kodama, a Santa Anita and Heart Mountain incarceree recruited by a local pastor to aid in resettlement. Each day, Kodama aided new residents with resettlement from 9 a.m. to 1:30 p.m., punched in at his full-time job at McCall Corporation from 2 p.m. to 10:30 p.m., rode the late bus home four miles outside the city, then woke up and started the process all over again. He fought for wartime housing for his fellow nikkei, and convinced McCall's nine labor unions to unanimously consent to Stan and nineteen other Japanese Americans joining them at the world's largest printing plant.

Color, strength, and size—that was how Stan would sort the paper for his stock route, delivering reams and reams of paper to the various departments that filled the cavernous building. *Redbook* needed different paper from *Bluebook*, while both needed different paper from *Mc-Call's*. After his shift he and a friend would walk to the YMCA and play pickup basketball against the club's white patrons. They held their own, he'd remember years later, because "we were quite a bit more agile and faster."

The Dayton winter soon passed, and Stan took a train from Fort Hayes in Columbus to Washington State's Fort Lewis. On his new path, he stared out the old cattle car, admired the vastness of Texas, and relived the memories of bedbugs by slapping mosquitoes day and night at the Fort Leavenworth campsite known as Gonorrhea Gulch. (Venereal diseases were so rampant in the U.S. military at the time that officials commissioned director John Ford to film a twenty-five-minute short entitled *Sex Hygiene* for the troops. It was released the same month he won the best director Oscar for *How Green Was My Valley*, his third such win.) In Washington, Stan was assigned to an engineering class: building bridges, learning demolition techniques, clearing land mines, and laying barbed wire. They sent him to typing school, a task so numbingly boring—and repetitive for someone who'd known how to type since ninth grade—that Stan requested a transfer to the Medical Corps. Barbed wire and land mines were replaced with enemas and stretchers. That request became the greatest regret of his military career.

During medical training, a friend from his engineering class stopped by Stan's barrack to say goodbye. He was headed to Europe to join the 442, he said. Stan was crestfallen. News of the regiment's bravery had trickled back to the States, tales of valor and sacrifice. Stan wanted to be a part of it. *I should have never left the combat engineers*, he thought to himself.

Tayzo had waited more than a year for his day in court and it lasted less than ten minutes. The attorney for him and the twenty-one other resisters picked up by the U.S. Marshals over the previous twelve months had arranged a deal with Judge Kennedy—no trial, two-year bids. Tayzo joined eighty-four of his fellow resisters from Heart Mountain and the other camps at Washington State's McNeil Island Federal Penitentiary, where he picked apples and tomatoes and slopped hogs at the prison's farm. There they settled back into what distracted them at Heart Mountain—sports. They built three teams of Heart Mountain resisters. Minidoka resisters formed another, Jehovah's Witness conscientious objectors two more, and the prison's African American incarcerees another two. The eight teams battled in football and baseball until August 1946, when the resisters were released on time served.

On Christmas Eve 1947, newspapers across the country blared a surprising headline. "1,523 Draft Violators Get Yule Pardons," declared *The Fresno Bee*. Earlier that year, Fair Play Committee and Southern California ACLU attorney A. L. Wirin had petitioned President Harry Truman for amnesty of not only his clients, but thousands like them across the United States. Truman established a committee to review the 15,803 men convicted of violating the Selective Service Act during the war.

Proclamation 2762 read, in part: "Upon consideration of the report and recommendation of the Board and the recommendation of the

Attorney General, it appears that certain persons convicted of violating the Selective Training and Service Act of 1940 as amended ought to have restored to them the political, civil, and other rights of which they were deprived by reason of such conviction and which may not be restored to them unless they are pardoned."

The Amnesty Board was more specific, saying that it "fully appreciate[d] the nature of their feelings and their reactions to orders from local Selective [Service] Boards. . . . Prior to their removal from their homes they had been lawabiding and loyal citizens. . . . Most of them remained loyal to the United States and indicated a desire to remain loyal to this country and to fight in its defense, provided their rights of citizenship were recognized." The board recommended pardoning the men "in the belief that they will justify our confidence in their loyalty."

Tayzo was drafted after leaving prison, then called up again during the Korean War. He went to Korea with the 38th Engineer Combat Battalion, and built the cribs, treadways, and bridges used to cross the Bukhan River. Many years later, in 1996, the JACL sought to reconcile with the draft resisters they so vehemently opposed during the war. Tayzo spoke with two members.

Interviewer: "You didn't have any problem being drafted now that you were out of camp, did you? I mean, now that you are free?"

Tayzo: "Yeah."

Interviewer: "Since there's no reason to object?"

Tayzo: "About what?"

The headline on the December 12, 1945, Associated Press story would've seemed impossible just a year before:

Babe Nomura of Los Angeles City College Is Nation's Top Japanese-American Gridster

Barry Brown was the fullback for the Los Angeles City College football team. Abe Fuhrman played tackle. Johnny Payne was a reserve; he played halfback. The one thing the three men had in common was that on December 7, 1941, they'd all just wrapped up football season at Hollywood High School. And, four years later, one of their old teammates had just dropped his bags in Los Angeles.

Babe worked his way back west from Hartford that spring and summer, stopping in Chicago and Wyoming along the way. In September he returned to Los Angeles, where he was greeted by his old friends. Out of competitive football for nearly two years, he quickly regained his form. That fall he picked apart the Metropolitan Conference, considered the strongest junior college football conference in the country. In front of ten thousand fans on October 26, Babe was responsible for all of LACC's points in a 20–13 loss to Compton College—two touchdown passes and a sneak for the conversion. At the end of the season Compton was rated the best two-year football program in the country. After the game, a sportswriter declared Babe "one of the best since Jackie Robinson," the baseball pioneer who had played quarterback at Pasadena Junior College. On November 9, against Robinson's alma mater, Babe slung three touchdowns and returned a punt 45 yards for another. After four years away, his name once again lit up the sports pages of the *Los Angeles Times*. He threw 15 touchdowns, tying the Southern California junior college record, and ran for another three touchdowns himself. His teammates voted him co-captain, and at the end of the season he was named first-team all-conference.

His coach, Don Newmeyer, former NFL player (and father of then future Tony Award–winner Julie Newmar) was succinct in his praise: "This boy is one of the greatest athletes I've ever seen."

As Babe, Horse, Stan, and Tayzo scattered across the globe, Keiichi stayed at Heart Mountain. The families capable of relocating already had, leaving the camp mostly full with the elderly and women with small children—neither group had the financial means to move. Incarceration had gutted most families' savings, and those unable to work in camp were especially vulnerable. Even those able to return refused, hoping that after the war ended they'd have a better chance at securing a job. In a poll taken by Heart Mountain officials at the end of February 1945, only 9 percent of the four thousand respondents said they could relocate under current conditions. A month after the WRA's closure announcement, just twelve families had made plans to return to the West Coast.

Robertson took steps to ensure that they'd all leave, and soon. In January he banned visitors, and in February he closed the first mess hall. In the springtime the decision was made not to plant summer crops, and the farm's tractors, plows, and seed were sold at fire-sale prices to local farmers. The fields that had stood fallow three years earlier were returned to the Reclamation Service, who in turn leased them in Cody and Powell to farmers eager to plant on the newly fertile dirt.

Three years and two months after signing Executive Order 9066, at 3:35 p.m., April 12, Franklin Delano Roosevelt died of a cerebral hemorrhage at his retreat in Warm Springs, Georgia. Every flag at Heart Mountain was lowered to half-mast; special services were added in honor of the president at the center's churches. The staff of the *Sentinel* wrote a letter to Eleanor Roosevelt on behalf of the camp's remaining incarcerees.

"Speaking for all Americans of Japanese ancestry and their loyal parents, we wish to express our profound sorrow on the passing of our great leader," it read. "Unforgettable to us are his words 'Americanism is a matter of mind and heart; Americanism is not, and never was, a matter of race or ancestry.' These words express in our minds the fundamental honesty, integrity, and belief of the world's greatest leaders against intolerance, bigotry, and fascism."

Keiichi, Yoichi, and the rest of the Eagles seniors graduated on May 24. Despite pleadings from the community council to remain open for fall classes, all Heart Mountain schools were closed after May 25. Any students who remained in camp would once again have no school to attend. In July, WRA director Dillon Myer announced the camp's November 15 closure date, a full two months earlier than originally scheduled. Families scrambled; nearly eight months after the War Department's announcement, only 2,200 incarcerees had left. The final issue of the *Sentinel* published on July 28; newspaper and mail service ended soon after.

Keiichi left for Denver on September 11, nine days after the Japanese surrender. There, he and a group of friends from San Jose formed a basketball team, and by the spring the Marusho Miks were the JACL Intermountain champions, defeating nisei teams from Colorado, Idaho, and Utah on their way to the title. His parents, two younger brothers, and little sister remained in Heart Mountain as everything around them shuttered: the stores, the mess halls, the latrines. Military police, no longer concerned, if they ever truly were, packed up in early October. Robertson informed the remaining incarcerees that if they refused to leave, their bags would be packed for them. As they clamored to find housing back on the West Coast, he sent them off with a final note.

"I feel sure that within a very short time all of Heart Mountain's people will again be reestablished in normal American communities where they will again be happy and free of care," he wrote on November 2, in the last public bulletin. "Best wishes for you all."

The Igawa family took a train to Santa Ana Army Air Base, where they were housed in a temporary camp. From there they were trucked to the sea, where they boarded a ship. Their decade of living on the mainland was enough; they'd spend the rest of their lives in Hawai'i. Babe's parents returned to Hollywood, took their keys from Marion Binder, and resumed operating the boardinghouse. The Ikeda family knew their lives were unalterably changed. Keiichi never asked his father what happened to the grocery store—it was just gone. Horse's mother and sister moved to Brighton, Colorado, in October, then continued on to San Jose. His mother died the following March while Horse was stationed in Japan.

At 8 p.m., November 10, 1945, the Ikeda family boarded the last train to leave Heart Mountain Relocation Center, bound once again for the unknown.

The New Year's Day halftime show featured one thousand flutists, trumpeters, tuba players, clarinetists, drummers, and cornetists, fifty majorettes, and an appearance by the Raisin Bowl Queen and her attendants. A Marine guard presented the colors, while an ROTC unit performed a drill exhibition. They filled Fresno, California's Ratcliffe Stadium field from end zone to end zone, as thirteen thousand fans cheered from the grandstands. As the show came to an end, the San Jose State College Spartans and their Associated Press All-West Coast halfback charged out of the tunnel.

Los Angeles City College coach Newmeyer predicted Babe would have his pick of universities, and he was right. Babe settled on San Jose State, which had a history of welcoming Asian American athletes and already featured another nisei, lineman Jake Kikuuchi. Babe made an immediate impact. He moved from quarterback to left halfback, allowing the team to utilize his speed. In the Spartans' first season after three war-canceled years, the team went 9-1-1 and won the California Collegiate Athletic Association conference title. After a week-two loss to Texas's Hardin-Simmons College, the Spartans exhibited Eagles-like dominance, shutting out four of their next five opponents.

On November 8 they faced coach Amos Alonzo Stagg's College of the Pacific Tigers. Stagg was—and remains—one of the greatest innovators in football history, creating such foundational tools as the center snap, the huddle, and the lateral pass, along with ephemera like varsity letters and uniform numbers. He created the T formation and Notre Dame Box, two of the offensive formations Babe used at Hollywood High and Heart Mountain. In 1951 Stagg was inducted into the College Football Hall of Fame as both a player and a coach, the only person to hold both honors for more than forty years. There are six football fields, three schools, a giant sequoia, and a Division III national championship game named after him, and on November 8, 1946, Babe and the Spartans whipped him so badly that his college chancellor asked him to resign.

Babe beat the Tigers without even scoring, dragging the Tigers to their own goal line three times before other Spartans crossed the goal line. The final score was 32–0, the Tigers' worst defeat to the Spartans in the schools' nineteen-year rivalry.

Wins against San Diego State, Fresno State, and the University of Portland earned Babe a spot on the Associated Press All-West Coast team, one of only three California Collegiate Athletic Association athletes to be named among the seventy-three selections, and the Spartans an invitation to the Raisin Bowl. With Babe leading the way, the Spartans outgained the Utah State Aggies 177–74 on the ground, en route to a 20–0 victory. A United Press report from the game declared the team "made mincemeat out of Utah State."

On the other side of the country, the New York Giants had just lost their fourth NFL championship in eight years, falling to the Chicago Bears 24–14. Looking to shore up their backfield for the future, they invited Babe to try out. The invitation was extraordinary on its face: no Asian American had ever played professional football in the United States. It was the opportunity of a lifetime, one that would've been unfathomable three years earlier, standing on a makeshift sideline in a concentration camp. It was also daunting for the same reason. Babe's return to the West Coast had been ameliorated by his presence on the football team, but he wasn't blind to reality. Although previously exclusionist politicians California governor Earl Warren and Los Angeles mayor Fletcher Bowron now preached tolerance and held ceremonies welcoming the return, groups like the California Preservation Association and Seattle's Remember Pearl Harbor League formed to fight resettlement.

Jobs were scarce for nikkei, and housing worse. Many found themselves in makeshift hostels in former Buddhist churches or once again in barracks in former Army facilities. (One group was even housed at Camp Kohler, a Sacramento facility that had been used as a temporary detention center less than four years earlier.) Families returning home were greeted with more than twenty shootings and untold arsons, graffiti, and threats. In the early morning hours of March 6, 1945, two miles outside San Jose, the Takeda family was awakened to the smell of gasoline. The house was soon consumed with flames. As the family ran outside, a car crept by, firing three shots. One sailed past the head of twelve-year-old Beverly and lodged in the outside of the house.

"We expected something unpleasant, but we didn't expect this," Joe Takeda told the *Pacific Citizen*, the JACL's newspaper out of Salt Lake City. "We have no bitterness. We realize we are the victims of circumstance. We have always wanted to help the war effort and have sent word to the farmers of the valley we would be glad to help on the farms where needed, especially those farms where sons are in service."

After the New York Giants' invitation came another: a tryout with the Boston Red Sox. An athlete so gifted that he was sought by not just two professional teams but two professional *sports*, Babe declined both.

Tayzo and Keiichi became landscapers, tending the shrubs and gardens of Southern California. Stan Igawa served in World War II, the Korean War, and the Vietnam War, before becoming an elementary school principal. Like his parents before him, he returned to Hawai'i. Between 1998 and his death in 2004, he logged more than three thousand hours as a volunteer at the Pearl Harbor National Memorial. Each day, Stan would put on his National Park Service uniform and his VFW Post 10276 cap and try to explain to visitors how he managed to find himself where he stood. He'd suffer the indignity of those who asked "What army did you serve?" and "What are you?," then wake up the next morning and do it all over again. Asked decades later how she'd describe her brother, Stan's sister Irene put it succinctly: "He bled red, white, and blue."

Babe hung a cigar out of his mouth at Pacific California Fish Company, where he worked alongside former Eagles center Yoichi Hosozawa. On May 9, 1949, at the First Congregational Church of Los Angeles, he married Kimiko, whom he'd first met outside a barrack in northwest Wyoming seven years earlier. Fifteen years before that, though, Kimiko crossed paths with another Eagle. Every morning while walking to elementary school in Mountain View, she'd pass a boy heading the other direction. They never became friends, or even spoke. At least until the boy became one of her husband's best friends, seated in the pews at First Congregational. Throughout the 1950s Babe returned to dominance in the nisei basketball, baseball, and softball leagues of Southern California. In September 1950, Los Angeles's *Shin Nichi-Bei* named its annual Nisei Athletic Union all-star softball team. Babe earned the spot at first base. Former Eagle Bill Shundo was next to him, at second. From the pitcher's mound, Tosh Asano. The author of the article, the first of nearly six hundred he'd write for the paper over the next eight years, was Horse Yoshinaga.

After he returned from the war, Horse followed his Heart Mountain friends and moved to Los Angeles. There he rented a small room near the corner of Cahuenga and Santa Monica Boulevards, at a Hollywood boardinghouse where Babe used to roam the halls, befriending lonely bachelors. He became a newspaper columnist, writing for the *Shin Nichi-Bei*, *Kashu Mainichi*, and *Rafu Shimpo* for nearly seventy years. Asked once by a reader to name the best nisei football player of all time, Horse didn't hesitate. "Nomura could do everything asked of him on the football field," he wrote. "He probably could have done equally as well as waterboy too." In second place he named Babe's former rival, Tosh.

In the late 1950s and early 1960s Horse appeared in three films, then moved to Japan, where he worked with Rikidōzan, the godfather of Japanese professional wrestling, who was stabbed to death by a member of the yakuza in 1963. Back in California, he founded George Yoshinaga and Associates, "specializing in sports and entertainment in the Orient." His company brought Japan's Meiji University basketball team to play the UNLV Runnin' Rebels, and introduced Japanese sumo wrestlers to an American audience. In 1968, Indiana real estate developer Walter Dilbeck had the idea to create a global baseball league, and sent Horse to Japan to find a team willing to join. He returned with the Tokyo Dragons; at one point forty Japanese professional baseball players lived in his small house in Gardena, and played catch in the street with his sons. When Tokyo's *Japan Times* wanted to stage an exhibition football game in the city's National Stadium, they called Horse. He sent letters to college coaches around the country, and on January 18, 1976, a line of sixty-eight thousand Japanese fans circled twice around the stadium waiting to watch the first American collegiate football game ever held on foreign soil. The tradition continued for the next seventeen years, drawing Heisman Trophy winners like Ty Detmer and Bo Jackson.

Over the years, Horse's columns grew more conservative, drawing the ire of the younger sansei generation, and other nisei. In 1993, a months-long debate with Frank Emi over the treatment of the Heart Mountain resisters—Horse considered them draft dodgers—spilled out of the *Rafu Shimpo* and into the front page of the *Los Angeles Times* under the headline "Draft Rift Lingers 50 Years Later." In an interview with a historian in 2010 he explained his thinking.

> *When I think back, a lot of the things that are said today never occurred to me, like, "Hey, my mother's locked up in camp and I'm fighting for the U.S.A. that locked her up." Those kinds of thoughts never entered my mind. I was there, I said "OK, I'm going to go to war and do whatever I can." . . . Today when they talk about [draft resistance] I say "What do you think would have happened to us if we all refused to go?" It would've changed our life completely, and because we went and served and the 442 did such a magnificent job we were able to re-establish ourselves more quickly. . . . If we all refused to go, where do you think we would've ended up? Probably in Tule Lake and on a ship going back to Japan where we'd never been.*

He excoriated younger incarcerees for claiming their time in camp was more brutal than it was, and wrote in opposition to the redress movement, which ultimately won the passage of the Civil Liberties Act of 1988 and provided a national apology and payments of $20,000 to surviving incarcerees. He disliked the term "concentration camps," preferring the WRA nomenclature of "relocation centers." While most former incarcerees understandably tried to forget the camp experience, Horse argued that there were in fact some *positive* outcomes. The reasoning behind their removal wasn't sound, he said, but "if it wasn't for evacuation I wouldn't have a college education, I'd be working on the farm."

Horse wouldn't have had to go far to find a differing opinion. While some boys fantasized about becoming pilots or baseball stars, Mas Ogimachi dreamed of being a certified public accountant. He would twirl calculations around in his head and spit them out as effortlessly as others recited the alphabet. Like most of his Eagles teammates, his grades had suffered in camp—a reality based on many factors, not least of which was the quality of the education—but he still held out hope for an accounting degree. After Heart Mountain closed, he returned to California and waited to be drafted. He would visit the Pasadena draft board incessantly. *If you're going to draft me*, he said, *do it so I can get it over with.* Just eighteen, he had already experienced a lifetime of fits and starts; he wasn't about to start college only to be drafted midsemester. So he would drive, back and forth, back and forth. He was finally drafted, but the war was over. He'd later earn a two-year accounting degree from Los Angeles City College, but never became a CPA.

"He resented the fact that he was interned," recalled his wife, Bunny, years later. "He'd say that they ruined his life because he couldn't even go to college . . . [H]e was full of resentment."

Every year until his death in 2017, Mas would do his taxes by hand, without a calculator.

Despite his political leanings, Horse's beliefs were complicated. He fought for the installation at Santa Anita Park of a plaque commemorating the Japanese American incarceration, and organized reunions of those imprisoned there. He was the most widely read nisei columnist in the United States. His efforts could be summed up by words written by a *Shin Nichi-Bei* colleague in July 1958: "There never was a nisei writer more lauded and yet more cursed at the same time."

Unlike his friend, Babe shied away from politics and controversy. Instead, he prowled the sidelines of the sporting endeavors of his children, finding a way to merge the two things he loved most. When his bones and joints finally said enough, he traded his baseball bat for a golf club, bending and willing that once-in-a-generation talent toward a 5 handicap. After nearly forty years at Pacific California Fish Company, he retired in 1989; his retirement party was a golf tournament. That first tournament was small—two foursomes, a local course. The Nomura Family Golf Tournament grew and grew until eight foursomes of family and friends piled onto a bus for weekends of golf in Las Vegas. He died on November 11, 2011. Under the *Rafu Shimpo* headline "His Speed Was the Stuff of Legend," Horse tried to sum up a friendship that survived two concentration camps and sixty-nine years. In lieu of jokes, he struck a solemn tone.

"This past week was a tough one," he wrote. "On Sunday, I lost my best friend."

Heading northeast on U.S. 14 out of Cody, you'll first pass over the stinking waters of the Shoshone River. Heart Mountain will snap into place next, sitting to your left as it has for the past 48 million years, a quiet sentinel on the basin. As the road flattens out the chimney will appear, the chimney that rose above the hospital, the hospital that welcomed 550 children, the children whose birth certificates were stamped Heart Mountain, Wyoming, the city that only existed for 1,187 days. You'll turn left before the smokestack, and cross the train tracks that brought fourteen thousand Americans from their homes and took them back again, the tracks that brought 654 men and women to the war, the tracks that brought eleven of those men to their deaths, the tracks that witnessed thousands of hellos and goodbyes, tears and last embraces. A small but mighty museum is next, then a shallow, steady hill climbing past the peeking root cellar that once stored the fruits of the camp's labor, piled to its subterranean ceiling with potatoes and daikon and carrots. At the top of the hill sits a memorial. And then—nothing. Hundreds, thousands of acres sprawl before you, with rivulets of irrigation trickling through, a living ode to the imprisoned men who took it upon themselves to finish what Buffalo Bill Cody could not. Strands of hay tremble where 459 barracks once stood, filling the streets and latrines and mess halls and sumo rings, the barracks sawed into thirds and sold to prospective homesteaders for $1 apiece. From this viewpoint, the only reminder of the third-largest city in Wyoming is a block of hollowed concrete surrounded by hay, the engineering room of the high school. Behind that the only tree, a plains cottonwood, the state tree of Wyoming, rises from what was once a high school football field, spreading its branches as it reaches for the sun.

Lean against the tree and listen and it won't take long to hear the crowd. There are thousands of them, more people than have ever been on that piece of earth in human history. They're warming their hands against the November chill as the Boy Scouts weave throughout, eagerly selling bottles of soda. The dust flits into your eyes as you squint, attempting to discern what seems unimaginable. Stan and Tayzo sit on the sidelines, hoping for the score to climb so out of reach that their services are warranted. Babe reads the defense and notices that the left end looks a bit weak, a bit vulnerable, and calls the play. Yoichi snaps the ball and bulls forward, stunning the opposing tackle and giving Keiichi just enough of a hole to bounce through. He cuts left and Horse sprints downfield, blocking the last remaining defender. There's nothing but open field.

6–0, Eagles.

ACKNOWLEDGMENTS

THIS BOOK WOULD not have been possible without Jan Morey. In May 2017, I sent a short email to Jan titled, "Journalist interested in Babe Nomura." She responded and, for reasons that remain a mystery to both of us, decided that I was the right person to tell her father's story. She called Keiichi Ikeda and the Yoshinaga family, on my behalf, and made introductions at the Japanese American National Museum. She helped me interview her mother, Kimiko, excavating seventy-five-year-old memories. Jan and her husband, Jack, not only welcomed me into their home, but let me stay the night on every Los Angeles reporting trip. On days when I reported in other parts of the city, Jan would make me breakfast and then send me off with a bag of snacks. There are many people who made this book possible, but Jan Morey sits at the top of that list.

Paul and Tim Yoshinaga opened up their father's archives to me, as did the children of Stan Igawa: DaVee Lopez, Ian Cayetano, and Erin Sauder. Irene Igawa described Stan to me in a way that only a younger sister could. Bunny Ogimachi spent hours on the phone explaining to me the ins and outs of teenage life at Heart Mountain.

In May 2018, I met and interviewed Keiichi Ikeda at the Japanese American National Museum in Los Angeles. The conversation drove this book to unexpected places, making connections to the history of Japanese American sports in the United States that I hadn't considered before. He was the only living Eagle I was able to interview for this book; I hope it honors his legacy.

On the opposite side of the ball, Charles Pearce was invaluable in sketching out the details of his father LeRoy's life.

In Wyoming, Dakota Russell, Kate Wilson, Danielle McAdams, Brandon Daake, Claudia Wade, Aura Newlin, Ray Locker, Sam Mihara, Doug Nelson, and Shirley Higuchi at the Heart Mountain Wyoming Foundation and Heart Mountain Interpretive Center kindly responded to every one of my increasingly frantic messages, and were even more helpful in person. Early on in this project, Bacon Sakatani mailed me a CD of every *Heart Mountain Sentinel* and *Echoes*, which allowed me to build a database of each story mentioning one of the Eagles players. Without those newspapers this book wouldn't exist.

Danielle Higa, Natasha Varner, and Brian Niiya at Densho served as willing sounding boards for my various theories and itches, and the group's digital archive and encyclopedia provided my crash course in Japanese American history.

Mike Mackey has spent much of his life chronicling life at Heart Mountain. His books were my first introduction to the camp, and the subsequent conversations we had guided my own research. I think just as highly of Eric Muller, who immediately responded when a stranger emailed him to ask if he'd be willing to share a very specific document. (He said yes.) I leaned on Mike, Eric, and Frank Abe's essential work when reconstructing the world of the Fair Play Committee.

Patrick Schmiedt built the Wyoming Football website as a labor of love, and it's grown into one of the most comprehensive high school football websites in the country. Nearly every record, score, all-state team, or schedule mentioned in this book is there only because of Patrick's work.

The scholarship of Roger Daniels, Valerie Matsumoto, Michi Weglyn, Tetsuden Kashima, Greg Robinson, Eiichiro Azuma, Erika Lee, Joel S. Franks, Gary Okihiro, Bill Hosokawa, Ty P. Kāwika Tengan, Jesse Makani Markham, Stephanie Hinnershitz, Chris Nielsen, Christina Chin, John R. Waggener, and Michael Mullan, among many others I'm surely forgetting, built the foundation of this story. Conversations with Oliver Wang, Duncan Ryūken Williams, Rob Buscher, Colleen Miyano, David Fujioka, Dale Kunitomi, Pat Hayes, Raymond Uno, Beth Hessel, Brandon Shimoda, and Don Kurtz were equally helpful.

Archivists! My beloved, underappreciated archivists! Jamie Henricks at the Japanese American National Museum, Rebecca Sharp at the National Archives in Washington, D.C., and Samantha Long at the Carbon County Historical Society in Red Lodge, Montana, all opened their minds and prodded the author of this book with documents and microfilm and manuscripts that I wouldn't have found without them. No request was too strange for the magicians in the interlibrary loan department of the Free Library of Philadelphia. The Franklin D. Roosevelt Presidential Library, the Bancroft Library at the University of California, Berkeley, the Charles E. Young Research Library of UCLA, the California State University Japanese American Digitization Project, San Francisco State University, the San Jose Public Library, the Montana State University Library's Merrill G. Burlingame Special Collections, the California Digital Library, the Park County (Wyoming) Archives, the Special Collections at the University of Southern California, the California Digital Newspaper Collection, the American Heritage Center at the University of Wyoming, the Federal Reserve Bank of St. Louis archives, the University of Hawai'i at Mānoa Library, the Huntington Park branch of the Los Angeles County Library, and the Special Collections and Archives at UNLV provided either in-person or online assistance.

To the archivists who spend their days digitizing our collective past so that we may learn from it in the future: Thank you.

Though I don't mention it in the book, I grew up in Hyde Park, New York, the same hometown as FDR. I attended middle school in a grand, Colonial Revival building constructed with Roosevelt-earmarked Public Works Administration funds, and dropped my mail off at a post office built with the same funds. (During construction, in

1940, architects would mail blueprints to Roosevelt for final approval.) My high school was Franklin D. Roosevelt High School; the mascot was the Presidents. I went into this project thinking of this book as a corrective to my upbringing, as a way to rebalance the narrative of Roosevelt's life, at least in my own mind. While that goal never slipped, it was joined by the memory of my high school English teacher, Rem Briggs. Years before I ever thought I'd be a writer, Mr. Briggs introduced me to new worlds, and pushed me to read texts critically and thoroughly. In eleventh grade he made our class memorize the opening of *Moby Dick*; I can still repeat it today. There's a very small mention of Herman Melville in this book—and that's for Mr. Briggs.

Garrett Graff, Eva Holland, Evan Ratliff, Brantley Hargrove, JK Nickell, Shea Serrano, Jason Fagone, and Matt Goodman provided advice and, during slumps of confidence, reassurance. I've never played a down of real football in my life, so Ben Montgomery graciously agreed to read an early draft of the book to ensure I hadn't made a fool of myself. Matt Giles pored over chapters to ensure my facts lined up with my narrative.

Hunter Hauk at *Cowboys and Indians* magazine assigned the story that first sent me to Wyoming in 2014. Without that I would've never walked into the Heart Mountain Interpretive Center, and I would've never met the Eagles. There's an alternate universe where Hunter assigns that story to another writer, and I never write this book.

I could use 1,000 words and it wouldn't be enough to express my thanks to my editor, Rakesh Satyal. He took a draft that was somehow both bloated *and* full of holes and pushed it to become the book that it is today. His encouragement lifted me up when I needed it most. Fred Chase caught more embarrassing errors in this text than I'll ever admit publicly. Loan Le kept this book on schedule even when a global pandemic actively fought that plan, and Kelli McAdams designed a cover that took my breath away when I first saw it. Additional thanks to Amar Deol, Joanna Pinsker, Maudee Genao, Peter Borland, Kathryn Higuchi, Jimmy Iacobelli, and Libby McGuire at Atria Books and Simon & Schuster.

My agent, David Patterson, knew this was a book before I did. He's the calmest person I know, a quality I often needed during this process. Aemilia Phillips was one of the first people to read this manuscript, and her encouraging words helped me tremendously during a time of self-doubt.

Deep in my inbox, I have a 2007 email saved from my grandfather. In it, I explain that I won't be able to come home for a family event; I was working my first job after college, and I unexpectedly needed to cover a story that weekend. His response was three words, in all caps: "GO GETUM TIGER." Whenever I'm weary I think of that note, and all the sacrifices my four grandparents made to allow their grandson to write books for a living.

My parents, Paul and Judy, encouraged and nurtured the strange tendencies of a child who preferred maps and globes over almost anything else. My siblings Drew, Tyler, and Rachel constantly make me want to be a better person.

Merrick and Clark: I hope you'll read this book someday and be proud that I'm your dad.

Kelleen: This, as is everything in my life, is for you.

NOTES

PART 1
Chapter One: City of Good Neighbors

3 *"Do you know what your people did?"*: "George Yoshinaga oral history interview conducted by Alisa Lynch in Las Vegas, Nevada, 2010-08-10" (GYOH). From Densho Digital Archive, Manzanar National Historic Site Collection, film, http://ddr.densho.org/interviews/ddr-manz-1-107-1/.

NOTE: Most of the family details in this chapter are derived from this oral history, hereafter abbreviated GYOH.

4 *One of the world's largest active volcanoes*: Oregon State University's Volcano World, "Aso," accessed May 19, 2020, http://volcano.oregonstate.edu/aso.

4 *Usaburo owned a dead smile*: The descriptions of the Yoshinagas are from family photos.

4 *For an overwhelming number of Japanese men*: Kelli Y. Nakamura, "Picture Brides," in *Densho Encyclopedia*, accessed May 19, 2020, http://encyclopedia.densho.org/Picture_brides/.

5 *some just minutes after the bride fainted*: Erika Lee, *The Making of Asian America: A History* (New York: Simon & Schuster, 2015), 113.

5 *By 1910 Japanese farmers*: Shelley Hang-See Lee, *A New History of Asian America* (New York: Routledge, 2013), 85.

5 *founded as a forgettable stop*: *Map of Mountain View, Los Altos and Vicinity*. Map, Mountain View: Mountain View City Council and Mountain View Chamber of Commerce, 1944, located in San Jose Public Library California Room, Ephemera Collection, accessed May 19, 2020, http://digitalcollections.sjlibrary.org/cdm/compoundobject/collection/sjplephemer/id/146/rec/1. The details regarding Mountain View's climate, fruit production, and crime in the subsequent paragraphs are derived from a pamphlet on the inverse of this map.

6   *The* Macon *was the world's largest helium-filled rigid airship*: Ben Koning and Anneke Metz, *Sunnyvale: Images of America* (Mount Pleasant, SC: Arcadia Publishing, 2011), 72.

6   *The building constructed to house the airship*: "U.S. Naval Air Station Sunnyvale, California, Historic District," September 3, 2017, National Park Service, https://www.nps.gov.

6   *the "architect of naval aviation"*: William F. Trimble, *Admiral William A. Moffett: Architect of Naval Aviation* (Annapolis: Bluejacket Books, 2007).

7   *Built in 1926, the Mission-style structure*: Nicholas Perry, *Mountain View: Images of America* (Mount Pleasant, SC: Arcadia Publishing, 2006), 62.

7   *Yoshinagas and Yamijis and Okamotos stood next to Gruenebaums and Popoviches and Mendozas*: Mountain View High School, *Blue and Gray* (Mountain View, California, 1940).

7   *twenty-eight players*: This description is from a Yoshinaga family photo.

7   *the youngest of Usaburo and Tsuru's five children*: GYOH.

8   *he once baked a lemon meringue pie in home economics*: Tim Yoshinaga, email message to author, February 20, 2019.

8   *His father was more volatile*: GYOH.

8   *back-to-back Santa Clara Valley Athletic League titles in 1940 and 1941*: The information here is from Yoshinaga family memorabilia.

8   *Usaburo died when George was thirteen*: Tim Yoshinaga, email message to author, September 19, 2018.

8   *On the second floor of the Mockbee Building*: Perry, *Mountain View*, 38.

9   *Founded in 1875 by General A. M. Winn*: Joseph R. Knowland, "California's 'Native Sons,'" *Overland Monthly*, February 1908, https://www.google.com/books/edition/_/VYHNAAAAMAAJ?gbpv=1.

9   *The man of the "sturdy pioneers" language*: Willard B. Farwell, *The Chinese At Home and Abroad* (San Francisco: A. L. Bancroft and Co., 1885), 30.

9   *"California was given by God to a white people"*: Roger Daniels, *The Politics of Prejudice: The Anti-Japanese Movement in California and the Struggle for Japanese Exclusion* (University of California Press, 1977), 79.

Chapter Two: Twinkletoes

10   *The boardinghouse sat one block north*: The descriptions in this paragraph and the next are from personal observations and 2017, 2018, and 2019 interviews with Jan Morey.

10   *On June 12, 1907*: "Canada Passenger Lists, 1881–1922," database with images, FamilySearch, https://familysearch.org/ark:/61903/3:1:S3HT-619R

-CV?cc=1823240&wc=36TT-1X9%3A981984601%2C982042401%2C9 81989001 : 22 May 2014, Victoria, BC_Jun 1907_Tosa Maru_image 8 of 11, Library and Archives Canada, Ottawa, Ontario.

10 *not until 1962*: Mandy Bartok, "Diving into Ise-Shima's Ancient Womanly Traditions," *Japan Times*, August 12, 2012, https://www.japantimes .co.jp/life/2012/08/12/travel/diving-into-ise-shimas-ancient-womanly-tra ditions.

11 *For three thousand years*: Ibid.

11 *Hyohei listed his profession as student*: Canada Passenger Lists, 1881–1922.

11 *Soon came a son*: Jan Morey interviews. The Nomura family details in this paragraph and the subsequent paragraphs come from those interviews and family photos.

11 *He was drawn to loners and the lonely*: Kimiko Nomura interview, February 25, 2019.

12 *Cole Field, the baseball diamond across the street*: "Paramount Nine Wins," *Los Angeles Times*, June 22, 1936; "St. Louis Signs Paramount Ace," *Los Angeles Times*, September 23, 1935; "Paramount Nine Wins," *Los Angeles Times*, January 8, 1934.

12 *Created in 1929 in San Francisco*: "Origins of the Nisei Athletic Union," Northern California Nisei Athletic Union, http://ncnau.org/history.

12 *he was named a second-team all-star outfielder*: "Kashu Sports Pick J.A.U. 'A' All-Star Nine," *Kashu Mainichi*, exact 1939 date unknown.

12 *Two years later*: "Dis 'n Dat," *Rafu Shimpo*, exact 1941 date unknown.

12 *At fifteen he tried basketball*: "Betsuin All-Star Cage Teams Selected by Rafu Shimpo Scribes," *Rafu Shimpo*, December 18, 1940.

13 *Rain showers flooded the infield*: "Weather Reports," *San Francisco Call*, January 3, 1909.

13 *Seven-thousand-seat capacity*: Joey Enos, "Pacific Coast League Baseball in Emeryville: The History of the Oakland Oaks Ballpark," April 21, 2016, *The E'ville Eye,* https://evilleeye.com/history/oakland-oaks/.

13 *the Imperials and the Fujis*: T. P. Magilligan, "Chinese Wrest Victory from Japanese in Football Battle," *San Francisco Call*, January 4, 1909.

13 *Police arrived to a melee of umbrellas*: "Slit-Eye Game Ends in Riots," *Los Angeles Daily Times*, December 27, 1909.

14 *In 1919, the Asahis and Mikados*: Joel S. Franks, *Asians and Pacific Islanders in American Football: Historical and Contemporary Experiences* (Lanham, MD: Lexington Books, 2018), 37.

14 *Issei football leagues launched*: Ibid., 37.

14 *the all-Chinese Yoke Choy Club*: Ibid., 34.

14 *The game spread to Southern California*: Keiichi Ikeda interview, May 31, 2018.

14 *Japanese American teens dotted the rosters*: Franks, *Asians and Pacific Islanders in American Football*, 132. The history of Japanese American football is painstakingly chronicled in Franks's book; this section of my book would've been impossible without his work.

15 *The article was just two sentences*: "Redshirts Win, 19–0," *Los Angeles Times*, October 25, 1940.

15 *The write-up was just as brief*: "Sheik Lightweights Trip Marshall, 6–0," *Los Angeles Times*, November 1, 1940.

15 *Babe was one of the Sheiks' smallest players*: The details in this paragraph come from Nomura family photos.

15 *For his entire life he'd be embarrassed by his teeth*: Kimiko Nomura interview, February 25, 2019.

16 *Pash was the son of a Russian Orthodox priest*: Boris T. Pash, "Checkmate!: How the Soviets Tried to Take Over the Japanese Orthodox Church, Using 'Diplomatic Channels,'" *American Legion* magazine, April 1958.

16 *born in San Francisco in 1900*: Register of the Boris T. Pash Papers, 1892/1989, Hoover Institution Archives, https://digitalcollections.hoover.org/objects/113.

16 *Pash traveled from Hollywood to Kezar Stadium*: Jack Schmale, "Orientals Set for Grid Test," *San Francisco Examiner*, December 23, 1934.

16 *After leaving Hollywood for active duty*: Sam Kean, *The Bastard Brigade: The True Story of the Renegade Scientists and Spies Who Sabotaged the Nazi Atomic Bomb* (New York: Little, Brown, 2019).

16 *investigated the communist sympathies of Robert Oppenheimer*: Vincent Jones, *Manhattan: The Army and the Atomic Bomb* (Washington, DC: United States Army Center of Military History, 1985), 261.

16 *the 1940 season had stumbled out of the gates*: Hollywood High School, *Poinsettia* (Los Angeles, California, 1941).

17 *an incandescent Judy Garland would walk the halls in the late 1930s*: John Blumenthal, *Hollywood High: The History of America's Most Famous Public School* (New York: Ballantine, 1988), 36.

17 *women allegedly passed out when Valentino appeared on-screen*: Susan King, "A Real Heartthrob and Oh, So 'Sheik,'" *Los Angeles Times*, July 11, 2002.

18 *"A football hero sure is he / what greater glory can there be?"*: Blumenthal, *Hollywood High*, 25.

18 *Before a 1924 game against Army*: Jim Lefebvre, "88 Years Ago Today, The 'Horsemen' Dominated," October 18, 2012, *Forever Irish,* http:// ndfootballhistory.com/88-years-ago-today-october-18-1924.

18 *Football was a demonstration sport in that summer's Olympic Games*: Herb Dana, "90,000 Expected to Witness Grid Battle at Olympic Stadium To-night," *San Francisco Examiner*, August 8, 1932.

19 *the Western All-Stars had defeated the East 7–6*: Jean Bosquet, "West Eleven Triumphs Over East in Hot Game," *Los Angeles Times*, August 9, 1932.

19 *Local press dubbed it the Dust Bowl*: Irving Marks, "Fairfax Plays Red-shirts in Opener Friday," *Hollywood Citizen News*, October 11, 1941.

19 *the game ended 7–7*: "Redshirts Tie Lincoln, 7–7," *Los Angeles Times*, October 4, 1941.

20 *the speed of the Fairfax High eleven overpowered Hollywood*: Hollywood High School, *Poinsettia* (Los Angeles, California; 1942).

20 *The rest of the season was equally dismal*: Ibid.

20 *Of the fifty-five boys who dressed for the Sheiks that fall*: The details in this paragraph come from Nomura family photos.

20 *"There is one thing I'm going to see as far as it is in my power"*: Blumenthal, *Hollywood High*, 50.

20 *Roosevelt's decision to move the United States' Pacific Fleet*: Michael Beschloss, *Presidents of War: The Epic Story, from 1807 to Modern Times* (New York: Crown, 2018), 361.

20 *In a Gallup survey*: Roger W. Lotchin, "A Research Report: The 1940s Gallup Polls, Imperial Japanese, Japanese Americans, and the Reach of American Racism," *Southern California Quarterly* 97, no. 4 (2015): 399–417.

20 *In lieu of social studies*: Hollywood High School, *Poinsettia*, 1942.

21 *of the 654 graduates of the class of 1940*: Hollywood High School, *Poinsettia*, 1941.

21 *six aircraft carriers bearing 414 airplanes*: "The Path to Pearl Harbor," December 6, 2018, The National WWII Museum, https://www.nation alww2museum.org/war/articles/path-pearl-harbor.

21 *"Mr. Vice President, Mr. Speaker"*: Franklin D. Roosevelt, "Speech by Franklin D. Roosevelt," *New York Transcript*, 1941, https://www.loc.gov /item/afccal000483/.

21 *Without the aid of speechwriters*: Robert J. Brown, *Manipulating the Ether: The Power of Broadcast Radio in Thirties America* (Jefferson, NC: McFar-land, 1998), 117–20.

22 *the largest radio audience in American history*: Ibid.

22 *Jeannette Rankin, the first woman ever to hold federal office, voted no*: Whitney Blair Wyckoff, "The First Woman in Congress: A Crusader for Peace," May 18, 2011, National Public Radio, https://www.npr .org/2011/07/14/135521203/the-first-woman-in-congress-a-crusader-for peace.

22 *two days later*: Blumenthal, *Hollywood High*, 52.

Chapter Three: *Furusato*

23 *By the afternoon of December 8*: Jacobus tenBroek, Edward N. Barnhart, and Floyd W. Matson, *Prejudice, War, and the Constitution: Causes and Consequences of the Evacuation of the Japanese Americans in World War II* (Berkeley: University of California Press, 1954), 101.

23 *The FBI's authority came via presidential warrant*: Bill Hosokawa, *Nisei: The Quiet Americans* (Boulder: University Press of Colorado, 1969), 239.

23 *"So long as aliens in this country conduct themselves"*: Select Committee Investigating National Defense Migration, U.S. House of Representatives, *Fourth Interim Report* (Washington, DC: U.S. Government Printing Office, May 13, 1942), 28.

24 *the great-great-grandson of the first attorney general of the United States*: Brian Niiya, "Francis Biddle," *Densho Encyclopedia*, accessed May 20, 2020, https://encyclopedia.densho.org/Francis_Biddle/.

24 *Under the shield of the Alien Enemies Act of 1798*: Tetsuden Kashima, *Judgment Without Trial: Japanese American Imprisonment During World War II* (Seattle: University of Washington Press, 2004), 49.

24 *Roosevelt expressed his concern in a letter*: Gary Okihiro, *Cane Fires: The Anti-Japanese Movement in Hawaii, 1865–1945* (Philadelphia: Temple University Press, 1991), 163.

25 *"The Imperial Japanese Government has agents in every large city in this country"*: Ibid., 172.

25 *By June 1940*: Kashima, *Judgment Without Trial*, 39.

25 *the FBI secured more than eleven thousand informants in the plants by the end of 1940*: Bob Kumamoto, "The Search for Spies: American Counter-intelligence and the Japanese American Community, 1931–1942," *Amerasia Journal* 6, no. 2 (1979).

26 *"the Japanese plan to utilize American Negroes for subversion and espionage"*: George Lipsitz, " 'Frantic to Join . . . the Japanese Army': The Asia Pacific War in the Lives of African American Soldiers and Civil-

ians," in *The Politics of Culture in the Shadow of Capital,* ed. Lisa Lowe and David Lloyd (Durham, NC: Duke University Press, 1997), 324.

26 *investigators went so far as to speculate that Japanese Americans had infiltrated A. Philip Randolph's March on Washington movement*: Ibid.

26 *more than one hundred cruises had left the United States for Japan*: Kumamoto, "The Search for Spies."

26 *the majority of issei would be loyal to the United States*: Duncan Ryūken Williams, *American Sutra: A Story of Faith and Freedom in the Second World War* (Cambridge: Harvard University Press, 2019), 36.

27 *"With the help of the J.A.C.L., which got to be very much on our side"*: Kumamoto, "The Search for Spies."

28 *a man-made amalgam of the former Rattlesnake and Deadman's Islands*: Anna Marie Hager, "A Salute to the Port of Los Angeles from Mud Flats to Modern Day Miracle," *California Historical Society Quarterly* 49, no. 4 (1970): 329–35.

28 *The first Japanese settled in the San Pedro Bay area in 1899*: Eiji Tanabe, "Japanese Fishermen Have Made Important Contributions to Progress of Industry," *Pacific Citizen*, March 27, 1948.

28 *Filipinos, Mexicans, Portuguese, Sicilians, and Slovenians occupied the eastern part of the island*: Lilian Takahashi Hoffecker, "A Village Disappeared," *American Heritage* 52, no. 8 (December 2001): 64–71, http://www.americanheritage.com/content/village-disappeared.

28 *Three thousand issei called the island home*: Ibid.

28 *They built a labyrinthine town*: Lilian Takahashi Hoffecker, "Terminal Island," *Densho Encyclopedia*, accessed May 20, 2020, https://encyclopedia.densho.org/Terminal_Island,_California/.

28 *A staccato blend of Japanese and English developed there*: Min Tonai oral history interview conducted by Tom Ikeda in Los Angeles, California, September 2, 2010," Densho Digital Archive, Densho Visual History Collection, film, https://encyclopedia.densho.org/sources/en-denshovh-tmin-01-0005-1/.

28 *Hoover saw the fishermen as little more than sardine-scented spies*: Kumamoto, "The Search for Spies."

28 *Naval Intelligence purchased 105 acres of land along San Pedro Bay*: Ibid.

29 *51,923 Italian nationals in California alone*: Select Committee Investigating National Defense Migration, U.S. House of Representatives, *Fourth Interim Report*, 230.

29 *Los Angeles's 8,726 Japanese nationals, 17,528 German-born residents*: Mau-

rice Alexandre, "Wartime Control of Japanese-Americans," *Cornell Law Quarterly* 28, no. 4 (June 1943): 385–458, http://scholarship.law.cornell.edu/clr/vol28/iss4/5.

29 *Amerika-Deutscher Volksbund boasting members in every state save for Louisiana*: Leland V. Bell, "The Failure of Nazism in America: The German American Bund, 1936–1941," *Political Science Quarterly* 85, no. 4 (December 1970): 585–99.

29 *American Nazis raised swastikas in Los Angeles parks*: Anna Diamond, "The Nazis' Plan to Infiltrate Los Angeles and the Man Who Kept Them at Bay," *Smithsonian*, October 26, 2017.

29 *only glancing effort to monitor the activities of Americans of German or Italian descent*: Greg Robinson, *By Order of the President: FDR and the Internment of Japanese Americans* (Cambridge: Harvard University Press, 2001), 59.

29 *"You needn't worry about the Italians"*: Committee on Internal Security, U.S. House of Representatives, Hearings Relating to Various Bills to Repeal the Emergency Detention Act of 1950, Vols. 8–15 (Washington, DC: U.S. Government Printing Office, 1970), 3552.

29 *In October 1940*: Hyohei Nomura evacuee file, Records About Japanese Americans Relocated During World War II, created 1988–1989, documenting the period 1942–1946, Record Group 210, National Archives, Washington, DC. Hereafter evacuee file.

30 *"Los Angeles is to the Japanese"*: Valerie Matsumoto, *City Girls: The Nisei Social World in Los Angeles, 1920–1950* (Oxford: Oxford University Press, 2016), 14.

30 *the nikkei in America had grown to 138,834*: *Personal Justice Denied: Report of the Commission on Wartime Relocation and Internment of Civilians* (Washington, DC: Commission on Wartime Relocation and Internment of Civilians, 1983), 36.

30 *Of those a full quarter*: Kevin Starr, *Material Dreams: Southern California Through the 1920s* (Oxford: Oxford University Press, 1991), 146.

30 *the number of nisei spiked*: Alexandre, "Wartime Control of Japanese-Americans."

30 *Much of the credit for the list*: Ken Ringle, "What Did You Do Before the War, Dad?," *Washington Post*, December 6, 1981.

31 *Category A comprised*: Williams, *American Sutra*, 37.

31 Sokoku, *however, was a Japanese nationalist magazine*: Kashima, *Judgment Without Trial*, 31.

31 *Leaders of both the Nippon Bunka Kyokai . . . and Nichibei Kinema*: Kumamoto, "The Search for Spies."

31 *removing two samurai swords from a dresser*: Hosokawa, *Nisei*, 233.

32 *radio transmitters, shortwave radio receiving sets, and cameras*: Richard Reeves, *Infamy: The Shocking Story of the Japanese American Internment in World War II* (New York: Henry Holt, 2015), 26.

32 *1,458 radios, 2,114 cameras, 1,652 sticks of dynamite, 2,592 guns, and 199,000 rounds of ammunition*: Ibid., 27.

32 *Biddle admitted the fallacy of the searches*: Hosokawa, *Nisei*, 253.

32 *she attempted to calm the nerves of Japanese Americans*: "No Seizure Is Due for 'Good' Aliens," *New York Times*, December 4, 1941.

33 *On overnight flights west*: Eleanor Roosevelt, *My Day* syndicated column, December 10, 1941, The Eleanor Roosevelt Papers Project, George Washington University, https://www2.gwu.edu/~erpapers/myday/displaydoc.cfm?_y=1941&_f=md056056a.

33 *In between civilian defense meetings*: Eleanor Roosevelt, *My Day* syndicated column, December 12, 1941, The Eleanor Roosevelt Papers Project, George Washington University, https://www2.gwu.edu/~erpapers/myday/displaydoc.cfm?_y=1941&_f=md056056b.

33 *"Our citizens come from all the nations of the world"*: Eleanor Roosevelt, *My Day* syndicated column, December 16, 1941, The Eleanor Roosevelt Papers Project, George Washington University, https://www2.gwu.edu/~erpapers/myday/displaydoc.cfm?_y=1941&_f=md056057.

34 *the* San Francisco Chronicle *reminded readers*: Gary Okihiro, *Storied Lives: Japanese American Students and World War II* (Seattle: University of Washington Press, 2011), 22.

34 *In the December 8 edition of the* Brawley News: Reeves, *Infamy*, 16.

34 *Grodzins studied the editorials of 112 California newspapers*: Gary Y. Okihiro and Julie Sly, "The Press, Japanese Americans, and the Concentration Camps," *Phylon* 44, no. 1 (1983): 66–83. All the facts and data in this paragraph are from this article.

35 *In a January 23 editorial*: "Dies and the Japs," *Los Angeles Times*, January 23, 1942.

35 *Five days later*: "Facing the Japanese Issue Here," *Los Angeles Times*, January 28, 1942.

35 *On January 2, Hearst columnist Damon Runyon*: Damon Runyon, "Coast 'Little Tokyo' Depleted by Raids," (Rochester, New York) *Democrat and Chronicle*, January 2, 1942.

35 *No transmitter was ever found*: Bill Hosokawa, *Nisei: The Quiet Americans* (Boulder: University Press of Colorado, 1969), 264.

35 *John B. Hughes began near-daily attacks*: Ibid.

35 *Walter Lippmann worked from the top down*: Greg Robinson, *By Order of the President: FDR and the Internment of Japanese Americans* (Cambridge: Harvard University Press, 2001), 112.

36 *McLemore made explicit what Lippmann left implicit*: Henry McLemore, "California's Alive with Japanese Who Could Duplicate the Tricks of Their Cousins at Pearl Harbor or Manila," *Austin American-Statesman*, January 29, 1942.

Chapter Four: How to Make It in America

37 *The westernmost tract of the North Pacific gyre*: Kunio Kutsuwada and Yoshihiko Sekine, "Seasonal Variation in Volume Transport of the Kuroshio South of Japan," *Journal of Physical Oceanography*, 24 (February 1994): 261–72.

37 *On the fifth day of the first month of 1841*: Hisakazu Kaneko, "The Man Who Discovered America," *American Heritage*, December 1956. The account of Manjiro in this book is derived from this magazine story, which is itself a condensed version of Kaneko's book, *Manjiro, The Man Who Discovered America*.

38 *Herman Melville left New Bedford on the* Acushnet: Wilson Heflin, *Herman Melville's Whaling Years* (Nashville: Vanderbilt University Press, 2004), editors' preface, xvii.

39 *Manjiro arrived in the New World 233 years after*: Zelia Nuttall, *The Earliest Historical Relations Between Mexico and Japan* (Berkeley: University of California Publications, 1906), 46.

39 *"They seem bold, not gentle and meek people"*: Doris Namala et al., *Annals of His Time: Don Domingo de San Antón Muñón Chimalpahin Quauhtlehuanitzin* (Stanford: Stanford University Press, 2006).

39 *By 1623, British traders found themselves driven out of the Japanese archipelago*: Bill Hosokawa, *Nisei: The Quiet Americans* (Boulder: University Press of Colorado, 1969), 10.

39 *twenty-two families landed in San Francisco*: Alan Ehrgott, "History of the Wakamatsu Tea and Silk Farm Colony," *Discover Nikkei*, January 25, 2018, http://www.discovernikkei.org/en/journal/2018/1/25/wakamatsu-colony/.

39 *In an effort to ward off Western imperialism*: Hosok O, "Cultural Analysis

of the Early Japanese Immigration to the United States During Meiji to Taisho Era (1868–1926)" (PhD diss., Oklahoma State University, 2010).

40 *The first Japanese immigrants had technically arrived*: Hosokawa, *Nisei*, 35.

40 *The Meiji Restoration*: Ibid., 38.

40 *Chinese workers had arrived in the United States*: Roger Daniels, *The Politics of Prejudice: The Anti-Japanese Movement in California and the Struggle for Japanese Exclusion* (Berkeley: University of California Press, 177), 16.

40 *the United States was predominantly a black and white society*: "1880 Overview," United States Census Bureau, https://www.census.gov/history /www/through_the_decades/overview/1880.html.

41 *Seventy-five boarded a train in San Francisco*: Anthony W. Lee, *A Shoemaker's Story: Being Chiefly About French Canadian Immigrants, Enterprising Photographers, Rascal Yankees, and Chinese Cobblers in a Nineteenth-Century Factory Town* (Princeton: Princeton University Press, 2008), 2.

41 *Cotton fields in Arkansas*: Byrd Gibbens, "Strangers in the Arkansas Delta: Ethnic Groups and Nationalities," in *The Arkansas Delta: Land of Paradox*, ed. Williard B. Gatewood Jr. and Jeannie M. Whayne (Fayetteville: University of Arkansas Press, 1996), 173.

41 *the first anti-Asian mass meeting in America*: Lucile Eaves, *A History of California Labor Legislation* (Berkeley: University of California Publications, 1910), 23.

41 *the room filled with manic applause*: "The Chinese and the Workingmen," *San Francisco Chronicle*, July 9, 1870.

41 *"The Chinese Must Go!"*: Daniels, *The Politics of Prejudice*, 17.

41 *On October 24, 1871*: Scott Zesch, "Chinese Los Angeles in 1870–1871: The Makings of a Massacre," *Southern California Quarterly* 90 (Summer 2008): 109–58.

42 *39,579 Chinese immigrants entered the country*: Kerry Abrams, "Polygamy, Prostitution, and the Federalization of Immigration Law," *Columbia Law Review* 105, no. 3 (April 2005): 641–716.

42 *tried to commandeer the California Constitutional Convention*: Daniels, *The Politics of Prejudice*, 18.

42 *many Chinese workers in Wyoming had transitioned into coal mines*: T. A. Larson, *History of Wyoming* (Lincoln: University of Nebraska Press, 1965), 141. The details throughout this paragraph are from Larson's work.

43 *Another's penis and testicles were cut off*: David T. Courtwright, *Violent Land: Single Men and Social Disorder from the Frontier to the Inner City* (Cambridge: Harvard University Press, 2009), 158.

43 *found work in the sawmills, restaurants, and more lascivious trades*: Bill Hosokawa and Robert Arden Wilson, *East to America: A History of the Japanese in the United States* (New York: William Morrow, 1980), 33.

43 *Japanese immigrants didn't surpass 1,000 per year until 1891*: Ibid., 44.

44 *An estimated 700,000 native Hawaiians*: Sara Kehaulani Goo, "After 200 years, Native Hawaiians Make a Comeback," *Pew Research Center*, April 6, 2015, https://www.pewresearch.org/fact-tank/2015/04/06/native-hawaiian-population/.

44 *In only thirty years*: Daniels, *The Politics of Prejudice*, 5.

44 *nearly eighteen thousand Chinese contract workers lived on the islands*: Ibid.

44 *subsidized the emigration of Japanese*: Ralph S. Kuykendoll, *The Hawaiian Kingdom: Volume 3—The Kalakaua Dynasty, 1874–1893* (Honolulu: University of Hawaii Press, 1979), 170.

44 *largest ship ever constructed in the United States*: "Another Great Steam-Ship," *New York Times*, May 14, 1874.

45 *At 9 a.m.*: Kuykendoll, *The Hawaiian Kingdom*, 164.

45 *sake lubricated the proceedings*: Franklin Odo and Kazuko Sinoto, *A Pictorial History of the Japanese in Hawaii, 1885–1924* (Honolulu: Bishop Museum Press, 1985), 39.

45 *Between the* ikkaisen's *1885 arrival and 1894*: Hosokawa and Wilson, *East to America*, 141.

45 *contracts stipulated three-year commitments*: Ibid.

45 *If workers claimed to be sick*: Hosokawa, *Nisei*, 458.

45 *Foremen on horseback held whips*: Erika Lee, *The Making of Asian America: A History* (New York: Simon & Schuster, 2015), 115.

45 *"The Hawaiian plantation was a Japanese frontier"*: Hilary Conroy, *The Japanese Frontier in Hawaii, 1868–1898* (New York: Arno Press, 1953), 86.

46 *by the fifteenth boat of migrants*: Ibid.

46 *workers on the Paia plantation refused to work*: Eric Saul, "Japanese American Chronology," personal website, http://www.easaul.com/japanese-amer-timeline.html.

46 *The sport was introduced in the islands in 1875*: Ty P. Kāwika Tengan and Jesse Makani Markham, "Performing Polynesian Masculinities in American Football: From 'Rainbows to Warriors,'" *International Journal of the History of Sport* 26, no. 16 (2009): 2412–31.

46 *In December 1890*: Dan Cisco, *Hawai'i Sports: History, Facts, and Statistics* (Honolulu: University of Hawaii Press, 1999), 130.

47 *By 1890*: Hosokawa, *Nisei*, 81.

47 *The first Japanese on the mainland*: Hosokawa and Wilson, *East to America*, 107.

47 *The Chinese and Japanese lived competitive but overlapping existences*: Joan S. Wang, "The Double Burdens of Immigrant Nationalism: The Relationship Between Chinese and Japanese in the American West, 1880s–1920s," *Journal of American Ethnic History* 27, no. 2 (2008): 28–58.

48 *Thousands of Japanese workers*: Hosokawa and Wilson, *East to America*, 146.

48 *more than 2,800 peasant uprisings took place in the empire*: Takashi Fujitani, "Cultures of Resistance," in *A Matter of Conscience*, ed. Mike Mackey (Powell, WY: Western History Publications, 2002), 142.

48 *On May 7, 1900*: Daniels, *The Politics of Prejudice*, 21.

49 *Phelan was born into privilege there*: Kevin Starr, *Inventing the Dream: California Through the Progressive Era* (Oxford: Oxford University Press, 1986), 241.

49 *Phelan's San Francisco experienced unrivaled prosperity*: Raymond Leslie Buell, "The Development of the Anti-Japanese Agitation in the United States," *Political Science Quarterly* 37, no. 4 (1922): 605–38.

49 *modeling his plan after Pericles's beautification of Athens*: Robert W. Cherny, "City Commercial, City Beautiful, City Practical: The San Francisco Visions of William C. Ralston, James D. Phelan, and Michael M. O'Shaughnessy," *California History* 73, no. 4 (December 1994): 296–307.

49 *On March 6, the body of Chick Gin*: Philip A. Kalisch, "The Black Death in Chinatown: Plague and Politics in San Francisco, 1900–1904," *Arizona and the West* 14, no. 2 (1972): 113–36.

50 *"The Japanese are starting the same tide of immigration"*: Daniels, *The Politics of Prejudice*, 21.

50 *an unstable, heterogeneous state*: Personal Justice Denied: Report of the Commission on Wartime Relocation and Internment of Civilians (Washington, DC: Commission on Wartime Relocation and Internment of Civilians, 1983), 31.

50 *Republican, Democratic, and Populist party platforms*: Daniels, *The Politics of Prejudice*, 22.

51 *victory stoked anti-Japanese accusations*: Personal Justice Denied: Report of the Commission on Wartime Relocation and Internment of Civilians, 33.

51 *the San Francisco Chronicle, introduced readers*: "The Japanese Invasion, the Problem of the Hour for the United States," *San Francisco Chronicle*, February 23, 1905.

52 *The political effect was immediate*: Daniels, The *Politics of Prejudice*, 27.

52 *for the next forty years*: Ibid.

52 *representatives from sixty-seven different organizations*: Ibid.

52 *"An eternal law of nature"*: Daniels, *The Politics of Prejudice*, 28.

52 *"We have been accustomed to regard the Japanese as an inferior race"*: "Representative Men Tell of Danger," *San Francisco Chronicle*, May 8, 1905.

53 *the board voted to move the district's Japanese students*: Daniels, *The Politics of Prejudice*, 35.

53 *the deadliest earthquake in U.S. history*: "The Great 1906 San Francisco Earthquake," U.S. Geological Survey, https://earthquake.usgs.gov/.

53 *between 1.3 and 1.8 percent of the country's gross national product*: Kerry A. Odell and Marc D. Weidenmier, "Real Shock, Monetary Aftershock: The 1906 San Francisco Earthquake and the Panic of 1907," *The Journal of Economic History* 64, no. 4 (2004): 1002–27.

53 *setting the stage for the New York Stock Exchange free fall*: Ibid.

53 *Donations and aid poured into the region*: Daniels, *The Politics of Prejudice*, 33.

54 *the league declared boycotts on Japanese restaurants and markets*: Herbert Buell Johnson, *Discrimination Against the Japanese in California: A Review of the Real Situation* (Berkeley: The Courier Publishing Company, 1907), 102. The details and accounts in the paragraphs that follow also come from Johnson's work in the immediately subsequent pages.

55 *seventeen months after its initial resolution*: Daniels, *The Politics of Prejudice*, 34.

55 *poorly translated versions of the events*: Hosokawa and Wilson, *East to America*, 123.

55 *Diplomatically, the timing couldn't have been worse*: "Metcalf Ignores Alarm Over the Japanese," *San Francisco Examiner*, May 18, 1905.

55 *Roosevelt delivered his annual congressional address*: Theodore Roosevelt, "Sixth Annual Message," Washington, DC, December 3, 1906, The American Presidency Project, https://www.presidency.ucsb.edu/docu ments/sixth-annual-message-4.

56 *Roosevelt was pummeled by the California press*: Daniels, *The Politics of Prejudice*, 42.

56 *The seeds of this plan*: Theodore Roosevelt to Elihu Root, December 5, 1906, in *Gentleman's Agreement of 1907,* San Francisco State University, https://diva.sfsu.edu/collections/ga1907.

57 *"[The] only way to prevent constant friction"*: Daniels, *The Politics of Prejudice*, 41.

57 *After weeks of negotiation*: Ibid., 42.

57 *Hyohei Nomura boarded the* Tosa Maru: Canada Passenger Lists, 1881–1922.

58 *Usaburo Yoshinaga had opposite plans*: GYOH.

58 *climbing emigration numbers and falling immigration ones*: Daniels, *The Politics of Prejudice*, 44.

58 *twenty-four Japanese men for every one Japanese woman*: Hosokawa and Wilson, *East to America*, 54–55.

59 *Instead of curbing the state's anti-Japanese sentiment*: Daniels, *The Politics of Prejudice*, 45.

59 *the Vaca Valley is greeted annually by two seasons*: Harold Rubin, *The Solano Water Story* (Davis, CA: Robert D. Kahn & Company, 1988), 14.

59 *The valley is eight miles long*: U.S. Senate, Reports of the Immigration Commission, *Immigrants in Industries: Part 25: Japanese and Other Immigrant Races in the Pacific Coast and Rocky Mountain States, Volume II* (Washington, DC: U.S. Government Printing Office, June 15, 1910), 175.

59 *produced small, sweet, dry fruit*: Kurt R. Richter and Alvin D. Sokolow, University of California Agricultural Issues Center, *The Economic Roots of Solano County Agriculture: Report II, Solano Agricultural Futures Project*, September 14, 2007, https://aic.ucdavis.edu/solano/econroots.pdf.

59 *four Japanese men in San Francisco ventured east*: Hosokawa and Wilson, *East to America*, 61.

59 *the men undercut their competitors*: Reports of the Immigration Commission, *Immigrants in Industries*, 176.

59 *first foray into the American agricultural market*: Hosokawa and Wilson, *East to America*, 60.

59 *four stores, three billiard parlors*: Reports of the Immigration Commission, *Immigrants in Industries*, 197.

59 *"The Japanese are ambitious"*: Ibid., 187.

60 *Japanese immigrants leased close to 75 percent of the Vaca Valley's*: Ibid., 175.

60 *the men had purchased a small, 290-acre cluster of orchards*: Ibid., 196.

60 *George Shima, a former domestic servant in San Francisco*: Donald Teruo Hata and Nadine Hata, "George Shima: The Potato King of California," *The Journal of the West* 25, no. 1 (January 1986): 55–63. All the biographical details included here are from this journal article.

61 *They leveled the ground*: Hosokawa and Wilson, *East to America*, 62.

61 *In Oregon's Hood River Valley*: Ibid., 70.

61 *The garlic industry in the San Juan Valley*: Hosokawa, *Nisei*, 65.

61 *five hundred Japanese workers and two hundred Mexican workers*: Tomás Amaguer, "Racial Domination and Class Conflict in Capitalist Agriculture: The Oxnard Sugar Beet Workers' Strike of 1903," in *Working People of California*, ed. Daniel A. Cornford (Berkeley: University of California Press, 1995), 183.

61 *"[The Californians] had seen the Japanese convert"*: Ronald Takaki, *Strangers from a Different Shore: A History of Asian Americans* (New York: Penguin, 1992),192.

62 *Bradford Smith puts it more directly*: Hosokawa, *Nisei*, 133.

62 *By the summer of 1909*: Hosokawa and Wilson, *East to America*, 64.

62 *venomous statement drafted by James Phelan*: Daniels, *The Politics of Prejudice*, 56.

63 *M. A. Mitchell stood before the committee*: Franklin Hichborn, *Story of the Session of the California Legislature of 1913* (San Francisco: Press of the James H. Barry Company, 1913), 225. The paragraphs that follow Mitchell's quote are derived from the same source.

64 *In 1910, nikkei farmers owned or leased*: Hosokawa, *Nisei*, 105.

64 *nikkei farmers operated less than 2 percent of that land*: California State Board of Control, *California and the Oriental: Japanese, Chinese and Hindus*, January 1, 1922 (Sacramento: California State Printing Office).

64 *"The Japanese nation is characterized by industry"*: Ibid., 236.

64 *Phelan and his band of exclusionists and racists*: Daniels, *The Politics of Prejudice*, 84.

64 *Representatives from groups as diverse*: Ibid., 144.

65 *Nearly three hundred Native Sons parlors*: Nancy Pratt Melton, "Native Sons of the Golden West Parlor Locations," 2005, *SF Genealogy,* https://www.sfgenealogy.org/caldatanook/nsgw/nsgw.htm.

65 *excoriated the Methodist Church*: "No Jap School," *The Grizzly Bear*, March 1922.

65 *Future California governor and chief justice of the Supreme Court Earl Warren*: Jim Newton, *Justice for All: Earl Warren and the Nation He Made* (New York: Penguin, 2007), 74.

65 *member Richard Nixon welcomed*: Richard S. Kimball and Barney Noel, *Native Sons of the Golden West* (Mount Pleasant, SC: Arcadia Publishing, 2008), 119.

65 *It passed in a more than three-to-one landslide*: Daniels, *The Politics of Prejudice*, 90.

66 *The American Legion produced the film* Shadows of the West: Tom Rice, *White Robes, Silver Screens: Movies and the Making of the Ku Klux Klan* (Bloomington: Indiana University Press, 2016), 183.

66 *The trade magazine* Moving Picture World: Sumner Smith, "Shadows of the West," *Moving Picture World*, November 27, 1920.

66 *no matter the reality*: *Personal Justice Denied: Report of the Commission on Wartime Relocation and Internment of Civilians* (Washington, DC: Commission on Wartime Relocation and Internment of Civilians, 1983), 34.

66 *the U.S. House Committee on Immigration and Naturalization traveled to California and Washington*: Doug Blair, "The 1920 Anti-Japanese Crusade and Congressional Hearings," The Seattle Civil Rights and Labor History Project, 2006, https://depts.washington.edu/civilr/Japanese_restriction.htm.

67 *wide swath of classes deemed "undesirable" by Congress*: Cherstin Lyon, "Immigration Act of 1917," *Densho Encyclopedia*, https://encyclopedia.densho.org/Immigration%20Act%20of%201917/.

67 *Albert Johnson introduced a bill*: Daniels, *The Politics of Prejudice*, 94.

67 *Takao Ozawa was born in Kanagawa*: Shiho Imai, "Ozawa v. United States," *Densho Encyclopedia*, https://encyclopedia.densho.org/Ozawa%20v.%20United%20States/.

68 *"My honesty and industriousness are well known"*: Ibid.

68 *Pacific Coast Japanese Association Deliberative Council*: Xiaojian Zhao and Edward J. W. Park, eds., *Asian Americans: An Encyclopedia of Social, Cultural, Economic, and Political History* (Santa Barbara, CA: ABC-CLIO, 2013), 598.

68 *The results were unanimously unfavorable*: Ozawa v. U.S., 260 U.S. 178 (1922).

69 *Los Angeles had more than doubled in population*: "Population Is Past 230,000," *Los Angeles Herald*, April 15, 1906.

69 *3,000 were ethnically Japanese*: City of Los Angeles, Department of City Planning, Office of Historic Resources, *Los Angeles Citywide Historic Context Statement: Japanese Americans in Los Angeles, 1869–1970*, https://planning.lacity.org/odocument/bf97b9b9-cb81-4661-8d20-62c02b9c1415/SurveyLA_JapaneseAmericanContextandResources_Aug2018.pdf. The facts and data in this paragraph were gleaned from this report, which goes into extensive detail about Japanese American life in Los Angeles.

69 *the number of Little Tokyo* nomiya: Ibid., 21.

69 *the inefficiency of the Los Angeles Pacific Railroad*: Nathan Masters, "How Prospect Avenue Became Hollywood Boulevard," *Los Angeles Magazine*, June 4, 2014.

70 *Hollywood's population grew from 5,000 residents to 36,000*: John Blumenthal, *Hollywood High: The History of America's Most Famous Public School* (New York: Ballantine, 1988), 52.

70 *Recreational indignities*: John Modell, *The Economics and Politics of Racial Accommodation: The Japanese of Los Angeles, 1900–1942* (Champaign: University of Illinois Press, 1977), 66.

70 *In late 1922*: Ibid., 62.

70 *By May the group had a name*: Koyoshi Ouno, "The Factors Affecting the Geographical Aggregation and Dispersion of the Japanese Residents in the City of Los Angeles" (MA diss., University of Southern California, 1927).

71 *A new publication called* Swat the Jap *was founded*: Ibid., 30.

72 *In March 1924*: Daniels, *The Politics of Prejudice*, 99.

72 *McClatchy also had a secret weapon*: Leo McClatchy, "May Investigate Gentleman Pact with Japanese," *Honolulu Star-Bulletin*, March 26, 1924.

72 *Born into a family of missionaries in the Marshall Islands*: Sandra C. Taylor, "Japan's Missionary to the Americans: Sidney L. Gulick and America's Interwar Relationship with the Japanese," *Diplomatic History* 4, no. 4 (1980): 387–407.

72 *He published* The American Japanese Problem: Greg Robinson, "Sidney Gulick," *Densho Encyclopedia*, https://encyclopedia.densho.org/Sidney%20Gulick/.

73 *Ever the internationalist*: McClatchy, "May Investigate Gentleman Pact with Japanese."

73 *The National Association of Manufacturers, the American Mining Congress, and the U.S. Chamber of Commerce*: Michael C. LeMay, *Guarding the Gates: Immigration and National Security* (Westport, CT: Greenwood Publishing, 2006), 118.

73 *Chinese, Czechs, Greeks*: Ibid., 127.

73 *both resigned in protest*: "Anti-American Feeling at Very High Pitch in Japan," *Eugene Guard*, June 9, 1924.

74 *when V. S. McClatchy stepped foot off the train*: "Passing of Jap Anger at Ban Seen," *San Francisco Examiner*, June 10, 1924.

74 *the adjutant of the California state American Legion*: "Keaton Is Named Legion Adjutant," *Madera Mercury*, October 16, 1921.

Chapter Five: 9066

75 *Ten hours after Pearl Harbor*: John T. Correll, "Disaster in the Philippines," *Air Force Magazine*, November 1, 2019, https://www.airforcemag.com/article/disaster-in-the-philippines/.

75 *Roosevelt's studies*: Michael Beschloss, *Presidents of War: The Epic Story, from 1807 to Modern Times* (New York: Crown, 2018), 361.

75 *stuffed with models, pamphlets, and documents*: Ibid., 362.

76 *At age eleven he picked up Admiral Alfred Thayer Mahan's seminal* The Influence of Sea Power upon History: Greg Robinson, *By Order of the President: FDR and the Internment of Japanese Americans* (Cambridge: Harvard University Press, 2001), 12.

76 *Roosevelts didn't fight in the War of 1812, the Mexican War, or the Civil War*: Beschloss, *Presidents of War*, 362.

76 *Delano bequeathed to his grandson an unusual obsession with China*: Robinson, *By Order of the President*, 10.

76 *In 1913 Roosevelt assumed the role of assistant secretary of the navy*: Ibid., 25.

77 *In a 1920 interview with the* Brooklyn Eagle: Frederick Boyd Stevenson, "Roosevelt Says 'Prepare for War' if U.S. Does Not Join the League," *Brooklyn Eagle*, July 18, 1920.

77 *Roosevelt doubled down*: Robinson, *By Order of the President*, 40.

78 *The parasols shone in the sun*: Hisakazu Kaneko, "The Man Who Discovered America," *American Heritage*, December 1956.

78 *Washington Street Christian Meeting-House*: "Washington Street Meetinghouse," Fairhaven, Massachusetts, Office of Tourism, https://fairhaventours.com/washington-street-meetinghouse/.

78 *He studied English and surveying in Fairhaven*: Kaneko, "The Man Who Discovered America."

79 *"My dear Dr. Nakahama"*: Franklin Delano Roosevelt to Toichiro Nakahama, June 8, 1933.

80 *FBI agent Robert Shivers filed a voluminous report*: Robinson, *By Order of the President*, 62.

80 *The head of the Honolulu Police Department's espionage division*: Duncan Ryūken Williams, *American Sutra: A Story of Faith and Freedom in the Second World War* (Cambridge: Harvard University Press, 2019), 30.

80 *"They are good law-abiding citizens"*: "Why Attack the People of Hawaii?," *Honolulu Star Bulletin*, November 18, 1941.

80 *political conditions in the French Caribbean colonies of Martinique and Guadeloupe*: Bob Kumamoto, "The Search for Spies: American Coun-

terintelligence and the Japanese American Community, 1931–1942," *Amerasia Journal* 6, no. 2 (1979).

80 *a DC native with a blue blood pedigree*: "Curtis Munson, Veteran of Two Wars, Was Farmer and Engineer in Canada," *Washington Post*, October 16, 1980, https://www.washingtonpost.com/archive/local/1980/10/16/curtis-munson-veteran-of-two-wars-was-farmer-and-engineer-in-canada/a81ce565-f51e-4300-adab-8102a57342eb/.

81 *after one failed marriage*: Judith Cass, "Edith Cummings Will Be Bride of New Yorker," *Chicago Tribune*, January 15, 1934.

81 *Ringle's contacts in the Japanese American community ran deep*: Ken Ringle, "What Did You Do Before the War, Dad?," *Washington Post*, December 6, 1981.

81 *"We do not want to throw a lot of American citizens"*: Robinson, *By Order of the President*, 66.

82 *Carter passed the report on to Roosevelt*: United States, *Personal Justice Denied: Report of the Commission on Wartime Relocation and Internment of Civilians* (Washington, DC: Commission on Wartime Relocation and Internment of Civilians, 1983), 53.

82 *Carter copied a five-point summary of the report*: Robinson, *By Order of the President*, 70.

82 *Its congressman was Leland Ford*: "Leland Merritt Ford," *Biographical Directory of the United States Congress*, https://bioguideretro.congress.gov/Home/MemberDetails?memIndex=F000264.

82 *A staunch antilabor and anti–New Deal Republican*: Martha Nakagawa, "Leland Ford," *Densho Encyclopedia*, https://encyclopedia.densho.org/Leland%20Ford.

83 *leading to a sit-down strike outside his office*: "Shirt with Large Padlock Presented to Supervisor," *Los Angeles Times*, February 27, 1938.

83 *The congressman fired off a telegram to Washington*: Morton Grodzins, *Americans Betrayed: Politics and the Japanese Evacuation* (Chicago: University of Chicago Press, 1949), 65.

83 *By February his tone flew past being impatient*: *Personal Justice Denied: Report of the Commission on Wartime Relocation and Internment of Civilians*, 34.

84 *released a statement drafted by Attorney General Francis Biddle*: Robinson, *By Order of the President*, 84.

84 *Western Defense Command head General John DeWitt*: Bill Yenne, "Fear Itself: The General Who Panicked the West Coast," *World War II Mag-*

azine, August 2017, https://www.historynet.com/fear-itself-the-general -panicked-west-coast.htm.

84 *He abandoned Princeton in 1898*: Eric L. Muller, *Free to Die for Their Country: The Story of the Japanese American Draft Resisters in World War II* (Chicago: University of Chicago Press, 2001), 20.

84 *"the creature of the last strong personality with whom he had contact"*: Roger Daniels, *Concentration Camps, North America: Japanese in the United States and Canada During World War II* (Malabar, FL: R. E. Krieger Publishing, 1971), 44.

85 *He couldn't accept Japanese American loyalty*: Robinson, *By Order of the President*, 85.

85 *every German, Italian, and Japanese national over the age of fourteen*: Ibid.

85 *Bendetson grew up in a Finnish neighborhood*: Klancy Clark de Nevers, *The Colonel and the Pacifist* (Salt Lake City: University of Utah Press, 2004), 47.

85 *Bendetson had enlisted in the Washington National Guard*: Klancy de Nevers, "Karl Bendetson," *Densho Encyclopedia*, https://encyclopedia .densho.org/Karl%20Bendetson/.

86 *he traveled to Kilauea Military Camp in Hawai'i*: de Nevers, *The Colonel and the Pacifist*, 62.

86 *Much of the city's newspapermen and War Department officers*: William K. Klingaman, *The Darkest Year: The American Home Front, 1941–1942* (New York: St. Martin's Press, 2019), 41.

86 *After receiving a call from his office*: de Nevers, *The Colonel and the Pacifist*, 77.

86 *he spent his days communicating with DeWitt in San Francisco*: Ibid., 89.

86 *"I'm very doubtful that it would be common sense procedure"*: Roger Daniels, *Prisoners Without Trial: Japanese Americans in World War II* (New York: Farrar, Straus & Giroux, 2004), 32.

87 *Roosevelt ordered the registration of foreign nationals on January 14*: Robinson, *By Order of the President*, 86.

87 *the Canadian government okayed the removal*: Masumi Izumi, "Japanese Canadian Exclusion and Incarceration," *Densho Encyclopedia*, https:// encyclopedia.densho.org/Japanese%20Canadian%20exclusion%20and%20 incarceration/.

87 *misinformation and pressure were growing in Roosevelt's cabinet*: Robinson, *By Order of the President*, 94.

87 *In a letter drafted by Bendetson*: de Nevers, *The Colonel and the Pacifist*, 91.

88 *Roosevelt tasked Supreme Court justice Owen Roberts to lead a commission*: Robinson, *By Order of the President*, 95.

88 *Mayor Earl Millikin offered the five hundred horsemen of the city's Cavalry Brigade*: Bill Hosokawa, *Nisei: The Quiet Americans* (Boulder: University Press of Colorado, 1969), 249.

88 *Earl Warren believed*: G. Edward White, *Earl Warren: A Public Life* (Oxford: Oxford University Press, 1982), 69.

88 *Los Angeles mayor Fletcher Bowron*: Martha Nakagawa, "Fletcher Bowron," *Densho Encyclopedia*, http://encyclopedia.densho.org/Fletcher_Bowron.

89 *Reflecting the fever of the turn of the century*: Daniels, *The Politics of Prejudice*, 127.

89 *nikkei produce production in California*: The data included in this paragraph was compiled by Morton Grodzins for the 1942 University of California, Berkeley, Japanese American Evacuation and Resettlement Study. It is found in various folders held at the school's Bancroft Library and available digitally here: https://bancroft.berkeley.edu/collections/jais/.

89 *"We're charged with wanting to get rid of the Japs for selfish reasons"*: Frank J. Taylor, "The People Nobody Wants: The Plight of Japanese-Americans in 1942," *Saturday Evening Post*, May 9, 1942, https://www.saturday eveningpost.com/2017/05/people-nobody-wants/.

90 *California governor Culbert Olson*: Robinson, *By Order of the President*, 96.

90 *Olson hosted two dozen nisei leaders from across the state*: Hosokawa, *Nisei*, 271–72. Other details from this section come from the notes of Togo Tanaka, held at UC Berkeley's Bancroft Library and available under call number BANC MSS 67/14 c, Folder A17.07 (3/4).

92 *Some of this clemency may be traced*: David Zurawik, "Insightful DiMaggio Biography Is a Jolt," *Baltimore Sun*, May 8, 2000.

92 *At 6-foot-2, 193 pounds, and twenty-six years old*: "Joe DiMaggio," *Life*, September 29, 1941.

92 *Japan's leaders were virtually unknown in America*: Hosokawa, *Nisei*, 247.

93 *bricks smashed through the front windows*: Ibid., 248.

93 *Restaurants posted signs*: Daniels, *The Politics of Prejudice*, 131.

93 *"Don't shoot! I'm a Chinaman!"*: Klingaman, *The Darkest Year*, 71.

93 *Teens chopped down four Japanese cherry trees*: Ibid., 70.

93 *the Parks Department placed a guard*: "City Razes Jap Pavilion as Result of Protests," *Brooklyn Eagle*, September 29, 1943.

93 *Rising Sun Baptist Church*: "As the Day Begins," *Indianapolis Star*, December 14, 1941.

94 *Insurance policies were canceled, leases broken*: Daniels, *The Politics of Prejudice*, 128.

94 *he saved particular spite for Franklin Roosevelt*: David Pietrusza, *Judge and Jury: The Life and Times of Judge Kenesaw Mountain Landis* (Lanham, MD: Diamond Communications, 2001), 432.

94 *"Landis wasn't much more welcome at the White House than the Japanese ambassador"*: Bill Gilbert, *The Seasons: Ten Memorable Years in Baseball, and in America* (New York City: Citadel Press, 2004), 6.

94 *Landis wrote in a January 14 letter*: Pietrusza, *Judge and Jury*, 432.

94 *"it would be best for the country to keep baseball going"*: Matt Cox, "Keep Baseball Going," National Baseball Hall of Fame, https://baseballhall.org/discover-more/stories/short-stops/keep-baseball-going.

94 *The previous month's issei roundup decimated the nikkei baseball leagues*: Bill Staples, *Kenichi Zenimura, Japanese American Baseball Pioneer* (Jefferson, NC: McFarland, 2011), 114.

95 *two men in dark suits walked onto a muddy practice field*: Brian Curtis, *Fields of Battle: Pearl Harbor, the Rose Bowl, and the Boys Who Went to War* (New York: Flatiron Books, 2016), 90. Many of the details in the following paragraphs are derived from this book.

95 *DeWitt worried the magnitude and visibility of the game made it a prime target*: "Tournament of Roses and Bowl Game Off," *Los Angeles Times*, December 15, 1941.

95 *Jack was born in Japan in 1921*: J. D. Chandler, *Hidden History of Portland, Oregon* (Mount Pleasant, SC: Arcadia Publishing, 2013).

95 *Jack grew, and grew*: Curtis, *Fields of Battle*, 63.

96 *Thirteen days later*: "Oregon State Beavers School History," *Sports Reference*, https://www.sports-reference.com/cfb/schools/oregon-state/.

96 *Bendetson met with a committee of West Coast congressmen*: Robinson, *By Order of the President*, 97.

96 *He armed himself with a new report*: Ibid., 100.

96 *At a statehouse meeting led by Warren*: "Warren Warns of Fifth Columnists," *San Francisco Examiner*, February 3, 1942.

97 *nikkei were either communicating with Japanese submarines*: Robinson, *By Order of the President*, 102.

97 *Biddle's staff suggested*: de Nevers, *The Colonel and the Pacifist*, 99.

97 *Images of the charred USS Arizona*: This information was gleaned by using newspapers.com to search newspapers across the country. Papers as geographically diverse as the *Palm Beach* (Florida) *Post, Denton*

(Texas) *Record-Chronicle,* and *The* (Munster, Indiana) *Times* all ran the images.

97 *Stimson wrote in his diary that night*: de Nevers, *The Colonel and the Pacifist*, 114.

98 *Bendetson was undergoing his own transformation*: Ibid., 116.

98 *DeWitt and Bendetsen cowrote a six-page, single-spaced memo*: John L. Dewitt, *Final Report: Japanese Evacuation from the West Coast, 1942* (Washington, DC: U.S. Government Printing Office, 1943), http://www .archive.org/details/japaneseevacuati00dewi.

99 *Biddle was still trying to convince the president*: Robinson, *By Order of the President*, 107.

99 *the group had secured the support of three firebrand Southerners*: Hosokawa, *Nisei*, 281. The quotes are from the *Congressional Record*, Vol. 88, Part 1 (January 5, 1942, to February 19, 1942).

100 *Executive Order 9066 was placed on Roosevelt's desk the next day*: Robinson, *By Order of the President*, 108.

PART 2
Chapter Six: A Question of Blood

103 *Hideo Murata lived alone in a small cottage*: Clarence W. Hall, "Exclusion Act 1942 Model," *Santa Ana Register*, October 26, 1942. Many of the details of Murata's life can be found in this story.

103 *a bottle of strychnine next to him*: David Middlecamp, "He Was Told He Couldn't Avoid Japanese Internment. He Opted for Suicide Instead," *San Luis Obispo Tribune*, November 2, 2016. https://www.sanluisobispo .com/news/local/news-columns-blogs/photos-from-the-vault/article1112 49922.html.

104 *JACL leaders urged cooperation with the government*: Lawrence Davies, "Coast Japanese Split on Ouster," *New York Times*, February 21, 1942.

104 *a man walked into a boardinghouse in Stockton, California*: "Japanese Alien Is Killed at Stockton," *Havre Daily News*, February 21, 1942.

104 *six men raided a nisei-operated asparagus farm*: "Armies of F.B.I. Agents Round Up Enemy Aliens in New Raids on Coast," *Spokane Chronicle*, February 21, 1942.

104 *Between December 7 and February 15*: *Personal Justice Denied: Report of the Commission on Wartime Relocation and Internment of Civilians* (Washington, DC: Commission on Wartime Relocation and Internment of Civilians, 1983), 88.

104 *at a conclave of California district attorneys and sheriffs*: Jim Newton, *Justice for All: Earl Warren and the Nation He Made* (New York: Penguin, 2007), 131.

105 *now used as the West Coast's air corps training center*: "War Department Names Moffett Training Center," *San Jose News*, July 15, 1940.

105 *"It is certainly evident that the Japanese population of California"*: Richard Reeves, *Infamy: The Shocking Story of the Japanese American Internment in World War II* (New York: Henry Holt, 2015), 55.

105 *redlining*: "Regional Redlining," Testbed for the Redlining Archives of California's Restricted Spaces, http://salt.umd.edu/T-RACES/.

105 *"Even before the war there was a lot of suspicion"*: GYOH.

105 *At an emergency meeting earlier that month in San Francisco*: Bill Hosokawa and Robert Arden Wilson, *East to America: A History of the Japanese in the United States* (New York: William Morrow, 1980), 198–201. The quotes in this section are all from these pages as well.

106 *Removal was voluntary at first*: Bill Hosokawa, *Nisei: The Quiet Americans* (Boulder: University Press of Colorado, 1969), 338.

107 *The governor of Kansas, Payne Ratner*: "A 'Keep Out' to Japanese," *Iola Register*, April 1, 1942.

107 *Gas station owners refused to sell them gas*: Hosokawa and Wilson, *East to America*, 205.

107 *the fishermen, canners, and shop owners of Terminal Island were next to go*: Lilian Takahashi Hoffecker, "A Village Disappeared," *American Heritage* 52, no. 8 (December 2001).

107 *they'd have forty-eight hours to leave*: "Japs' Ouster Demand Rises," *Los Angeles Times*, February 27, 1942.

107 *a Japanese B1 submarine surfaced a half-mile off the California coast*: "Shelling of Oilfield Described by Eyewitness" and "Submarine Shells Southland Oil Field," *Los Angeles Times*, February 24, 1942.

108 *a coastal radar picked up an unidentified object over the Pacific*: "Army Says Alarm Real," *Los Angeles Times*, February 26, 1942.

109 *That morning on Terminal Island*: "State Board Ousts Japs in Employ," *Los Angeles Times*, February 28, 1942.

110 *Japanese Americans of Hawai'i experienced a different fate*: Charles S. Bouslog, "Hawaii Shows Japan—And Asia," *Asia and the Americas* 43, no. 2 (February 1943), via the California State University Japanese American Digitization Project, https://cdm16855.contentdm.oclc.org/digital/collection/p16855coll4/id/8424.

110 *the entire territory was placed under martial law*: Alan Rosenfeld, "Barbed-Wire Beaches: Martial Law and Civilian Internment in Wartime Hawai'i," *World History Connected* 8, no. 3 (2011): 1–18.

110 *A Shinto priest was fined $500*: Bruce Dunford, "Blackout, Martial Law After Japanese Attack," Associated Press, December 9, 1996.

110 *98.4 percent of trials ended in a guilty verdict*: Daniel Immerwahr, *How to Hide an Empire* (New York: Farrar, Straus & Giroux, 2019), 176.

110 *The rule was to give fifteen days' credit*: Thomas H. Green, *Martial Law in Hawaii: December 7, 1941–April 4, 1943* (unpublished manuscript), via Library of Congress, http://www.loc.gov/rr/frd/Military_Law/pdf/Martial-Law_Green.pdf.

110 *The Army temporarily closed all Japanese-language newspapers and schools*: *Personal Justice Denied: Report of the Commission on Wartime Relocation and Internment of Civilians*, 267.

111 *Much of the agricultural work on the islands was still performed by Japanese Hawaiians*: Ibid., 269.

111 *DeWitt's order left no ambiguity*: John L. Dewitt, *Final Report: Japanese Evacuation from the West Coast, 1942* (Washington, DC: U.S. Government Printing Office, 1943), http://www.archive.org/details/japanesee vacuati00dewi.

112 *One farmer who lived west of Portland, Oregon*: "Miscellaneous File," File Unit: Reel 9, 3/18/1942–6/30/1946, Series: San Francisco Branch Evacuee Property Files, 3/18/1942–6/30/1946, Record Group 210: Records of the War Relocation Authority, 1941–1989, [ARC Identifier 48540905].

113 *in a memo with the subject line "HALF-BREEDS"*: Ibid.

113 *The Los Angeles Realty Board*: Ibid.

113 *"Dear Sir:"*: Ibid.

113 *the market effects of liquidating San Francisco's 120 nikkei-owned dry cleaners*: William B.Pollard, Memorandum to Files, Box 38, Folder 18, Item 13, Marriner S. Eccles Papers, https://fraser.stlouisfed.org/archival/1343/item/468233.

114 *"We have been asked"*: NARA "Miscellaneous File."

114 *a flock of GIs arrived on the island and tacked posters up on utility poles*: "Bainbridge Island," University of Washington Special Collections' Japanese American exhibit, https://www.lib.washington.edu/specialcollec tions/collections/exhibits/harmony/exhibit/bainbridge.

114 *two million pounds of the fruit*: "Pre WWII—Lives of Bainbridge Island Nikkei Before the War," Bainbridge Island Japanese American

Community, https://bijac.org/history/bainbridge-island-before-wwii
/pre-wwii-lives-of-bainbridge-island-nikkei-before-the-war/.

115 *currently repairing five of the six surviving battleships from the Pearl Harbor
attack*: Daryl C. McClary, "Puget Sound Naval Shipyard," HistoryLink
.org, November 4, 2003, https://historylink.org/File/5579.

115 *On the dock were classmates of the thirteen Bainbridge High School students*:
"Evacuation," Bainbridge Island Japanese American Community, https://
bijac.org/history/exclusion-and-internment/evacuation/.

115 *the case of the residents at 1841 Redcliff Street*: NARA "Miscellaneous File."

116 *"He showed himself a little Hitler"*: "Clark Winning Respect on the Supreme Court," (Santa Rosa, California) *Press Democrat*, February 3, 1950.

Chapter Seven: Japanita

117 *The federal government created fifteen temporary detention centers*: Konrad
Linke, "Assembly Centers," *Densho Encyclopedia*, http://encyclopedia
.densho.org/Assembly_centers/.

117 *stretching from the arid flats of Santa Cruz County, Arizona, to the glaciers
of Washington's Cascade Mountains*: Western Defense Command, *Map of
the Japanese Evacuation Program*, San Francisco, 1942, from the CSU
Japanese American Digitization Project, https://scalar.usc.edu/works
/csujad-exhibit/media/sjs_fla_0072.jpg.

117 *For the rest of his life*: GYOH.

118 *Patriotism flooded the halls of Hollywood High*: Margaret Rudi, "Patriotism Emphasized," *Los Angeles Times*, April 29, 1942.

118 *the district's students were tending to nearly ten thousand rabbits and chickens*:
William K. Klingaman, *The Darkest Year: The American Home Front,
1941–1942* (New York: St. Martin's Press, 2019), 159.

118 *nine hundred mattresses filled the gym floor*: "School Canteen," *Life*, April
10, 1944.

118 *In an editorial entitled "Japs or Jalopies?"*: John Blumenthal, *Hollywood
High: The History of America's Most Famous Public School* (New York:
Ballantine, 1988), 174.

118 *Three FBI agents*: GYOH.

118 *George passed a schoolmate*: Tim Yoshinaga email message.

119 *The Nomuras left the keys to the boardinghouse*: Hyohei Nomura evacuee file.

119 *emigrated to the United States in 1913 from Yokohama*: Binder's biography
here was re-created using census documents, marriage certificates, and
naturalization records.

119 *past the studio where Charlie Chaplin shot his silent classics*: "Charlie Chaplin Studio," Los Angeles Historic Resources Inventory, http://historic placesla.org.

120 *They divvied up his bicycles and sporting equipment*: GYOH.

120 *His brother sold the strawberry farm for $400 an acre*: Ibid.

120 *The land is assessed at more than $3 million an acre*: Though difficult to pinpoint exactly, I used the address of the Yoshinagas' family farm and compared that to 2018 tax assessments on that same land today. As of this writing, a branch of Microsoft Research occupies the land.

120 *Forty thousand visitors left their stockings on the chimney*: The scene from Santa Anita Park's opening day was re-created from a variety of *Los Angeles Times* articles from December 24, 25, and 26, 1934. The paper sent both sports reporters and society reporters to cover the opening, and printed no fewer than a dozen stories about the new park over the three days.

121 *staid Colonial Revival and the aerodynamic curves of the Streamline Moderne style of Art Deco*: Isabelle Taylor, Paul Roberts, and Laurence Weatherly, "Racecourse Architecture: Stately Santa Anita," thorough bredracing.com, October 25, 2014, https://www.thoroughbredracing .com/articles/race-course-architecture-stately-santa-anita/.

121 *Field artillery battalions weighed heavy*: *Personal Justice Denied: Report of the Commission on Wartime Relocation and Internment of Civilians* (Washington, DC: Commission on Wartime Relocation and Internment of Civilians, 1983), 136.

121 *"For some it is a vacation"*: "Life in Japanita," *Los Angeles Examiner*, April 8, 1942, via USC Regional History Collection, http://digitallibrary.usc .edu/cdm/landingpage/collection/p15799coll75.

122 *greeted by a bronze statue of the legendary horse Seabiscuit*: "All Was Not Horse That Galloped," *Santa Anita Pacemaker*, October 7, 1942, via Densho Digital Repository, http://ddr.densho.org/ddr-densho-146-53/.

122 *The first 7,182 incarcerees were herded into stables*: Ibid.

122 *Workers removed and replaced fourteen inches of dirt*: Lynn A. Thomas interview with Lynn Bowman, March 15, 1976, via *California Revealed*, https://californiarevealed.org/islandora/object/cavpp%3A20393.

122 *every dish had to be used and washed three times*: "Greatest Feeding Problem of Evacuation Movement," *Santa Anita Pacemaker,* farewell issue (exact 1942 date unknown), via Densho Digital Repository, http://ddr .densho.org/ddr-janm-5-1/.

122 *a fifth of the usual consumption rate*: Klingaman, *The Darkest Year*, 128.

122 *a shortage of toilet paper*: *Personal Justice Denied: Report of the Commission on Wartime Relocation and Internment of Civilians*, 139.

123 *The temporary detention centers spent only an average of 39 cents*: Ibid., 142.

123 *accustomed to eating rice in a bowl with chopsticks*: This detail, and many others in this section, are from a collection of incarceree letters housed at the Japanese American Evacuation and Resettlement collection at UC Berkeley's Bancroft Library. These letters are found under call number BANC MSS 67/14 c, Folder B12.49. Wherever a specific citation is not provided, the information is most likely held within one of these many correspondences.

124 *The Army made no effort to create a formal education system*: Konrad Linke, "Santa Anita (detention facility)," *Densho Encyclopedia*, https:// encyclopedia.densho.org/Santa_Anita_(detention_facility).

124 *All classes were held under the grandstands*: "Awaiting the School Opening," photo, via University of Southern California Regional History Collection, http://digitallibrary.usc.edu/cdm/ref/collection/p15799coll75/id /1787.

124 *"the birth rate is going to go to spectacular proportions"*: Carey McWilliams, "Inspection of Centers at Pomona and Santa Anita," June 15, 1942, Japanese American Evacuation and Resettlement Study, BANC MSS 67/14 c, Folder B9.50.

124 *Due to a lack of barbershops*: "The barbers in Santa Anita Assembly Center set up in the street," photo, via USC Regional History Collection, http://digitallibrary.usc.edu/cdm/ref/collection/p15799coll75/id/1775.

124 *Santa Anita was twice-guarded*: Linke, "Santa Anita (detention facility)."

124 *"The high fences and the presence of the military police"*: *Personal Justice Denied: Report of the Commission on Wartime Relocation and Internment of Civilians*, 147.

125 *DeWitt had established a wage schedule*: Ibid., 146.

125 *tagged as a "farm boy" and "prune picker"*: GYOH.

125 *someone in need of a friend*: Jan Morey interviews.

125 *On the afternoon of March 10*: Stephen E. Ambrose and Richard H. Immerman, *Milton S. Eisenhower: Educational Statesman* (Baltimore: Johns Hopkins University Press, 2009), 59.

126 *A sickly child, Milton favored academia*: Paul W. Valentine, "Dr. Milton S. Eisenhower, Public Servant and Educator, Dies," *Washington Post*, May 3, 1985.

126 *tasked by Roosevelt to study all the war-related informational services*: Brian
Niiya, "Milton Eisenhower," *Densho Encyclopedia,* http://encyclopedia
.densho.org/Milton_Eisenhower/.

126 *he wrote to his former boss, Agriculture Secretary Claude Wickard*: Ambrose
and Immerman, *Milton S. Eisenhower,* 61.

127 *Eisenhower flew from San Francisco to Salt Lake City*: Ibid., 62.

127 *he spoke fluent Spanish and socialized with the small issei community in the
town of La Jara*: William Wei, *Asians in Colorado: A History of Persecution
and Perseverance in the Centennial State* (Seattle: University of Washington Press, 2016), 206.

128 *In a radio address three days after Pearl Harbor*: Ibid.

128 *Colorado, he said, would open its doors*: Roger Daniels, *Concentration
Camps, North America: Japanese in the United States and Canada During
World War II* (Malabar, FL: R. E. Krieger Publishing, 1971), 94.

128 *"If you harm them you must harm me"*: Richard Reeves, *Infamy: The
Shocking Story of the Japanese American Internment in World War II* (New
York: Henry Holt, 2015), 99.

128 *Not wanting to be outshone by the invective of Maw or Clark*: Eric L.
Muller, "Apologies or Apologists—Remembering the Japanese American Internment in Wyoming," *Wyoming Law Review* 1, no. 2 (2001):
473–95.

128 *"The whole picture is much worse than anyone can imagine"*: Ibid.

129 *a twenty-three-year-old University of Washington senior*: Richard Gold-
stein, "Gordon Hirabayashi, World War II Internment Opponent, Dies
at 93," *New York Times,* January 3, 2012.

129 *highest bar exam score in the state of Colorado*: Kerry S. Hada and Andrew
S. Hamano, "Five of the Best: A Tribute to Outstanding Lawyers in
Colorado History," *The Colorado Lawyer* (July 1998).

129 *he took a job as a speechwriter and translator at the Japanese consulate in
Chicago*: Gil Asakawa, "Minoru Yasui," *Densho Encyclopedia*, http://en
cyclopedia.densho.org/Minoru_Yasui.

129 *He reported for active duty only to be denied nine times*: "Minoru Yasui,"
Encyclopedia of Japanese American History, ed. Brian Niiya (New York:
Facts on File, 2001), 423.

129 *Yasui's ire grew*: Asakawa, "Minoru Yasui."

130 *Fred Korematsu's first plan after Pearl Harbor was to enlist*: Karen Korematsu, "Fred T. Korematsu," Korematsu Institute, http://www.kore
matsuinstitute.org/fred-t-korematsu-lifetime.

131 *the spotlight shone brightest on Anita Chiquita*: "Anita Funita Events," *Santa Anita Pacemaker*, July 1, 1942, via Library of Congress, www.loc.gov /item/sn83025574/1942-07-01/ed-1/.

131 *Babe picked up a bat*: Kimiko Nomura interview.

131 *George spent his mornings running laps*: GYOH.

131 *entertained up to two thousand dancers in front of the grandstand*: Sherrie Tucker, *Dance Floor Democracy: The Social Geography of Memory at the Hollywood Canteen* (Durham, NC: Duke University Press, 2014).

131 *George didn't know how to jitterbug*: GYOH.

131 *One of the largest enterprises in the camp was a camouflage netting factory*: Michi Weglyn, *Years of Infamy: The Untold Story of America's Concentration Camps* (New York: William Morrow, 1976), 80–82.

131 *The net was gradually raised*: Macsd, "Life In Santa Anita," YouTube video, 4:52, March 2008, https://www.youtube.com/watch?v=RjVcZLNiCKU&t=4s.

131 *volunteering for the factory flagged*: Weglyn, *Years of Infamy*, 81.

132 *"Here is a chance to show your patriotism'"*: This is found in the same Bancroft collection as cited earlier, BANC MSS 67/14 c, Folder B12.49.

132 *handbills made their way across camp*: Weglyn, *Years of Infamy*, 82.

132 *On June 18, after the morning head count*: The events portrayed on pages 139–46 were re-created using reports from the FBI and the Department of Justice's Alien Enemy Control Unit, along with personal letters, found at UC Berkeley's Bancroft Library, call number BANC MSS 67/14 c, folder B7.01 (2/3).

138 *the WCCA released a statement about the events*: "Troops Quell Jap Riot of 2000 at Santa Anita," *Los Angeles Times*, August 9, 1942.

139 *"The camp is now proceeding with normal routine on a quiet basis"*: FBI report held at UC Berkeley's Bancroft Library.

139 *"I suppose riots at Japanese centers are not really our problem"*: Department of Justice Alien Enemy Control Unit report held at UC Berkeley's Bancroft Library.

139 *Every morning when George woke up*: GYOH.

140 *One day in late August*: Ibid.

Chapter Eight: 58 Minutes

141 *crocodiles swam in the warm waters above the Arctic Circle*: Will Clyde and Kirk Johnson, *Ancient Wyoming: A Dozen Lost Worlds Based on the Geology of the Bighorn Basin* (Golden, CO: Fulcrum Publishing, 2016), 52.

141 *five-hundred-square-mile slab of dolomite and limestone*: "Heart Mountain,

Wyoming," NASA Earth Observatory, https://earthobservatory.nasa
.gov/.

141 *lurching into its final resting place just thirty minutes later*: Corey Binns,
"Land Speed Record: Mountain Moves 62 Miles in 30 Minutes," *Live
Science*, May 19, 2006, https://www.livescience.com/796-land-speed-re
cord-mountain-moves-62-miles-30-minutes.html.

141 *its movement aided by either hydrothermal fluids*: "Giant Rock Slab Slid on
Hot Lube," *New Scientist*, May 4, 2005, https://www.newscientist.com
/article/mg18624985-400-giant-rock-slab-slid-on-hot-lube/.

142 *"If the active racism of the West Coast"*: Roger Daniels, *Japanese Americans:
From Relocation to Redress* (Seattle: University of Washington Press,
2013), 114.

142 *located a safe distance from "strategic installations"*: Bill Hosokawa, *Nisei:
The Quiet Americans* (Boulder: University Press of Colorado, 1969), 339.

142 *To call the sites unattractive would be an overstatement*: The physical descriptions of each camp, unless otherwise noted, are from their accom-
panying *Densho Encyclopedia* page.

143 *winning the Pulaski County sheriff's race with the backing of the Ku Klux
Klan*: Charles C. Alexander, "White Robes in Politics: The Ku Klux
Klan in Arkansas, 1922–1924," *The Arkansas Historical Quarterly* 22, no.
3 (1963): 195–214.

143 *a part of the state so physically removed from the rest*: Lawrence Woods,
Wyoming's Big Horn Basin to 1901: A Late Frontier (Norman, OK: Arthur H. Clark, 1997), 10.

143 *Fur trappers explored the region in the early nineteenth century*: Emilene
Ostlind, "The Bighorn Basin: Wyoming's Bony Back Pocket," *Wyoming
History*, November 8, 2014, https://www.wyohistory.org/encyclopedia
/bighorn-basin-wyomings-bony-back-pocket.

143 *An altitude of four thousand feet meant little precipitation*: Louis S. Warren,
Buffalo Bill's America: William Cody and the Wild West Show (New York:
Vintage, 2005), 476.

143 *take a meager snowfall and convert it into a blizzard*: John McPhee, *Rising
from the Plains* (New York: Farrar, Straus & Giroux, 1986), 62.

143 *a two-day wagon ride away*: Warren, *Buffalo Bill's America*, 475.

144 *Staring west from the top of Bighorn Mountain*: Ibid., 479.

144 *"The settler's cabin and the stockman's ranch house and corrals"*: Ibid., 473.

145 *The Chicago, Burlington and Quincy Railroad*: Lynn Johnson Houze,

"Cody, Wyoming," *Wyoming History*, November 8, 2014, https://www
.wyohistory.org/encyclopedia/cody-wyoming.

145 *Debs ignored the invitation*: Warren, *Buffalo Bill's America*, 485.

145 *Cody begged the Wyoming Board of Land Commissioners*: "Shoshone Project," U.S. Department of the Interior Bureau of Reclamation, April 5, 2013, http://www.usbr.gov/projects.

145 The Cody Enterprise *began its fear-mongering*: "Unfound Rumors Current Here; Enemy Aliens to Local Camps," *Cody Enterprise*, February 25, 1942.

145 *"One stick of explosive in the Corbett Tunnel"*: Mike Mackey, *Remembering Heart Mountain: Essays on Japanese American Internment in Wyoming* (Powell, WY: Western History Publications, 1998), 58.

145 *the news was announced*: multiple stories, *Cody Enterprise*, May 27, 1942.

146 *weary to the point of insomnia*: Stephen E. Ambrose and Richard H. Immerman, *Milton S. Eisenhower: Educational Statesman* (Baltimore: Johns Hopkins University Press, 2009), 63.

146 *complaining and commiserating about the position*: Richard Drinnon, *Keeper of Concentration Camps: Dillon S. Myer and American Racism* (Berkeley: University of California Press, 1987), 8.

146 *before packing his desk*: Ambrose and Immerman, *Milton S. Eisenhower*, 64–65.

147 *He helped write his brother Dwight's 1961 farewell address*: Sam Roberts, "In Archive, New Light on Evolution of Eisenhower Speech," *New York Times*, December 10, 2010, https://www.nytimes.com/2010/12/11/us/politics/11eisenhower.html.

147 *he cherished a desk-size bonsai tree*: Ambrose and Immerman, *Milton S. Eisenhower*, 65.

148 *One man with a heart ailment*: University of Wyoming, American Heritage Center, John A. Nelson Papers, Accession Number 5325, Box 1, "Diary Notes."

148 *Trains were sidetracked for hours*: GYOH.

148 *Just after midnight on August 12, 1942*: Mieko Matsumoto, "Heart Mountain," *Densho Encyclopedia*, https://encyclopedia.densho.org/Heart_Mountain.

148 *The barracks were constructed in sixty days*: Mackey, *Remembering Heart Mountain*, 53.

149 *Construction crews left messages on the walls*: There's a barrack on the site of the former camp; I viewed these markings myself.

149 *the camp put out a bulletin welcoming the new residents*: Bill Hosokawa, "Facts About Heart Mountain," general information bulletin, August 25, 1942. Due to the kindness of Bacon Sakatani, I possess digital copies of every bulletin and *Heart Mountain Sentinel*. This book wouldn't have been possible without them.

149 *the third-largest city in Wyoming*: Mackey, *Remembering Heart Mountain*, 212.

149 *"Our city really looks like something at night"*: John A. Nelson diaries, September 11, 1942, University of Wyoming, American Heritage Center.

150 *apartment A in the tenth building of the twenty-fourth block*: Heart Mountain Relocation Center roster, Record Group 210, National Archives, Washington, D.C. The National Archives provides a search function to look up former incarcerees; their files include their exact camp addresses.

150 *Just four days after the camp opened*: "General Information Bulletin—Series 3," August 29, 1942.

150 *steeling themselves against the first snowflakes of winter*: "David Yamakawa diary," Heart Mountain Wyoming Foundation, 2011.032, Folder 9.

150 *Horse scorched his right pinkie toe*: George Yoshinaga evacuee file, Records About Japanese Americans Relocated During World War II, created 1988–1989, documenting the period 1942–1946, Record Group 210, National Archives, Washington, D.C.

151 *Medical care was just as haphazard*: Mackey, *Remembering Heart Mountain*, 102.

151 *while transporting an incarceree to an eye specialist in Billings, Montana*: Velma Berryman Kessel, *Behind Barbed Wire* (Casper, WY: Mountain States Lithographing, 1992), 19. Kessel was a nurse at Heart Mountain for three years. This is a printed version of her diary that I found in George Yoshinaga's belongings, held by his son, Paul.

151 *The first of 552 babies born in camp arrived September 4*: "General Information Bulletin—Series 7," September 10, 1942.

151 *the first of the camp's 183 deaths was on August 28*: Ibid.

151 *replaced by a baseball diamond*: Ibid.

151 *The industrious residents of Block 22, Barrack 26*: "General Information Bulletin—Series 11," September 15, 1942.

152 *The first school opened at 8:30 a.m., September 30, 1942*: "General Information Bulletin—Series 20," October 1, 1942.

152 *Desks didn't arrive until January 1943*: "Makeshifts in Education Fail to Deter Students," *Heart Mountain Sentinel*, August 12, 1944.

152 *a teacher sprinted between barracks*: Ibid.

153 *many students didn't know where they fell, grade-wise*: Interview with Bunny Ogimachi, July 20, 2018.

153 *A handful of incarcerees*: Mackey, *Remembering Heart Mountain*, 77.

154 *"Well, at first I had a little prejudice"*: Ibid., 76.

154 *conversion of sugar to industrial alcohol for use in synthetic rubber was skyrocketing*: Louis Fiset, "Thinning, Topping, and Loading: Japanese Americans and Beet Sugar in World War II," *The Pacific Northwest Quarterly* 90, no. 3 (1999): 123–39.

154 *"Here is a real opportunity"*: "General Information Bulletin—Series 23," October 8, 1942.

154 *George found work in a mess hall*: George Yoshinaga evacuee file

154 *Babe joined the camp's garbage crew*: Tamotsu Nomura evacuee file, Records About Japanese Americans Relocated During World War II, created 1988–1989, documenting the period 1942–1946, Record Group 210, National Archives, Washington, D.C.

Chapter Nine: Kannon-sama Is Crying

155 *On December 22, 1934, Amelia Earhart left Los Angeles*: Amelia Earhart, "My Flight from Hawaii," *National Geographic*, May 1935, https://www.nationalgeographic.com/news/2014/7/140727-amelia-earhart-history-flight-airplanes-adventure-explorer/#close.

155 *the brick-red Zen Buddhist temple*: Jerry Shimoda, "National Register of Historic Places registration form," March 1994, National Park Service, https://npgallery.nps.gov/NRHP/GetAsset/NRHP/94000382_text.

156 *Eizo immigrated to Hawai'i from Japan in 1896*: "United States Census, 1930," database with images, FamilySearch (https://familysearch.org/ark:/61903/1:1:XH18-H72), accessed May 24, 2020, Eizo Igawa, North Kohala, Hawaii, Hawaii, United States; citing enumeration district (ED) ED 60, sheet 4A, line 20, family 68, NARA microfilm publication T626 (Washington, DC: National Archives and Records Administration, 2002), roll 2631; FHL microfilm 2,342,365.

156 *He deserted the plantation and fled as far as he could*: Before he died in 2004, Stanley Igawa wrote down many of the stories of his life in an unpublished memoir. When I began working on this book, his children graciously allowed me to read and use the memoir in my reporting. I confirmed many of the factual details independently through camp records, ship manifests, interviews, and other means. Details and anec-

dotes in this chapter that do not come from Stan's memoir are cited. I am eternally grateful for the Igawa family's help, and trust.

156 *bartering with them for a chicken*: Irene Igawa interview, November 26, 2018.

156 *Three months before Stan's fourth birthday*: "California, Los Angeles Passenger Lists, 1907–1948," database with images, FamilySearch (https://familysearch.org/ark:/61903/1:1:KZQ9-VDV : 13 March 2018), Kimiko Igawa, 1930; citing Immigration, ship name *City of Los Angeles*, NARA microfilm publication M1764 (Washington, DC: National Archives and Records Administration, n.d.), roll 29; FHL microfilm 1,734,633.

158 *hazel-eyed Marshall student Rosemary LaPlanche*: "Blond Wins Beauty Test," *Los Angeles Times*, July 26, 1941.

158 *they were willing to overlook the fact that she had falsified her age*: "1941: Rosemary LaPlanche," Miss America, 2004, http://www.missamerica .org/our-miss-americas.

158 *including Grease, A Nightmare on Elm Street, and Pretty in Pink*: Chris Eggertsen, "How John Marshall High School Became a Hollywood Star," *Curbed*, December 20, 2017, https://la.curbed.com/2017/12/20/16717840 /john-marshall-high-school-movies-grease.

158 *a cavernous ice rink wedged between Paramount Studios and the Hollywood Cemetery*: Eve Babitz, *Eve's Hollywood* (New York: New York Review of Books Classics, 2015), 60.

159 *the men were viewed by both military and civilian officials as a national security threat*: Duncan Ryūken Williams, *American Sutra: A Story of Faith and Freedom in the Second World War* (Cambridge: Harvard University Press, 2019), 21.

159 *"The temple was filled with soldiers"*: Ibid., 26.

160 *an arrow was rammed through his penis*: Richard Hardoff, *The Custer Battle Casualties: Burials, Exhumations, and Reinterments* (El Segundo, CA: Upton & Sons, 1989), 21.

160 *the Holly Sugar company opened a 23,000-square-foot processing plant*: Lorna Thackery, "Hardin Remembers Sugar Factory," *Billings Gazette*, December 20, 2010.

161 *labor training manuals were translated into German and Spanish*: G. H. Bingham and George W. Gustafson, "Pulling, Piling, Topping, and Loading Sugar Beets: A Labor Training Manual in English, Spanish, and German," Montana State College Agricultural Extension Service, September 1945, https://arc.lib.montana.edu/msu-extension/objects/ext1-000290.pdf.

161 *The average American man in 1910*: This paragraph uses data from a few

different charts consolidated by Max Roser, Cameron Appel, and Hannah Ritchie at https://ourworldindata.org/human-height.

161 *After a beet field was plowed*: Bigham and Gustafson, *Pulling, Piling, Topping, and Loading Sugar Beets*.

161 *a foot-long cross between a machete and a butcher knife with a three-inch hook at the end*: Jackie Sojico, "When Things Speak: The Beet Knife," NET Nebraska, May 2, 2015, http://netnebraska.org/article/culture/971728/when-things-speak-beet-knife.

162 *the nikkei laborers harvested as much as 25 percent of the season's crop*: Louis Fiset, "Thinning, Topping, and Loading: Japanese Americans and Beet Sugar in World War II," *The Pacific Northwest Quarterly* 90, no. 3 (1999).

Chapter Ten: "Trapped Like Rats in a Wired Cage"

163 *He'd ballooned, packing thirty pounds onto his previously lanky frame*: Tamotsu Nomura evacuee file.

163 *Heart Mountain High School was officially voted a member of the Wyoming High School Athletic Association*: "Makeshifts in Education Fail to Deter Students," *Heart Mountain Sentinel*, August 12, 1944.

164 *the incarceree-led Pacemaker was overseen*: Brian Niiya, "Santa Anita Pacemaker (newspaper)," *Densho Encyclopedia*, https://encyclopedia.densho.org/Santa_Anita_Pacemaker_(newspaper)/.

164 *At a time when absences were common*: Mike Mackey, *Remembering Heart Mountain: Essays on Japanese American Internment in Wyoming* (Powell, WY: Western History Publications, 1998), 81.

164 *finagled a short profile of his new best friend from Hollywood*: George Yoshinaga, "Meet the Champ," *Echoes*, November 25, 1942.

165 *the Santa Anita Jackrabbits met the Valley Sportsmen*: "Rabbits Triumph Over Sportsmen, 13–6," *Heart Mountain Sentinel*, November 28, 1942.

165 *before 6,500 fans at the Los Angeles Coliseum*: "Compton High Tracksters Grab Southland C.I.F. Championship," *Los Angeles Times*, May 19, 1940.

165 *His high school accomplishments*: "CAT Athletes Awards Given," *Arcadia Tribune*, June 13, 1940.

166 *The colleges would play not only against each other*: "Citrus College Year by Year," Citrus College Owls, https://www.citrusowls.com/sports/fball/Citrus_College_Football_Composite_Year_by_Year.pdf.

166 *Five games into the season*: This season was re-created using box scores and game stories from the *Los Angeles Times*, *The Santa Ana Register*, and the *Bakersfield Californian*.

166 *While at Citrus he got a call from Red Strader*: Melissa Masatani, "Citrus College Grants Honorary Degrees to Japanese-American Former Students," *San Gabriel Valley Tribune*, August 30, 2017.

166 *a 14–6 loss to San Diego State's freshman team*: "Aztec Frosh Win," *Los Angeles Times*, November 15, 1941.

167 *a combined Boy Scout drum and bugle corps assembled*: "Makeshifts in Education Fail to Deter Students," *Heart Mountain Sentinel*.

167 *"should produce a total of an additional 16,800"*: in *A Matter of Conscience*, ed. Mike Mackey (Powell, WY: Western History Publications, 2002), 41.

167 *wrote Colonel M. W. Pettigrew*: Takashi Fujitani, *Race for Empire: Koreans as Japanese and Japanese as Americans During World War II* (Berkeley: University of California Press, 2013), 405.

168 *the* Sentinel *suggested do-it-yourself Christmas gifts*: "White Christmas in Store for Colonists This Year," *Heart Mountain Sentinel*, November 7, 1942.

168 *To aid parents struggling on the WRA's measly salaries*: The details in this paragraph are from multiple stories in the January 1, 1943, *Sentinel*.

168 *For the first time in many of the incarcerees' lives, it snowed on Christmas*: Stanley Hayami diary, Gift from the Estate of Frank Naoichi and Asano Hayami, parents of Stanley Kunio Hayami, Japanese American National Museum (95.226.1).

169 *Camp officials had first felt a jolt of unrest in October*: Mike Mackey, *Heart Mountain: Life in Wyoming's Concentration Camp* (Powell, WY: Western History Publications, 2000), 71.

169 *camp officials began erecting a barbed wire fence*: "Protest Petition Sent to WRA Director," *Heart Mountain Sentinel*, November 21, 1942.

169 *an anonymous poem began circulating not only at Heart Mountain*: "Poem Written in Camp," Densho Digital Repository, http://ddr.densho.org /ddr-densho-126-1/.

Chapter Eleven: Everything Is Going Along Fine

171 *the temperature had never dropped below freezing*: I determined this using CurrentResults.com, which tracks historical temperature extremes for major U.S. cities.

171 *The recreation department flooded twenty-two blocks to create ice-skating rinks*: Mike Mackey, *Heart Mountain: Life in Wyoming's Concentration Camp* (Powell, WY: Western History Publications, 2000), 70.

171 *The mayor of Lovell*: "Editorials," *Heart Mountain Sentinel*, February 6, 1943.

171 *Babe and a dozen teammates piled into a truck*: Keiichi Ikeda interview, May 31, 2018.

172 *Lovell had been a town for twelve years before the Mormons arrived*: Darcee Barnes, "Mormon Colonizers in Wyoming's Bighorn Basin," *Wyoming History*, August 3, 2015, https://www.wyohistory.org/encyclopedia/mor mon-colonizers-wyomings-bighorn-basin.

172 *the Church of Jesus Christ of Latter-day Saints held the Mutual Improve-ment Association Basketball Conference championship*: Les Goates, "Tro-phy Goes Back to Lovell, Wyoming," *The Improvement Era*, May 1942.

172 *2,500 spectators would pile into Salt Lake City's sweltering, musty Deseret Gymnasium*: Jessie L. Embry, "Spiritualized Recreation: LDS All-Church Athletic Tournaments, 1950–1971," *BYU Studies Quarterly* 48, no. 3 (2009), Article 8, https://scholarsarchive.byu.edu/byusq/vol48/iss3/8.

172 *In 1940*: Les Goates, "New Champions of M Men's Basketball," *The Im-provement Era*, May 1940.

172 *Roberts had grown up in Lehi, Utah*: "Charles Roberts Signs to Coach," *Lehi Free Press*, June 15, 1939.

172 *he lettered in basketball, football, and track, and played intramural tennis when he grew bored*: "Charles Roberts," BYU Cougars, https://byucou gars.com/athlete/m-basketball/12244/Charles-Roberts.

173 *The game was never close*: George Kinshita, "Sports Tidbits," *Heart Mountain Sentinel*, February 20, 1943.

173 *the outfit sweated out a win over Byron High School, 40–37*: "All-Stars Trounce Byron," *Echoes*, February 12, 1943.

173 *Kaihatsu, a Hollywood High graduate named to all-league status in Los Angeles*: Joel S. Franks, *Asian American Basketball: A Century of Sport, Community and Culture* (Jefferson, NC: McFarland, 2016), 111.

174 *"Lovell Drubs Prep Cagers"*: "Lovell Drubs Prep Cagers," *Heart Moun-tain Sentinel*, March 6, 1943.

174 *The only highlight of the trip*: Keiichi Ikeda interview

174 *attendance for film screenings topped 600,000*: Mackey, *Heart Mountain*, 67.

174 *camp administrators recognized that recreational programming was best left to the incarcerees*: T. J. O'Mara, "Heart Mountain Relocation Center Com-munity Activities Section Final Report," 1945. Details from this paragraph are provided by O'Mara's report. Mike Mackey gifted me a stack of bind-ers full of each of the camp's final reports. I'm indebted to his kindness, and his seemingly unending contributions to Heart Mountain scholarship.

175 *a 16-by-8-inch depiction of Hyohei's voyage to America*: This sign is in the

possession of Jan Morey, Hyohei's granddaughter and Babe's daughter.

175 *the school administration held a pep rally*: "Rally Dance Held Friday Deemed a Success," *Echoes*, March 17, 1943.

176 *Horse was crushed*: GYOH.

176 *The actual tally wasn't nearly as dire*: "Fujioka Polls 885 Votes to Win Prep Election," *Heart Mountain Sentinel*, February 6, 1943.

176 *Byron beat Heart Mountain*: "Byron Swamps Eagles," *Echoes*, March 17, 1943.

176 *the student body took to the polls*: "Blue and White and Eagles Chosen as School Color and Name," *Echoes*, March 17, 1943.

177 *nearly 5,000 nisei were enlisted as soldiers*: Eric L. Muller, *Free to Die for Their Country: The Story of the Japanese American Draft Resisters in World War II* (Chicago: University of Chicago Press, 2001), 42.

177 *on Easter Sunday 1943*: "An Army Tune for the President," *Miami News*, April 30, 1943.

177 *forty-two nisei soldiers were driven ten miles away*: Linda Tamura, *Nisei Soldiers Break Their Silence: Coming Home to Hood River* (Seattle: University of Washington Press, 2012), 106.

177 *marched in single file into an airplane hangar and wedged onto temporary bleachers*: Muller, *Free to Die for Their Country*, 42.

177 *After sitting in silence for four hours*: Tamura, *Nisei Soldiers Break Their Silence*, 107.

177 *it granted the Office of War Information an important piece of propaganda*: Muller, *Free to Die for Their Country*, 46.

178 *"It is the inherent right of every faithful citizen"*: "Stimson Opens Army to Nisei," *Heart Mountain Sentinel*, January 30, 1943.

178 *proved its opponents right with an editorial supporting Stimson's plan*: "Vindication," *Heart Mountain Sentinel*, January 30, 1943.

178 *the distribution of Selective Service Form 304A*: Cherstin Lyon, "Loyalty Questionnaire," *Densho Encyclopedia*, https://encyclopedia.densho.org /Loyalty_questionnaire/.

179 *a point system designed by Census Bureau statistician Calvin Dedrick*: Duncan Ryūken Williams, *American Sutra: A Story of Faith and Freedom in the Second World War* (Cambridge: Harvard University Press, 2019), 197.

180 *He gave a series of informational speeches*: Lieutenant Ray McDaniels, "Speech at Heart Mountain Relocation Center," February 1943, via CSU Japanese American Digitization Project, https://cdm16855.contentdm .oclc.org/digital/collection/p16855coll4/id/9597.

180 *His messages back to Washington were optimistic*: Muller, *Free to Die for Their Country*, 54.

180 *five hundred incarcerees calmly approached McDaniels*: Ibid.

180 *He met with the men*: McDaniels, "Speech at Heart Mountain Relocation Center."

180 *The crowd, crammed into a mess hall, wasn't buying it*: Mike Mackey, *Remembering Heart Mountain: Essays on Japanese American Internment in Wyoming* (Powell, WY: Western History Publications, 1998), 126.

181 *Many disagreed*: Ibid., 127.

181 *strong-armed the* Sentinel *into avoiding coverage of the debacle*: Ibid.

181 *"The eyes of the nation are upon you"*: "General Information Bulletin—Series 36," February 25, 1943.

182 *he chided them for their registration efforts*: "Robertson Places Responsibility for Enlistment on Block Heads," *Heart Mountain Sentinel*, March 6, 1943.

182 *Behind the scenes, things were falling apart for Robertson*: The quotes here are derived from a series of letters available at the National Archives within the "Field Basic Documentations of the War Relocation Authority, 1942–46." The Heart Mountain documents can be found on microfilm rolls 56–64, at NARA's Washington, DC, headquarters.

182 *Babe filled out the form in pencil*: Tamotsu Nomura evacuee file.

183 *Horse filled out his form entirely in capital letters*: George Yoshinaga evacuee file.

183 *Only nineteen were inducted into the Army*: Mackey, *Remembering Heart Mountain*, 127.

Chapter Twelve: A Determined Effort to See the Job Through

184 *On the morning of April 13, 1943*: "Two Die, Pair Caught in Alcatraz Break; Guards Overpowered," *San Francisco Examiner*, April 14, 1943.

184 *He'd spent the prior weeks scoffing at the War Department's loyalty questionnaire*: *Personal Justice Denied: Report of the Commission on Wartime Relocation and Internment of Civilians* (Washington, DC: Commission on Wartime Relocation and Internment of Civilians, 1983), 221–22.

185 *his plan was wending its way to the U.S. Supreme Court*: "Evacuation Question Goes to Supreme Court," *Heart Mountain Sentinel*, April 10, 1943.

185 *"I don't want any of them here"*: *Personal Justice Denied: Report of the Commission on Wartime Relocation and Internment of Civilians*, 221–22.

185 *DeWitt held an off-the-record meeting with reporters*: Ibid.

186 *In a statement that ran in newspapers across California*: "Gen. DeWitt's View on Japs Is Supported by Native Sons," *Santa Rosa Press Democrat*, April 18, 1943.

186 *Ads flooded the* Sentinel: The jobs mentioned here are an assortment of opportunities offered in the April 13, 20, and 26 Heart Mountain bulletins.

187 *Racism only compounded that difficulty*: Brian Niiya, "Hostels," *Densho Encyclopedia*, https://encyclopedia.densho.org/Hostels/.

187 *sponsored by Quaker, Baptist, Lutheran, Unitarian, and other Christian communities*: Beth Hessel, "'Let the Conscience of Christian America Speak': Religion and Empire in the Incarceration of Japanese Americans, 1941–1945" (PhD diss., Texas Christian University, 2015).

187 *Demand was high*: Niiya, "Hostels."

187 *On April 1, Babe submitted his first leave request*: Tamotsu Nomura evacuee file.

187 *60-degree sun*: "Weather Report," *Heart Mountain Sentinel*, May 1, 1943.

187 *Incarcerees cleared and leveled 1,100 acres and dug a mile-long canal*: Karl Lillquist, *Imprisoned in the Desert: The Geography of World War II–era, Japanese American Relocation Centers in the Western United States* (Ellensburg: Central Washington University, 2007), 77. The other facts and data in this paragraph are also from Lillquist's work.

188 *Industrious groups scoured the base of Heart Mountain for wild black mustard grass*: "Residents Use Wild Mustard Grass to Prepare 'Tsukemono,'" *Heart Mountain Sentinel*, June 12, 1943.

188 *a number that would've made the crowd the sixth-largest city in Wyoming*: This is from 1940 U.S. Census data.

188 *That April afternoon the Lovell High Bulldog's*: George Kinoshita, "Sports Tidbits," *Heart Mountain Sentinel*, May 1, 1943.

189 *the first couple's relationship had been strained*: Blanche Wiesen Cook, *Eleanor Roosevelt, Volume 3: The War Years and After, 1939–1962* (New York: Penguin, 2006), 416–21.

189 *Mrs. Roosevelt received a letter from a Seattle woman named E. Harriet Gipson*: Selected Digitized Correspondence of Eleanor Roosevelt, 1933–1945, at the Franklin D. Roosevelt Presidential Library & Museum, Series 1, Myer, Dillon S., 1943–1944, http://www.fdrlibrary.marist.edu/_resource s/images/ersel/ersel073.pdf.

190 *a Japanese American family move into the White House was rejected*: Greg

Robinson, "Eleanor Roosevelt," *Densho Encyclopedia*, http://encyclope
dia.densho.org/Eleanor_Roosevelt.

190 *After a state dinner with Mexican president Manuel Ávila Camacho*: "Reserved Outreach," Associated Press, August 30, 2017.

190 *the Roosevelts inspected a naval air station in Corpus Christi, Texas*: "President Franklin Roosevelt Seated in His Car," photo, *World War II Database*, https://ww2db.com/image.php?image_id=24375.

190 *She spent the night at the Hotel Westward Ho*: "Eleanor Roosevelt Visits
Phoenix, Rivers Jap Camp," *Arizona Republic*, April 24, 1943.

190 *"desert country which flowers only when water is brought to it"*: Eleanor
Roosevelt, *My Day* syndicated column, April 26, 1943, The Eleanor Roosevelt Papers Project, George Washington University, https://www2
.gwu.edu/~erpapers/myday/displaydoc.cfm?_y=1943&_f=md056480.

190 *She met alone with six members of the camp's community council*: Brandon
Shimoda, "State of Erasure: Arizona's Place, and the Place of Arizona,
in the Mass Incarceration of Japanese Americans," Asian American
Writers' Workshop, January 20, 2017, https://aaww.org/state-erasure
-arizona/.

190 *all they asked for was a cooler for the hospital*: "Eleanor Roosevelt Visits
Phoenix, Rivers Jap Camp," *Arizona Republic*.

190 *an interview at the* Los Angeles Times *three days later*: Timothy Turner, "Mrs.
Roosevelt Here to Visit Hospitals," Los Angeles Times, April 23, 1943.

191 *wrote an article for* Collier's *magazine*: Eleanor Roosevelt, "A Challenge
to American Sportsmanship," *Collier's*, October 16, 1943.

191 *it was a total takedown of Heart Mountain*: Jack Carberry, "Hostile Group
Is Pampered at Wyoming Camp," *Denver Post*, April 24, 1943.

192 *Camp director Guy Robertson fired back*: "WRA Chiefs Investigate Denver
Paper's Charges, Senate Probe Looms," *Heart Mountain Sentinel*, May 1,
1943.

192 *Angry letters flooded the offices of Wyoming's senators*: Mike Mackey, *Remembering Heart Mountain: Essays on Japanese American Internment in
Wyoming* (Powell, WY: Western History Publications, 1998), 43–44.

192 *passing a blatantly unconstitutional bill that February*: Eric L. Muller,
"Apologies or Apologists—Remembering the Japanese American Internment in Wyoming," *Wyoming Law Review* 1, no. 2 (2001).

192 *took to the Senate floor and accused the WRA*: "Says We 'Pamper' Internees in the West," *New York Times*, May 7, 1943.

192 *incarcerees who passed a dam on the way to the camp's sawmill may sabotage*

the installation: "Petting Disloyal Japs Must Stop, Senator Warns," *Indianapolis Star*, May 7, 1943.

193 *He never visited the camp*: "Senator Robertson, in Cody, Declines Invitation to Center," *Heart Mountain Sentinel*, June 12, 1943.

193 *The instigator of all the lies was an unlawful resident*: Mike Mackey, *Heart Mountain: Life in Wyoming's Concentration Camp* (Powell, WY: Western History Publications, 2000), 97.

193 *the Wyoming state commander of the American Legion took to the stage*: "Valedictory Address," *Heart Mountain Sentinel*, June 12, 1943.

193 *Nevertheless, school officials allowed him to graduate*: Tamotsu Nomura evacuee file.

194 *"The Northern Pacific Railroad Company is seeking two crews of 80 men each"*: "General Information Bulletin—Series 49," March 23, 1943.

194 *the best analog on earth of Mars's outflow channels*: Isaac Larsen and Michael Lamb, "Progressive Incision of the Channeled Scablands by Outburst Floods," *Nature* 538 (2016): 229–32, https://doi.org/10.1038/nature19817.

194 *the camp had sprouted a dozen social clubs*: "Clubs Make Plans for Joint Social," *Heart Mountain Sentinel*, May 27, 1944.

194 *They'd find a kind mess hall cook willing to let them use their building*: Bunny Ogimachi interview.

195 *Babe worked a stretch between Lind and Ellensburg*: "Northern Pacific Railway, 1910," map, https://upload.wikimedia.org/wikipedia/commons/f/f5/Northern_Pacific_Railroad_map_circa_1900.jpg.

195 *Babe sent a handwritten note to Frank A. Brown*: Tamotsu Nomura evacuee file.

PART 3
Chapter Thirteen: 13 Days

199 *Toyoshi Kawasaki was 5 feet 6 inches" and 190 pounds*: Toyoshi Kawasaki evacuee file.

199 *he toured California with Los Angeles's famed Olivers baseball club*: "Olivers Baseball Team in Guadalupe, 1930," *Discover Nikkei*, March 30, 2011, http://www.discovernikkei.org/en/nikkeialbum/albums/84/slide/?page=30.

199 *At Lincoln High*: "Lincoln Lighties in 6–2 Grid Victory," *Los Angeles Times*, November 1, 1929.

199 *in front of five thousand fans*: "Santa Ana Junior College Wins Southern California Title by Beating Cub Team, 7–6," *Los Angeles Times*, December 10, 1933.

199 *the most points the school had ever scored in a football game*: "Los Angeles

Jaysee Eleven Passes to 32–0 Victory Over Invading Taft Aggregation," *Los Angeles Times*, December 1, 1933.

199 *he earned $30 a week working at a produce stand in Los Angeles's Grand Central Market*: Toyoshi Kawasaki evacuee file.

200 *The goal was not just to adhere to Wyoming regulations*: Jack Kunitomi, "Sports Tidbits," *Heart Mountain Sentinel*, September 11, 1943.

200 *The boys lived in Gebo*: Chuck Harkins, "Extra Points," *Casper Star-Tribune*, May 15, 1976.

200 *the Thompson brothers scored more points than the rest of the competitors combined*: "Thermopolis Captures Track Meet, Casper High Is Second," *Casper Star-Tribune*, May 6, 1923.

201 *Thompson spent middling seasons coaching*: "University Prep Buckaroos," Wyoming Football, http://wyoming-football.com/index.php/results/results-by-team/university-prep-buckaroos/. Most of the historic records, scores, schedules, and awards cited in this book come from the Wyoming Football website, which chronicles the first one hundred years of football in the state. The site was created by Patrick Schmidt. This book would be much thinner without his tireless (and volunteer) efforts.

202 *led the Broncos to their only winning season between 1925 and 1949*: *2018 University of Wyoming Football Media Guide,* 210, https://s3.amazonaws.com/sidearm.sites/wyoming.sidearmsports.com/docments/2018/7/22/2018_Wyoming_Football_Media_Guide.pdf.

202 *The Associated Press named him second-team all-conference*: "Utah Places Five Players on All-Conference Eleven," *Casper Star-Tribune*, November 29, 1931.

202 *returning seven from the previous year's starting eleven*: "Grid Team Plays Host to Worland," *Heart Mountain Sentinel*, September 25, 1943.

202 *Thompson and forty teenage boys met on the rocky field behind the new school's auditorium*: Ibid.

202 *the only nisei player on the Phineas Banning High varsity football team*: "Banning Gridders Play Gardena in League Opener," *Wilmington Daily Press Journal*, October 17, 1941.

202 *"Food, of course, is of much importance to him"*: "Sportraits," *Echoes*, November 9, 1943.

202 *at 125 pounds*: Yoichi Hosozawa evacuee file.

202 *the straight-A son of a fisherman*: Bunny Ogimachi interview.

202 *Tayzo Matsumoto, who spoke English, Japanese, and Spanish*: Teruo Matsumoto evacuee file.

202 *He grew up in an apartment behind his parents' laundry off Skid Row*: "Teruo Matsumoto oral history interview conducted by Frank Chin and Paul Tsuneishi in Torrance, California, September 13, 1996." From Heart Mountain Wyoming Foundation.

202 *"very disturbed about the evacuation"*: Teruo Matsumoto evacuee file.

203 *watching the world's fastest humans swim at Griffith Park*: Keiichi Ikeda interview.

203 *Issei and nisei jammed the stadiums, natatoriums, and grandstands of the Games*: Eriko Yamamoto, "Memories of the 1932 Olympics: A Page in Japanese American History," *Discover Nikkei*, February 10, 2016, http://www.discovernikkei.org/en/journal/2016/2/10/1932-olympics.

203 *The victory set off an explosion of the sport in Japan*: Olympic Channel, "How Japan Changed Swimming Forever," YouTube video, 4:14, July 15, 2018, https://www.youtube.com/watch?v=Ka2tjzijvRw.

203 *newspapers mocked the athletes as "little brown men"*: Frank Roche, "The Olympic Torch," *Los Angeles Times*, July 25, 1932.

203 *The Japanese team won gold in five of the six men's events*: "Swimming at the 1932 Los Angeles Summer Games," *Sports Reference*, https://www.sports-reference.com/olympics/summer/1932/SWI/.

204 *Autograph seekers hounded the team*: Yamamoto, "Memories of the 1932 Olympics."

204 *a laborer at a tofu factory in Little Tokyo*: Keiichi Ikeda interview. The details in the paragraphs that follow are all from this conversation.

Chapter Fourteen: Warriors

205 *Twenty-five thousand people visited the self-proclaimed Lettuce Capital of the World*: Alan J. Stein, "Kent—Thumbnail History," *HistoryLink.org*, September 24, 2001, https://historylink.org/File/3587.

205 *The harvest was the work of the area's nikkei community*: Mildred Tanner Andrews, "Japanese-American Legacies in the White River Valley: Historic Context Statement and Inventory," prepared for the King County Landmarks and Heritage Program, December 19, 1997, https://www.kingcounty.gov/~/media/services/home-property/historic-preservation/documents/resources/JapaneseAmericanLegaciesWhiteRiverValley.ashx?la=en.

205 *Saito owned the White River Packing Company*: Ken and Dahlynn McKowen, *Best Oregon and Washington Mansions, Museums, and More: A Behind-the-Scenes Guide to the Pacific Northwest's Historical and Cultural Treasures* (Berkeley: Wilderness Press, 2009), 396–97.

205 *Every summer*: George Nakagawa, *The Cross on Castle Rock: A Childhood Memoir* (Bloomington, IN: iUniverse, 2004), 68.

206 *he was detained and interrogated by the Federal Bureau of Investigation*: This information is from a Freedom of Information Act request, fulfilled by FOITimes.com. It is categorized as Custodial Detention (Arrest Warrants), Japanese 1941, File Number 100-2-60, Section: 30, and available at https://www.foitimes.com/internment/Arrest30.pdf.

206 *he, his white wife, Augusta, his stepdaughter (and 1935 Lettuce Queen), Thelma, and his son, Ray*: "United States Census, 1920," database with images, FamilySearch (https://familysearch.org/ark:/61903/3:1:33S7-9RJ3 -Q63?cc=1488411&wc=QZJY-VFJ%3A1036474601%2C1037581801%2C 1037137901%2C1589332282 : 14 September 2019), Washington_King_Oak Lake_ED 51_image 10 of 30; citing NARA microfilm publication T625 (Washington, DC: National Archives and Records Administration, n.d.).

206 *traveled to the Lonely Acres Skating Rink*: Determined by finding the Saitos' address in 1940 U.S. Census records, then comparing it to the collection of Civilian Exclusion Orders held at UC Berkeley's Bancroft Library, found here: https://digitalassets.lib.berkeley.edu/jarda/ucb/text /cubanc6714_b016b01_0001_1.pdf.

206 *The Hanada family avoided removal*: Nakagawa, *The Cross on Castle Rock*, 68.

206 *Each ticket was hand-typed*: This ticket is located at the Heart Mountain Interpretive Center.

206 *Four thousand fans, more than a third of all the incarcerees at Heart Mountain*: Crowd numbers, box scores, play-by-play, and other details in this and other game re-creations are mostly derived from *Heart Mountain Sentinel* and *Echoes* stories.

206 *During gym class that week*: Keiichi Ikeda interview.

207 *they'd segregate all the incarcerees deemed "disloyal" by the questionnaire*: Barbara Takei, "Tule Lake," *Densho Encyclopedia*, https://encyclopedia .densho.org/Tule_Lake.

207 *428 bleary-eyed Tuleans deboarded the train*: "428 In, 434 Out; Segregation All in Day's Work for Evacuees," *Heart Mountain Sentinel*, September 25, 1943.

208 *His father, Oscar, played football as early as 1919*: Cheri Housley, Marie Lundgreen, and Kathy Jones, *Images of America: Richmond* (Mount Pleasant, SC: Arcadia Publishing, 2011), 97.

208 *He was known in Worland simply as "Mr. Baseball"*: Don Zupan, "The Sports Beat," *Billings Gazette*, June 22, 1957.

208 *a team that didn't score a single point in four of its five games*: "Lander Tigers," Wyoming Football, http://wyoming-football.com/index.php/re sults/results-by-team/lander-tigers/.

208 *yell leader Dempsey Maruyama egged them on*: "Field Basic Documentations of the War Relocation Authority, 1942–46," microfilm rolls 56–64, National Archives, Washington, D.C.

209 *The Eagles took the field in white jerseys with gold pants*: "High School Athletics Given New Life," *Heart Mountain Sentinel*, August 12, 1944.

209 *they wrapped their legs with cardboard*: Jan Morey interviews.

209 *using an unbalanced offensive line and switching between single and double wingback formations*: This detail and those that follow are from stories found in the October 2, 1943, edition of the *Heart Mountain Sentinel*.

Chapter Fifteen: Coyotes

212 *the coal mines that give Carbon County its name drew thousands of Finns, Italians, Scots, Russians, Serbians, Germans, Norwegians, Croats, and Greeks*: Bonnie Christensse, " 'Nothing up Here but Foreigners and Coal Slack': World War I and the Transformation of Red Lodge," *Montana: The Magazine of Western History* 52, no. 3 (2002): 16–29.

212 *the normally short, serene whistle of the mine switched to a longer, more frantic pitch*: Mike Kordenbrock, "75 years ago, the Smith Mine Disaster decimated the small Montana coal town of Bearcreek," *Billings Gazette*, February 27, 2018, https://billingsgazette.com/news/state-and-regional /montana/years-ago-the-smith-mine-disaster-decimated-the-small-mont ana/article_9bacd94f-a98f-5386-a408-2c93204da392.html.

213 *"Good bye wifes and daughters:"* Kayde Kaiser, "Smith Mine Disaster," *This Is Montana,* https://www.umt.edu/this-is-montana/short-notes/sto ries/smith-mine-disaster.php.

213 *two starters quit in the middle of the 1942 season to join the Navy*: Frank Hyde, "Here and There," *Billings Gazette*, October 9, 1942.

213 *In the first week of practice*: "Red Lodge Gridders Meet Laurel Friday," *Billings Gazette*, September 20, 1943.

213 *Carbon County ground out a 0–0 tie*: "Carbon, Lovell Deadlock, 0–0," *Billings Gazette*, September 26, 1943.

213 *the straight-line buck*: "Football ABC's," *Santa Cruz Evening News*, November 10, 1931.

214 *The 1,100-person student body filled the sidelines once again*: This game was re-created using articles from the October 9 and October 16, 1943,

editions of the *Heart Mountain Sentinel* and the October 19, 1943, edition of *Echoes*.

216 *During the postgame Pep Club dance*: "Wanted: Jitterbugs," *Echoes*, October 19, 1943.

217 *"Your team is much faster, shiftier, and better all-around"*: Jack Kunitomi, "Sports Tidbits," *Heart Mountain Sentinel*, October 16, 1943.

Chapter Sixteen: Bulldogs

218 *a simple play purported to have been written by Anglo-Irish fantasy author Lord Dunsany one afternoon between his lunch and afternoon tea*: "Lord Dunsany Drama Analysis," eNotes, https://www.enotes.com/topics/lord-dunsany.

218 *a trio of sailors steal a ruby from an idol in an Indian temple*: Lord Dunsany, "A Night at an Inn," 1916, Project Gutenberg Canada, https://gutenberg.ca/ebooks/dunsany-night/dunsany-night-00-h-dir/dunsany-night-00-h.html.

219 *the eligibility requirements for the Wyoming Athletic Association were straightforward*: "State Athletic Association Sets Basketball Regulations," *Echoes*, November 16, 1943.

219 *The Sentinel broke the news with an October 23 headline*: "Nomura's Loss Big Blow; Backfield Reshuffled for Today's Grid Game," *Heart Mountain Sentinel*, October 23, 1943.

219 *Babe joined the ash crew*: Tamotsu Nomura evacuee file.

220 *The high school closed after the camp ran out of coal*: "Lack of Heat Closes School," *Echoes*, October 23, 1943.

220 *the camp experienced one of its most harrowing moments*: "Oil Worker Is Charged with Felony," *Heart Mountain Sentinel*, October 23, 1943.

220 *the shop owners of Cody were less welcoming*: Mike Mackey, *Heart Mountain: Life in Wyoming's Concentration Camp* (Powell, WY: Western History Publications, 2000), 74.

221 *The Heart Mountain High School band gave its first performance*: "Band Plays for Football Rally," *Echoes*, October 26, 1943.

221 *A 3–2–1 season in 1942*: "Lovell Bulldogs," Wyoming Football, http://wyoming-football.com/index.php/results/results-by-team/lovell-bulldogs.

221 *Bill Shundo would take over for Babe*: This game was re-created using articles from the October 23 and October 30, 1943, editions of the *Heart Mountain Sentinel* and the October 26, 1943, edition of *Echoes*.

223 *sports editor Jack Kunitomi raked the teens and Tubby*: Jack Kunitomi, "Sports Tidbits," *Heart Mountain Sentinel*, October 30, 1943.

223 *A radio announcer for KPOW*: Kunio Otani, "Sports Tidbits," *Heart Mountain Sentinel*, November 13, 1943.

224 *Kaz Sugiyama was named first-team all-Marine League*: "Banning High Places 3 on All-Marine 11," *Wilmington Daily Press-Journal*, November 21, 1939.

224 *Kinoshita [as Lloyd Kino] later went on to a nearly fifty-year career as a Hollywood character actor*: "Lloyd Hiroya (Kino) Kinoshita obituary," *Los Angeles Times*, August 26, 2012.

225 *ghosts, black cats, witches, and jack o'lanterns*: "Halloween Social Is Huge Success," *Heart Mountain Sentinel*, November 6, 1943.

225 *The conditions thinned the crowd from the usual thousands to just three hundred*: This game was re-created using articles from the November 6, 1943, edition of the *Heart Mountain Sentinel*.

226 *Cheyenne's* Wyoming Eagle *newspaper named its annual all-state football team*: "All-state: 1940s," Wyoming Football, http://wyoming-football .com/index.php/recognition/all-state-teams/all-state-1940s/.

226 *The tables were topped with miniature goalposts*: "Varsity Football Team Honored," *Echoes*, December 14, 1943.

227 *George earned a B and Babe a C*: George Yoshinaga and Tamotsu Nomura evacuee files.

227 *coaching the Block 7 elementary school football team*: "Eagle Gridders Coach Grade School Tuffies," *Echoes*, November 9, 1943.

227 *the team spent two hours after school every day passing, dribbling, and practicing weave drills*: "Basketball Ratings Listed for Wyoming Schools," *Echoes*, November 30, 1943.

227 *eighty-five teenagers pulled on their long underwear*: "Eighty-Five Carolers and a Carol," *Echoes*, December 28, 1943.

Chapter Seventeen: 4-F

228 *True to form, the announcement was blunt*: "Selective Service Opens for Nisei," *Heart Mountain Sentinel*, January 22, 1944.

228 *After pleading with the War Department to send them to battle*: Franklin Odo, "100th Infantry Battalion," *Densho Encyclopedia*, https://encyclope dia.densho.org/100th_Infantry_Battalion/.

229 *The likelihood of a large contingent of nisei soldiers fighting in the Pacific theater was nil*: "Letter from Executive to Assistant Secretary of War Harrison Gerhardt to Samuel Menin, March 4, 1944," University of Hawaii, 442nd Veterans Club Collection, Series 3: National Archives Docu-

ments, RG 107: Records of the Office of the Secretary of War, 1791–1947, Box 49, Folder 1, http://hdl.handle.net/10524/61863.

229 *Kiyoshi Okamoto . . . jolted awake*: Mackey, *A Matter of Conscience*, in *A Matter of Conscience*, ed. Mike Mackey (Powell, WY: Western History Publications, 2002), 53.

229 *Okamoto had spent the past year fighting for quality-of-life improvements*: Ibid., 53.

230 *Nakadate was bookish, an insurance salesman*: Brian Niiya, "Paul Nakadate," *Densho Encyclopedia*, http://encyclopedia.densho.org/Paul_Naka date.

230 *Selective Service, they argued, was morally corrupt and legally indefensible otherwise*: Mackey, *A Matter of Conscience*, 53.

230 *Cigarette smoke poured out of the windows*: Eric L. Muller, *Free to Die for Their Country: The Story of the Japanese American Draft Resisters in World War II* (Chicago: University of Chicago Press, 2001), 79.

230 *Emi and his brother bought a mimeograph machine*: Ibid.

230 *Guntaro Kubota translated the proceedings from English into Japanese for issei parents*: Mackey, *A Matter of Conscience*, 53.

230 *he met with Horse's mother to convince her to try to get him to change his mind*: GYOH.

230 *Babe and his two brothers took seasonal clearance*: This was determined by scouring each week's leave notices in the *Sentinel*.

231 *"When your constitutional rights are deprived"*: "Teruo Matsumoto oral history interview conducted by Frank Chin and Paul Tsuneishi in Torrance, California, September 13, 1996." From Heart Mountain Wyoming Foundation.

231 *twenty-nine-year-old George Fujii was arrested and charged with sedition*: Eric L. Muller, "A Penny for Their Thoughts: Draft Resistance at the Poston Relocation Center," *Law and Contemporary Problems* 68, no. 2 (2005): 119–57.

231 *the FBI held five nisei after they failed to report for their induction physicals*: "General Information Bulletin–Series 174," February 24, 1944.

232 *The women read the mealymouthed letter as "too weak," and wrote their own*: Mira Shimabukuro, *Relocating Authority: Japanese Americans Writing to Redress Mass Incarceration* (Boulder: University Press of Colorado, 2015), 176–77.

232 *Robertson resorted to the same tactics of fear and intimidation*: "General Information Bulletin–Series 170," February 10, 1944.

232 *He spent weeks trying to cultivate spies within the meetings*: Mike Mackey, *Heart Mountain: Life in Wyoming's Concentration Camp* (Powell, WY: Western History Publications, 2000), 112.

232 *urged church groups to discuss the draft*: Muller, *Free to Die for Their Country*, 86.

232 *even meeting with an FBI special agent*: Mackey, *Heart Mountain*, 112.

232 *Okamoto wrote a letter to the community*: "Essay by Kiyoshi Okamoto entitled 'We Should Know,' 2/25/1944," National Archives at Denver, Record Group 21: Records of District Courts of the United States, 1685–2009, Series: Criminal Case Files, 1890–1949 File Unit: *United States of America vs. Kiyoshi Okamoto, et al.*, ARC Identifier: 292808.

233 *Okamoto and Emi crafted their message and posted it across camp*: Mike Mackey, *Remembering Heart Mountain: Essays on Japanese American Internment in Wyoming* (Powell, WY: Western History Publications, 1998), 134–35.

234 *The chrome bumper of the Burlington Trailways bus nudges out of Heart Mountain*: The details in this anecdote come from a report from *Heart Mountain Sentinel* reporter John Kitasako in the paper's March 18, 1944, edition. The pure luck of Kitasako choosing this specific trip to chronicle is not lost on me.

234 *the bus lights shimmering off the sandstone walls*: This detail came from a very deep internet rabbit hole that dragged me to an eBay auction for a CB&Q Burlington Bus & Railroad Depot postcard. The price was $8. I did not purchase it, but know that the details are accurate.

234 *the first fully operational Air Force intercontinental ballistic missile base*: "F. E. Warren History," F. E. Warren Air Force Base, February 28, 2018, https://www.warren.af.mil/About-Us/Fact-Sheets/Display/Article/3312 81/fe-warren-history/.

235 *where they are prodded, x-rayed, measured, squeezed, electrocardiogrammed*: "Physical Standards in World War II," Medical Department, United States Army, 33, https://apps.dtic.mil/dtic/tr/fulltext/u2/a291761.pdf.

235 *The best athlete in Heart Mountain has flat feet:* Jan Morey interviews.

Chapter Eighteen: Letter from Laramie County Jail

236 *the* Sentinel *had lost any sense of serving its readers*: "Our Cards on the Table," *Heart Mountain Sentinel*, March 11, 1944.

236 *committee members were branded "Janus-faced" and "rat-like"*: "Provocateurs," *Heart Mountain Sentinel*, March 18, 1944.

236 *Omura blasted the* Sentinel: Roger Daniels, *Asian America: Chinese and Japanese in the United States Since 1850* (Seattle: University of Washington Press, 2011), 270.

237 *"The editors of the* Sentinel *said in today's issue"*: "Letter from camp internee Frank Emi to the editors of the Heart Mountain Sentinel, 3/19/1944," National Archives at Denver, Record Group 21: Records of District Courts of the United States, 1685–2009, Series: Criminal Case Files, 1890–1949 File Unit: *United States of America vs. Kiyoshi Okamoto, et al.*, ARC Identifier: 292812.

237 *On March 6, two refused to board the bus to Cheyenne*: Eric L. Muller, *Free to Die for Their Country: The Story of the Japanese American Draft Resisters in World War II* (Chicago: University of Chicago Press, 2001), 84.

237 *his sparsely populated district didn't require another grand jury to be called until early May:* Ibid., 88.

237 *Sackett was born in 1876 in a sod house in southwestern Nebraska*: Ibid., 96.

238 *Carl would climb to the top of Sackett Hill and watch as Plains Indian tribes arranged their tepees*: Carl Sackett, "Carl Sackett Knew What the West Was Really Like," *Sunday Tribune-Eagle*, July 20, 1980.

238 *One of the first actions Franklin D. Roosevelt took following his inauguration*: "Carl L. Sackett of Sheridan Is Named for U.S. Attorney," *Casper Star-Tribune*, June 4, 1933.

238 *The arrests made national news*: Papers as wide-ranging as the *Hawaii Tribune-Herald, Arizona Republic, Tampa Bay Times*, and *The* (Louisville) *Courier-Journal* carried the news.

238 *Emi and a Fair Play Committee colleague, Minoru Tamesa, walked from their barracks to the front gate of the camp*: Mackey, *A Matter of Conscience*, in *A Matter of Conscience*, ed. Mike Mackey (Powell, WY: Western History Publications, 2002), 54.

238 *military police lobbed tear- and vomit-gas grenades into a crowd*: Tetsuden Kashima, "Homicide in Camp," *Densho Encyclopedia*, http://encyclopedia.densho.org/Homicide_in_camp. The details in this paragraph are all from this article and the primary source documents contained within.

239 *Later in the week they were summoned to Robertson's office for a hearing*: Mackey, *A Matter of Conscience*, 54.

240 *He first summoned Okamoto for a leave clearance hearing*: Daniels, *Asian America*, 271.

241 *No Wyoming jail was large enough to hold the sixty-three men arrested at Heart Mountain*: Mackey, *A Matter of Conscience*, 68.

241 *a two-story building so dark and claustrophobic*: W. Dean Hirsch, "Laramie County Jail Not Fit for Human Habitation," *Casper Star-Tribune*, August 15, 1984.

241 *sunlight would reflect off the neighboring building and trickle into the cells*: William Hohri, *Resistance: Challenging America's Wartime Internment of Japanese-Americans* (Self-published, 2001), 63.

241 *soaked with the urine and vomit of former residents*: Mackey, *A Matter of Conscience*, 68.

241 *the men played bridge feet away from their cellmates on the toilet*: Hohri, *Resistance*, 66.

241 *they were allowed no reading materials other than letters*: Ibid., 76.

241 *the $200 bond would've been difficult for many of the men to gather under normal circumstances*: Teruo Matsumoto oral history.

241 *they wrote letters to Emi*: Muller, *Free to Die for Their Country*, vii.

242 *After dinner on April 28, Joe Grant Masaoka and Min Yasui arrived at the jail*: Ibid., 97.

242 *To be identified as a criminal or, perhaps worse, a coward could bring shame not only to the man but to his family*: Hohri, *Resistance*, 68.

243 *where it landed on the desk of J. Edgar Hoover*: Muller, *Free to Die for Their Country*, 91.

243 *He fought against the distribution of Bibles in Denver's public schools*: Ibid., 103.

243 *in 1942 defended a Jehovah's Witness minister on draft evasion charges*: "Ft. Collins Man Convicted of Draft Evasion," *Greeley Daily Tribune*, June 18, 1942.

243 *he punched an opposing attorney so hard he broke his left hand*: "O. Otto Moore, Samuel Menin Trade Punches," *Greeley Daily Tribune*, March 8, 1940.

244 *Kennedy had endorsed placing educational requirements on voting*: Muller, *Free to Die for Their Country*, 107.

244 *he referred to the sixty-three defendants not by name but as "you Jap boys"*: Mackey, *A Matter of Conscience*, 69.

245 *During a May 26 cabinet meeting*: Fred Barbash, "The West Coast Turns into a War Zone," *Washington Post*, December 8, 1982. The quotes that follow also come from this article, which relied on documents newly released by the Commission on Wartime Relocation and Internment of Civilians.

246 *The hailstones fell from the sky as if they were mad at the ground*: "Hail-

stones As Big As Baseballs Cause Heavy Damage at Cheyenne," *Casper Star-Tribune*, June 12, 1944.

246 *passed under the federal courthouse's limestone frieze*: "U.S. District Court for the District of Wyoming (1933–1965)," photo, National Archives, RG 121-BS, Box 97, Folder QQ, Print 1817 (ca. 1933), https://www.fjc .gov/history/courthouse/cheyenne-wyoming-1933.

246 *the courtroom was nearly empty*: "Little Interest Shown at Trial," *Heart Mountain Sentinel*, June 17, 1944.

246 *Sackett's goal was to keep the scope of the trial narrow*: Muller, *Free to Die for Their Country*, 110.

246 *he convinced some of the men to shave their heads*: Ibid., 187.

247 *the staff wrote in an editorial*: "Two Objectives," *Heart Mountain Sentinel*, June 17, 1944.

247 *Kennedy denied the motion*: "Dismissal of Charges Sought in Draft Case," *Heart Mountain Sentinel*, June 17, 1944.

247 *Menin threw his last bomb*: Muller, *Free to Die for Their Country*, 110.

247 *Kennedy found that they had "willfully and intentionally neglected and refused to obey the order"*: United States v. Fujii, 55 F. Supp. 928 (D. Wyo. 1944), https://www.courtlistener.com/opinion/2312600/united-states-v-fujii/.

248 *On July 3, Kennedy walked back into his courtroom*: T. Blake Kennedy, "Remarks on Naturalization Day," July 3, 1944, T. Blake Kennedy Collection, American Heritage Center, University of Wyoming, Laramie. This document was kindly shared with me by Eric Muller, whose essential work is cited frequently throughout this book.

Chapter Nineteen: Boys of Summer

249 *The Heart Mountain High School class of 1944 gathered in the auditorium*: "302 Seniors Graduate," *Echoes*, May 9, 1944.

249 *"What are we, you and I?" he asked his peers*: "Valedictory Address: Citizenship Carries Responsibility," *Heart Mountain Sentinel*, May 13, 1944.

250 *Fort Logan, eight miles outside the city*: Tom Munds, "Fort Logan Was 1st Federal Military Post in Denver Area," Colorado Community Media, July 25, 2001, https://coloradocommunitymedia.com/stories/fort-logan -was-1st-federal-military-post-in-denver-area,121284.

250 *winning the junior batting title by nearly 100 points*: "Bat Title Goes to Matsumoto," *Heart Mountain Sentinel*, September 30, 1944.

250 *He never learned who paid the $200*: "Teruo Matsumoto oral history inter-

view conducted by Frank Chin and Paul Tsuneishi in Torrance, California, September 13, 1996." From Heart Mountain Wyoming Foundation.

250 *he was hired in the camp's auto shop*: Teruo Matsumoto evacuee file.

250 *Tosh Asano left on June 8*: "General Information Bulletin –Series 203," June 6, 1944.

250 *Northern Pacific Railway's Extra Gang #6 was looking for men*: Stanley Igawa unpublished memoir.

251 *the town's lumberjacks click-clacking their way down the sidewalk in their spiked caulk boots*: Billie Jean Plaster, "Timber Town," *Sandpoint Magazine*, Summer 1994, https://www.sandpointonline.com/sandpointmag/sms94/timber_loggers_logging.html.

251 *Horse embarked on his own new career*: GYOH.

252 *he had worked as an office boy, a truck driver, a guard, a maintenance worker, and helped in a mess hall*: George Yoshinaga evacuee file.

252 *On July 20, the FBI arrived at Tule Lake*: "Four Japs Nabbed for Opposing Draft," *Fort Collins Coloradoan*, July 21, 1944.

252 *they thought he was Irish*: William Hohri, *Resistance: Challenging America's Wartime Internment of Japanese-Americans* (Self-published, 2001), 65.

252 *But the FBI and the U.S. Attorney's Office saw his role differently*: "James M. Omura interview with Arthur A. Hansen," August 22–25, 1984, Japanese American Project of the Oral History Program at California State University, Fullerton, available at the Online Archive of California: http://www.oac.cdlib.org/.

253 *the first two soldiers from Heart Mountain to die in battle*: "Two Heart Mountaineers Killed on Italian Front," *Heart Mountain Sentinel*, July 29, 1944.

253 *Both of his legs were blown off by an 88mm shell*: Dorothy Matsuo, *Boyhood to War: History and Anecdotes of the 442nd Regimental Combat Team* (Honolulu: Mutual Publishing, 1992), 144.

253 *It was the Fourth of July*: "Kei Tanahashi," National Japanese American Memorial Foundation, https://www.njamemorial.org/kei-tanahashi.

253 *Aoyama's actions were memorialized in issue #34 of* Heroic Comics: Cord A. Scott, "Comics and Conflict: War and Patriotically Themed Comics in American Cultural History From World War II Through the Iraq War" (2011), Dissertations, 74, https://ecommons.luc.edu/luc_diss/74.

254 *A switch-hitter who could play all nine positions*: Christen Sasaki, "Kenichi Zenimura," *Densho Encyclopedia*, http://encyclopedia.densho.org/Kenichi_Zenimura.

254 *he teamed up with Negro league legend Lonnie Goodwin*: Dexter Thomas,

"The Secret History of Black Baseball Players in Japan," *NPR Code Switch*, July 14, 2015, https://www.npr.org/sections/codeswitch/2015/07/14/412880758/the-secret-history-of-black-baseball-players-in-japan.

254 *Zenimura would attempt to make a world-class baseball community out in the middle of the Sonoran Desert*: David Davis, "A Field in the Desert That Felt Like Home: An Unlikely Hero Sustained Hope for Japanese-Americans Interned in World War II," *Sports Illustrated*, November 16, 1998, https://vault.si.com/vault/1998/11/16/a-field-in-the-desert-that-felt-like-home-an-unlikely-hero-sustained-hope-for-japanese-americans-interned-in-world-war-ii.

255 *The team was mostly a re-creation of the prewar San Jose Asahis, plus Babe and Tosh Asano*: Bill Staples Jr., *Kenichi Zenimura, Japanese American Baseball Pioneer* (Jefferson, NC: McFarland, 2011), 136–37.

255 *40 to 50 degrees higher than the temperature at Heart Mountain that week*: "Weather Report," *Heart Mountain Sentinel*, September 18, 1943.

255 *Only five players were able to play in all thirteen games*: Jack Kunitomi, "Sport Tidbits," *Heart Mountain Sentinel*, September 25, 1943.

255 *The team they met in Heart Mountain had been decimated by the draft and relocation*: George Yoshinaga, "Sport Tidbits," *Heart Mountain Sentinel*, August 26, 1944.

Chapter Twenty: Chasing Perfection

256 *Ray Thompson resigned a week before classes started*: George Yoshinaga, "Sport Tidbits," *Heart Mountain Sentinel*, August 26, 1944.

256 *Rudolph and his wife, Mona, moved into camp from Big Piney*: "High School Gridders Launch Football Practice," *Heart Mountain Sentinel*, September 9, 1944.

256 *a two-hundred-person Wyoming town so cold its nickname was the Ice Box of the Nation*: Kelly McEvers, "Why Three Towns Are Fighting to Be the 'Ice Box of the Nation,'" *All Things Considered*, NPR, https://www.npr.org/2018/01/15/578172751/why-three-towns-are-fighting-to-be-the-ice-box-of-the-nation.

256 *the Rudolphs had spent the past two decades bouncing from state to state*: This was a bit convoluted, but I determined this by searching public records and newspapers.com for the Rudolphs and mapping their residences.

257 *Jack Sakamoto was a twenty-one-year-old Jackrabbit*: Much of this information is contained in Sakamoto's evacuee file at the National Archives.

257 *now attending his third high school in as many years after his family relocated to El Paso, Texas*: Mas Yoshiyama evacuee file.

257 *Both became starters on their new teams*: George Yoshinaga, "Sport Tidbits," *Heart Mountain Sentinel*, October 28, 1944.

258 *forty-five Heart Mountain high schoolers met their new coaches*: "High School Gridders Launch Football Practice," *Heart Mountain Sentinel*, September 9, 1944.

258 *Yasui had started at left tackle for the Jerome High School team*: "Denson High Tigers Play Monroe Tomorrow," *Denson Tribune*, November 19, 1943, from Library of Congress, https://www.loc.gov/resource/sn82016475/1943-11-19/ed-1/?sp=6&r=-0.316,-0.004,1.78,0.901,0.

258 *The camp bought new shoulder pads and helmets for the team*: George Yoshinaga, "Sport Tidbits," *Heart Mountain Sentinel*, September 9, 1944.

259 *they'd lost nearly their entire second string to the potato harvest*: "This Week's Heroes," *Heart Mountain Sentinel*, October 7, 1944.

259 *their last season above .500 was 1938*: "Cody Broncs," Wyoming Football, http://wyoming-football.com/index.php/results/results-by-team/cody-broncs/.

259 *Dr. E. W. J. Schmitt, the pastor of a church in suburban Philadelphia, Pennsylvania*: "Methodist Pastor Criticizes 'Prejudice' in Town of Cody," *Heart Mountain Sentinel*, August 5, 1944.

260 *an incarceree was punched in the face by a military police officer*: Mike Mackey, *Heart Mountain: Life in Wyoming's Concentration Camp* (Powell, WY: Western History Publications, 2000), 124.

260 *The rules of the scrimmage were laid out plainly*: "Eagle Pigskinners Look Impressive, Rout Cody Broncos in Scrimmage," *Heart Mountain Sentinel*, September 23, 1944.

260 *rail thin and with a hedgehog for a haircut*: Shuzo Sumii evacuee file.

261 *Chuck Harkins was a barrel of a boy*: This description was created after consulting stories in the *Billings Gazette* and *Casper Star-Tribune*.

261 *they were faster and lighter than the 1943 team*: "Worland Invade Eagles," *Echoes*, September 22, 1944.

262 *spent the past months taking heavy losses in Italy*: "Nisei at war in Europe with the 100th and 442nd," Nisei Veterans Legacy, https://www.nvlchawaii.org/nisei-war-europe-100th-and-442nd.

262 *Ed Yasuda traveled to Fort Logan for his Army physical*: George Yoshinaga, "Sport Tidbits," *Heart Mountain Sentinel*, September 20, 1944.

262 *After an opening 35-yard drive down to the Worland 34*: This game was re-created using stories and box scores from the September 23, 1944, *Heart Mountain Sentinel*.

263 *Coach Sakamoto packed his bag*: Youngren Mishima, "Sport Tidbits," *Heart Mountain Sentinel*, September 20, 1944.

264 *"Coaches are getting as scarce as new jalopies"*: Al Himsl, "Sports Soundings," *Billings Gazette*, July 30, 1944.

264 *The district hired Frank Ward as athletic director and football coach*: "Red Lodge Wins, 13–6, Over Colts," *Billings Gazette*, November 4, 1944.

264 *a 33–6 beatdown at the hands of the Cody Broncs*: "Cody Broncs," Wyoming Football, http://wyoming-football.com/index.php/results/results -by-team/cody-broncs/.

264 *a more respectable 19–12 loss to the Lovell Bulldogs*: "Football Results," *Billings Gazette*, September 24, 1944.

264 *Resembling General Patton*: Youngren Mishima, "Sports Tidbits," *Heart Mountain Sentinel*, October 23, 1944.

265 *It took the Eagles only five plays from kickoff to land on the Coyotes' 10*: This game was re-created using stories from the October 7, 14, and 21, 1944, editions of the *Heart Mountain Sentinel* and October 20, 1944, *Echoes*.

266 *the most points scored by a Wyoming varsity eleven since Powell dropped 66 on Basin High School in November 1940*: "Results by year," Wyoming Football, http://wyoming-football.com/index.php/results/results-by-year/.

266 *the Eagles' 1943 record outshined seven*: "1943 Wyoming High School Football Standings," Wyoming Football, http://wyoming-football.com /index.php/standings/all-time-standings/1943-wyoming-high-school-foot ball-standings/.

266 *His uncle, Johnny Winterholler, was the greatest athlete in Wyoming during the 1930s*: Robert Cantwell, "An Era Shaped by War," *Sports Illustrated*, November 11, 1964.

267 *the Rolling Devils, the first wheelchair basketball team*: André B. Sobocinski, "When Johnny Came Home," *Navy Medicine Live*, https://navy medicine.navylive.dodlive.mil/archives/5368.

267 *his mother would receive a sixth star for her service flag*: "Lovell Family's Sixth Son Enlists," *Billings Gazette*, December 1, 1944.

267 *Four plays after kickoff, right end Jack Funo took an end-around to the house*: This game was re-created using stories from the October 21 and 28, 1944, editions of the *Heart Mountain Sentinel* and October 27, 1944, edition of *Echoes*.

268 *Horse took up their cause*: George Yoshinaga, "Sport Tidbits," *Heart Mountain Sentinel*, October 28, 1944.

269 *Abraham Lincoln Wirin found himself blindfolded and bound*: "Johnson

Still Said Hiding in Imperial Area," *San Bernardino County Sun*, January 25, 1934.

269 *Wirin was born in Russia and as a child moved to Boston*: Greg Robinson and Brian Niiya, "A. L. Wirin," *Densho Encyclopedia*, http://encyclopedia.densho.org/A.L._Wirin. Much of the biographical sketch of Wirin is derived from this article.

269 *as a child he was arrested and fined $5 for protesting assaults perpetrated by sailors during a peace march*: "A. L. Wirin, First Counsel to Civil Liberties Union," *New York Times*, February 5, 1978.

270 *ACLU founder and executive director Roger Baldwin dismissed any support of the Fair Play Committee*: Eric L. Muller, *Free to Die for Their Country: The Story of the Japanese American Draft Resisters in World War II* (Chicago: University of Chicago Press, 2001), 90.

270 *Judge Eugene Rice was called to Cheyenne*: Ibid., 114.

270 *Wirin was honest with the men from the outset: the prospects weren't good*: Mackey, *A Matter of Conscience*, in *A Matter of Conscience*, ed. Mike Mackey (Powell, WY: Western History Publications, 2002), 58.

270 *Wirin built the case with appeal in mind*: Muller, *Free to Die for Their Country*, 119.

271 *One day, a neighbor of Frank Emi's took the stand*: Mackey, *A Matter of Conscience*, 58.

271 *a bulletin came across the Associated Press wire*: "Mustang Eleven Will Play Heart Mountain," *Casper Star-Tribune*, November 1, 1944.

Chapter Twenty-One: November 4, 1944

272 *Joe Schwartz couldn't find enough cars*: "Casper Mustang Team Goes to Heart Mountain," *Casper Star-Tribune*, November 3, 1944.

272 *a snaking gap of tectonic-molded rock that climbs to heights of more than 2,500 feet*: "Wind River Canyon, Part One," Geology of Wyoming, https://www.geowyo.com/wind-river-canyon-part-1.html.

272 *Schwartz's team would play its fewest games since 1921*: "Natrona Mustangs," Wyoming Football, https://wyoming-football.com/index.php/results/results-by-team/natrona-mustangs/.

273 *The team's last losing season was 1926*: Ibid.

273 *a terra-cotta Collegiate Gothic–style masterpiece funded with 1920s oil boom cash*: "Natrona County High School," National Register of Historic Places Collection registration form, December 9, 1993, https://npgallery.nps.gov/NRHP.

273 *the undisputed king of Wyoming football*: "Cheyenne Central Indians," Wyoming Football, http://wyoming-football.com/index.php/results/results-by-team/cheyenne-central-indians/.

273 *LeRoy was a 210-pound mortar round of a teen*: "Champ Bond Salesmen," *Casper Star-Tribune*, November 15, 1942.

273 *at the state track championships*: Murl Hendrickson, "Mustangs Pile Up 65 Points to Lead State Track Teams," *Casper Star-Tribune*, May 21, 1944.

273 *the son of Herbert and Lucile Pearce*: Charles Pearce email to author, September 23, 2018. The biographical details of Pearce's life derive from this email from his son.

274 *Wirin urged Judge Rice to release the men on bail while he appealed the case*: "7 Fair Play Leaders Convicted," *Heart Mountain Sentinel*, November 4, 1944.

274 *They lived among the murderers and drug dealers common in high-security prisons*: Mackey, *A Matter of Conscience*, in *A Matter of Conscience*, ed. Mike Mackey (Powell, WY: Western History Publications, 2002), 59.

275 *The men petitioned to be treated like equals, like their white countrymen*: Shirley Castelnuovo, *Soldiers of Conscience: Japanese American Military Resisters in World War II* (Westport, CT: Praeger, 2008), 71.

275 *Emi and the rest of the Fair Play Committee put on judo demonstrations*: Mackey, *A Matter of Conscience*, 59.

275 *The day was a picturesque, built-in-a-lab day for football.* This game was re-created using stories from the November 4 and 11, 1944, editions of the *Heart Mountain Sentinel*.

278 *former student body president Ted Fujioka would be killed as the 442 fought in France*: "One Killed, Three Wounded in France," *Heart Mountain Sentinel*, November 25, 1944.

278 *Horse wrote his final* Sentinel *column*: George Yoshinaga, "Sport Tidbits," *Heart Mountain Sentinel*, November 4, 1944.

278 *His mother and sister would walk him to the front gate*: GYOH.

Chapter Twenty-Two: Going About Like Eagles

279 *Endo was a twenty-two-year-old clerk for the California Department of Motor Vehicles on December 7, 1941*: Brian Niiya, "Mitsuye Endo," *Densho Encyclopedia*, https://encyclopedia.densho.org/Mitsuye%20Endo/.

279 *Political machinations from the Roosevelt cabinet delayed the announcement just long enough to blunt its impact*: Mike Mackey, *Remembering Heart Mountain: Essays on Japanese American Internment in Wyoming* (Powell, WY: Western History Publications, 1998), 147.

280 the *War Department announced in a December 17 press release*: "Proclamation of Army Considered Vindication," *Heart Mountain Sentinel*, December 23, 1944.

280 *who spent his court recesses as a lieutenant colonel in the Army Reserve and once appeared in court not in his robe but his uniform*: Shannon M. Grammel, "Old Soldiers Never Die: Prior Military Service and the Doctrine of Military Deference on the Supreme Court," *Military Law Review* 223 (2015): 989–1033.

280 *In the 155-year history of the Court it was the first time the word "racism" was used in an opinion*: Robert Havey, "The Dissenter," The University of Michigan's Bentley Historical Library, https://bentley.umich.edu /news-events/magazine/the-dissenter/.

281 *Politicians and professional bigots along the West Coast were furious over the announcement*: All three of these examples come from separate stories from the same December 18, 1944, edition of the *Los Angeles Times*.

281 *A full-scale model of a Hawaiian village was built outside Los Angeles City Hall and then leveled with explosives*: "Village Burns to Teach Pearl Harbor Day Crowd Bomb Control," *Los Angeles Times*, December 8, 1942.

281 *seven thousand residents of Imperial County, California, met on the football field of Brawley High School*: "California County Protests Possible Jap Return to Coast," *The Palladium-Item*, December 8, 1944.

281 *At the annual California Farm Bureau Federation convention*: "Farm Bureau Opposed to Return of Japs," *Hanford Sentinel*, November 22, 1944.

282 *The Panthers were 6–1*: "Powell Panthers," Wyoming Football, http://wy oming-football.com/index.php/results/results-by-team/powell-panthers.

282 *Talbot Rudolph received a call from Panthers head coach L. A. Kohnke*: "Heart Mountain Eagles Claim Basin Title," *Heart Mountain Sentinel*, November 18, 1944.

282 *The declaration didn't sit well with one Powell resident*: Youngren Mishima, "Sport Tidbits," *Heart Mountain Sentinel*, November 25, 1944.

283 *Cheyenne's* Wyoming State Tribune *named its top five teams in the state*: "Rated Second," *Wyoming State Tribune*, November 18, 1944.

283 *When the paper announced its all-state team, it was much the same as the previous year*: "All-State," Wyoming Football, http://wyoming-football .com/index.php/recognition/all-state-teams/.

283 *The Office of the Provost General prohibited Babe from working in plants or facilities "important to the war effort"*: Tamotsu Nomura evacuee file.

284 *S&N was widely known for its Asian employees*: "6 Javanese Seamen Held in Roundup," *Hartford Courant*, April 29, 1943.

284 *read a* Hartford Courant *sports column on October 26, 1944*: Bill Lee, "With Malice Towards None," *Hartford Courant*, October 26, 1944.

284 *Kiyoto "Ken" Nakaoka was joined on the team by Kay Kiyokawa, a 4 feet 11 inch back*: Dom Amore, "From the Sports Pages of UConn History, A Stand Against Anti-Japanese Racism," *Hartford Courant*, June 30, 2014.

284 *University president Albert Jorgensen saw how German universities kowtowed to Hitler's demands*: Jeff Tyson and Lucy Nalpathanchil, "From Internee to College Student: UConn's Enrollment of Japanese-Americans During World War II," Connecticut Public Radio, February 14, 2017.

285 *Horse was sitting among the palmettos and pines*: The remembrances in this section are from the George Yoshinaga oral history.

285 *In 1945, the camp's mission expanded in a new direction: counterintelligence*: "History and Mission of the Counter Intelligence Corps in World War II," CIC School, Counter Intelligence Corps Center, https://fas.org/irp/agency/army/cic-wwii.pdf.

286 *It was summertime when the SS* Pennant *steamed across the Pacific*: Ronald W. Charles, *Troopships of World War II* (Washington, DC: The Army Transportation Association, 1947), 297, https://history.army.mil/documents/WWII/wwii_Troopships.pdf.

286 *in rough seas the bottom bunks would be drenched with vomit*: "Soldiers in Bunks on Army Transport, S.S. Pennant," photo, *World War II Database*, https://worldwar2database.com/gallery/wwii1035.

286 I'm finally going to set foot on Japanese soil: "Nisei in His Imperial Majesty's Service: Japanese Americans Who Served the Fatherland During World War II," interview with George Yoshinaga for the Mansell Center for Research, an online study of Allied POWS Under the Japanese, http://www.mansell.com/eo9066/NIHIMS/Nisei_IHIMS.html.

287 *his own unit called him "Blanket Ass," a slur they usually reserved for Eskimos and Native Americans*: GYOH.

287 *Jazz was always on the record player at the Dayton, Ohio, boardinghouse*: Stan Igawa unpublished memoir.

287 *More than 150 nikkei moved to Dayton between 1943 and 1946, practically the first ever to do so*: Paul Michael Dankovich, "The Japanese American Resettlement Program of Dayton, Ohio: As Administered by the Church Federation of Dayton and Montgomery County, 1943–1946" (MA diss., Wright State University, 2012).

287 *The city throbbed with the war effort*: Eileen McClory, "4 Ways Dayton Contributed to WW II Effort," *Dayton Daily News*, August 15, 2015.

288 *Guiding the new residents was Robert Kodama*: Dankovich, "The Japanese American Resettlement Program of Dayton, Ohio," 29.

288 Color, strength, and size: Stan Igawa unpublished memoir.

288 *officials commissioned director John Ford to film a twenty-five-minute short entitled* Sex Hygiene *for the troops*: Quentin Turnour, "John Ford: Other Directions," *Senses of Cinema*, April 2004, http://sensesofcinema.com/2004/cteq/john_ford/.

289 *Tayzo had waited more than a year for his day in court and it lasted less than ten minutes*: Teruo Matsumoto oral history.

289 *On Christmas Eve 1947, newspapers across the country blared a surprising headline*: "1,523 Draft Violators Get Yule Pardons," *Fresno Bee*, December 24, 1947.

289 *A. L. Wirin had petitioned President Harry Truman for amnesty of not only his clients, but thousands like them*: Lorraine K. Bannai, "Taking the Stand: The Lessons of the Three Men Who Took the Japanese American Internment to Court," *Seattle Journal for Social Justice* 4, no. 1 (December 2005), Article 29.

289 *Truman established a committee to review the 15,803 men convicted of violating the Selective Service Act*: "1,523 Draft Violators Get Yule Pardons," *Fresno Bee*.

289 *Proclamation 2762 read*: "Granting Pardon to Certain Persons Convicted of Violating the Selective Training and Service Act of 1940 as Amended," Proclamation 2762, Federal Register, https://www.archives.gov/federal-register/codification/proclamations/02762.html.

290 *The Amnesty Board was more specific*: Bannai, "Taking the Stand."

290 *Tayzo spoke with two members*: Teruo Matsumoto oral history.

290 *The headline . . . would've seemed impossible just a year before*: "Babe Nomura of Los Angeles City College Is Nation's Top Japanese-American Gridster," Associated Press, December 12, 1945.

291 *on December 7, 1941, they'd all just wrapped up football season at Hollywood High School*: This information was gleaned from Babe Nomura's Los Angeles City College game programs, shared with me by Jan Morey.

291 *In front of ten thousand fans on October 26*: "Tartars Thump Cub Grids, 20–13," *Los Angeles Times*, October 27, 1945.

291 *a sportswriter declared Babe "one of the best since Jackie Robinson"*: "Compton Beats L.A. City College, 20–13," *Long Beach Independent*, October 28, 1945.

291 *against Robinson's alma mater, Babe slung three touchdowns and returned a punt 45 yards for another*: "Cubs Outscore Bulldogs," *Los Angeles Times*, November 10, 1945.

291 *"This boy is one of the greatest athletes I've ever seen"*: Alex Troffey, "Jap-American Heads Grid Team," United Press, November 14, 1945.

291 *leaving the camp mostly full with the elderly and women with small children*: Mike Mackey, *Heart Mountain: Life in Wyoming's Concentration Camp* (Powell, WY: Western History Publications, 2000), 132–33.

292 *The staff of the* Sentinel *wrote a letter to Eleanor Roosevelt*: "Center Mourns Sudden Death of President," *Heart Mountain Sentinel*, April 14, 1945.

292 *all Heart Mountain schools were closed after May 25*: Mackey, *Heart Mountain*, 136.

293 *Keiichi left for Denver on September 11*: Keiichi Ikeda interview.

293 *by the spring the Marusho Miks were the JACL Intermountain champions*: "Basketball Scoreboard," *Salt Lake Tribune*, March 24, 1946.

293 *His parents, two younger brothers, and little sister remained in Heart Mountain as everything around them shuttered*: Camp records indicate the rest of the Ikeda family left on the final train departing Heart Mountain.

293 *"Best wishes for you all"*: "General Information Bulletin—Series 363," November 2, 1945.

294 *The New Year's Day halftime show featured one thousand flutists, trumpeters, tuba players, clarinetists, drummers, and cornetists*: "Utah State Grid Squad Arrives for Jan. 1 Tilt," *Hanford Sentinel*, December 27, 1946.

294 *thirteen thousand fans cheered from the grandstands*: "San Jose Tramples Utags 20–0 in Raisin Contest," United Press, January 2, 1947.

294 *which had a history of welcoming Asian American athletes*: Joel S. Franks, "Asian Americans and Sport in the Santa Clara Valley During the Mid-Twentieth Century," in *San Francisco Bay Area Sports: Golden Gate Athletics, Recreation, and Community*, ed. Rita Liberti and Maureen Smith (Fayetteville: University of Arkansas Press, 2017), 113–28.

294 *already featured another nisei*: Joel S. Franks, *Crossing Sidelines, Crossing Cultures: Sport and Asian Pacific American Cultural Citizenship* (Lanham, MD: Rowman & Littlefield, 2010), 130.

294 *one of the greatest innovators in football history*: Edwin Pope, *Football's Greatest Coaches* (Atlanta: Tupper & Love, 1955), 231–32.

295 *Babe and the Spartans whipped him so badly that his college chancellor asked him to resign*: "Stagg Resigns When Offered Inactive Role," Associated Press, December 8, 1946.

295 *Babe beat the Tigers without even scoring*: "San Jose Routs Foe," *San Francisco Examiner*, November 9, 1946.

295 *With Babe leading the way*: Keith Pope, "Spartans Roll Over Utah 20–0 to Win Raisin Bowl Tilt," *Spartan Daily*, January 3, 1947, https://schol arworks.sjsu.edu/spartandaily/7930/.

295 *the Spartans outgained the Utah State Aggies 177–74 on the ground*: "Spartans Power 20–0 Utah Aggies Win," *Santa Rosa Republican*, January 2, 1947.

295 *Looking to shore up their backfield for the future, they invited Babe to try out*: Jan Morey and Kimiko Nomura interviews.

295 *groups like the California Preservation Association and Seattle's Remember Pearl Harbor League formed to fight resettlement*: Brian Niiya, "Return to West Coast," *Densho Encyclopedia*, https://encyclopedia.densho.org/Re turn_to_West_Coast.

296 *the Takeda family was awakened to the smell of gasoline*: "Night Riders Attack Returned Evacuee Family on San Jose Farm with Fire, Gunshots," *Pacific Citizen*, March 10, 1945. Decades' worth of *Pacific Citizen* editions have recently been digitized, and are a fascinating way to examine the shifting role of the JACL in Japanese American life over the past century: https://www.pacificcitizen.org/digital-archives/.

296 *Between 1998 and his death in 2004, he logged more than three thousand hours as a volunteer at the Pearl Harbor National Memorial*: "Secretary Norton and Governor Lingle Honor Outstanding Volunteers at USS Arizona Memorial," U.S. Department of the Interior, January 11, 2004, https://www.doi.gov/sites/doi.gov/files/archive/news/archive/04_News _Releases/040112a.htm.

296 *Stan would put on his National Park Service uniform and his VFW Post 10276 cap*: iConnectCAST—Pearl Harbor 75th Anniversary, "Stan Igawa," You-Tube video, 1:51, https://www.youtube.com/watch?v=fdCKmCiH8xY.

296 *He'd suffer the indignity of those who asked "What army did you serve?" and "What are you?"*: Geoffrey M. White, *Memorializing Pearl Harbor: Unfinished Histories and the Work of Remembrance* (Durham, NC: Duke University Press, 2016).

296 *"He bled red, white, and blue"*: Irene Igawa interview.

297 *On May 9, 1949, at the First Congregational Church of Los Angeles, he married Kimiko*: Jan Morey interviews.

297 *Every morning while walking to elementary school in Mountain View, she'd pass a boy heading the other direction*: Kimiko Nomura interview.

297 *Los Angeles's Shin Nichi-Bei named its annual Nisei Athletic Union all-star softball team*: George Yoshinaga, "Sports . . . ," *Shin Nichi-Bei*, September 5, 1950.

297 *he rented a small room near the corner of Cahuenga and Santa Monica Boulevards*: Jan Morey interviews.

297 *Asked once by a reader to name the best nisei football player of all time*: George Yoshinaga, "Horse's Mouth," *Shin Nichi-Bei*, October 3, 1956.

297 *who was stabbed to death by a member of the Yakuza in 1963*: Kenji Nakano, "Looking Back at the Death of Rikidozan," *Tokyo Reporter*, May 10, 2013, https://www.tokyoreporter.com/japan-news/tabloid/looking-back-at-the-death-of-wrestler-rikidozan/.

297 *His company brought Japan's Meiji University basketball team to play the UNLV Runnin' Rebels*: "UNLV 'Rebels' vs. MEIJI," University of Nevada, Las Vegas (1984), https://digitalscholarship.unlv.edu/basketball_programs/106.

298 *real estate developer Walter Dilbeck had the idea to create a global baseball league*: Brian McKenna, "Global League," Society for American Baseball Research, https://sabr.org/bioproj/topic/global-league.

298 *at one point forty Japanese professional baseball players lived in his small house in Gardena, and played catch in the street with his sons*: Paul Yoshinaga interview.

298 *68,000 Japanese fans circled twice around the stadium*: "They Even Played a Bowl in Japan," Associated Press, January 19, 1976.

298 *In an interview with a historian in 2010 he explained his thinking*: GYOH.

299 *wrote in opposition to the redress movement, which ultimately won the passage of the Civil Liberties Act of 1988*: Guy Aoki, "Into the Next Stage: The Long and Bumpy Ride of George 'Horse' Yoshinaga," *Rafu Shimpo*, August 27, 2015, http://www.rafu.com/2015/08/into-the-next-stage-the-long-and-bumpy-ride-of-george-horse-yoshinaga.

299 *"if it wasn't for evacuation I wouldn't have a college education, I'd be working on the farm"*: GYOH.

299 *Ogimachi dreamed of being a certified public accountant*: Bunny Ogimachi interview.

300 *His efforts could be summed up by words written by a* Shin Nichi-Bei *colleague in July 1958*: Fred Taomae, "So Long, George," *Shin Nichi-Bei*, July 23, 1958.

300 *The Nomura Family Golf Tournament grew and grew*: This was gleaned from Nomura family photo albums.

INDEX

ABOUT THE AUTHOR

Bradford Pearson is a journalist whose work examines everything from magicians to technology to his own kidnapping. He's written for *The New York Times*, and *Esquire*, *Time*, and *Philadelphia* magazines, and is the former features editor at *Southwest: The Magazine*. He is a recipient of the German Marshall Fund of the United States' Marshall Memorial Fellowship, which took him to Europe to study media on the continent. He lives in Philadelphia with his wife and two children.

CPSIA information can be obtained
at www.ICGtesting.com
Printed in the USA
LVHW041208211022
730778LV00002B/2